The Users Guide to GPS
The Global Positioning System

by Bonnie Dahl

Richardsons' Publishing
88 Hatch Street, Suite 403
New Bedford, MA 02745

Cover art: *A GPS Block IIR Space Vehicle*
courtesy of GE Astro Space

ISBN 0-932647-12-x

To Ron, Peter and Kristin, who have given unending patience, support, and assistance in the writing of this book.

ACKNOWLEDGEMENTS

Many individuals and agencies made invaluable contributions to the writing of this book. I would like to thank those consultants at Magellan, Magnavox, Micrologic, Garmin, and the Coast Guard who gave technical assistance on different aspects of the GPS system and on radionavigation concepts in general. I would also like to thank Wayne Spangler and David Nixon for the access to hundreds of navigational charts that were used as resources for illustrating various concepts discussed in the text.

Graphic and photographic materials used to illustrate different concepts in the text were provided by a number of manufacturers and companies. They are:

Cetrek Autopilot & Control Sys.

Eastern Land Navigation Sys.

Electronic Systems Co.

Furuno U.S.A., Inc.

Garmin International, Inc.

GE Astro Space

Magellan Systems Corp.

Micrologic

Motorola, Inc.

NAVSTAR GPS Joint Program Office

Ray Jefferson, Magnavox

Richardsons' Marine Publishing

Techsonic Industries, Inc.

Trimble Navigation, Ltd.

U.S. Coast Guard

A very special note of appreciation goes to those individuals who read different chapters for technical error. They are:

Steve Ault, Magnavox Electronic Systems Co.

Peter Dahl, HPC Research Fellow, Army High Performance Computing Research Center

Marc Rubenstein, Magellan Systems Corp.

Larry Weill, Ph.D., Magellan Systems Corp. and California State University, Fullerton

Larry Vallot, Senior Research Staff Scientist, Honeywell Systems and
Research Center
Emile Yacoub, Magellan Systems Corp.

Finally, I want to thank my husband, Ron, who spent countless hours
proofing copy and providing invaluable assistance in researching
and field testing the GPS system. I also want to thank our son, Peter,
who provided technical assistance in the explanation of different
GPS concepts.

Bonnie Dahl

TABLE OF CONTENTS

CHAPTER THREE

CHAPTER FOUR

CHAPTER FIVE

General Mechanics in Using GPS

CHAPTER SIX

CHAPTER SEVEN

CHAPTER EIGHT

GPS Applications & Uses

FOREWARD

In the last quarter of the twentieth century, there has been a proliferation of navigation systems, many of which use the principles of determining position with radiowaves. Many of these are terrestrial-based systems such as DECCA, VOR/DME, and Loran-C. Others are products of the Sputnik legacy and receive their signals from satellites circling the globe. Since the time of its inception in the mid-1970's, the NavStar Global Positioning System has been long awaited as the system with the promise of providing very precise continuous worldwide positioning. Now on the brink of the twenty-first century, GPS has become a reality, carrying with it the potential for revolutionizing all applications of position fixing.

Historically, the marine user community has been one of the largest users of radionavigation systems, and it is for this group that this book is primarily written. Nevertheless, many sections should prove useful for other user groups. For example, the chapters on radionavigation history, system characteristics, program development, theory, and accuracy are basic to the GPS system, regardless of who is using it and for what application.

The civil marine user community represents a fairly diverse user group, and it has been a challenge to write a book that is applicable to all users. For example, some are just beginning to use radionavigation and GPS is their first and only radionavigation, system. Thus, it may be beneficial for the novice to concentrate on the basics presented in the sections on System Characteristics in Chapter 2, Part I in Chapter 3 on Theory, Chapter 4 on Receivers, and Chapter 5 on General Mechanics in using GPS. On the other hand, years of using Loran-C and Transit (Sat Nav) have produced another segment of the user community that is fairly adept at using radionavigation systems. For these users access to receiver functions, data entry and retrieval, and waypoint navigation all come as second nature. For those users who wish to expand their knowledge of radionavigation and, in particular of GPS, other segments have been included in the book such as Part II in the chapter on Theory, Chapter 6 on Accuracy and Chapter 7 on Navigating with GPS. To assist all users, an Appendix on Abbreviations and Acronyms and a Glossary are included at the back of the book.

Although GPS has been designed and implemented primarily as a military utility, I have tried to keep away from military applications for

1

several reasons. One is that the main emphasis of the book is for the civil user. Another reason is that, aside from being classified, often military applications are so technical and numerous that they are beyond the scope of this text. It is also important to note that this book is not written for the engineering community. For those who require more technical information on the GPS system, hundreds of papers and resources are available that are far more detailed than the material in this book. Some of these sources are listed in the Bibliography.

Admittedly, many readers will not pick up this book and read it from cover to cover but will go to those sections that interest them most. Therefore, I feel I must address the issue of redundancy. Because I expected that the book would be read in fragments, certain topics are discussed in more than one section. For example, topics such as selective availability (SA) and differential GPS (DGPS), which are becoming basic to the GPS system, are discussed in a number of different sections. Likewise, the concepts of pseudorandom codes, GPS signal propagation on the two L bands, the effects of satellite geometry on the accuracy of a fix (HDOP), and segments of the navigation message (almanac and satellite ephemerides) are examples of topics that are discussed in many of different contexts.

Within this book, charts and diagrams are provided to illustrate various aspects of the concepts discussed. While every effort has been made to make these visuals as accurate as possible, it should be noted that the charts are not intended to be, nor should they be, used for actual navigation.

By far one of the most frustrating chapters to write was the last chapter on GPS applications. I would just get a section finished and some new application would come out in the media—and I am sure that I have missed more than a few. It would be presumptuous to assume that I could note all the possible applications, and in addition, many innovative uses of GPS are coming on line even as the book is being printed. Yet, I feel it is important to acknowledge the widespread potential of GPS, and it was my intent in including the last chapter to give the reader an idea, however incomplete, of GPS system capabilities.

Finally, I think it is important to note that although GPS has been touted as "the system that is the be-all and end-all in radionavigation," it may be just a forerunner of systems to come. Already there are those in the field who are beginning to talk of "what's coming after GPS." As we turn the corner into the twenty-first century, new technologies and new systems undoubtedly will explore and expand the capabilities of precise positioning, timing, and velocity determinations.

Bonnie Dahl

.

.

CHAPTER ONE

Radionavigation: Past, Present, & Future

Since earliest times people have looked to the heavens to assist in their travels around Earth. Whether using the periodic movements of the sun and its planets or the stars themselves, people quickly learned to determine relative position based on the movements of these heavenly bodies. At best, position fixing using these methods could be described as more of an art than a science. Even with the assistance of small computers to perform the necessary mathematical calculations, fixes still lack the accuracy of contemporary requirements. However, as we near the end of the twentieth century, we have returned once again to the stars with a newfound precision in position fixing. The only difference is that the stars are now made by humans, a product of modern technology.

A notable characteristic of the twentieth century has been an information explosion unequaled in human history. The body of accumulated knowledge is now doubling every few years, resulting in technological spin-offs that have affected every aspect of our lives. As in many areas, the field of navigation, particularly radionavigation, has seen tremendous accomplishments in the past few decades. Thanks to advances in applied science and microchip technology, we are now able to pinpoint position and solve navigational problems as never before.

I. Forerunners of the Radionavigation Concept

The Electromagnetic Spectrum

All forms of radio location are alike in one respect: they measure certain propagation characteristics of radio waves, which are part of the electromagnetic spectrum. The electromagnetic spectrum consists of a continuum of all kinds of electric, magnetic, and visible radiation, from incredibly small gamma rays that have a wavelength of 0.001 angstrom to waves with a wavelength of more than 1 million kilometers. The spectrum includes infrared, ultraviolet, and X-rays along with radio waves. Radio waves, or Hertzian waves as they are often called, are found towards the end of the spectrum that has longer wavelengths and lower frequencies. Loran-C, AM, FM, TV, and radar transmissions are all part of the Hertzian band of the spectrum. (See

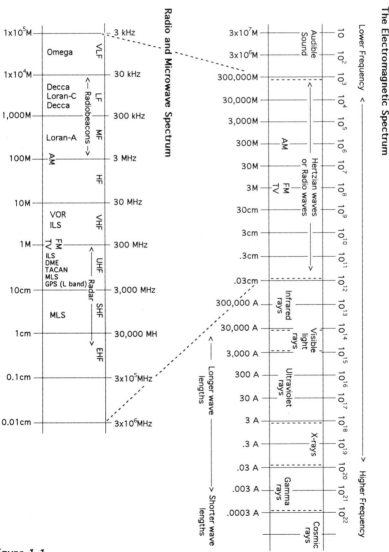

Figure 1.1

Figure 1.1.) For a summary of radio frequency bands see Figure 1.2.

Existence of the electromagnetic spectrum was first predicted in the 1860's by a British physicist, James Clerk Maxwell. It wasn't until 1887 that the first radio waves were actually produced by a German physicist, Heinrich Hertz. Initial applications were largely in the field of communication, and it wasn't until 1925 that radio waves were used for detecting distant objects. In their classic experiments, two American physicists, Gregory Breit and Merle Tuve, bounced short radio pulses off the ionosphere and calculated its height by measuring the transmission time of the reflected signals. Many scientists consider these experiments to have constituted the first practical use of radar.

In the 1930's, British, French, German, and American researchers developed experimental radars that could be used to detect planes and ships within a limited range. Just prior to World War II, the British developed experimental radar stations along England's south and east coasts for defense against sea and air attacks. The war brought further demands on the radar concept and produced other very important radio navigational aids — DECCA and Loran-A.

Very Low	VLF	Below 30 kHz
Low	LF	30 to 300 kHz
Medium	MF	300 to 3,000 kHz
High	HF	3,000 kHz to 30 MHz
Very High	VHF	30 to 300 MHz
Ultra High	UHF	300 MHz to 3 GHz
Super High	SHF	3 to 30 GHz
Extremely High	EHF	30 to 300 GHz

Figure 1.2   Radio Frequency Bands

Contemporary Radar

Today radar remains a unique radionavigational tool in that it is the only system that operates independently of external stations to generate radio signals. It is similar to many contemporary radionavigation systems in that it operates on the basic principle that radio signals, like all signals in the electromagnetic spectrum, travel at a specific speed in space—186,000 statute miles/second or 982 feet/microsecond. By measuring the time it takes a radio signal to travel from the source of transmission (or reflection, as in the case of radar), the range or distance to an object can be determined — i.e., time becomes synonymous with distance.

Although radar was initially designed as a system to detect the presence and range of other objects (hence, its name — (RAdio Detecting And Ranging), radar can also be used in accurate position fixing in a number of different ways. One of these is to make range measurements from two or more different landmasses via the distance rings on the screen. These distances are transferred to a chart and where they cross determines your position.

Radar can also be used to determine the bearing (direction of arrival) of a reflected signal from a distant object. Position can then be determined by crossing two or more bearings. It can also be determined by crossing the range and bearing from the same target. (See Figure 1.3.) A decided advantage in contemporary radar units is the addition of electronic range and bearing indicators that give precise digital readouts for position fixing.

The following is a brief discussion of radio navigation systems in use in the twentieth century. It is not within the scope of this chapter to go into a detailed discussion of each system. Nor are all systems in use discussed — especially those in the private sector. Instead, the intent is to show the wide variety of radionavigation systems that have emerged in the second half of the twentieth century and to look at the radio navigation systems of the future.

II. Terrestrial-Based Transmission Systems

Radiobeacons

Radiobeacons are omnidirectional radio-transmitting stations that operate in the low and medium frequency bands to provide ground wave signals. Radiobeacons are used by both the marine and aviation communities: nondirectional beacons in the 190 – 415 kHz and 510 – 535 kHz bands; maritime radiobeacons at 275–335 kHz. Signals from marine beacons are transmitted in two different ways: as a continuous signal or sequenced with other beacons on an assigned frequency. Continuous beacons generally have shorter ranges and are used as homing devices to identify harbor entrances. Some of the longer range marine beacons operate with others in a group on the same frequency and are time sequenced to prevent interference. (See Figure 1.4 for

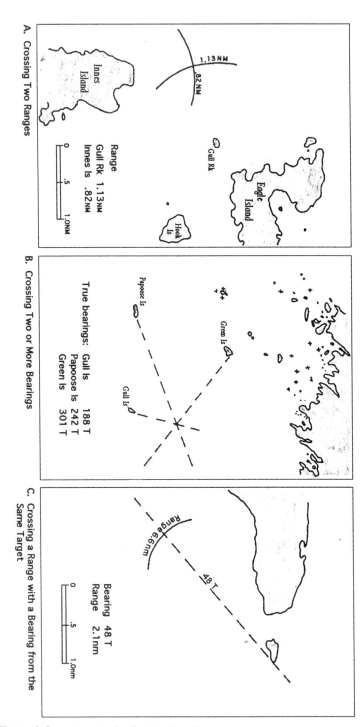

A. Crossing Two Ranges

Range
Gull Rk 1.13 NM
Innes Is .82 NM

1.13 NM
.82 NM

Innes Island

Gull Rk

Eagle Island

Hook Is

0   .5   1.0 NM

B. Crossing Two or More Bearings

True bearings: Gull Is   188 T
                Papoose Is   242 T
                Green Is   301 T

Papoose Is

Green Is

Gull Is

C. Crossing a Range with a Bearing from the Same Target

Range 6.6 nm

48 T

Bearing 48 T
Range   2.1 nm

0   .5   1.0 nm

Figure 1.3   Using Radar for Position Fix

8

PACIFIC
OCEAN

ATLANTIC
OCEAN

Coverage

Taken from the 1990 Federal Radionavigation Plan

Figure 1.4   Conterminous U.S. Marine Radiobeacon Coverage

Conterminous U.S. Marine Radiobeacon Coverage.)

Signals are accessed via a radio direction finder (RDF), which is used to measure the bearing of the transmitter with respect to a vessel or an aircraft. One line of position (LOP) results from each beacon. Crossing two or more LOPs establishes a fix. However, in remote areas, because of distance or station geometry, it may not be possible to obtain accurate two point bearings. In some areas, long-range sequenced beacons are being changed to short-range continuous beacons because they are more effective in providing homing characteristics.

In the early 1990's, the United States Coast Guard developed a modernization plan for its marine radiobeacon system, which consists of approximately 200 beacons. The plan called for:

1. Elimination of all sequenced radiobeacons.
2. Relocation of difficult-to-maintain and costly-to-operate radio beacons.
3. Reduction of interference.
4. Development of a system of homing beacons for desired coverage areas.

The use of radiobeacons has taken on new importance in the 1990's because of the decision to use some of their broadcast signals as the communications link for Differential GPS (DGPS). DGPS is an accuracy and integrity enhancement technique in which GPS signals are corrected for timing, satellite, and transmission errors by using a receiver positioned at a known site. These corrections are then transmitted to the user by a communications link, which in this case are marine radiobeacons. This service will be on-line and in use by 1996. For a more thorough discussion of DGPS, see that section in Chapter Six on Accuracy.

DECCA

The DECCA NAVIGATOR system, one of the oldest radiolocation systems, was developed in the mid-1940's. Until the early 1990's, it has been a major navigation system for maritime and air use in Western Europe, the Baltic area, South Africa, the Arabian Gulf, India, Japan, and Australia. Of the 44 DECCA chains in operation, most are located in the European sector. European coverage is extensive in the northern areas and covers most coastal regions down to the northern coast of Spain.

DECCA is similar to Loran-C in that it uses hyperbolic lines of position determined by measuring time-delay differences between three or more stations to determine horizontal position. This is done by measuring the phase angle between the synchronized transmissions of a master and slave signal. The system operates on five low frequency (LF) subbands located on two main bands at 70 – 90 kHz and 110 – 130 kHz. Accuracy is approximately 340 nm. Further degradation occurs during nighttime due to sky wave limitations. Many of the DECCA transmitters will soon need to be replaced, which will be expensive. Given other available radio navigational systems (Loran-C and GPS), DECCA's future remains uncertain.

Omega

Omega was originally designed to meet U.S. Department of Defense (DOD) requirements for general worldwide navigation but has evolved into a system that is now used primarily by the civil community. It is a multinational system with eight continuous wave transmitting stations located in seven different countries (Argentina, Australia, France, Japan, Liberia, Norway, and the United States), which provide coverage over most of the earth. Because the stations are located approximately 6,000 miles apart, signals from at least four stations are provided at any given point. Worldwide position coverage became possible when the Australian station became operational in 1982. (See Figure 1.5.)

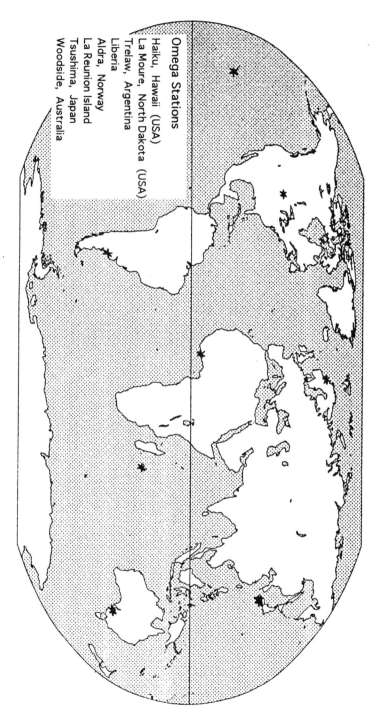

Omega Stations

Haiku, Hawaii (USA)
La Moure, North Dakota (USA)
Trelaw, Argentina
Liberia
Aldra, Norway
La Reunion Island
Tsushima, Japan
Woodside, Australia

Figure 1.5   *The Omega System*

11

Omega stations transmit time-shared signals in ten-second periods on very low frequencies: 10.2 kHz, 11.05 kHz, 11.33 kHz, and 13.6 kHz. Usable signal ranges are from 4,000 to 10,000 miles. Two-dimensional fixes are determined from two or more hyperbolic LOPs, which are achieved by measuring relative phase differences of received Omega signals. It is necessary to know estimated position within a set of lines called lanes. Lane identification is resolved with an internal receiver counter, which keeps track of lanes crossed. In case of interrupted reception, lane identification can be resolved by using transmissions on other frequencies. Fixes are plotted on special Omega charts overprinted with hyperbolic lines or on regular charts by using Latitude/Longitude (Lat/Lon) coordinates derived from Omega position tables or Lat/Lon conversion in receiver Read Only Memory (ROM).

Accuracy of the system (1 to 2 nm) is limited by the type of user equipment, location, time of day, and accuracy of sky wave propagation corrections that must be applied to individual receiver readings. These corrections are in the form of mathematical tables, which may be entered into the receiver manually or stored in the memory of computerized receivers. Accuracy can also be improved by using differential Omega, which uses single monitor stations that calculate a correction factor. This is done by comparing received Omega signals with the predicted signal for a given area. The correction factors are usually transmitted over existing radiobeacon systems. Along the European coastline and the Mediterranean, there are approximately 15 of these stations, which can improve accuracies to within 0.3 nm at 50 miles and 1 nm at 500 miles.

Radionavigation Systems Specific for the Airways

Three systems use radio transmissions for en route guidance of aircraft. **VHF Omnidirectional Range (VOR)** provides aircraft with bearing information relative to a VOR ground station and magnetic north. It operates in the VHF frequency range (108 to 118 MHz). Predictable ground station errors are +1.4 degrees, which translates to 0.25 nm at a range of 10 nm or 2.5 nm at 100 nm. There are, however, other errors such as course selection and receiver and flight technical errors that can add up to +4.5 degrees.

Distance Measuring Equipment (DME) provides aircraft with distance information from the aircraft to a DME ground station. It operates in the UHF frequency range (960–1213 MHz). Predictable ground station errors are less than +0.1nm. Overall system error is less than +0.5 nm or 3% of the distance, whichever is greater. These two systems are usually combined as a VOR/DME facility. They both have line-of-sight limitations that restrict ground coverage to 30 nm or less. At altitudes above 5,000 feet, the range is approximately 100 nm; at 20,000 feet it is 200 nm.

Tactical Air Navigation (TACAN) is a short-range UHF (960 to 1215 MHz) radionavigation system designed primarily for military aircraft. It provides both range and bearing to a selected station. Ground station bearing errors vary from +1.0 to +4.5 degrees. Range errors are the same as DME errors. As with the other two systems, line of sight limits coverage: ground coverage to 30 nm; at 5,000 feet, to 100 nm; at 18,000 or above, range approaches 130 nm. TACAN stations are often collocated with VOR facilities and are then known as VORTACs.

In addition to en route navigation, two systems are designed to provide precision approaches to landing at an airport runway. In the early 1990's, **Instrument Landing System** (ILS) was the standard precision landing system approved by the International Civil Aviation Organization. It consists of a localizer facility (VHF:108–112 MHz), which provides accurate, single path horizontal guidance; a glide slope facility (UHF:328.6 – 335.4 MHz), which provides precise single path vertical guidance; and two or three VHF markers.

Another system, **Microwave Landing System (MLS)**, is being developed by Department of Transportation (DOT), Department of Defense (DOD), and National Aeronautic Space Administration (NASA) to be implemented in 1998 as the international standard precision approach system. The system transmits signals that produce precise bearing, elevation angle, and range to aircraft. All angle functions operate in the Super High Frequency (SHF) 5.0 – 5.25 GHz band. Ranging is provided by precise DME operating in the UHF 0.96 – 1.22 GHz band. Because MLS is transmitted through a large volume of space, multiple aircraft and multiple approach paths can be served, thereby ensuring greater flexibility in air traffic control and safety. Another advantage is that MLS transmissions are less sensitive to the effects of snow, terrain, and other structures, which will increase the reliability of the system. MLS is expected to eventually replace ILS in national and international civil aviation after simultaneous operation of both systems during a transition period.

Racal Pulse 8	100 kHz	Hydrotrac	1720 kHz
Geoloc	1600-2300 kHz	Maxiran	430 MHz
TORAN	1800-2000 kHz	Syledis	430 MHz
Raydist-N/RAC	1650 kHz, 3300 kHz	Racal Microfix	5520/5560 MHz
Raydist-DRS	1650 kHz, 3300 kHz	Mini-Ranger (Motorola)	5570/5480 MHz
Racal Hyperfix	1600/3400 kHz	Trisponder	9480/9325 MHz
ARGO	1646.7 kHz		

* This is only a partial listing of radiolocation systems which have operated in the private sector

Figure 1.6   Radiolocation Systems in the Private Sector *

The Private Sector

There are a number of radionavigation systems that are privately developed and operated. They employ a variety of measurement techniques and are used in areas where coverage is not available or that lack specific accuracy requirements. Note: Not all of these are terrestrial-based systems. For example, ARGO, which was used in the BOC Challenge and Whitbread round-the-world sailboat races in the late 1980's and early 1990's, is a privately operated satellite radiolocation system. A partial list of these systems and their operating frequencies is found in Figure 1.6.

Loran-C

Without a doubt, Loran-C, has put the little guy in the driver's seat in twentieth- century radionavigation. Never before in the history of navigation has a single nav-aid been so eagerly embraced by the maritime community. It has also found increased use in the airways, and by the early 1990's, the user community was rapidly approaching 1 million.

The word "loran" is an acronym that stands for LOng RAnge Navigation. The original system, Loran-A, was originally developed during World War II and provided a moderate range of 600–800 nm with an average fix error of 1 to 2 nm. In the early 1970's, as accuracy requirements increased, a national commitment to an official radionavigation aid for the navigable waters of the U.S. produced a new breed of loran, Loran-C.

A loran chain consists of three to six stations that provide reliable ground wave coverage over an area 1000 miles across. In each chain, one of the stations is designated as the master while the others are called

14

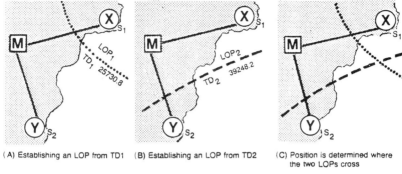

(A) Establishing an LOP from TD1   (B) Establishing an LOP from TD2   (C) Position is determined where the two LOPs cross

Taken from *"The Loran-C Users Guide"*   Published by Richardsons' Marine Publishing

Figure 1.7   *Plotting a Loran-C Fix with TDs*

secondaries. Each station transmits a series of coded pulses on a LF 100 (90-110) kHz band. A loran receiver measures the time difference (TD) between receiving the signal from a master and a given secondary. The TDs, as measured in microseconds, establish position relative to the two stations as a hyperbolic LOP. To get a fix, another TD measurement must be made from a second master-secondary pair to produce another LOP. Position is established where the two LOPs cross. (See Figure 1.7.)

Originally designed to provide accuracies of 1/4 mile 95% of the time, actual loran use consistently demonstrates a much higher accuracy level (typically 50 to 200 feet), especially in the repeatable mode. Accuracies can also be improved by using a technique called Differential Loran-C in which TD signals are monitored at a fixed site and error corrections are subsequently broadcast to the user. The inherent potential of this method is in providing the greater precision required for use in inland waterways and harbor approaches.

Although there are numerous chains located throughout the world, coverage has been most extensive within the coastal waters of the United States and Canada. It is important to note, however, that in the early 1990's, loran coverage was brought to the interior of the North American continent. The impetus for this expansion came from increased use of loran in the aviation community. For years, use of loran in the airways was limited by a "mid-continental gap" between coverage by coastal chains. With the Loran-C Mid-Continent Expansion Project, a joint effort of the Coast Guard and the Federal Aviation Administration, work began in 1986 to close this gap. By dual rating some of the stations in existing chains and adding just four new stations, two completely new chains were added to the loran system. (See

15

A. GRI 8290 NOCUS Loran-C Coverage

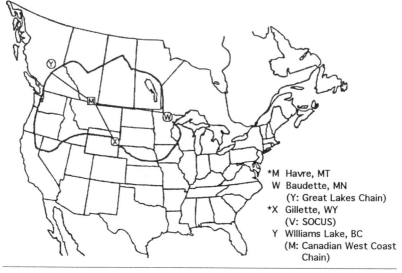

*M Havre, MT
W Baudette, MN
 (Y: Great Lakes Chain)
*X Gillette, WY
 (V: SOCUS)
Y Williams Lake, BC
 (M: Canadian West Coast
 Chain)

B. GRI 9610 SOCUS Loran-C Coverage

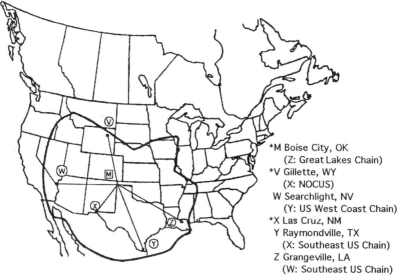

*M Boise City, OK
 (Z: Great Lakes Chain)
*V Gillette, WY
 (X: NOCUS)
W Searchlight, NV
 (Y: US West Coast Chain)
*X Las Cruz, NM
Y Raymondville, TX
 (X: Southeast US Chain)
Z Grangeville, LA
 (W: Southeast US Chain)

* New transmitter stations added in Mid-Continent Expansion Project
( ) Dual rated stations which also serve in other Loran-C Chains

Figure 1.8   *Closing the Mid-Continential Gap in Loran-C Coverage*

Figure 1.8.)

The South Central U.S. Chain (SOCUS) became operational in late

16

December 1990, the North Central U.S. Chain (NOCUS) in April 1991. The SOCUS Chain bears special mention because it represents a milestone in loran navigation as the first chain to have five secondaries. A new station at Boise City, Oklahoma, was incorporated into the Great Lakes Chain to increase its coverage. Another part of the expansion project was to increase coverage of the Gulf of Alaska Chain by dual rating one of the stations (Port Clarence) in the North Pacific Chain. For a complete picture of loran coverage within the conterminous United States and Canada and surrounding waters, see Figure 1.9.

Worldwide a number of chains are constructed/operated by the U.S. Coast Guard in conjunction with a host country. Also numerous chains are operated independently by a given country. The late 1980's and early 1990's saw expansion of loran coverage in many areas such as Europe, Saudi Arabia, and China. In 1990, the United Kingdom announced that subject to international agreement, Loran-C would replace the deteriorating DECCA Navigator system as its standard marine radionavigation system.

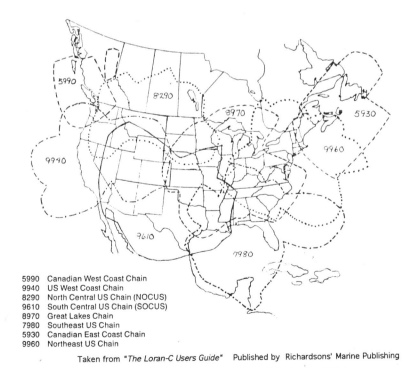

5990   Canadian West Coast Chain
9940   US West Coast Chain
8290   North Central US Chain (NOCUS)
9610   South Central US Chain (SOCUS)
8970   Great Lakes Chain
7980   Southeast US Chain
5930   Canadian East Coast Chain
9960   Northeast US Chain

Taken from *The Loran-C Users Guide*   Published by Richardsons' Marine Publishing

Figure 1.9   Loran-C Coverage in the Contiguous U.S. in the 1990s

The Russian counterpart of the U.S. loran system is called Chayka. It consists of two basic chains serving European Russia and the waters off eastern Siberia with another chain being built for Arctic regions. Agreements signed between the U.S. and USSR in the late 1980's established a basis for integrating operation of the two systems, creating a Loran/Chayka chain (Bering Sea Chain) in the Bering Straits between Alaska and the Soviet Union.

In the early 1990's, Loran-C emerged as the most widely accepted precision navigation aid in the world. Interestingly, despite the advent of GPS with all of its promise and potential, advocates of the loran system are predicting that Loran-C will remain the primary commercial navigation system to the end of this century.

III. Satellite-Based Systems

Although a distinct advantage of loran use is continuous position fixing, its main disadvantage is that because its stations are land based, coverage is limited to within 800–1000 miles of transmitting stations. Therefore, total worldwide coverage with Loran-C isn't feasible; vast areas of open water have no coverage. Although Omega provides coverage on the high seas, there are disadvantages in maintaining accurate lane counts and updating position by comparing to a fix obtained with another navigation system or maintaining an accurate fix by dead reckoning (DR). For many, the answer to these problems has been navigation via satellite.

Satellite navigation had its beginning in 1957 when the Russians became the first to enter the space age with their historic launch of the earth's first artificial satellite, *Sputnik*. While the rest of the world marveled at the Russians' accomplishment, scientists turned their attention to tracking the satellite and collecting data. It quickly became apparent that by measuring the Doppler Shift in the frequency of the satellite's "bleep, bleep" as it passed overhead, its range could be determined. By knowing receiver position and a series of range determinations, scientist's could calculate the satellite's path (position). By reversing the process, that is, by knowing the satellite's position as it passes while Doppler measurements are made yielding subsequent ranges, scientists could determine position on the earth.

Transit

In the early 1960's, the U.S. Navy used the above principles to develop the first satellite navigation system, NNSS (Navy Navigation Satellite System), which was used to help position *Polaris* submarines. Also called Transit, or more commonly, Sat Nav, the system became operational in January 1964 and was released for nonmilitary use in July 1967. A Russian equivalent to Sat Nav called Tsicada was also put into use in the late 1960's.

The Transit system consists of a "nest" of four or five satellites that circle the earth in low (640 miles) polar orbits. It differs from many of the other navigational systems such as loran, DECCA, etc., which require more than one transmitting station, in that position can be determined from just one satellite.

Essentially, the satellite is tracked by measuring the change in the frequency of its radio waves during a two-minute period as it moves closer to or farther away from your position (Doppler Shift). During this time, the satellite also transmits its precise position, which it knows from information periodically fed into it by a land-based station. From this information, a Sat Nav receiver calculates an LOP based on the range differences from the satellite. Subsequent two-minute periods yield other LOPs, which can be crossed to establish a fix. (See Figure 1.10.) Within a 12- to 15-minute satellite pass, as many as six LOPs can

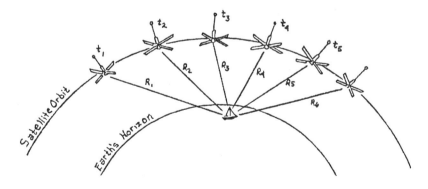

t_1 through t_6 represent satellite's position at different times and successive transmissions which occur at 2 minute intervals.

R_1 through R_6 represent the respective ranges or distances between the satellites and receiver at these positions as determined by Doppler Shift.

An LOP is determined from each satellite's spatial position and each subsequent range.

Figure 1.10   Determining a Fix from a Satellite in the Transit System

be calculated to produce a very precise fix (0.1 nm/600 feet)—as long as you are stationary.

One of the main disadvantages with Sat Nav is the 15-minute time element required to track a satellite and calculate a fix. If you are moving, speed and heading must be accurately fed into the receiver or position will be off—i.e., an error of 1 knot in speed can throw a fix off by as much as 0.2 nm. Because of this tracking time element and the fact that it produces only two-dimensional fixes, Sat Nav is used primarily to calculate position of low dynamic vehicles, has little use in a high-dynamic environment (aircraft, missiles), and thus lacks value as a military utility.

Another disadvantage in navigating with Sat Nav is that it isn't continuous. You have to wait for a satellite to pass by, and in latitudes close to the equator, theoretically, the wait can be as long as 110 minutes. Also a satellite pass may not necessarily guarantee a fix. If the elevation angles are too low or high for the receiver to accurately read the signal or the time that the satellite is in direct line of sight is too short for an adequate number of Doppler counts, the pass will be rejected. Thus, several hours may lapse between fixes, and some means must be made to dead reckon between fixes, either electronically or otherwise. Note: In the early 1990's, a constellation of seven satellites provided the best system coverage since Sat Nav's initiation in 1964.

Regional Satellite Systems

A couple of smaller satellite systems provide coverage only over a specific region. These satellites are usually communication satellites in geo-stationary orbits. Undegraded accuracies are often in the order of 5–25 meters. These systems come under the general heading of Radio Determination Satellite Systems (RDSS) and are operated in the commercial sector.

One of these systems is Star-Fix, which provides positioning service in the Gulf of Mexico and the Midwestern United States. It is used primarily by the oil industry and comes with a day-rate service fee. Another system is Geostar, which combines satellite communications with Loran-C. Coverage is primarily in the North American continent, but a similar European system, Locstar, is proposed for use beginning in the mid–1990's. Another proposed European system is NAVSAT, which also uses geo-stationary satellites along with high-orbiting satellites similar to those used in the GPS system. Although some of these systems have yet to become reality, they are mentioned here primarily to indicate the worldwide interest in the potential of using satellite-based navigation systems.

NAVSTAR GPS

There are advantages and disadvantages with each of the radionavigation systems described so far. For example, Loran-C provides continuous position-fixing capabilities but lacks worldwide coverage. Loran accuracy is often affected by adverse weather conditions and inconsistent transmission times over varying terrain (ASF). Sat Nav offers worldwide coverage but only intermittently. It also suffers from errors obtained during the time it takes to track a given satellite. GPS combines the best of both loran and Sat Nav: continuous coverage, everywhere, in all kinds of weather with a high degree of potential accuracy.

The name "GPS" is an abbreviation for Navstar GPS, which stands for **NAV**igation Satellite Timing And Ranging Global Positioning System. It is a satellite-based three-dimensional positioning system that also provides precise time and velocity information. The Russian counterpart to GPS is called Glonass, which is derived from **GLO**bal **NA**vigation Satellite System.

The Navstar GPS concept began in 1973 when personnel from the United States Air Force, Army, Navy, Marine Corps, and Defense Mapping Agency integrated their technological resources to produce a highly accurate satellite-based navigation and timing system. Years of studies and tests demonstrated system feasibility, and with the launching of 11 experimental Block I satellites (10 successfully launched into orbit) from 1978 to 1985, it became apparent that a precise, continuous global solution to position fixing and navigation was a realizable goal.

The GPS system consists of a constellation of 24 satellites in six orbital planes, which will provide a 98% probability of having 21 or more satellites operational at any time. The satellites are placed in very high orbits (10,900 nm) with an inclination angle of 55 degrees to the equator and an approximate 12-hour period (11 hours 56 minutes). It is because of the high orbits and precise spacing of satellites that continuous position fixing is assured with a minimum of five satellites always in view to users worldwide. (Glonass satellites are in slightly lower orbits arranged in only three orbital planes.)

The theory behind GPS is somewhat similar to that of Sat Nav in that an LOP is established by calculating the position and range of a specific satellite at a given moment in time. Like Sat Nav, GPS depends on accurate and continuous knowledge of the spatial position of each satellite in the system. It differs from Sat Nav in that instead of using the Doppler Effect to calculate the range, GPS actually determines the range at a specific time by measuring how long it takes a radio signal to reach a receiver from the satellite. This signal transfer time is achieved by synchronizing the satellites and GPS receivers so that they generate the same code at the same time. By measuring the time difference in receiving the satellite code, distance from the satellite can be computed to establish an LOP. In actuality, the distance is called a pseudo-range because of receiver clock error. This error is resolved mathematically with computations from additional satellites. (For further discussion of system characteristics and GPS operation, see Chapters 2 and 3.)

To get a two-dimensional fix, another LOP is calculated from a second satellite and where the LOPs cross is your position, similar to loran theory. To resolve the time element, a third satellite is needed to determine a two-dimensional fix, and a fourth satellite if a three-dimensional fix is required. (See Figure 1.11.)

While the advantages of continuous position fixing anywhere in the world are obvious, accuracy is where the GPS system exhibits its greatest potential. Noncivil accuracy in the predictable mode is 22 meters or better, a little more than the width of an average street. Yet, in the early days of GPS, with less than a full complement of satellites, accuracies of 5–15 meters were often achieved depending on the dynamics (stationary

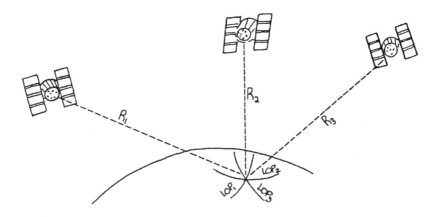

R = Actual range from each satellite to user.

Note: GPS differs from Transit in that each LOP is determined from a different satellite. Transit LOPs are determined from the same satellite over a given tracking period.

Figure 1.11   Determining a Fix with GPS Satellites

applications) of the user. The ultimate in accuracy, however, is in the extension of the system called Differential GPS. With this technique, position errors are measured at a known location and then used to update subsequent fixes in the area. In this mode, accuracies of 1 meter or better at a fixed location are possible.

At this point, it is important to note that these degrees of accuracy are not available to all users. GPS provides two different services for position fixing: Precise Positioning Service (PPS) and Standard Positioning Service (SPS). PPS (22 meters 2 drms or better accuracy) requires the use of certain cryptographic keys and is limited to military and official government users. SPS is a degraded system that is available to all users and provides 100 meters 2 drms or better positioning accuracy. (See Chapter 6 for a discussion of 2 drms.)

IV. The Future of Radionavigation

From the foregoing discussion, it should be obvious that at the close of the twentieth century there is a proliferation of radionavigation systems worldwide. Present use, along with inherent potential, has assured radionavigation high priority in the contemporary array of nav-aids. Virtually every major country on the planet is planning to establish or continue some form of radionavigation that will meet its needs.

Amid the diversity of systems, one bright star that seems to exceed the promise and potential of all others emerges: GPS. In the early 1990's, GPS was purported to be the ultimate in radionavigation. Yet, as the new technology emerges, questions are being asked about the fate of the old technologies. Given GPS's availability and accuracy, there exist some real concerns about the future radionavigation systems mix.

The FRP and Federal Radionavigation Systems

Users of radionavigation systems are not the only ones who express concern about the future of present radionavigation systems. Agencies of the U.S. Federal Government, DOD and DOT, which are responsible for the development and maintenance of many of these systems, including GPS, are also taking a hard look at the future and addressing the problems of overlap and redundancy.

It is the responsibility of DOT to ensure safe and efficient transportation in all areas, a responsibility that includes the use of radionavigation systems. DOD is responsible for the development, implementation, and maintenance of aids to navigation and equipment required for national defense. Together, these agencies have complied the Federal Radionavigation Plan (FRP), which is the official source of radionavigation planning and policy for the Federal Government.

The FRP was first released in 1980 and is updated biennially. Covering nine different navigation systems, its main goals are to:

1. Select a <u>mix</u> of those common-use civil/military systems that meet diverse user requirements for accuracy, reliability, availability, integrity, coverage, operational utility, and cost;
2. Provide adequate capability for future growth;
3. Minimize unnecessary duplication of service.

Because of national commitment to GPS and if its full civil capabilities are to be realized, DOT will consider phasing out some of the existing radionavigation systems. Since some of the Federally sponsored navigation systems exist outside of the U.S., the FRP also has an impact on international radionavigation planning. Decisions to discontinue Federal operation of an existing system will depend on a number of factors. (See Figure 1.12.)

The FRP makes it quite clear that DOD is putting all its navigational eggs into the GPS basket. Yet, it is also sensitive to the needs of the civil community, particularly concerning those systems that have low-cost access and large user communities or that are lacking alternatives. Even though DOD requirements will cease for most systems in December 1994, many systems will continue for civil use into the twenty-first century.

1. Resolution of GPS accuracy, coverage, integrity, and financial issues.
2. Determination that the systems mix meets civil and military needs currently met by existing systems.
3. Availability of civil user equipment at prices that would be economically acceptable to the civil user.
4. Establishment of a transition period of 10-15 years.
5. Resolution of international commitments.

* Taken from the 1992 Federal Radionavigation Plan.

Figure 1.12   Factors Affecting Discontinuation of Federal Operation of existing Radionavigation Systems. *

Two of these systems are radiobeacons and Omega. Both maritime and aeronautical radiobeacons serve the civilian user community with low-cost radionavigation and will continue to be used into the next century. Marine radiobeacons have an additional utility in providing the communications link in DGPS. Many of those beacons that don't provide differential corrections may be phased out after the year 2000. Because Omega is the sole means of navigation for both maritime and aviation users in some oceanic areas, it is expected to remain as part of the radionavigation mix into the next century. However, because the United States operates the system in conjunction with six other nations, Omega's future is dependent upon continued participation of these countries under bilateral agreement.

Most of the systems serving the airways will remain at least to the year 2000. Civil use of VOR/DME as an international standard in controlled airspace will continue as a short-range navigation system into the next century. However, in the early 1990's, the Federal Aviation Administration (FAA) initiated steps towards authorizing the use of Loran-C and GPS as stand-alone alternatives to VOR/DME for Instrument Flight Rules operations. DOD requirements for VOR/DME and TACAN will terminate when GPS becomes an approvedsystem for sole-means navigation in national and international controlled airspace. That target date is near the close of the century. As stated earlier, MLS is expected to gradually replace ILS in national and international aviation.

The one system that has absolutely no future in the radionavigation mix is Transit. Even early in its history, Sat Nav was considered an interim system until the advent of fully operational GPS. This was particularly due to inherent problems with the system, such as lack of three-dimensional fixes and intermittent position fixing that prevented its use in a high dynamic environment. Originally it was scheduled to be discontinued in 1992, but the Space Shuttle disaster in January 1986 pushed this date back and Sat Nav was given a few years' reprieve. The FRP clearly states that the DOD requirement for Transit will cease, and system operation will terminate in December 1996.

Probably the single system for which there is the greatest concern, at least within the United States, is Loran-C. With a user community of over 1 million and receivers costing only a few hundred dollars, Loran-C use has far exceeded original expectations. The early 1990's even saw expansion of the system with the addition of two new mid-continent chains to provide continuous coverage for aviation use. While the military requirement for Loran-C will cease December 31, 1994, it is important to note that FRP policy states that those chains serving the continental United States, Alaska, and coastal areas will continue to remain in operation until 2015.

Outside the continental United States, the picture is quite different. Overseas loran stations, including those in the Hawaiian Islands, which are operated by the U.S. Coast Guard, will be phased out or transferred to host governments. A good example of this occurred in October 1989 when Korea took over the operation of two loran stations in the Commando Lion Chain located in that country. Along with the transfer and plans for future expansion, the name of the chain was changed to the East Asian Chain.

The impetus of the FRP is, of course, the introduction of GPS, which will have wide military and civil applications on a global basis. In the FRP, GPS is represented as DOD's primary radionavigation system well into the next century. It goes on to describe in detail two levels of service: the Standard Positioning Service (SPS), which will have a degraded form of accuracy available for civil users, and the Precise Positioning Service (PPS), which provide highly accurate positioning, velocity, and timing determinations only for military and authorized users.

Non-Federal Systems

Outside the Federally operated systems, others throughout the world are taking a close look at their navigational needs. For example, in 1990, the United Kingdom announced its commitment to Loran-C to replace the deteriorating DECCA system for United Kingdom waters. Subject to international agreement, the proposal also chose Loran-C as the standard marine radionavigation system during the 1990's for northwest Europe and the North Atlantic. Norwegians are looking to expand their loran chain, and India is looking to replace some of its deteriorating DECCA stations with Loran-C. Other countries that either are considering expansion of or have renewed interest in loran are Canada, South Africa, and a number of South American countries.

Of the satellite systems, Glonass, the Russian counterpart of GPS, holds the most promise. Regional systems, such as those proposed for European coverage, could also expand to worldwide coverage. In the private sector, certain regional systems provide services for those with high-precision accuracy requirements that are not available in the degraded form of GPS.

In The Final Analysis

Everyone says GPS is going to be big, but no one really seems to know how big. Certainly, widespread application is inherent in all aspects of use, including surveying, marine exploration, monitoring land vehicles, and air and marine navigation. Accurate projections are hard to come by, and the U.S. Government, which is usually conservative in its estimates, doesn't extend beyond the mid-1990's in projecting surface civil use. Modest projections are that non Government civil use will grow rapidly and will far outweigh military use by the year 2000.

The future of GPS seems to hinge on two factors: availability and accuracy. The FRP does not quibble; it warns that all Federally operated systems are operated only as long as the United States and its allies receive greater military benefit than do their adversaries, and the systems don't jeopardize national defense. Subject to national emergency, these systems may cease operations or change signal characteristics and formats.

It is, however, the concept of accuracy that will have the most profound effect on how much GPS is used or which other radionavigation systems will continue into the next century. Compared to GPS in the degraded form, many of the existing systems provide equal or better position-fixing capabilities. On the other hand, if the full accuracy potential of GPS is realized, particularly in the differential mode, the applications on land, sea and in the air are unlimited—a promise for the future no crystal ball can predict.

CHAPTER TWO

System Characteristics & Program Development

Since the early 1960's, the military has actively pursued the concept of a continuous worldwide space-based positioning system that would provide highly accurate positioning and navigation capabilities for a large spectrum of users. Forerunners of the concept were the Transit system and Timation (a program for developing high stability oscillators and two-dimensional navigation), both sponsored by the Navy. Another forerunner was a continuous service three-dimensional navigation system called System 621 B, which was tested by the Air Force.

The actual beginnings of the GPS concept date back to 1973 when the Air Force, Army, Marine Corps, and Navy, along with the Defense Mapping Agency (DMA), combined the results of years of tests and technological resources toward the common goal of a continuous global positioning system. In April 1974, the U.S. Deputy Secretary of Defense designated the Air Force as the executive service to combine these concepts, and the GPS system emerged as the one that kept the best features of previous satellite systems.

The new system was developed and managed by the Joint Program Office (JPO) located at the Air Force Systems Command, Space Division, Los Angeles Air Force Station in California. It combined participation of all military services along with the DOD, DOT, NATO personnel, and allied nations. National commitment to the project is clearly demonstrated by the $10.14 billion price tag required to get the system operational by 1993. A large portion of this money goes to the network of satellites and their launches into orbit. The development and acquisition of the GPS program have been divided into three segments: the space segment, the control segment, and the user segment. (See Figure 2.1.)

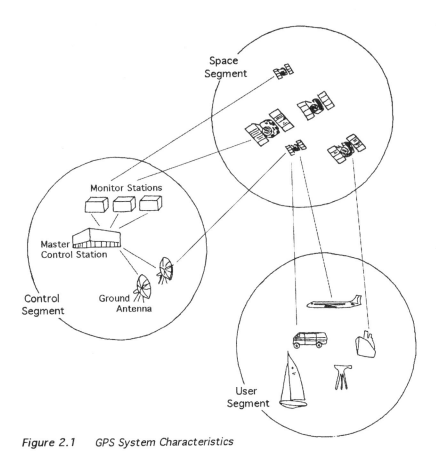

Figure 2.1   GPS System Characteristics

I. The Space Segment

Satellites

The GPS system consists of a constellation of 24 satellites positioned in six orbital planes. The contract to build the first two blocks of satellites was awarded to Rockwell International's Satellite & Space Electronics Division located at Seal Beach, California. To accommodate the demand for producing "assembly line" spacecraft, Rockwell International and its subcontractors invested over $50 million to streamline their production facilities.

The satellites were designed and produced in two different generations: Block I and Block II. Block I consisted of 11 space-based satellites designed to test system feasibility. This developmental and concept-validation phase of the GPS program was an overwhelming success. Exceeding initial expectations, three-dimensional position parameters to within 50 feet, velocity measured to fractions of a foot/second, and time to 100 parts in a trillion became a reality. Although Block I satellites were designed with an expected life span of five years, many far exceeded that span, and one was still operating 11 years after it had been launched.

Block II satellites consist of more than 65,000 parts with a central unit housing controls, and electronic, propulsion, and telegraphic equipment. In orbit they weigh approximately 1900 lbs. Most of their electrical power is supplied by arrays of honeycomb solar panels, which when extended to each side, produce a total complex that measures approximately 17 feet. The solar panels also help stabilize the satellite as do balancing wheels controlled by powerful magnets. To provide electrical power when they move into earth-eclipse, the satellites are supplied with battery back-up. Key elements in the precision timing of each satellite are four atomic (rubidium or cesium) clocks, which gain or lose only one second every 70,000 years. Another important feature is that the satellites can be maneuvered in space to adjust for gaps in the system if any satellites become unreliable or cease to function.

Nine regular Block II satellites were produced and launched in the late 1980's and in 1990. In 1990, a new breed of Block II's, the Block IIA, was produced. The Block IIA satellite carries a heavier payload than its predecessors as well as additional onboard systems that "harden" some elements for improved military survivability. Interestingly, after a long run of successful launches and subsequent satellite operation of first-generation Block II satellites, the first Block IIA satellite (SVN 23) caused a glitch in the system. Due to electrical failure of a control unit that automatically positions the solar arrays toward the sun, the satellite's panels were put into a locked position. The satellite was still able to function, but only with time-consuming manual control from the ground. Subsequent launches in 1991 were set back from January until midsummer when the problem was resolved.

To keep the GPS system continuously functional, a third generation of satellites, the Block IIR (replenishment) satellites, are being produced. These will be used to replace Block II satellites as they reach the end of their usable life span. The contract to produce 20 replenishment satellites was awarded to General Electrics Astrospace in Princeton, New Jersey.

The core of the Block IIR satellite without extensions measures 60"W x 76"D x 75"H and has an in-orbit weight of 2370 lbs. The Block IIR has a number of performance advances over earlier Block II's including longer autonomous satellite operation without ground control corrections (six months), improved user navigation accuracies through autonomous crosslink ranging, improved reliability, and increased service life and survivability (design life: 10 years). A fourth generation of satellites, the Block IIF (follow-on), is in the planning stages for future replacement as older satellites become unusable.

Orbital Configuration

Initially, the GPS system was designed for a constellation of 21 operational satellites and three orbital spares. In December 1979, these numbers were reduced to 18 operational satellites and three orbital spares because of budget cuts. Then in 1982, the three orbital spares were put back actively into the system, and in March 1989, the plan for the original 24-satellite constellation was approved.

The satellites are positioned in very high orbits (10,900 miles/20,180 km) in the familiar birdcage constellation of six orbital planes: A, B, C, D, E, and F. The 10 Block I satellites, which were used primarily for testing system feasibility, were placed in two orbital planes—A and C. To provide maximum coverage for the main military testing at Yuma Proving Grounds in Arizona, they were positioned with inclinations of approximately 64 degrees between the orbit plane and the earth's equator with 120 degrees phasing between each plane.

Design for the completed system calls for four satellites in each of the six orbital planes positioned with an inclination angle of 55 degrees. To ensure maximum coverage, the ascending nodes of orbits in adjacent planes are separated by 60 degrees. The positions of the satellites in each plane are such that there will always be at least five satellites and often more in view to the earth-based user.

The 12-hour period (one revolution around the earth) of each satellite is within one minute of 1/2 sidereal day, which is approximately four minutes shorter than one solar day. To make sure that it's antenna is always pointed toward earth, the satellite rotates once per orbit on an axis perpendicular to the orbital plane.

It is interesting to note that the orbital configuration of the Glonass system differs in a number of ways from GPS. Although the Glonass satellites are placed in somewhat lower orbits (10,200 miles/19,100 km), the main difference is that they are positioned in only three orbital planes. These planes are positioned with an inclination of 65 degrees and a phase angle of 120 degrees. (See Figure 2.2.) Another difference is that the Glonass orbital period is somewhat shorter, 11 hours 15 minutes, which means that the satellites do not appear at the same point in space each day as GPS satellites do (minus 4 minutes). For a comparison of orbital characteristics of the two systems, see Figure 2.3.

Launch Schedule and Operation

Block I satellites were launched from Vandenburg Air Force Base in California using Atlas E/F rockets. The first launch took place on 22 February 1978 and the final launch in the series on 9 October 1985. Each launch is identified by a Space Vehicle Number (SVN). There were 11 launches in all with only one failure, SVN #7 on 18 December 1981. It is important to note that each satellite is further identified by a PRN

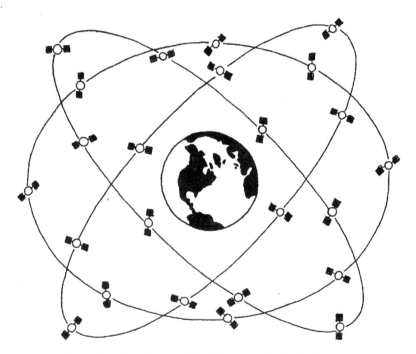

21 operational satellites plus 3 orbiting spares in 3 orbital planes

Figure 2.2   The Glonass Constellation

	GPS	GLONASS
Number of satellites	21 + 3 spares	21+ 3 spares
Orbital altitude	10,900 miles/20,180 km	10,200 miles/19,100 km
Orbital planes	6	3
Inclination to equator	55	64.8
Phase angle between planes	60	120
Period	12 hrs	11 hrs, 15 min

Figure 2.3   Comparing GPS and GLONASS Orbital Characteristics

number that refers to a unique Pseudo Random Noise code of the satellite. For a summary of Block I launching dates and satellite usage, see Figure 2.4.

The operating lives of Block I satellites varied from three years (SVN #7/PRN #2) to 11 years (SVN #4/PRN #8 and SVN #6/PRN #9) and an unexpected 13 1/2 years (SVN #3/PRN #9). One satellite, SVN #6/ PRN #9, had an interesting history. It was shut down on 11 December 1990 because of faulty wheel balancing, which prevented it from obtaining proper earth alignment for continuous transmission. Then, when it became apparent that war with Iraq was imminent in the Persian Gulf, SVN #6 was set usable and repositioned so that it would provide cover-

SVN #	PRN #	Orbital Plane	Launch Date	Operational Date	Deactivation Date	Performance Notes
1	4		22 Feb, '78	29 Mar, '78	17 Jul, '85	
2	7		13 May, '78	14 Jul, '78	16 Jul, '81	
3	6		06 Oct, '78	09 Nov,'78	29 Apr, '92	
4	8		11 Dec, '78	08 Jan, '79	14 Oct, '89	
5	5		09 Feb, '80	27 Feb, '80	28 Nov, '83	
6	9		26 Apr, '80	16 May,'80	06 Mar, '91	I
7			18 Dec, '81			II
8	11	C3	14 Jul, '83	10 Aug,'83	operational*	
9	13	C1	13 Jun, '84	19 Jul, '84	operational*	
10	12	A1	08 Sep, '84	03 Oct, '84	operational*	
11	3	C4	09 Oct, '85	30 Oct, '85	operational*	

SVN - Space Vehicle Number

PRN - Satellite identification number by pseudorandom noise code

I - Satellite was shut down 11 Dec, '90 because of a faulty balancing wheel, then repositioned
    and reactivated to provide two hours coverage over the Persian Gulf during the Gulf Crisis,
    and finally shut down permanently 6 Mar, '90.

II - Launch failure

* - as of January 1993

Figure 2.4   Summary of Block I Launches and Satellite Usage

age for about two hours/day and supplement coverage in the Persian Gulf. After the cease-fire with Iraq, SVN #6 was removed from system operations on 6 March 1991 by the Second Satellite Control Squadron at Falcon Air Force Base in Colorado, which is responsible for managing GPS operations. The satellite was then turned over to the First Satellite Control Squadron for two months of data collection before it was permanently boosted approximately 15 km out of orbit. These events are recounted to illustrate the flexibility of the GPS system in the manual control and positioning of satellites to adjust for system defects and requirements.

Originally, Block II satellites were to have been launched by the Space Transportation System (Space Shuttle), but the delays that followed the *Challenger* disaster in January 1986 forced the Air Force to seek an alternative launch vehicle, an improved Delta rocket, the Delta II. Block II satellites were launched on the expendable Delta II's from the Cape Canaveral Air Force Station adjacent to the Kennedy Space Center. The first launch occurred on 14 February 1989, just a little more than three years after the *Challenger* disaster—a setback that pushed the original 1989 GPS system completion date into the early 1990's. By 1991, with a constellation of 15 operational satellites (five Block I's and ten Block II's), two-dimensional coverage of more than 20 hours/day worldwide was a reality. Subsequent satellite function delays with second-generation Block II satellites pushed the completion date to the mid-1990's. However, beginning in 1992, satellites were launched and declared operational with clockwork regularity. By early 1993, there were 21 functioning satellites: four Block I's, nine Block II's and

SVN #	PRN #	Orbital Plane	Launch Date	Operational Date	Deactivation Date	Performance Notes
14	14	E1	14 Feb, '89	15 Apr, '89	operational*	
13	2	B3	10 Jun, '89	11 Jul, '89	operational*	
16	16	E3	18 Aug, '89	14 Oct, '89	operational*	I
19	19	A4	21 Oct, '89	26 Nov, '89	operational*	
17	17	D3	11 Dec, '89	06 Jan, '89	operational*	
18	18	F3	24 Jan, '90	16 Feb, '90	operational*	
20	20	B2	24 Mar, '90	18 Apr, '90	operational*	
21	21	E2	02 Aug, '90	22 Aug, '90	operational*	
15	15	D2	01 Oct, '90	15 Oct, '90	operational*	

I - Had original rubidium clock which was changed to cesium clock in early 1991.

* - as of January 1993

Figure 2.5   Summary of Block II Launches and Satellite Usage

34

eight Block IIA's. For the first time, this 21-satellite operational constellation provided three-dimensional 24 hours/day coverage. (See Figure
2.5 for a Summary Launch Schedule of Block II Satellites and Figure 2.6
for a similar schedule of Block IIA satellites.)

Interestingly, with each successive satellite launch, the time required
to get each satellite to operational status was substantially shortened.
For example, 2 1/2 to 3 months of in-orbit testing were required for
PRN #14 launched on 14 February 1989. By 1990, this testing period
had been shortened to approximately two weeks.

II. The Control Segment

The GPS concept is predicated on obtaining two important pieces of
information: the distance from a transmitting satellite to the user and

SVN #	PRN #	Orbital Plane	Launch Date	Operational Date	Deactivation Date	Performance Notes
23	23	E4	26 Nov, '90	10 Dec, '90	operational*	1
24	24	D1	4 Jul, '91	30 Aug, '91	operational*	
25	25	A2	23 Feb, '92	24 Mar, '92	operational*	
28	28	C2	10 Apr, '92	25 Apr, '92	operational*	
26	26	F2	7 Jul, '92	23 Jul, '92	operational*	
27	27	A3	9 Sep, '92	30 Sep, '92	operational*	
32	1	F1	22 Nov, '92	11 Dec, '92	operational*	2
29	29	F4	18 Dec, '92	8 Jan, '93	operational*	
22	22	B1	3 Feb, '93	30 Mar, '93	operational*	
31	31	C3	4 Apr, '93	13 Apr, '93	operational*	
37	7	C1	13 May, '93	13 Jun, '93	operational*	3
39	9	A1	NET 26 Jun, '93			
35	5	B4	NET 2 Sep, '93			
30	30	D4	NET 28 Oct, '93			
34	4	C1	NET 2 Mar, '94			

1 - 12 Dec, '90, solar panels put in locked position due to failure of solar array drive electronics.
Further launch schedules delayed until mid-summer '91.

2 - Initially was called PRN 32, but was changed to PRN 1.

3 - Marked the completion of a 24 operational satellite constellation: Four Block I, Nine Block II,
Eleven Block IIA satellites.

NET - No Earlier Than
NET dates are subject to change due to unforseeable problems.

* - as of June, 1993

Figure 2.6   Summary of Block I IA Launches and Satellite Usage

precise and continuous information about the exact spatial position of each satellite in the constellation with respect to time. It is the function of the Ground Control Segment or Operational Control System (OCS), which is operated by the Air Force Space Command, to provide and update the information on satellite position that is transmitted as part of the satellite message.

Fortunately, one of the advantages of the very high orbits used with GPS is that they are well outside of the earth's atmosphere and thus are very stable and mathematically predictable. Yet, in the interest of absolute precision, the Control Segment of the GPS system continuously monitors its satellites via five Monitor Stations and three Ground Antennas longitudinally spaced throughout the world. Three of these stations are located on small islands that are used mainly for military purposes: Ascension Island, Diego Garcia, and Kwajalein. These three stations also have ground antennas, which are used to transmit and receive satellite control and monitoring signals and to upload the corrected data back to the satellites. The other two stations are located in Hawaii and at the Falcon Air Force Station in Colorado Springs, Colorado. The Colorado Springs station also serves as the Master Control Station (MCS) for the group. A back-up MCS is positioned at the Onizuka Air Force Base in Sunnyvale, California. (See Figure 2.7.)

Using GPS receivers, the monitor stations passively track all satellites in view collecting their pseudorange and carrier-phase data. This information is transmitted back to the MCS where it is processed via sophisticated computer software models that predict the satellites' future orbits. This new set of orbital parameters, called the *ephemeris*, is transmitted back to those stations with ground antennas where it is uploaded to a specific satellite.

Updated ephemerides may be injected to the satellites up to three times/day. However, as a safeguard to the system in case of interrupted service from the Ground Control Stations, the Block II satellites can store updated orbital information for up to 14 days. The Block IIA's can store corrected ephemerides for 180 days and the Block IIR's for six months.

In addition to calculating and injecting orbital information into the satellites, another function of the Control Segment is to disseminate the orbital information to the user. This is done in a number of ways, the most important of which is direct transmission of the ephemeris from the satellite to the receiver. Another type of transmitted satellite message is the *almanac*, a "health message" that defines the orbits and health of

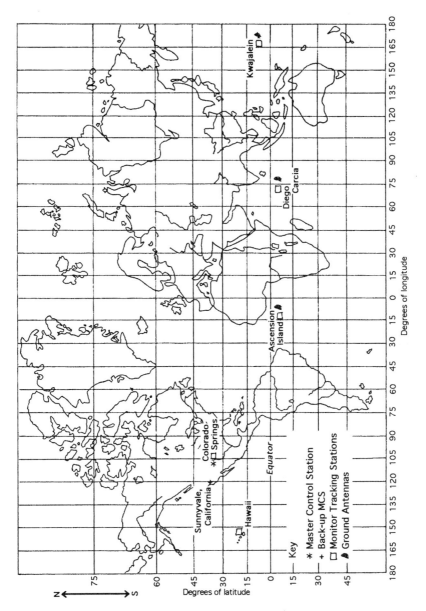

Figure 2.7   *Ground Stations Serving the GPS Control Segment*

all the satellites in the system. This information is used by the receiver to assist in acquiring those satellites that are above the horizon but not yet tracked.

Another way the user can access system status information is

37

through a number of Operational Advisory Broadcasts (OAB's). These broadcasts originate from the Coast Guard GPS Information Center (GPSIC), which is located at the Coast Guard Omega Navigation System Center in Alexandria, Virginia. Information is supplied to the center from the U.S. Air Force Second Satellite Operations Squadron, which operates the MCS in Colorado Springs. The broadcasts consist of:

1. Current constellation status
   (satellites healthy/unhealthy)
2. Recent outages
3. Future scheduled outages
4. Almanac data for predicting satellite visibility
   and coverage

The GPS Information Center uses two primary means of disseminat

I. Operational Broadcasts from the GPS Information Center

Voice Telephone Recording* (703) 313-5905	Summarizes current constellation status
Computer Bulletin (703) 313-5910 for modem speeds of 300 to 14,400 bps	Summarizes current constellation status plus more detailed information which includes the almanac.

II. Other Information Sources

WWVIWWVH HF radio broadcasts* 5, 10, 15, and 20MHz	Voice information WWV - minutes 14 and 15 WWVH - minutes 43 and 44
Defense Mapping Agency (DMA) Weekly Notices to Mariners*	Section III summarizes voice or data broadcast warning of GPS status information.
DMA Broadcast Warnings* (NAVAREA, HYDROLANT, HYDROPAC)	Issued via voice and CW. Generally geared for the offshore mariner.
DMA NavInfoNet. Automated Notice to Mariners System.	Data base which contains data on GPS status, outages and almanac.
USCG Broadcast Notices to Mariners*	Local and coastal information broadcasts.
NAVTEX Data Broadcast* 518 kHz	Worldwide chain of coastal radio stations that transmit navigation and meteorologic information by radio telex.

* no almanac

Figure 2.8   GPS Information Sources

ing this information: a voice telephone recording and a computer bulletin board system. The voice recording provides a brief summary of constellation status. The computer bulletin board system gives more detailed information.

The information is also given via a number of voice/data broadcasts, and in March 1990, GPS status information was added to WWV and WWVH broadcasts. In August 1990, status information was provided for inclusion in the weekly DMA Notice to Mariners. The information is also disseminated in the DMA's broadcast warning and the Coast Guard's broadcast notice to mariners. A summary of these sources of GPS information can be found in Figure 2.8. Further information on GPS or the Information Center can be obtained by writing:

Commanding Officer (GPSIC)
U.S. Coast Guard ONSCEN
7323 Telegraph Road
Alexandria, VA 22310-3998

III. The User Segment

The user segment consists of all areas in which GPS signals are used to determine navigation and time information. Although GPS was designed primarily as a military utility with extensive use in most military mission areas, it is expected that civil use and applications will far exceed military use by the year 2000. Federal projections for the GPS user community are seen in Figure 2.9.

At the heart of the user community is the GPS receiver or user equipment (UE). To assist in the development of UE, NATO nations were encouraged to participate, and in 1978, 10 NATO nations signed a Memorandum of Understanding directed toward the development of GPS. In addition to the formal involvement with NATO countries, the DOD worked with other allied nations, including Australia, in developing and testing UE. Much of what was learned has filtered down and has direct applications on all types of UE. Even before GPS was fully operational, the civil market offered commercial receivers, many of which exhibited spin-off technology from early military testing contracts.

Although user community applications of GPS may be quite varied, receivers can be divided into three types based on the dynamics of the

Calendar Years

Facilities/Users	1990	1991	1992	1993	1994	1995	1996	1997	1998	1999	2000	2001	2002	2003
Development Satellites	6	5	4	3	0	0	0	0	0	0	0	0	0	0
Operational Satellites	10	15	20	24	24	24	24	24	24	24	24	24	24	24
DOD Users	2,300	4,500	6,000	7,000	9,000	12,000	16,000	21,000	26,000	28,000	33,000	38,000	43,000	48,000
Civil Aviation Users [1,2,4]	400	750	1,200	1,800	2,400	4,000	6,000	10,000	20,000	40,000	80,000	100,000	150,000	200,000
Civil Land Users [1,4,5]	2,500	3,750	5,600	8,400	12,600	18,900	28,400	[3]						
Civil Maritime Users [1,4]	4,000	6,000	9,000	13,500	20,250	30,375	45,600	[3]						

1 Includes non-DOD Federal users.
2 Civil use of GPS/SPS is not authorized for IFR until DOD declares the GPS fully operational and until civil user equipment is approved by FAA.
3 Data necessary for projections beyond this year are not available.
4 Worldwide.
5 Includes survey and time users.

Taken from 1990 Federal Radionavigation Plan

Figure 2.9   *GPS User Community Projections*

user while GPS signals are being processed:

Low-dynamic sets operate in an environment with a velocity of less than 25 meters/second or approximately 48 knots. Examples would be fixed-base operations such as surveying, soldier-carried "manpacks", land vehicles, and most boats.

Medium-dynamic receivers operate with a velocity between 25 m/sec and 150m/sec or approximately 290 k. Certain military applications such as the UH-60 helicopter and CV-64 aircraft carrier are in this category.

High-dynamic applications range from 150m/sec and above. Examples would be commercial and military aircraft. Navy submarines and surface ships are also in this category, but for other reasons than dynamics.

Note that these divisions are really just categories for general classification. A further discussion of the different types of UE is found in Chapter Four and of applications in the User Segment in Chapter Eight.

IV. GPS Program Development and Implementation

The development and acquisition of the GPS program can be divided into three major phases and a number of subphases. (See Figure 2.10.)

PHASE I: Concept Validation (1973-1979)

In December 1973, the Joint Program Office received approval to begin the concept validation phase for the Navstar GPS program in which all segments of the GPS concept were tested for system feasibility. The first year permitted companies to compete for the design and development contracts for the first generation Block I satellites, Phase I Control, User Segments, and equipment for the test range in Yuma, Arizona.

Space Segment: Initially, with no satellites positioned in space, an inverted range was constructed at the Yuma Proving Ground to simulate four GPS satellites using ground transmitters. The contract to provide the test range was awarded to General Dynamics.

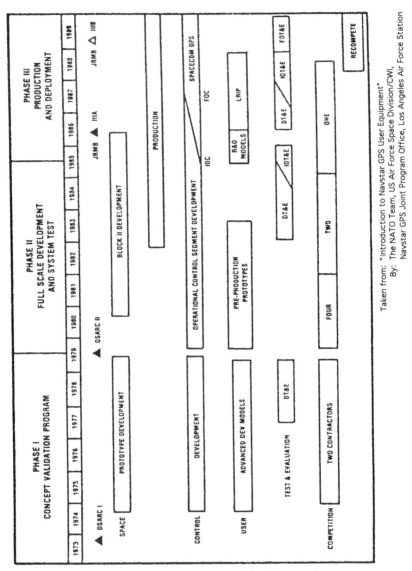

Figure 2.10   GPS Program Development and Implementation

In June 1974, Rockwell International was given the contract to provide three prototype GPS satellites. This contract was subsequently
increased to 11 satellites and one GPS navigation payload to be used on
a U.S. Naval Research Laboratory (NRL) satellite. The first GPS space
signals came from the NRL satellite, which was launched in June 1977
but malfunctioned after only seven or eight months. The first Block I
satellite was launched in February 1978, and as more satellites were put

into orbit, a combination of ground transmitters and satellites was used for testing. Limited two-dimensional navigation using only three satellites was first possible in October 1978, and limited three-dimensional navigation with four satellites in December 1978.

Control Segment: The contract for the Control Segment was awarded to General Dynamics in October 1974. In this phase, the Control Segment consisted of a MCS at Vandenberg Air Force Base in California and Monitor Stations at the Naval Communications Station in Hawaii and at Air Force Bases at Vandenberg, Guam, and Elmendorf, Alaska. The only Ground Antenna was at the Vandenberg Air Force Base.

User Segment: The contract for the User Segment was also awarded to General Dynamics in October 1974 but subsequently subcontracted to Magnavox. Initial User Equipment (UE) tests began at the Yuma Proving Ground in March 1977. Shipborne UE was first tested off the coast of California in October 1978. During Phase I, a variety of test platforms were provided by the Air Force, Army, Navy, and DMA. Tests in vehicle rendezvous, landing approach, harbor navigation, and clock synchronization provided excellent positioning and time transfer data and showed the potential for operational utility.

PHASE II: Full-Scale Development & Testing of GPS Segments (1979-1985)

Space Segment: In this phase, more Block I satellites were produced and launched to augment the existing satellite constellation and to replenish those Block I satellites that were reaching the end of their useful life. In December 1980, the contract for the development and production of Block II satellites went to Rockwell International. Production of Block II satellites began in the last quarter of 1982.

Control Segment: An Interim Control Segment (ICS) was developed to fill the gap between the Phase I Control System and the final Operational Control System (OCS). The contract for both ICS and OCS was awarded to IBM in September 1980.

User Segment: The User Segment in Phase II is divided into two stages: Phase IIA and IIB. Beginning in July 1979, Phase IIA involved four contractors: Magnavox, Rockwell/Collins, Texas Instruments, and Teledyne, which were selected to conduct tests on performance analyses and preliminary design of UE. In 1982, Magnavox and Rockwell/Collins were selected to continue design refinement and development of prototype UE in Phase IIB. Testing took place at the Yuma

Proving Ground and at the Naval Ocean Systems Center at San Diego, California. Test platforms included trucks, an aircraft carrier, a submarine, helicopters, and a variety of aircraft. Results substantiated the success of GPS in a military environment under different mission-oriented conditions.

PHASE III: Production and Deployment (1985-1993)

Space Segment: This phase featured continued launching of satellites and deployment of the full constellation to become fully operational by mid-1993. After a three-year delay in launch schedules due to the *Challenger* disaster, launching of satellites resumed in February 1989 with the first Block II satellite. In the next two years, a string of 10 successful launches of Block II's and Block IIA's greatly increased satellite coverage. Limited two-dimensional coverage was achieved in 1990, and limited three-dimensional coverage in 1991.

The improved version of the Block II satellite, the Block IIA, was first launched in November 1990. Unfortunately, the Block IIA satellites were beset with a number of problems so that additional launches were subsequently delayed.

To replace existing satellites that were no longer, useful a new replenishment satellite, the Block IIR, was designed. The contract to build the replenishment satellites was awarded to General Electrics Astrospace at Princeton, New Jersey.

Control Segment: The interim Initial Control Segment (ICS) was replaced with the final Operational Control Segment (OCS) first with initial operational capability in 1985 and then full operational capability in 1987. The new MCS was located at the Consolidated Space Operations Center at the Falcon Air Force Station in Colorado Springs. This transition from Vandenberg Air Force Base to Colorado Springs took place in 1985/86. A redundant system of additional Monitor Stations and Ground Antennas was established throughout the world so that the deactivation of any one station (sabotage/enemy attack) would not seriously jeopardize operational capability of the overall system.

User Segment: In 1985, Rockwell International's Collins Avionics and Communications Division was awarded the contract for low-rate initial production of GPS UE for the military. Initial production of receivers began in 1986 with full-scale production beginning in 1988. During this phase, testing continued with UE in a variety of military applications.

44

By the late 1980's, a number of commercial manufacturers began developing receivers for the nonmilitary community. By the early 1990's, a number of these receivers were available to the nonmilitary community, even though coverage fell short of 24 hours.

In previous phases, military UE performance was excellent but still below reliability and maintainability requirements, so a large part of the testing in Phase III was dedicated to verifying reliability-related test improvements. Interestingly, the first real test of GPS implementation as a military utility came during Phase III, before the system was fully operational, with the Persian Gulf crisis from August 1990 through March 1991.

By maneuvering existing satellites, GPS was able to provide 24 hours of two-dimensional coverage that accommodated most land and sea operations and 21 hours of the three-dimensional coverage required by aircraft in the Persian Gulf. By the time Iraq invaded Kuwait in early August 1990, over 4,000 military-designed GPS receivers had been delivered to the military. These were primarily built by Rockwell/Collins and consisted of one-channel "manpacks", two-channel aircraft receivers, and five-channel air and naval units. However, the military had to turn to other manufacturers to supplement its needs, and military specification units were also supplied by Texas Instruments and Magnavox. An additional 8,000 lightweight units, SLGRs or Sluggers, were ordered from Trimble and Magellen, which also supplied British, French, and Saudi troops with GPS receivers.

The use of commercially manufactured UE produced a dilemma for the DOD. These nonmilitary receivers were designed to access only the COurse Acquisition (C/A) code signal, whereas the military sets, which could also acquire the Precise code (P code), were able to produce a higher degree of accuracy. Accuracy was further limited for C/A code users by Selective Availability (SA), which had been turned on in March 1990. Thus, with many of our troops using commercial units that could acquire only the C/A code, the decision was made to turn off SA in early fall 1990. This meant, however, that any Iraqis with GPS receivers purchased before the crisis would also have access to a high degree of accuracy.

In the final days of Phase III implementation, the question arose as to what constitutes a **fully operational constellation**. The initial definition from the Joint Program Office for the fully operational GPS constellation was 21 operational satellites and three orbiting spares. If Block I satellites were accepted in the operational constellation, then

GPS could be declared fully operational by mid-1993. However, since the Block I satellites were nearing the end of their useful lives (one had been in operation for 10 years), it was questionable how much longer they could be counted on.

To address these questions, the 1992 Federal Radionavigation Plan identified two different levels of operational capability. The first to be achieved is Initial **Operational Capability (IOC)**, which will be attained when there are 24 GPS satellites (Block/I/II/IIA) operating in their assigned orbits and capable of delivering Standard Positioning Service for navigation use. This level was reached in mid-1993.

The second level, **Full Operational Capability (FOC)**, is of more concern to the DOD as it defines the condition when full and supportable military capability can be provided by the system. This level will be reached when 24 operational satellites (Block II/IIA) are operating in their assigned orbits <u>and</u> the constellation has successfully completed testing for operational military functionality. FOC is expected to take place in 1995. A fully operational constellation of all Block II satellites is planned to be in place by early 1994—16 years after the launch of the first Block I prototype satellite.

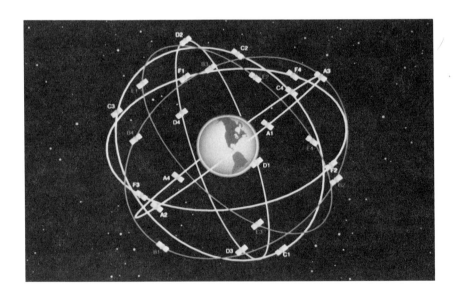

CHAPTER THREE

How GPS Works

I. Basic Theory

GPS is based on the concept of simultaneous timing/ranging to multiple satellites. The following is a brief discussion of the basic concepts used in position fixing with GPS. For a more thorough explanation of system characteristics, see Section II of this chapter.

Using Range to Determine Position

Ranging is not a new idea for navigators; in fact, it is the basic premise used in determining position in many navigation systems such as radar. For example, suppose you know your range from two or three different landmasses as measured with rings on a radar screen. Via radar, you know that your position is 2.98 nm from one island, 2.28 nm from another, and 3.17 nm from the third. Using a compass like the kind used in school geometry classes, you can transfer distance onto a navigational chart as an arc (segment of a circle of position or COP) from the landmass. Position is somewhere along the COP. Where two or more arcs cross is your fix or actual position. (See Figure 3.1.) The key is that you have to know two things: your distance from each landmass, and the known position of each landmass as displayed on a chart. The same is true with GPS. To compute your position, you need to know only two basic pieces of information:

1. The distance between you and a number of satellites.
2. Satellite positions when these distances are computed.

Satellite Ranging

If you know that your distance from a given satellite is 12,000 miles, then you know that your position is somewhere on the surface of a sphere that has a radius of 12,000 miles from the center where the satel

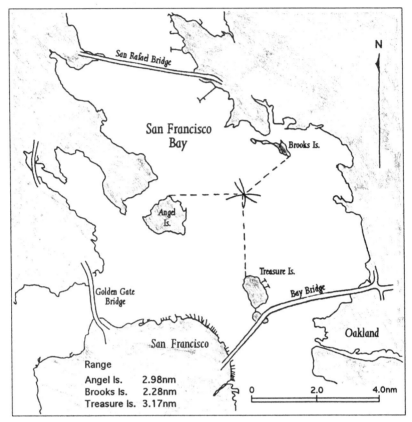

Range

Angel Is.	2.98nm
Brooks Is.	2.28nm
Treasure Is.	3.17nm

Figure 3.1   Determining Position by Using Radar Ranges

lite is located. (See Figure 3.2 A.)

As with radar, you can narrow this position down by adding another "sphere of position" calculated from the range of another satellite. Position would then be somewhere on a circle where the two spheres intersect. (See Figure 3.2 B.) If a third "sphere of position" is added from the calculated range of yet another satellite, position is now narrowed down to being at one of two points where the three spheres intersect. (See Figure 3.2 C.) Of the two possible positions, one can be ruled out as being way off — a ridiculous navigation solution — from your actual position.

For mariners and those determining position on land, the problem is simplified as they already know they are somewhere on the earth's surface. Think of the earth's surface as being one of the three "spheres of position." Thus, a two-dimensional fix is all that is required to determine position.

Suppose you are navigating on the ocean and your distance from Satellite A is 11,500 nm. This means that your position must be somewhere on an imaginary COP drawn on the surface of the earth that is exactly 11,500 miles at all points from the satellite. Now if you are also 13,200 miles from Satellite B, you are also located somewhere on another COP that is at all points 13,200 nm from the second satellite. Crossing the two COPs (just like crossing two LOPs with Loran-C or any other navigation system) will give you a fix. (See Figure 3.3.) Again there are two possibilities, one of which can be ruled out as being a ridiculous solution nowhere near your actual position and confirmed by determining a range from yet another satellite.

Thus, to determine a two-dimensional fix, the ranges from two different satellites are needed — theoretically. Actually, a third satellite is required to determine the time element, but more on that later. Airborne

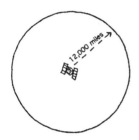

Position is somewhere on the surface of a sphere which is at all points 12,000 miles from the satellite.

A. Sphere of Position obtained with one satellite.

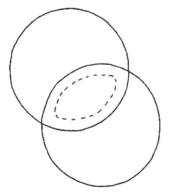

B. Circle of Position obtained where Spheres of Position from two satellites intersect.

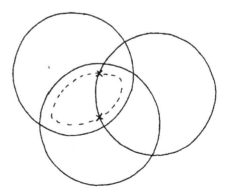

C. Two Points of Position obtained where Spheres of Position from three satellites intersect.

Figure 3.2   Determining Position by Satellite Ranging (3D)

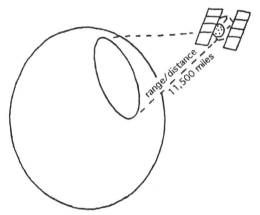

A. Position is somewhere on this Circle of Position (COP).

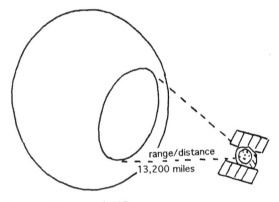

B. Position is also somewhere on this second COP.

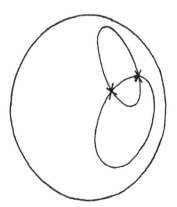

Note: Sketches are only diagramatic.
Distances and COPs are not drawn to scale.

C. A fix is established at one of the two points where the COPs cross.

Figure 3.3   Determining Position by Satellite Ranging (2D Fix)

navigators need three satellites to determine a three-dimensional fix, plus a fourth satellite for time adjustment.

Determining Satellite Range

(Time is of the Essence)

To determine the distance between you and a given satellite, you use the equation of speed multiplied by time:

Distance = speed x time

Because radio waves are a part of the electromagnetic spectrum (see Chapter 1) and travel at the speed of light (186,000 miles/second), it doesn't take long for the satellite signals to reach your receiver—even if they are 11,000 miles away. Therefore, the time in the equation is going to be incredibly small and is measured to the nearest nanosecond, or billionth of a second. Since the speed is a known constant, all you need to know to determine the distance from a satellite is the transmission time of a satellite-generated radio signal. In other words, distance becomes synonymous with time.

A binary digital code of 0's and 1's

0 1 0 0 0 1 1 0 1 0 1 0 1 1 0 0 1 1 1 0 1 0

Figure 3.4   The Pseudorandom Code

To measure this travel time, the GPS system uses a few neat tricks and some very sophisticated timing devices. One of the tricks is to have the satellite transmit the radio signal in a digital code that is made up of 1's and 0's, which at first glance looks like a random arrangement but, in actuality, is made up of very complicated repeated patterns. This is called a pseudorandom code. (See Figure 3.4.)

A GPS receiver generates an internal code at the same time that is an exact duplicate of the satellite code. The receiver matches the time difference between reception of a particular part of the satellite code with the same part of its own code. It does this by shifting its own code <u>in time</u> until it matches up with the satellite code. (See Figure 3.5.) Once the receiver knows the signal transmission time, range can be computed.

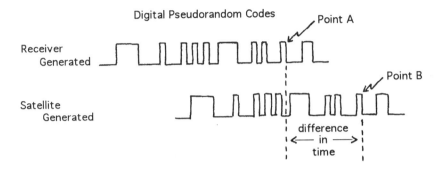

Digital Pseudorandom Codes

Receiver Generated

Point A

Satellite Generated

Point B

difference
←— in —→
time

Satellite transmission time is determined by comparing how late a specific point (B) is received in comparison to the same point (A) in the internal receiver generated code.

The receiver does this by shifting its own code in <u>time</u> until it matches up with the satellite code.

Figure 3.5   *Using Pseudorandom Codes to Determine Satellite Signal Transmission Time*

This process sounds simple, but the trick is to make sure that the satellite and receiver are generating the coded signals <u>at the same time.</u> At the satellite end, time is no problem. Satellites have very expensive cesium or rubidium atomic clocks, four in each satellite at $100,000 each. Any errors, however infinitesimally small, are periodically corrected by data uplinks from a ground control station just to make sure the satellites have the correct time — exactly.

At the receiver end, cost prohibits the use of such expensive atomic clocks so the range calculated between the satellite and the receiver is not correct. Other errors caused by the ionosphere, troposphere, and other sources make up a total error budget (all accumulated errors — see Chapter 6) that further contaminates the calculated range. Therefore, it is not a true range but a pseudorange. (See Figure 3.6.)

To correct for these receiver timing errors, GPS uses another trick by introducing another range measurement (remember that third satellite with a two-dimensional fix). This means getting another distance/range measurement from another satellite. In determining a two-dimensional fix with two LOPs (segments of COPs), a receiver would have no idea if it were off or not. For example, if the receiver clock is too fast, computed range would be greater than it really is, and actual position would not be where the two LOPs cross (as in Figure 3.7A), but in each case proportionately closer to the satellites. Note: If true ranges could be measured directly, then just two satellites would be needed to determine a two-dimensional fix and three satellites for a three-dimensional fix.

Introducing a third LOP produces the familiar "cocked hat" fix—if receiver timing is off, which it will be because of inaccurate receiver clocks. (See Figure 3.7B.) Here high technology and the computer age take over. GPS receivers are equipped with a built-in program that takes the information from the three LOPs and solves it algebraically until the three LOPs meet — exactly. These calculations involve solving three simultaneous equations for each pseudorange for the three unknowns: latitude, longitude, and clock error. In simpler terms, the calculations involve adding or subtracting specific time corrections until the error is calculated and the three LOPs meet. For a three-dimensional fix, four pseudoranges are required: one for each dimension and one to correct for receiver clock error.

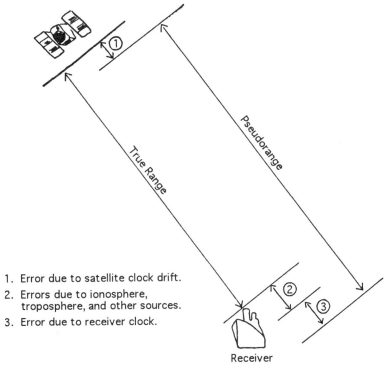

1. Error due to satellite clock drift.
2. Errors due to ionosphere, troposphere, and other sources.
3. Error due to receiver clock.

Figure 3.6   *Pseudorange Measurements*

Determining Satellite Position

Going back to the example of determining a radar fix, recall that it requires two pieces of information: the range to a given target or landmass AND the known position of that target as displayed on a chart. Thus, in addition to knowing the range to a given satellite, it is also necessary to know the position of the satellite at the time when that range was determined.

The GPS concept is predicated upon precise and continuous information of the spatial position of each satellite in the system. Fortunately, one of the advantages of the very high orbits used in GPS is that they are well outside of the earth's atmosphere and thus are very stable and mathematically predictable. Yet, in the interest of absolute precision, the Control Segment or Operational Control System continuously monitors its satellites via five Monitor Stations and Ground Antennas located throughout the world. (See Chapter 2.) Data from these stations is processed by the Master Control Station located at Falcon AFB in Colorado Springs, and the updated information with corrections is transmitted back to the satellites via the Ground Antennas.

GPS satellites transmit a number of messages to users' receivers here on earth. One, of course, is the pseudorandom code, which is used in time determination to measure satellite range. But they also transmit updated "ephemeris data," which precisely defines satellite position as a function of time. Another message is the almanac, which is a "health message" defining the orbits and health of all the satellites in the system.

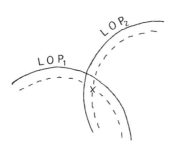 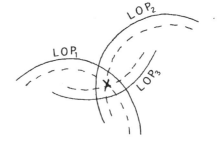

A. With only 2 LOPs exact position is not really known.
For example: If the receiver clock is too fast correct position would be somewhere near X.

B. If receiver clock is correct the 3rd LOP would intersect exactly.
Incorrect receiver timing is demonstrated by the 3rd LOP being off.
Receiver programs use this information to mathematically calculate a time correction which will allow the 3 LOPs to cross exactly.

Figure 3.7   Using a Third Range to Determine Receiver Timing Errors

For a more detailed description of the clock, ephemeris, and health messages, see Part II.

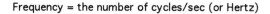

Frequency = the number of cycles/sec (or Hertz)

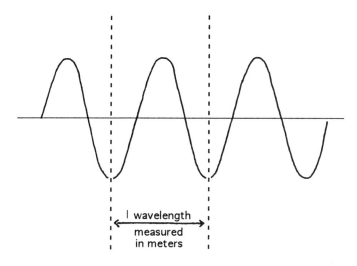

I wavelength
measured
in meters

Figure 3.8   A Typical Sine Wave Form

II. A Closer Look

The following discussions are not necessary for normal GPS use. They are included only to provide some further insight about system characteristics. Nor are these presentations meant to be exhaustive on GPS theory. They are addressed to the average GPS user who has an interest in pursuing system concepts.

The GPS Clock

The GPS system is designed to produce highly accurate position, velocity, and time determinations. Not only is time important from the standpoint of initiating satellite signal transmissions and measuring signal propagation time, but it is also the basis on which the whole system is constructed.

To the novice, time is usually represented by some kind of a time-

55

keeping device such as a quartz watch. In the world of electronics (and even a simple quartz watch), time is determined by measuring the oscillations or frequency of a stable signal such as sine wave. Frequency is how often the signal pattern repeats itself and is measured in cycles per second or equivalently, Hertz. (See Figure 3.8.)

All clocks contain an oscillator in which a resonator generates a signal of a given frequency. A resonator is anything that oscillates with a known frequency when excited. Examples of resonators are string instruments, such as a harp or violin, or pendulums, such as the movement of a metronome, used when practicing the piano. Unfortunately, these oscillations slowly deteriorate due to energy loss and need to be frequently stimulated or energized. For example, with the quartz watch, a small electric current is used to stimulate a quartz crystal, which causes it to continually oscillate with a given frequency.

The basis of time in the GPS system is the atomic clock, which has the most stable oscillator currently known to man — excited atoms that generate predictable and stable wavelengths of electromagnetic energy as they fall from a higher energy state to a lower one. The frequency of the waves is directly proportional to the change in energy of the atom. Since the energy states in atoms are quantized (occur only in certain combinations), the frequency of the waves produced is predictable.

There are two different types of atomic clocks in GPS space vehicles: cesium and rubidium. Cesium clocks are well known for their long-term stability (how well they stay on frequency) with a typical stability of 1 to 2 parts in 1012 in a 24-hour period. This translates to an error of approximately 2 – 5 meters in the determination of the pseudorange. Rubidium clocks come very close to cesium clocks in short-term stability (one day) but tend to wander over longer periods of time. Block II satellites contain two cesium and two rubidium clocks. This redundancy is not only provided as back-up in case of clock failure, but is also utilized to check one clock against another for enhanced accuracy and to determine GPS Time (see next section).

To provide a common time reference for the system, it is essential that all the satellite clocks are synchronized to the same frequency and that they drift at the same rate. Atomic clocks perform best with minimum adjustment. Thus, one of the tasks of the Control Segment is to monitor all satellite clocks and periodically uplink any corrections to the corresponding satellite. Until 1990, all satellites were compared to a single atomic clock at one of the Monitor Stations. GPS Time is now determined by comparing all the clocks in satellites and Monitor Stations.

These satellite clock corrections are then included in the broadcast Navigation Message, and the corrections are made on the receiver end.

The fundamental frequency of GPS clocks is nominally set prior to launch to operate at a frequency of 10.23 MHz. [One MHz (megahertz) equals 1 million cycles per second.] Actually to compensate for the effects of relativity, this clock frequency in the satellites is set slightly less. As demonstrated in Einstein's Special Theory of Relativity, a clock moving with a constant speed such as that in a satellite will appear to run slower than a clock on earth. However, according to his General Theory of Relativity, clocks are also affected by different gravitational potentials resulting in the satellite clocks running faster than earth clocks because they are farther away from the gravitational effects of the earth's center of mass. These two effects don't quite cancel each other out, with the net result being that a satellite clock gains 38.4 microseconds (microsecond = 1 millionth of a second) per day as compared to a clock on the ground. Because of this gain, all satellite clocks are set at a slightly reduced frequency — at 10.22999999545 MHz.

It is important to note that all the frequencies in the GPS system (i.e., code transmissions and carrier frequencies) generated from the satellites are a function of this fundamental clock rate of 10.23 MHz.

In the interests of national security, after all these efforts to achieve highly precise time determinations, **selective availability** (SA) intentionally degrades or introduces clock errors into the satellite transmissions. This process involves changing or dithering the satellite clock frequency by introducing an unknown, slowly varying delay into the time of the satellite signal transmission. Consequently, not only are errors introduced into the calculated pseudoranges and carrier-phase measurements, but the accuracy with which GPS Time can be determined from these measurements is also affected.

GPS Time

It is important to have an accurate timekeeping device, but it is also important to reference the time to an accurate time scale. Historically, there have been a number of different time systems, the earliest of which used the earth's rotation in respect to the sun — solar time. This, of course, varied depending on a person's position on the planet, as noon was defined when the sun crossed the local meridian. Within the last 100 years, we have become more sophisticated with our time scales with the introduction of 24 time zones of approximately 15 degrees of longitude in width in which time is related to Greenwich Mean Time. With the advent of atomic clocks and stellar observations, this concept has been further refined by a time scale called Universal Time Coordinated or UTC, which was introduced in 1961. To keep UTC concurrent with even more sophisticated systems, leap seconds have to be periodically introduced into the time scale. For example, a leap second was inserted into UTC just before midnight on 31 December 1990.

The time scale used in the GPS system is GPS Time. It is referenced to UTC but differs from it in that GPS Time doesn't contain periodic adjustments for leap seconds. To introduce leap seconds into GPS Time would necessitate a disruption in the continuous availability of satellites for navigation. Initially, GPS Time equalled UTC in 1980, but due to the insertion of leap seconds in UTC, GPS Time was 9 seconds ahead of UTC by 30 June 1993. GPS Time is continuously monitored by the United States Naval Observatory and corrected on a periodic basis. Disregarding the differences due to leap seconds, GPS Time is geared to be within approximately 1 microsecond of UTC over the long run.

GPS Time is further measured in recurring periods or epochs as the number of seconds that have elapsed since the previous Saturday/Sunday midnight at Greenwich, England. In order to be relevant, it is necessary to know which week the epoch is. These epochs begin with 6 January 1980 as week 0 and are numbered consecutively. For example, Friday, 24 December 1993 would be in GPS week 727.

The beginning of an epoch is important because it signifies the changes in an individual satellite's week-long segment of the very long P code (see section on Pseudorandom Codes, page 63). It is also important because each epoch is divided into smaller epochs of 1.5-second intervals called "Z-counts," beginning at midnight each Saturday. There are 403,199 of these Z-counts in each week, which are then re-initialized to zero at midnight each Saturday. Z-counts are important because they indicate the "address," or how far into the week a given P code has progressed, and they assist authorized receivers in locking into the correct portion of the P code at a given time during the week. These 1.5-second intervals are identified in the HOW (handover word) portion of the satellite Navigation Message (see section on the Navigation Message, page 67.)

The GPS Carrier

All GPS information is transmitted on two different carrier frequencies located on a segment of radio frequencies on the electromagnetic spectrum called the L-band. Centered at approximately 1500 MHz, the L-band frequencies are nearly 10 times greater than the marine VHF radio band frequencies, which are transmitted at approximately 160 MHz.

Both carrier frequencies are determined as a function of the basic satellite clock rate of 10.23 MHz. The L1 frequency is centered on 1575.42 MHz or 154 times the basic clock rate of 10.23 MHz. This carrier wavelength is 0.19 meters or 19 centimeters. The L2 frequency is centered on 1227.6 MHz, which is a multiple of 120 times the 10.23 MHz clock rate. It has a longer wavelength of 0.24 meters or 24 centimeters. Note: It is because of these short wavelengths (around 20 cm), that the antennas for GPS receivers are so small (as compared to those of loran receivers) as required antenna size is proportional to wavelength.

The C/A code is transmitted only on the L1 band, whereas the P-code is transmitted on both bands. Most civilian receivers track only the C/A code on the L1 band. However, more expensive receivers can also track the P code on both bands, and "codeless" receivers track the carrier on both bands. The military and authorized users have access to the C/A code and the encrypted form of the P code (the Y code) on both bands.

It is important to note that the transmitted carrier frequencies are centered on the given frequency. In modulating the carrier (superimposing information on it), the frequencies are actually spread out over a wider bandwidth so they aren't exactly at 1575.42 MHz and 1227.6 MHz. (See section on Pseudorandom Codes.) In effect, this changes the signal from one whose power is concentrated into a narrow bandwidth to one whose power is spread over a wide bandwidth. Signal processing theory dictates that a wide bandwidth signal is necessary for accurate measurement of range from a satellite to the receiver. In the early days of radar, the required bandwidth for range measurement was achieved by using very short signal pulses. Because the pulses were so short, they had to have a high peak power level to obtain enough energy to be detectable at the receiver. At GPS frequencies, such high peak power is very difficult to generate. The use of the spread spectrum signal achieves the wide bandwidth objective at low peak power levels. In fact, when the signal arrives at the receiver, its power is spread out over such a large bandwidth that when received it is below the thermal noise level that is present in any receiver. When the signal is correctly matched by the receiver-generated code, all of the signal power is again concentrated into a narrow bandwidth, but the thermal noise is still spread out over a large bandwidth and can be filtered out without affecting the signal. (See Figure 3.9.)

By making the two carriers multiples of the same fundamental frequency, a special relationship exists between them that can be used to improve accuracy. This is done by screening out the effects of transmis-

A. Original carrier signal with narrow frequency band.

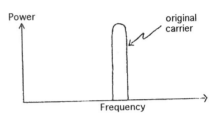

B. Code modulation spreads the band width into a lower power wide band width.

@ 2 MHz for C/A code
@ 20 MHz for P code
See Figure 3.13

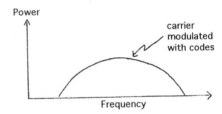

C. Signals as it arrives at the receiver.

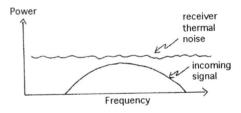

D. Signal collapses into original higher power narrow band width as it is amplified with the receiver code match.

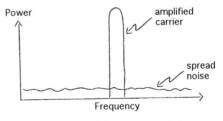

Modified from "Navstar GPS User Equipment" developed by members of the "NATO-TEAM" at US Air Force Space Systems Division, Navstar-GPS Joint Program Office at Los Angeles Air Force Base, California, USA.

Figure 3.9   GPS Spread Spectrum Transmission

sion retardation by the ionosphere. Basically, radiowaves are bent or slowed down when they encounter particles in the ionosphere, which in turn affects the accuracy of a pseudorange determination. This rate of retardation is inversely proportional to the wavelength of the transmission. In other words, the higher the frequency, the less the retardation. By comparing the amount of retardation on each frequency, it is possible to calculate the amount of error and correct for it. It is this technique that in part produces enhanced accuracy for the military and other users who track both carriers.

It is interesting that one of the main differences between GPS and Glonass lies in the transmission of the carriers. Both systems use two different carriers, L1 and L2, with the Glonass transmissions centered on 1607.0 MHz and 1250.0 MHz, respectively. The difference is in satellite identification. With GPS, individual satellites are identified by a unique code or an assigned segment of a code (P code) on one or both of the carrier frequencies. With Glonass, each satellite transmits with a slightly different but assigned offset frequency from the main L band.

Carrier Modulation

In order for information to be transmitted on a carrier frequency, it needs to be modulated. **Modulation** is a way of encoding a message sig-

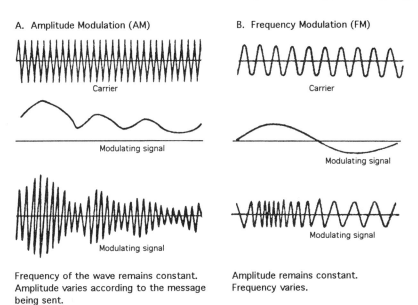

A. Amplitude Modulation (AM)

Carrier

Modulating signal

Modulating signal

Frequency of the wave remains constant. Amplitude varies according to the message being sent.

B. Frequency Modulation (FM)

Carrier

Modulating signal

Modulating signal

Amplitude remains constant. Frequency varies.

Figure 3.10   Carrier Signal Modulation

61

nal on top of a carrier, which can then be decoded at a later time. There are a number of ways in which a carrier signal can be modulated.

One way is by altering the height of different wavelengths, or amplitude modulation. (See Figure 3.10A.) This is the way in which radio signals are sent in AM radio broadcasts. In this type of modulation, the frequency remains constant, and the amplitude and thus the strength of the signal varies. One disadvantage with this type of modulation is that the signal is easily corrupted by static and noise, especially if the signal is weak. Another type of modulation is to encode the message by changing the frequency, or frequency modulation, which is used in FM radio. In this type of modulation, the amplitude remains constant, and the carrier frequency varies in step with the program information. (See Figure 3.10B.) FM has the advantage of better sound quality because static and noise have less effect on frequency modulation than on amplitude mod

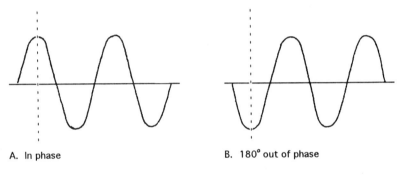

A. In phase   B. 180° out of phase

Figure 3.11   Phase Modulation

ulation. But because of its higher frequency and shorter wavelength, FM radio waves are not reflected back by the earth's ionosphere, and hence the range of reception is much less than with AM transmissions.

GPS uses a third kind of modulation — phase modulation. This technique reverses the phase of the carrier so that it is transmitted 180 degrees out of phase as though it were flipped over, as in Figure 3.11. The GPS code, which is binary (a series of 1's and 0's), lends itself nicely to this technique since a transmission of a series of cycles that are in phase could be used to represent, for example, the 1's, and a series of cycles that are out of phase could then be used to represent the 0's, as shown in Figure 3.12.

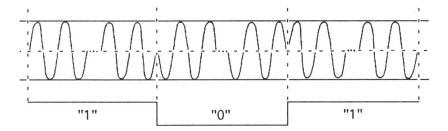

"1"   "0"   "1"

Figure 3.12   Using Phase Modulation to Represent a Binary Code

The Pseudorandom Codes

The carrier frequencies are modulated or encoded with message signals on top of the carrier, which can be decoded at a later time. One of these messages is the pseudorandom code. The pseudorandom code has two functions. One is the identification of the individual satellites. The other is the measurement of signal transmit time by shifting the same receiver-generated code until it matches up with the satellite code.

The codes are called PRN (pseudorandom noise) codes because to the casual observer, they appear as random noise without any specific pattern. The codes are binary and consist of long sequences of 1's and 0's. Even though they are transmitted in repeating patterns, because of their length, the codes appear random and thus the term "pseudorandom."

There are two different pseudorandom codes. The **C/A** (coarse acquisition) **code** is a relatively short code consisting of 1023 bits with a bit being either a 1 or 0. In some circles, the 1's and 0's composing a pseudorandom code are referred to as "chips" instead of bits because the code carries no information. It is merely a pattern of 1's and 0's that can be recognized and tracked by the receiver to determine range to the satellite. The C/A code is generated only on the L1 band and takes 1 millisecond (ms) to repeat. The frequency of the C/A code is 1.023 MHz or 1/10 of the basic clock frequency. Actually, it is transmitted at a shifted frequency centered at 1575.42 MHz with a bandwidth of a little more than 2 MHz. (See Figure 3.13.)

1.023 MHz or 1.023×10^6

1023 bits/message or 1.023×10^3

$$\frac{1.023 \times 10^6}{1.023 \times 10^3} = 10^3 \text{ or 1000 messages/second}$$
$$\text{or 1 message in .001 seconds}$$

This short transmission time of the C/A code makes it very easy to perform a bit-by-bit search for code correlation, and thus access is relatively easy and the code is quick to lock on to.

Although all satellites transmit on the same carrier frequency, they are identified by a different assigned C/A code. Thus, each satellite is identified by a PRN number such as PRN #18 or PRN #26. In addition to satellite identification and range determinations, the C/A code has a third function, which is to assist authorized users to gain access to the more complicated P code.

The **P code** (sometimes called the "precise" or "protected" code) is the second type of pseudorandom code and is transmitted on both the L1 and L2 bands. Utilization of the P code on both bands produces more precise range determinations by eliminating most of the errors caused by ionospheric delay. The P code can be protected by replacing it with the Y code (see section on Y code). The P code frequency is set equal to the clock rate or 10.23 MHz. In the L1 band, it is centered at 1575.42 MHz with a bandwidth of 20.46 MHz; in the L2 band, it is centered at 1227.6 MHz with a bandwidth of 20.46 MHz. (See again Figure 3.13.)

The P code is a much longer pseudorandom code than the C/A code. It takes 267 days to go through a complete cycle of the P code as opposed to 0.001 second for the C/A code. Each satellite is assigned a unique and mutually exclusive seven-day segment of the P code, which is changed at midnight Saturday each week.

Because of its length, the P code is much more difficult to acquire, that is, to know exactly where to jump in during the seven-day sequence to begin searching for a match. Thus, it is usually acquired by first locking on to the C/A code and then utilizing the handover word (HOW) in the Navigation Message, which gives the Z-count in 1.5-second intervals for the week. The Z-count gives the receiver a clue about what part of the P code to start shifting and searching for a match. Note that with some receivers with extremely accurate clocks that are precisely synchronized with GPS Time (usually by a precise timing signal reference from another receiver) and knowledge of approximate position (within two–four miles), it is possible to bypass the C/A code and lock on to the

A. The L₁ Signal Spectrum

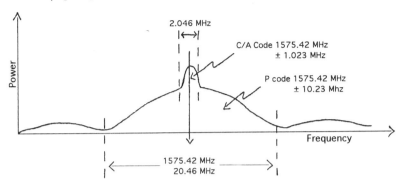

B. The L Signal Spectrum

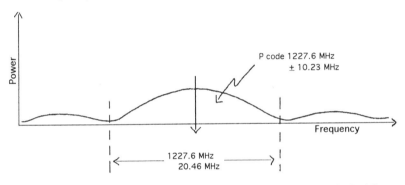

Modified from "Navstar GPS User Equipment" developed by members of the "NATO-TEAM" Air Force Space Systems Division, Navstar-GPS Joint Program Office at Los Angeles Air Force Base, California, USA.

Figure 3.13   Frequency Spectrum of the GPS Signal

P code directly.

Interestingly, there are historical reasons for the design of the system that provided a frequency rate for the P code 10 times that of the C/A code (10.23 MHz vs. 1.023 MHz). In early system design, this rate was set up intentionally because it was believed that the resolution of range accuracy with the lower 1.023 MHz frequency for the C/A code would be only about 30 meters. When combined with ionospheric propagation delays, satellite clock errors, etc., in the error budget, it was intended that these errors would add up to positioning accuracy of 100 meters. The P code with a frequency that was 10 times greater was expected to have a range resolution in the order of 3 meters, which when combined with the negation of ionospheric errors by using both L bands, would give the military its much-needed edge on accuracy. It was discovered early on, however, that the range resolution with the C/A code was actually very close to that obtained with the P code. Because the system was proving to have a much higher degree of accuracy resolution than had been originally intended, there had to be some way in which to differentiate position fixing capabilities between the military and civil user; hence, the inception of Selective Availability.

A third pseudorandom code, the Y code, will be employed when the GPS system is fully operational. Its purpose is to limit the performance of GPS to nonmilitary or unauthorized users. The technique is called anti-spoofing (AS), and it has two purposes. The first is to prevent spoofing, or the generation of false P code signals. The other is to prevent enemy access to the superior jamming resistance of the P code. The Y code is also very long and complicated, but unlike the P code, it is secret and not published. It is encrypted with specialized keys that can be accessed only by those with authorized receivers equipped with decryption keys.

Codeless GPS/Carrier-Aided Tracking

It is possible to track the signal carrier as well as the pseudorandom codes. The signal carrier can be used by itself for relative position fixing or to enhance range accuracy (and thus position) determined from the codes.

In tracking the carrier, the receiver's carrier tracking loop generates the L1 carrier frequency. This frequency will differ from the incoming satellite carrier frequency because of a Doppler shift that is proportional to the relative velocity between the satellite and the receiver and any error in the receiver frequency oscillator. The carrier tracking loop scales the receiver-generated carrier and shifts it until it matches the phase of the incoming carrier frequency. Because the receiver also knows the satellite's precise position, it is thus able to calculate the relative velocity between the receiver and satellite. By using three satellites and three range rate equations (for two-dimensional navigation), the frequency error offset in the receiver oscillator can be corrected in the same way as solving for receiver clock error by using the ranges from three satellites for two-dimensional navigation and four satellites for three-dimensional navigation.

One distinct advantage to carrier-aided tracking is that it enables the receiver to get an exact lock on the edge of the pseudorandom code. In order to match up the satellite-generated code with the receiver replica code, the receiver must do two things:

1. The center frequency of the replica must be scaled to the same center frequency of the satellite signal.
2. The phase of the replica needs to be lined up with the phase of the satellite code.

Tracking the carrier enables the receiver to more accurately determine the center frequency of its replica by correcting the frequency offset (error) in its frequency oscillator. This correction produces better timing measurements, which in turn deliver more precise position-fixing capabilities. It also permits the receiver to measure and track the pseudorange better by smoothing out the noise; thus, the term "carrier-aided smoothing." Another advantage of carrier-aided tracking is that the receiver can calculate velocity with higher accuracy.

The Navigation Message

In addition to transmitting the pseudorandom codes, the satellite signal must dispense a certain amount of information to provide the receiver with the necessary data to perform the operations and computations for position fixing and navigating with GPS. Included in the message is information on the status (health) of the satellite and parameters for computing its exact position in space as a function of time (ephemeris). The message also provides information on the positions and health of other satellites in the system (almanac). Within the message is specific time synchronization information, a handover word (HOW), needed for access to the P code. The message also includes GPS Time along with parameters for computing satellite clock corrections and coefficients to calculate Universal Time Coordinated. It also contains coefficients for calculating a propagation delay model due to ionospheric retardation for C/A code users. Finally, it includes provisions for special messages. (See Figure 3.14 for a summary of the Navigation Message.)

The Navigation Message is an additional modulation of the carrier above that of the pseudorandom codes. It is transmitted at a rate of 50 bits/second. (Note in this case these are true bits and not chips as they do carry specific information.) The entire Navigation Message contains 25 data pages or frames with each page consisting of 1500 bits with a transmission time of 30 seconds. Thus, it takes 12.5 minutes to receive all 25 pages. Each page is divided into three blocks of data plus an addi

1. Satellite health and ephemeris
2. System almanac
3. GPS time
4. Satellite clock corrections

5. Coefficients for UTC
6. Handover word for P code access
7. Corrections for propagation delays
8. Special messages

Figure 3.14   *The Navigation Message*

tional special message block, which are formatted in 5 subframes. Each subframe is made up of 300 bits with a transmission time of 6 seconds. (See Figure 3.15.)

Subframes 1, 2 and 3 are exactly alike on all 25 pages. This is so the critical navigation data on these frames can be readily accessed every 30 seconds. Each subframe begins with a 30-bit telemetry word, which

Data Message = 25 pages
Data rate = 50 bits/sec

Each page or frame:

= 1500 bits
= 30 sec transmission time

$$\frac{1500 \text{ bits}}{50 \text{ bits/sec}} = 30 \text{ sec}$$

Therefore: it takes 12.5 min to receive the full 25 page message.

Each page or frame is divided into 5 subframes:

= 300 bits each
= 6 sec transmission time

$$\frac{1500 \text{ bits each page}}{5 \text{ subframes}} = 300 \text{ bits/subframe}$$

$$\frac{300 \text{ bits each subframe}}{50 \text{ bits/sec}} = 6 \text{ sec}$$

Figure 3.15   *Navigation Message Parameters*

facilitates access to the data message. This is followed by another 30-bit message, the handover word (HOW), which transmits the Z-count that measures the time in the week in 1.5-second intervals from midnight of the previous Saturday. It is this Z-count that enables P code receivers to know exactly where to jump in to access the week-long segment of the P code.

Block I data, which is transmitted in Subframe 1, includes satellite clock correction parameters. These are updated each hour by the Control Segment, which also provides values for each hour in the 24-hour period following the update. It is these clock corrections that are "dithered" in the implementation of Selective Availability. Subframe 1 also includes coefficients that are used in correcting the model for determining ionospheric propagation delays for users who have access to only the C/A code.

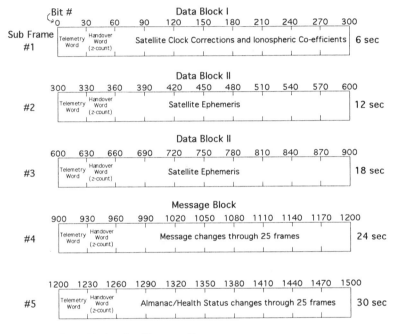

Figure 3.16   Navigation Message Format

Block II data is transmitted in Subframes 2 and 3. This data contains the ephemeris prediction parameters of the particular satellite being tracked. These are defined by 15 sets of numbers or coefficients that describe the satellite orbit using a Keplerian model. (Kepler was a sixteenth-century physicist who developed a very precise way of describing the movement of orbiting bodies.) This information is also updated hourly by the Control Segment with future predictions based on the update. By changing these numbers that describe satellite position as a function of time, the military has another method for controlling the level of accuracy for nonauthorized users.

Subframe 4 is a Message Block, which is reserved for special messages. This Subframe is not the same on each page and changes through the 25 pages.

Block III data is formatted on Subframe 5. It contains the almanac data of the whole satellite constellation. The almanac consists of all the ephemerides, clock correction parameters, and signal propagation corrections for all the satellites. It also includes a health word that identifies the status of each satellite. This information is important to receivers because it enables them to identify which satellites are in view and in the best positions to provide the best geometry and thus the best navigation solution. The almanac also enables the receiver to calculate the approximate range to each satellite, which assists the receiver in shifting its own generated code as a function of time as it searches for a code match.

Because of the large volume of information, the almanac is transmitted on continuing pages of the 25-page Navigation Message and takes 12.5 minutes to acquire. For this reason, it may take 12 – 15 minutes to begin tracking satellites and thus navigating on a "cold start." Without an almanac stored in memory, the receiver must search randomly for a satellite until it finds one that it can lock on to. Once one satellite is being tracked, the receiver can demodulate the Navigation Message and collect the almanac on the other satellites in the constellation, which then provides the necessary information for tracking additional satellites. Fortunately, most receivers retain enough information from the almanac in their memory to lessen this "time to first fix" considerably. The almanac information in their memory banks is then updated as tracking of satellites and navigation continue.

The Overall Picture

When viewed in its entirety, the GPS system emerges as a highly complex system that is designed to deliver precise position, velocity, and timing determinations. Yet in many respects, the design of the system is quite simple, based on a few key parameters.

Fundamental to the system is the element of time, which is set at a basic clock frequency of 10.23 MHz. All other frequencies are derived from and synchronized with integrals of this standard. (See Figure 3.17.) The carrier frequencies are multiples of the basic clock rate:

L1 = 154 x 10.23 MHz or 1575.42 MHz
L2 = 120 x 10.23 MHz or 1227.6 MHz

The code frequencies are also related to this basic standard, with the

Basic clock rate: 10.23MHz

L_1 Carrier	
frequency	= 154 x 10.23 MHz
	= 1575.42 MHz
wavelength	= 0.19 meters

C/A Code	
frequency	= 0.1 x 10.23 MHz
	= 1.023 MHz
wavelength	= 30 meters
time	= 1 mS
band width	= 2.046 MHz
Navigation Message = 50 bits/sec	
HOW (z-count) = 1.5 sec intervals	

P Code (Y Code)	
frequency	= basic clock rate
	= 10.23 MHz
wavelength	= 3 meters
repeat time	= 267 days
broken into 1 week segments	
band width	= 20.46 MHz
Navigation Message = 50 bits/sec	
HOW (z-count) = 1.5 sec intervals	

L_2 Carrier	
frequency	= 120 x 10.23 MHz
	= 1227.6 MHz
wavelength	= 0.24 meters

P Code (Y Code)	
frequency	= basic clock rate
	= 10.23 MHz
wavelength	= 3 meters
repeat time	= 267 days
broken into 1 week segments	
band width	= 20.46 MHz
Navigation Message = 50 bits/sec	
HOW (z-count) = 1.5 sec intervals	

Figure 3.17   The Overall Picture

P code set equal to the clock frequency and the C/A code at 1/10 of the clock frequency:

C/A code frequency = 1.023 MHz
P code frequency   = 10.23 MHz

Even the width of the spread spectrum that results from the modulation of the codes on the carriers is a multiple of these basic numbers:

C/A spread spectrum width = + 1.023 MHz or 2.046 MHz
P code spread spectrum width = + 10.23 MHz or 20.46 MHz

The number of bits (or chips) in the C/A code is set at 1023 so that an entire code sequence is generated in just 0.001 seconds. This short time enables users quick access to the code as receivers search for a match with their own internally generated codes.

It is also important to point out that a number of distinct advantages result from the simplicity of generating pseudorandom codes. One advantage is that the satellites can all transmit on the same frequency without interfering with each other. Identification is achieved with different codes as in the case of the C/A codes or an assigned portion of the

P code. Another advantage is that because the signals are amplified when they are matched up with receiver-generated codes, the signals can be transmitted with very low power. Finally, the generation of pseudorandom codes allows the military a means to control access to the system in times of national emergency. Not only can the codes be changed, but the complexity of the P code makes it almost impossible to jam. (See Figure 3.18.)

The system also lends itself nicely to different degrees of accuracy. By utilizing transmissions on the two different carrier frequencies, ionospheric errors can be largely reduced. By changing the Navigation Message parameters, the military can select the degree of accuracy, made available to nonauthorized users. But the system also lends itself to ways of getting around accuracy degradation for those who require enhanced precision in specific applications. Even without military receivers, it is possible to compensate for errors induced by the ionosphere and SA. By using differential GPS where the errors are computed at a known location and then transferred to the receiver by a communication link, accuracies exceeding those achieved with Precise Positioning Service (PPS) are possible. Finally, as the technology progresses, there are now ways of tracking the phase angle of the carrier in static known positions so that accuracies within centimeters are possible, which can be utilized for further position fixing.

1. All satellites can transmit on the same frequency
2. Identification of individual satellites
3. Accurate range measurement with low peak power signal transmission
4. Immunity to interference
5. Military control
   a. Can change codes
   b. Anti-jamming qualities of P code

Figure 3.18   Advantages of Using Pseudorandom Codes

CHAPTER FOUR

The GPS Receiver

With the space segment and control segment on line, it is within the user segment that we will continue to see advances in product technology and a wide variety of user applications. At the heart of the user segment is the GPS receiver. As projections exceed 500,000 units/year sold after 1994, manufacturers of GPS receivers have been tooling up to meet the demands of an ever-growing user community. When it comes to choosing a GPS receiver, however, it is no longer a simple matter of considering price, number of waypoints, screen display, etc., as it was in purchasing a Loran-C receiver. With GPS receivers, differences in internal architecture also have a significant impact on performance.

Manufacturers are well aware of these differences and, in some instances, use them to their advantage in advertising. Other manufacturers' promotional literature may gloss over how the receiver performs its tasks so that you really are not sure what you are getting. In order to understand some of these differences, it is important to take a closer look at the basic functions of any GPS receiver.

I. Receiver Functions

1. The first task of a GPS receiver is **to acquire** or **lock on to the satellites** that are to be tracked. Current time and almanac information assist the receiver in selecting those satellites that are in the best position to provide the best fix. Acquisition involves searching for the different unique codes of the satellite signals and aligning them with the receiver's internal oscillator. Acquisition also involves searching the different ranges that are transmitted in a code sequence and matching them up with the receiver's own internally generated code. Depending on receiver design, it can take 30 to 60 seconds to acquire a satellite. It is important to note that it takes much greater signal strength (five times greater) to achieve acquisition than it does to maintain tracking once satellite acquisition has occurred. Acquisition also requires more power than

1. Acquire the satellites
2. Make pseudorange measurements
3. Read the Navigation Message
   a. Time Corrections
   b. Ephemeris data - satellite's precise spacial position
   c. Almanac - orbits and health of all the satellites in the constellation

Figure 4.1   Tasks Performed by a GPS Receiver

satellite tracking.

2. The second task of the receiver is to **make pseudorange measurements,** that is, to determine how far away the satellite is from the receiver position. The receiver does this by moving its internally generated code as a function of time until it matches up with the incoming satellite signal, which, in effect, calculates the time delay for the signal to travel from the satellite to the receiver. This time delay is converted into the range between the satellite and receiver as time becomes synonymous with distance. The term "pseudo" is used because the range really isn't accurate due to inaccuracies in the receiver clocks and propagation errors. A mathematical solution is used to compensate for these inaccuracies and get the time right. This solution requires a third satellite for a two-dimensional fix and at least four satellites to determine three-dimensional position. (For a more thorough discussion of these topics, see Chapter 3 on "How GPS Works.")

3. To determine receiver position, the receiver also needs to know the satellite's exact position when its range is determined. Thus its third task is to **read the satellite's Navigation Message.** In addition to obtaining time corrections for the satellite clock, this process involves reading the ephemeris data of the particular satellite being tracked. This data consists of position coefficients that allow the receiver to calculate the satellite's position as a function of time. This data is transmitted by the satellite as part of its Navigation Message during the first 18 seconds of every 30-second data frame, which is continuously repeated. (Actually, the ephemeris is transmitted on Subframes 2 and 3, each of which are 6 seconds long. Again, see Chapter 3.)

Another function in reading the Navigation Message is to read the almanac data, which is a rough listing of the ephemerides of all the satellites in the constellation. The almanac can be thought of as a table predicting which satellites will be available for navigation, given the GPS receiver's time and last known location. The almanac is transmitted in segments during the final 6 seconds of each 30-second data frame in the Navigation Message. It takes 12 1/2 minutes to obtain a complete almanac with a "cold start." Note, however, that most receivers maintain the almanac from previous use in protected memory. (See Figure 4.1.)

II. Types of GPS Receivers

Although all GPS receivers receive the same GPS data and must perform the same three functions, the manner in which they do this can be quite different. There are three distinct levels in receiver technology based on the number and kinds of channels used to track the satellites and assimilate their information. (See Figure 4.2.) Broadly speaking, there are two basic methods. One is to **sequentially** acquire and move through a set of satellites with a single channel to solve for position. The other method, which is more costly, is to **simultaneously** acquire and solve each individual satellite's data using parallel channels, each of which is dedicated to a single satellite. Within these broad divisions are distinct variations that have direct impact on receiver performance.

Sequencing Receivers

Originally, slow and fast sequencing receivers were designed for the marine market. Because of fairly simple internal architecture, they are less costly to build and are therefore less expensive for the consumer. On the downside, they do not always provide continuous navigation because of the time taken out of the data frame to number crunch for certain housekeeping chores.

Many sequencing receivers use a single channel to perform all three receiver functions on a given satellite. Then they drop the satellite and switch to another. Once acquisition has occurred, it takes 5 or more seconds to sequence through four satellites and obtain a complete set of

Sequencing:
    1. Slow or fast sequencing receivers
    2. Multiplex receivers
Parallel:
    3. Multiple dedicated channel receivers

Figure 4.2   *Basic Types of GPS Receivers*

measurements for a fix. However, because it takes 30 seconds of acquisition time to acquire sufficient data (clock correction and ephemeris) from each satellite's Navigation Message, it may take up to 2 minutes to obtain a "first fix."

Sequencing receivers can be divided into four main types: starved power single channel, single channel slow sequencing, two channel slow sequencing, and single channel fast sequencing (multiplex). The word "slow" is only a relative term used to distinguish some receivers from multiplex receivers, which sequence through a set of satellites at a much faster rate.

1. Starved Power Single Channel. These receivers are like single channel slow sequencing receivers but with one important difference. Because they are designed for portability, starved power single channel receivers often run off small batteries. To save on battery power, they may take position data only one or two times a minute and then turn themselves off inbetween. Sometimes these receivers are advertised as having a "sleep mode."

One disadvantage with this type of unit is that navigation isn't continuous, so depending on your speed, accuracy is degraded. Also these units cannot accurately measure velocity—which may or may not be an important requirement in a low-dynamic marine environment. Another disadvantage is that these receivers cannot track the satellite carrier phase, which enhances accuracy performance. The main advantage with these receivers is their portability. They lend themselves nicely to use in the cockpit or flying bridge as a back-up GPS or in the dinghy going to a favorite fishing hole or diving spot on a reef. Their small size is also an advantage for those users with restricted space in the nav-station.

It is important to note that not all portables perform solely as starved power receivers. Many are capable of hooking into the ship's 12-volt system and providing continuous operation. Also a number of multiplexing and even dedicated channel portables offer a sleep or battery-saver mode. The starved power mode is then used only when the portable is relying on battery power for operation. For example, one manufacturer provides a four fix/hour mode that extends use on battery power from 14 hours to 100 hours. Yet, when drawing from ship batteries, the unit performs as a sophisticated multichannel receiver.

2. Single Channel Slow Sequencing. These types of receivers use one basic sequencing channel to move through a set of satellites making pseudorange measurements and calculating position. They do have an advantage over the starved power units in that they are more accurate and can measure velocity as long as there are no significant changes in speed and course.

In the marine environment, taking 5 seconds or so to sequence through a set of satellites to obtain a fix doesn't sound too bad. But there are a couple of drawbacks. Every so often, these receivers have to stop navigating to update the ephemeris data, which can take between 1 1/2 to 2 minutes. There is also a problem when satellites go out of view and new satellites have to be acquired. Depending on receiver design, it may take 30 to 60 seconds to make a code and range search to add a new satellite to the working constellation. During these time delays, position cannot be determined, and continuous navigation is interrupted. Because of these problems with velocity and discontinuous navigation, single channel receivers are unsuitable for the high dynamics of the aviation community.

Another disadvantage with this type of unit is that each satellite must be reacquired prior to each measurement. Finding and locking onto a satellite signal is the most difficult task the receiver has to perform. Because vulnerability to interference is greater during signal acquisition, there is greater chance of signal loss with these receivers than with sets that have enough channels to track signals continuously. Signal acquisition also requires a signal strength many times greater than that needed when tracking. Thus, weak satellite signals near the horizon may be lost, reducing the number of satellites that can be tracked. Also where intermittent blocking or shading occur (i.e., a sailboat with wet sails), it may be difficult to lock on to low-strength signals. Again, it should be noted that these receivers are unable to track the carrier phase which improves accuracy in the navigation solution. Because of these disadvantages, very few, if any, single channel units are on the market today.

3. Two Channel Slow Sequencing. To solve the problem of interrupted position fixing, some manufacturers add a second channel to do the housekeeping chores, leaving the other channel free to make the pseudorange measurements without interruption. In these receivers, one channel sequences through all the satellites under track, collecting positioning data. The other channel acquires the next satellite and collects the current ephemeris data from all visible satellites. This means that each satellite is "ready to go," and the tracking channel can read through each with no interruptions. Some manufacturers improve on these capabilities by adding a third channel.

The decided advantage of two or three channel sequencing

receivers is continuous navigation, which allows for more precise velocity measurements. Again, disadvantages are the signal strength needed for reacquisition along with the problems of intermittent blocking or shading and the inability to track the phase of the carrier. Other disadvantages are that these receivers cost more to produce and they may use more power.

4. Single Channel Fast Sequencing (Multiplex). In a way, fast sequencing multiplex receivers are a sort of halfway house between slow sequencing receivers and multiple/parallel channel receivers. These units operate in the same way as a single channel slow sequencing unit except they sequence through the satellites under track at a much faster rate, a few milliseconds every 20 milliseconds, which translates into at least 50 times per second. At this rate, the receiver is able to read all the messages from all the satellites under track, which in effect is the same as reading the satellite's data message at the same time the receiver is making pseudorange measurements. The rate is so fast that the tracking loops maintain continuous lock and, in many respects, multiplex units perform as though they were operating with several continuous channels. *See Chapter 4 photo#1 for an example of a multiplex - ing handheld unit.*

The overall result is virtually continuous navigation, which means that these receivers are more responsive in high-dynamic environments. Another advantage is that the time to acquire a "first fix" is less than with slow sequencing receivers and comes close to the same overall effect as a receiver with dedicated multiple channels. If the multiplexing is fast enough (the receiver must visit all satellites seen over a 20-millisecond data bit), the unit performs much like a continous parallel channel receiver. Thus, with many multiplexing units, it is also possible to track the carrier phase. One of the advantages of tracking the carrier phase is that over a period of time, it can improve the receiver synchronization with the C/A code. Another advantage is that the receiver can make an immediate measure on the Doppler shift of the signal so that the user can get a better response in velocity for low-dynamic applications. Until the use of very fast multiplexing, these advantages were possible only with parallel dedicated channels.

On the downside, a penalty with multiplexing is a degraded signal to noise ratio, which may result in reduced performance in marginal tracking conditions. Searching for new satellites and acquisition are also more difficult than with parallel channels. As with all sequencing receivers, there is a limit to the number of satellites that can be tracked at one time. Many units can track up to five satellites, and a few can even track up to eight. Another disadvantage with these receivers initially was that because of more complex circuitry, they cost more than single channel slow sequencing receivers. However, in the race to obtain a corner of the consumer market, prices for these receivers have dropped so much that they have become a very important choice option. *See Chapter 4 photo #2 for an example of a dual channel multiplexing receiver.*

Multiple/Parallel Channel Receivers

Multiple channel receivers have from four to 12 (or up to 24 for some military units) independent channels, each of which is dedicated to tracking a single satellite. Because the satellites are tracked simultaneously, the receivers are also sometimes called parallel multichannel receivers. *See Chapter 4 photo #3 for an example of a parallel channel unit.*

One advantage of having separate channels to track each satellite simultaneously is receiving instantaneous position and velocity data. Each channel remains locked on both the carrier and tracking loops, providing continuous pseudorange and carrier phase data. This means that these receivers are well suited to high-dynamic and high-accuracy environments in aircraft and surveying. Because these receivers don't have the recurrent problems of acquisition, they also require less signal strength and aren't affected as much by weak low elevation signals near the horizon or signals obscured by shadows (e.g., wet sails). Tracking more satellites also increases the possibility that the LOPs from some satellites will provide better crossing angles (dilution of precision) and thus improve accuracy. Other advantages are continuous satellite message updates and a shorter time to first fix.

Probably the biggest disadvantage with multiple channel receivers is cost. With the increased hardware for each channel, these units are usually more expensive than sequencing or multiplex receivers. However, a competitive market offers a number of parallel dedicated channel receivers priced just a few hundred dollars more than their multiplexing cousins. *See Chapter 4 photos #4, 5, 6 for examples of 6 channel units.*

Receiver Type	General Description	Advantages	Disadvantages
Sequencing Starved-power, single channel	Portable, operates on battery power. Intermittent satellite tracking, turns off in between fixes	Portability, use in more than one vehicle. Use in restricted nav-stations.	Interrupted navigation Degreded accuracy Cannot accurately measure velocity
Single channel, slow sequencing	One channel acquires and sequences through a series of satellites to determine a fix.	Improved accuracy and velocity measurements over starved power receivers. Cost-less than 2 channel, multiplex or multiple channel.	Interrupted navigation – has to periodically stop tracking satellites to update ephemeris. Difficulty in tracking weak siganls. Cannot track the carrier
Two channel, slow sequencing	One channel performs acquisition of satellites and collects ephemeris. One channel tracks satellites' pseudorandom codes.	Continuous navigation. Improved accuracy and velocity measurements.	Cost - more expensive than single channel receivers. Difficulty in tracking weak signals. Cannot track the carrier
Single channel, fast sequencing (multiplex)	Tracks many satellites very fast - 50 times/sec.	Continuous navigation More responsive to high dynamics. Less time to first fix. A few can track the carrier.	Reduced performance in marginal conditions (compared with multi -channel receivers.) Cost - more expensive than single channel receiver
Multi-channel, simultaneous tracking	4 - 12 separate channels for acquiring and tracking individual satellites.	Continuous navigation Greater sensitivity Less time to first fix Less signal strength required Responsive to high dynamics Improved accuracy Carrier aided tracking	Cost - most expensive type of receiver.
Hybrid/Integrated	GPS "black box" integrated with existing Loran or Sat Nav receivers.	Utilizes equipment at hand Alternative navigation in GPS coverage gaps.	Reciever failures stop navigation in both systems.

Figure 4.3   Advantages/Disadvantages of Different Types of Receivers

Hybrid Receivers

In the early days of GPS use before system completion, some manufacturers addressed the concept of integrating existing navigational systems with GPS by adding on a GPS "Black Box." Examples of this technology might involve tying GPS in with a Loran-C or Sat Nav receiver.

This approach had the advantage of getting the user in on the "ground floor" of GPS while still retaining present navigational capabilities. It also had certain appeal in the final days before GPS was fully operational, in that the original system could take over when the receiver did not have enough GPS satellites to track. For example, in November and December 1991, all 11 Block II satellites were declared unusable while they underwent testing (two different tests, each lasting three days), leaving only the five prototype Block I satellites for navigation during these periods.

A disadvantage of this type of integration is that you are putting "all your navigational eggs in one basket." Should a component common to both systems (i.e., the display screen) fail, you are left without any electronic navigation. In this instance, a better choice would be to have two completely separate systems.

Finally, it may be relevant to note that in the early days of GPS (before system completion), single channel receivers were in greater use than they are today. As more satellites were launched, manufacturers devoted their product development programs to more complex units. Today the majority of receivers on the market are either multiplex or parallel multichannel units. For a summary of the strengths and weaknesses of the different types of GPS receivers, see Figure 4.3.

III. Factors in Selecting a GPS Receiver

Aside from the internal architecture that a GPS receiver employs to access and track satellites, a number of other important considerations affect the type of receiver chosen. These range from performance parameters and options to a myriad of "bells and whistles" that are a product of the ever-expanding capabilities of the electronics/computer industry. Not only can the contemporary GPS receiver determine position and solve many navigation problems, it can also tell you when your anchor is dragging, when the sun will set, and when it is time to go back on watch by ringing an alarm.

Performance

Does the receiver do what it is supposed to do? It doesn't matter how many bells and whistles a GPS receiver has if it can't perform its basic function—tracking satellites and providing accurate position fixing, speed, and course determinations. A key factor is the amount of time the receiver takes to acquire satellites and begin navigating, or the Time To First Fix (TTFF).

There are two types of receiver start-ups: **the cold start**, which occurs the first time you use the new receiver with no information in its memory; and the **warm start**, which occurs in day-to-day use with almanac information retained from previous use. Another circumstance requiring a cold start would be if you were to move the receiver a long distance (e.g., from the New England states to a charter cruise in the Caribbean) from its last known position. Cold starts differ from receiver to receiver. In receivers with more sophisticated software, all you have to do is press the "on" button. Other receivers may require some initialization assistance with approximate time and position input. Cold start TTFF varies from 15 to 30 minutes or more. Warm start TTFF varies from 2 to 5 minutes and is a function of both software and internal hardware architecture.

Another performance parameter is receiver **accuracy**. Here some discretion must be exercised in accepting manufacturers' claims. Although the manufacturer may advertise what seems like incredible accuracy, it is important to remember that the military has the final say on accuracy with the implementation of Selective Availability (SA). A receiver may be designed to deliver speed readings accurate to 0.1 knots and headings within 1 degree, yet SA degradation may cause these values to fluctuate erratically. Most manufacturers make their claims about positioning accuracy without mentioning the effects of SA. Implementation of SA is supposed to degrade position accuracy to 100 meters 95% of the time for nonmilitary receivers. Yet, actual use often reveals much better accuracy—on the order of 40-70 meters. Carrier-aided tracking (locking on to the phase angle of the carrier) tightens up on the signal transmission time element to determine a more accurate range (and thus position) between the receiver and satellite. However, these effects are also largely reduced by SA degradation. The best way to get the ultimate in accuracy performance is to use a receiver with differential capabilities.

The DC **power requirement** needed to perform receiver functions is another important part of receiver performance. Again, the advances in the electronics industry with more efficient microprocessors have resulted in receivers which aren't nearly as power-hungry as those used in the early years of concept validation. Today it is possible to purchase receivers that consume between 250 ma (milliamps) to 2 amps of current. It can be confusing, however, as some manufacturers list their unit's power requirements in volts where others list them in watts or amperes. The following equation can be useful in converting these units for comparison:

Power (W) = Voltage (V) x Current (A)
With formula derivations of:

$$V = {}^W\!/_A \qquad A = {}^W\!/_V$$

If power consumption is a concern, many receivers on the market today require less than 1 amp of current for operation. At least one manufacturer includes an emergency power supply in case of ship power failure.

Many receivers have the ability to change the **performance options** used with different receiver functions. For example, it is possible to change waypoint realization parameters, alarm parameters, true vs. magnetic readings, and nautical vs. statute miles.

Housing

Receiver-case construction is usually heavy-duty plastic or cast aluminum, with a trend in the industry toward increased use of the plastic. Some units are waterproof; others are only water-resistant. Another trend in receiver design is toward smaller, more compact units, again a product of the electronics industry's ability to miniaturize individual chips and utilize sophisticated menu-driven software for efficient function management. Some receivers are so small that they can easily fit in the palm of your hand. With fixed-mount receivers, there are two basic profiles: flat, broad-faced units or deeper units with less exposed surface area on the front face. If space is at a premium in the nav-station, it may make a difference which type of receiver is purchased.

Some receivers on the market are not contained in basic receiver housing. Often called "Black Box" receivers, these units are housed directly in the antenna assembly without a control/display module. Instead, data is displayed on another system with which the GPS is interfaced, such as radar, a chart plotter, or a fishfinder with plotter capabilities. A few manufacturers provide modular navigation units controlled by a central nav-center in which a GPS "Black Box" can be added. It is even possible to have a GPS receiver on a computer expansion board designed to run on a personal computer. *See Chapter 4 photo #7 for an example of this type of unit.*

In the interest of cutting costs, some manufacturers have taken GPS chips and software and put them into existing loran or Sat Nav boxes. In many respects, this combination is not a bad idea. First, there is the advantage of proven technology—why re-invent the wheel? Second, this practice also speeds up the product development phase. Users have the advantage of working with units they are familiar with, particularly in the area of programming characteristics (accessing data, etc.). Finally, any cost saved in product development could potentially filter down to the consumer.

A part of the receiver housing is a working face unit that contains two basic parts: the screen display and the keypad.

Screen Display

While GPS receivers tend to be smaller than their early counterparts, there is a definite trend away from small two-line displays to screens that can present up to 10 lines of information. More sophisticated models divide the screen into separate "fields," which can display a large amount of data. Some receivers allow user access to these fields so that you can tailor the screen to display functions according to individual needs. Other receivers provide a variety of different "pages" with different combinations of information. *See Chapter 4 photos #8, 9 for examples of excellent screen display.*

It is important that the **display contrast** of the screen is sharp and crisp, providing high readability under all conditions. Here there are two different types of technology. One is a regular liquid crystal display (LCD); the other is a backlit Supertwist LCD. In either case, you shoul be able to read the screen from a variety of viewing angles and under differing conditions of light. To enhance the readability of the screen, some manufacturers provide lighting options where the backlight and contrast can be adjusted. Another nice option is the ability to invert the daytime screen, which has a light background and dark characters, to a night screen, which displays white characters on a black background.

In actual **character display**, there are two basic techniques. One is to use seven-segment bar displays, which were used in the loran industry and which provide a clear, crisp display. The other is to use dot matrix characters, which are a little easier to read. (See Figure 4.4.) The dot matrix technique also allows a far wider range of characters, including lowercase letters, which increases the ability to present a large variety of information. Although some receivers tend to put a lot of data on the screen, it can be quite valuable to have a large character display option in which just a few lines can be easily seen from the cockpit.

Many GPS receivers offer **graphic capabilities** in the display of information. The simplest type is a graphic steering display of cross-track

A. Using Dot Matrix Letters

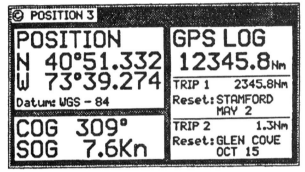

Information is divided into different fields with many lines of display.

B. Large Character Display Option

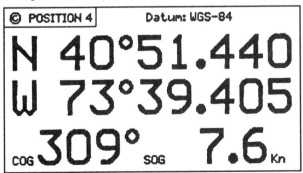

Information is easily read from a distance such as in a cockpit.

Courtesy of Magnavox
Government and Industrial Electronics Co.
Torrence, California

Figure 4.4   Different Types of Screen Displays

error. This can take the form of a bar, an arrow, or a boat that moves from side to side as course drifts off the center of the rhumb line to a waypoint. The outer limits of the graph can usually be set by the user. Some receivers also display an indicator that depicts the way to steer to correct the error. (See Figure 4.5A.)

Another type of graphic display used in some receivers is the **track-plotter function**. This is a more sophisticated display that shows where you have been and your continuing track in real time. Zooming capabilities vary with receivers. For example, it may be possible to zoom down to a one-mile scale for detail and accuracy and then zoom out to 100 miles or more for an overview of your trip. Navigation information such as position, waypoint range and bearing, course and speed over the ground, and cross-track error are usually displayed on the screen along with the graphic. User input can change cross-track variables and enter waypoints. The latter is particularly valuable for sailboaters tacking

A. Showing Cross-track Error

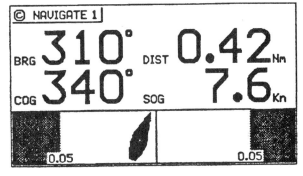

B. Using a Track-plotter

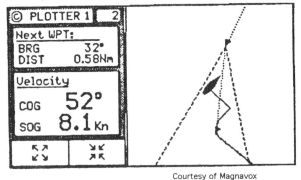

Courtesy of Magnavox
Government & Industrial Electronics Co.
Torrence, California

Figure 4.5   Graphic Displays

toward a given waypoint as they can see their actual course and distance made good with each tack. (See Figure 4.5B.)

Keypad

Another trend with GPS receivers is to move away from sealed membranes to the use of real keys or buttons in the keypad. Whichever method is used, the keys should be well-labeled and large enough for your fingers. It is also important that there is some kind of tactile feedback, either a click or beep that acknowledges function or data entry. Another important feature is backlighting the keys for night work.

Basically, there are two different approaches in the distribution of key functions. One is to have the function keys separated from the numeric keys. The other is to have the function and numeric keys collocated. The second approach requires more sophisticated menu-driven software to keep the unit operating smoothly and to provide intuitive keystrokes for the user. On some of the more sophisticated receivers, yet another section of "soft keys" are used for a wide variety of changing functions, thereby greatly expanding receiver performance options and user imput. Finally, it is important that the keys have both alpha and numeric functions for user input in waypoint identification.

Waypoints

One of the biggest assets of any radionavigational instrument is waypoint navigation. A waypoint is a "position event" that is described by a specific latitude and longitude. It may be the entrance to a harbor, positions where important turns are required in a tight channel, or just a point on a long run that is used to determine arrival time or elapsed distance.

Receivers on the market today generally provide storage of between 100 and an incredible 500 waypoints. Most receivers offer the option of organizing waypoints in routes that may be stored and used again. A handy function is route reversal, which provides waypoint information for the trip back home or for retrieval of fishing nets or lobster pots.

Waypoints can be stored either automatically with one keystroke as present position or with manual input. With manual input, ease of entry is the most important factor—particularly in how the alpha portion of the keys are accessed for naming waypoints. With some units, alphabet letters are chosen with a minimum of keystrokes. With others, the num

Position Functions	Dead Reckoning Functions	Steering Functions
Lat/Lon	Course over ground	Course to steer (true)
Present position	Speed over ground	Course to steer (mag)
storage	Velocity made good	Cross-track error
Man overboard	Distance traveled	Course corrections
Warning area	Distance to waypoint	Graphic display
Waypoint arrival	Elapsed time	Autopilot Interface
Anchor watch	Time to go	
	ETA	

Figure 4.6   Navigation Functions

ber and kind of strokes required are so complicated as to discourage the naming of waypoints. It is also important that the receiver provides quick access to the waypoint bank and easy retrieval for navigation. It is in the area of waypoint management that large differences between manufacturers are worth noting when selecting a GPS receiver.

Navigation Functions

The navigation functions of a GPS receiver can be divided into three broad areas: position functions, enroute functions, and steering functions. (See Figure 4.6.)

1. Position functions. Basic position functions are, of course, position readout as latitude and longitude. Most receivers express these readouts as degrees, minutes, and decimal fractions of minutes. Some provide a calculator function for converting latitude and longitude to degrees, minutes, and seconds.

A very nice option in most receivers is quick storage of <u>present position</u> as a temporary waypoint. This feature is an advantage when conditions are such that it isn't convenient to write the waypoint down as in rough weather or when navigating in tight quarters. Present position can then be converted into a regular waypoint later on if you want it stored for future retrieval.

One of the most important position functions is the <u>Man Overboard</u> (MOB) function. It operates very much like storage of present position, but with an important difference. Not only are the Lat/Lon of the overboard event recorded, but the position is immediately treated as a waypoint giving range and bearing directions back to the MOB position. Receivers with track plotters will display additional information showing the event and the vessel track back to the overboard position.

Should outside assistance be required (the Coast Guard or other boaters), knowledge of the overboard position is invaluable.

Another important position function is establishing a waypoint as a warning area. This could be used if there is a particular shoal or wreck that should be avoided. A warning area is defined as a circle around a waypoint, the radius of which can be determined by user input. Once a warning area is set and activated, an alarm will sound if the circle is penetrated. Receivers vary in the number of warning areas that can be entered; 8--10 are common.

Other position functions are notification of waypoint arrival and anchor watch. In anchor watch, the present position is stored as a waypoint. A user-determined distance around the waypoint is set and if the boat drags beyond this distance, an alarm will sound.

2. Enroute functions. Enroute functions are computed from position functions that are continuously updated and thus provide a vessel's course and speed relative to its change in position. Course/heading as course over the ground (COG) values can be displayed as true or magnetic, speed over the ground (SOG) as knots or statute miles/hour. Unfortunately, because of SA, these values may jump around somewhat with nonmilitary receivers. It is also important to note that the SOG given by a GPS receiver often will not correlate with the vessel's speed as indicated by a knotmeter. The GPS speed is based on the change in geographic position giving the true SOG, whereas a ship's knotmeter measures how fast the water is going by the boat and is influenced by seas and currents. A number of more sophisticated receivers will also calculate velocity made good (VMG), which combines speed and heading, to a waypoint.

With waypoint input, a receiver can determine the distance traveled from a previous waypoint or the distance to the next waypoint. It can also calculate the elapsed running time from the previous waypoint and the time to go and estimated time of arrival (ETA) to the next waypoint. It is important to note that these last three functions are computed not only on distance from/to waypoints, but also on present speed. Should the speed readout change, for example, due to the result of SA degradation, these readings will have a tendency to jump around. Fortunately, these fluctuations will decrease as the waypoint distance decreases because the amount of induced error is magnified over large distances.

Because the GPS receiver is also a very accurate timekeeping device, it is useful for displaying time enroute for normal dead reckoning navigation. This function is particularly helpful when GPS navigation is interrupted by lack of satellites in view or poor satellite geometry.

3. Steering functions. With the entering of waypoints, the receiver can determine what <u>course to steer</u> (also called waypoint bearing) to achieve the waypoint. This can be displayed either as a true or magnetic course. By comparing the actual course made good to the waypoint bearing, <u>cross-track error</u> and <u>course corrections</u> are also determined. These can be depicted either as specific steering instructions or as a <u>graphic display</u> such as an on-course meter or track plotter.

A very popular application of steering functions is <u>to interface</u> a GPS receiver <u>with</u> an <u>autopilot</u>. One disadvantage, however, of using the receiver to drive the boat is that the receiver will do just that and only that. Should an obstacle come in the way (i.e., another boat) it is important to have someone on watch for a quick connect. It is also important to keep a close watch on continued navigation as a wrongly entered waypoint could drive the boat up on the rocks. *See photo #10.*

Diagnostic Functions

It is important that the receiver has some way of displaying the health and status of the satellites (almanac information) and the accuracy of a fix. Receivers display this information in different ways with varying degrees of sophistication. When displaying satellite status, some units will indicate only whether a satellite is healthy or not. Others will additionally list current position parameters and signal to noise ratios. (See Figure 4.7.)

An indication of the accuracy of a fix is also important. Some receivers display a number from a given scale, for example, 1–10. Others display the HDOP value that is determined by satellite geometry (See Chapter 6 on Accuracy.) More sophisticated units present this information in the form of a graphic display. The degree of current position accuracy, or the level of uncertainty, may also be displayed as a numerical representation in nautical miles, statute miles, or kilometers.

Depending on satellite status and fix accuracy the receiver should also have some method of warning when position fixing and navigation are questionable. This warning may be expressed as alarms, lights, or specialized codes. Some receivers just stop navigating when these conditions occur. Others can be forced to continue to navigate with limited accuracy. At any rate, it is important that the user has diagnostic access to information on the accuracy of a fix.

PRN	AZ (°)	EL (°)	S/N*
13	232	30	49
2	86	88	49
14	109	6	46
15	58	38	49
12	328	3	37
26	269	9	48

PRN satellite epseudorandom noise code identification number
AZ   azimuth
EL   elevation
S/N signal to noise ratio

* Note: Manufacturers may have different ways of representing S/N. For example, some refer to this simply as signal quality, rating it from 0-9, with 9 being the best.

Figure 4.7   Satellite Status Readout

Computer Functions

In many respects, the GPS receiver is a very sophisticated computer. Not only does it perform the countless computations in determining position and navigation problems, but it can also be a valuable asset in assisting the user to solve his or her own calculations. Some receivers provide basic mathematical functions—add, subtract, multiply, and divide. These functions can be useful in solving daily problems as a supplement/check on GPS navigation such as subtracting the ship's log for distance run or in dead reckoning.

One of the most valuable computer functions is the ability to convert Latitude/Longitude from minutes and decimal fractions to minutes and seconds and vice versa. This function is a nice option as some navigational charts divide the minutes into units of six instead of 10. Similarly, many large-scale harbor charts are printed in minutes and seconds. In both cases, it is easier to plot position in seconds as opposed to decimal fractions. When lifting waypoints off these charts for receiver input, it is also nice to be able to convert back into minutes and decimal fractions.

With some receivers, it is possible to add and subtract time, which can be useful in dead reckoning, determining engine running time, etc. Other units will even calculate the time of sunrise and sunset based on your position or another waypoint. These calculations are particularly helpful if you want to be assured of good light when navigating a tricky area or timing your arrival into a harbor or to an anchorage before nightfall.

Other Functions

An important function of any GPS receiver is its ability to alert the user at the onset of certain events by visual or audible <u>alarms</u> or both. Heading the list of alarms are those that warn the user of discontinued navigation or high uncertainty in position and navigation. Other alarms announce waypoint arrival, exceeding preset cross-track error, entering a warning area, or anchor dragging. It is even possible to use a GPS receiver as an alarm clock to wake you up in the morning or to indicate when it is time to change watch or receive a weather report.

Most receivers give the option of <u>chart datum selection</u> to ensure that the receiver read-out of latitude and longitude is compatible with the chart in use. Not all charts have been compiled by the same techniques of geodetic survey. The GPS system uses the World Geodetic System 1984 (WGS 84) datum, which is comparable to North American Datum 1983 (NAD 83) now used by the National Oceanic and Atmospheric Administration (NOAA) on most of its charts. However, should you take a charter in Fiji and want to bring along your GPS receiver, you will need to switch to another datum. Therefore, it is important that receivers have the function of user chart datum input. Many units provide the choice of approximately 50 different datums; some offer over 100.

The ultimate in accuracy for the nonmilitary user may well be the use of <u>differential GPS</u> (DGPS). (See Chapter 6 on Accuracy.) DGPS is an accuracy enhancement technique in which received GPS signals at a known reference site are corrected for ranging errors, and these differential corrections are transmitted to the user by a separate communications link. The United States Coast Guard is in the process of upgrading coastal marine radiobeacons for broadcasting these corrections to the user for harbor and harbor approach (HHA) navigation. The receiver then uses this data to calculate a better position solution. Not all receivers, however, have the capability of receiving this information. If you are going to be using GPS in an area where DGPS is available, you may want to select a receiver that has the option to upgrade for the reception of DGPS corrections. It is important to note, however, that not all applications require 10 meter or less accuracy. While adding DGPS capability to a GPS receiver is primarily a software problem that can be added with little increase in receiver price, the real isn providing the communications link to the DGPS signal network. It is important, therefore, to look at your accuracy requirements and the total cost package when determining whether you need a

DGPS receiver.

With the variety of bells and whistles that come with GPS receivers on the market today, it is impossible to describe or even list them all. Certainly, sophistication in radionavigation has come a long way since the early days of Loran-C when all the user got from a loran receiver was a read-out in TDs. It is in the area of extra options that there is the greatest diversity among receivers as manufacturers compete for the expanding market by providing a host of additional functions.

Accessories

Probably one of the nicest accessories to have with a GPS receiver is a remote <u>read-out</u> for use in the cockpit, flying bridge, or owner's cabin. These small units, which are extensions of the parent receiver, can be accessed to call up important position and navigation functions such as Lat/Lon, waypoint bearing and distance, waypoint ETA, cross-track error and direction to steer, COG, and SOG. When selecting a remote, make sure that the unit is waterproof and not just water-resistant. Another consideration is whether the screen can be backlit for nighttime navigation.

A variety of other systems or sensors can be integrated with a GPS receiver. Most of these are separate systems in their own right, but when combined with a GPS unit, they can provide a wealth of additional functions. Accessories can be made by the manufacturer of your GPS receiver or by different manufacturers. However, in order for the integration to work, they must be able to "talk" to each other electronically.

To standardize the connecting ports for integration, the National Marine Electronics Association (NMEA) develops standards for the marine electronics industry. The most recent and popular standard, NMEA 0183, was established in 1983 and is found on most contemporary GPS receivers. Another output standard, NMEA 0180, is also provided on some receivers. A word of caution, however, is necessary. Just because a receiver has a serial output for NMEA 0183 data, doesn't necessarily mean it will interface with all units with the same output. Although the receiver meets the NMEA standard, there are a variety of manufacturer interpretations of formats (sentences) in which the data can be expressed. Therefore, if you wish to integrate with another system, it is advisable that you verify that the receiver is capable of sending and receiving messages to and from those external sensors that you wish to integrate with your GPS receiver.

In addition to integrating with an autopilot, it is also possible to integrate with radar, loran, fishfinders, and electronic charts where GPS data is displayed on the other system's screen. With radar and fishfinders, GPS position and navigation information is displayed on the screen in addition to the unit's normal functions. Loran integration is a nice back-up for those times when not enough satellites are in view to produce a GPS fix or the GPS system may be "down" because of testing or national security. But it is with the system of electronic charts that the full capabilities of electronic integration are realized. GPS puts your position on the chart and you can see your boat move in real time relative to surrounding landmasses, shoals, buoys, etc. Zooming in and out to change the scale of the chart can be accomplished with just a touch of a finger. With some systems, a simple movement of the cursor to any point on the chart will give an instant read-out of range and bearing to the point or record it as a waypoint. (See Chapter 8 for additional discussion of electronic charts.) *See Chapter 4 photo #11 for an example of a chart plotter which can be integrated with GPS.*

Some more sophisticated GPS units provide integration with external sensors, making the GPS receiver a central data collection station for important information. Examples of such sensor are the vessel's speed log, compass, fuel flow, depth sounder, barometer, and waypoints from external sources. With the compass function, it is possible to enter in your own deviation data, which the GPS receiver will then combine with local variation for steering information output. If you choose this option, steering directions, such as bearing and COG, will be directly comparable to your steering compass without your having to add/subtract for variation and deviation. The depth sounder input allows you to display read-outs of water depth below the surface, below the transducer, or below the keel. Another nice accessory for sailboats is the integration of wind sensors. These provide not only the display of apparent wind angle and speed but use these values, combined with user-entered tack angle, to compute the sailboat's approach to a layline, indicating when to change tack in approaching a given waypoint. *See Chapter 4 photo #12 for an example of an integrated system.*

User-Friendly Receivers

In the final analysis, one of the most important considerations in selecting a GPS receiver is whether it is user friendly. It shouldn't require a course in computer programming to operate the unit. The keystroke sequences should be intuitive and held to a minimum to access different functions. There should be sufficient plain English screen prompts so that you don't have to refer to the manual each time you perform an operation. Initial user input time should not exceed one or two hours before basic navigation is achieved. With many receivers, this initial period is assisted by a built-in demonstration mode that "walks" you through basic receiver functions and a sample trip with waypoints. Some manufacturers provide a videotape that explains the parts of the receiver, their uses, waypoint navigation, trip planning, etc. Some manufacturers provide an optional AC adapter so that you can learn to use your receiver in the comfort of your home.

Complementing basic ease of operation, the manual accompanying the receiver should be logically organized and well written with clear concise instructions. It should have good illustrations depicting actual screen displays of different functions. It should contain a section devoted to trouble-shooting so that you don't have to call your dealer every time there is a problem. The manual should also include a thorough index so that you can quickly find a given function or topic. Some manuals come with a listing of abbreviations and their meanings, which is very helpful to the beginning user. Often these abbreviations are expanded into a glossary that provides definitions not only of terms related to the receiver, but also of basic navigation terms and terms specific to the GPS system. One handy device provided by many manufacturers is a "cheat card" or small quick reference feature that outlines basic receiver functions.

Since many users are installing their own receivers, an accompanying installation manual should also be user friendly. Again, it should be clearly written, with logical steps, well-labeled parts, and easy-to-understand illustrations.

IV. Portable vs. Fixed-mount Receivers

In the early to mid-1990's, sales of portable, handheld GPS receivers exceeded those of fixed-mount units. And with good reason. Other than a sacrifice in screen display size, portable units can match performance and accuracy parameters with some of the more sophisticated, larger fixed-mount units. Portable receivers are versatile and flexible, going from a cockpit to a dinghy to a duffel for a charter in the Caribbean. They also have the advantage of quick removal to take home in areas where boat security is a problem. Another advantage is that the receivers can be brought home to learn how to use or to program in waypoints for future trips. Competitive pricing, which often brings portables in at hundreds of dollars below larger fixed-mount receivers, makes them an attractive option for many GPS users.

When shopping for a GPS portable, all of the features previously discussed such as good performance, ease of use, display screen characteristics, etc., still apply. However, with portable units, there are some additional important considerations.

1. Power options. It is important to note what type of batteries the unit runs on. Many units use inexpensive alkaline batteries, which must be thrown away after becoming discharged. An improvement over this technology is the use of a rechargeable NiCAD battery pack similar to those we have been using with our portable computers for years. It is also advantageous to be able to recharge the battery packs by the ship's 12V DC as well as by AC.

The amount of actual running time or battery life is also important. Some receivers provide only 4–5 hours of use, which doesn't allow much navigation time in a long day's run. This time, of course, can be extended by using the starved power mode with the sacrifice of discontinuous navigation. An advantage with most portables is the ability to plug into the ship's 12-volt system with a power cord/data cable, thus reserving battery use for those occasions when you are away from the main vessel. Some manufacturers even provide the option of a cigarette lighter power cord for recharging your GPS receiver in your car on the way to your boat.

2. Fixed-mount option. Along with the ability to run off the ship's batteries, the portable should be able to be mounted in different locations, i.e., nav-station or cockpit. The mounting bracket should solidly constructed of heavy-duty construction that will hold the unit securely in rough conditions. The mount should also be versatile lending itself to use in a variety of locations and angles. It may be advantageous to have a number of brackets around the nav-station and cockpit for flexible use. *See Chapter 4 photo #13 for an example of a fixed-mount receiver.*

3. Antenna. Some portables have an internal "patch" antenna, which allows for a more streamlined case design and has the potential for being more waterproof. The disadvantage with this type of antenna is that in some circumstances, it may have difficulty tracking low-altitude satellites. Other portables have a quadrifilar antenna that is attached externally to the unit. In some instances, this antenna may be more sensitive in tracking satellite signals. Many portables offer an external remote antenna option for use when the receiver is attached to a fixed mount.

4. Screen characteristics. The screen size of portables is definitely going to be smaller than that of a larger, permanently fixed unit. Yet, a number of manufacturers have been able to produce four-line displays, providing several functions on one page. On the downside is the inability to present the information in large characters that can be seen from a distance. Portables also differ with respect to the number of characters displayed for waypoint names. Some units provide up to 10 characters, allowing for a more thorough labeling of waypoints. A final point worth noting is that portable screens are difficult, if not impossible, to read when wearing polarized sunglasses because the screens themselves are polarized to provide a better character contrast in sunlight.

5. Waterproofing. Because of the diverse environments where they are likely to be used (i.e., cockpits and dinghies), portable receivers must be completely waterproof. Some units are advertised as being only fog- and mist-proof. Those units designed for land use are often only water-resistant. Another relevant feature is positive buoyancy. It could spoil anyone's day, let alone the whole trip or vacation, to drop a GPS receiver overboard while skimming over the surf in the dinghy to go out for some reef exploration.

6. Total cost package. Although portables are generally lower priced than larger fixed-mount receivers, it is important to look at the total cost package. By the time you add on a remote mounting kit with its external antenna and mounting bracket, you may well exceed the cost of many higher-priced receivers. Find out whether the 12-volt DC power cord is included with the basic package or is an extra option. Other considerations are the costs of extra battery packs and mounting brackets—all of which can increase the total financial outlay.

In the final analysis, all GPS receivers perform the same basic functions: They calculate your position (based on a known coordinate system); they calculate course and speed over ground; they provide accurate time updates; and they provide basic navigation to at least one waypoint. Beyond that, every GPS receiver is different. Which unit is selected depends on the choice of features, capabilities, receiver architectures, and prices that best meet individual needs.

Photo #1: Micrologic Supersport GPS is waterproof, provides 250 waypoints and 133 chart datums and comes with an optional external antenna and remote display/control unit. Courtesy of M i c r o l o g i c , Chatsworth, CA.

FURUNO GP-70

Photo #2: An example of a dual channel multiplexing receiver which can track up to 8 satellites. A completely water-tight package that features cast metal enclosures and a water-tight membrane keypad. Courtesy of Furuno U.S.A., Inc.

Photo #3: Magellan handheld Portable GPS Receiver uses 5 parallel channels, is differential-ready, is completely waterproof and floats. Note the use of an external quadrifilar antenna. Courtesy of Magellan Syatems Corporation.

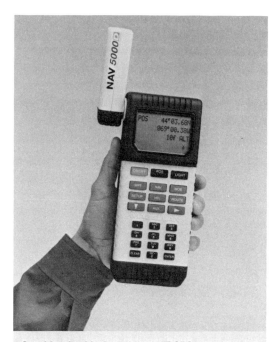

Capable of achieving 10-meter DGPS accuracy, the Magellan NAV 5000D is the only portable GPS receiver that is differential-ready, that is truly water proof and that floats.

Photo #4: Trimble's 6 channel Ension XL GPS comes with differential capability and NMEA output for transmission of position data to autopilots, radars, and repeater displays. Its built-in patch antenna allows a sleek-designed unit about the size of a cellular phone. Courtesy of Trimble Navigation, Ltd.

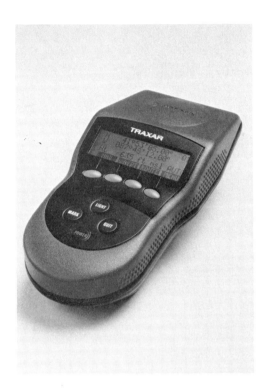

Photo #5: Motorola's TRAXAR 6-channel portable GPS uses just 8 keys to access its easy-to-use menu-driven software. Its internal patch antenna allows sleek contemporary housing which easily fits into the shape of your hand. Courtesy of Motorola.

Photo #6: Magnavox MX 100, A state of the art multiple channel receiver with 6 dedicated channels. It includes a graphic display of cross-track error and built-in track plotter. Note use of "soft keys" below screen. Courtesy of Magnavox Electronic Systems Company.

Photo #7: The Acutis DGPS is a high performance 6 channel DGPS receiver and antenna integrated in a compact waterproof enclosure which mounts like an antenna. Data is displayed on another system such as radar, a chart plotter, or fishfinder. Courtesy of TrimbleNavigation, Ltd.

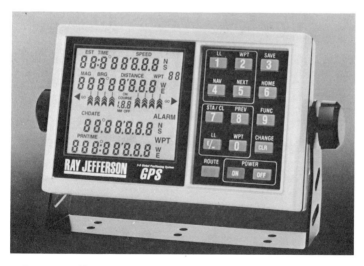

Photo #8: Ray Jefferson's GPS-6 multiplexing receiver tracks up to 5 satellites. Note use of 7 segment bar display, large screen size and easy-to-use keypad. Courtesy of Ray Jefferson Marine Electronics.

Photo #9: Garmin's GPS 75 uses its patented MultiTrac™ operating system to constantly track up to 8 staellites. Note screen display which shows satellite signal and lock on information. Courtesy of Garmin International, Lenexa, KS.

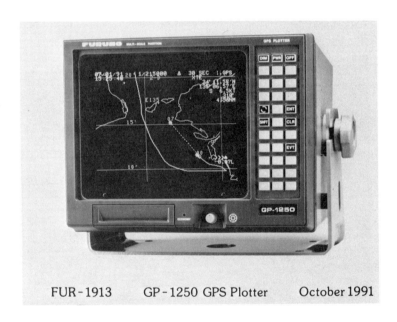

FUR-1913   GP-1250 GPS Plotter   October 1991

Photo #12: The Furuno GP-1250 is a totally integrated GPS receiver and videoplotter in one unit. Factory digitized charts are supplied on an optional ROM card with a maximum of 7 charts per card. From Furuno U.S.A., Inc.

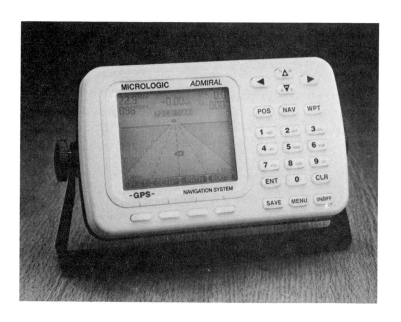

Photo #10: Micrologic Admiral GPS, a state of the art multiplexing receiver which tracks 5 satellites simultaneously. Includes a large display for presenting data and cross track error, a track plotter and a position database for over 14,000 lights and bouys for the coastal U.S., Great Lakes, Alaska, Hawaii, and Canada. A European version contains lights and bouys for the Mediterranean, Spain, France, Britain, Scandinavia and the Baltic Sea. The South Pacific version includes Australia, New Zealand, Indonesia, Pacific Islands and the west coast of Mexico, Central and South America. Courtesy of Micrologic, Chatsworth, CA.

Photo #11: Chartpilot™ is an integrated chart plotter and autopilot which can be interfaced with GPS to provide position, future course, speed and heading on a single screen Courtesy of Cetrek U.S.A., 640 Lewis Rd., Limerick, PA.

Capable of achieving 10-meter DGPS accuracy, the differential-ready Magellan NAV 5200D can be either bracket- or flush-mounted at the ship's nav station.

Photo #13: Magellan's fixed-mount receiver is housed in rugged cast-aluminum which is waterpfoof. It uses 5 parallel channels to track up to 11 satellites and is differential compatible. Courtesy of Magellan System Corporation.

104

CHAPTER FIVE

General Mechanics in Using GPS

GPS is not only the "smartest" navigation system to come on line in the last quarter of the twentieth century, it is also one of the easiest systems to use since the advent of radionavigation. Despite the system's intricate complexity in the timing and sending of radio signals, GPS has emerged as one of the most user-friendly systems available in the world of navigation and position fixing.

A major reason for this development is that the technological advances gained in the electronics industry have rapidly filtered down from the drawing board, passed through product development, and become available on the common user market with mind-boggling geometric progression. No longer do users have to struggle with complex manuals as they did in the early days of Loran-C technology. Miniaturization of microprocessors makes GPS receivers more sophisticated than their loran cousins of yesteryear. Advanced software programs lead users quickly through a minimum of intuitive steps to access functions that were hardly thought of a decade ago.

Not only has the electronics industry rapidly advanced in recent decades, but the user community has also become more sophisticated. We learned a lot in our years with Loran-C and Sat Nav and have entered the world of GPS no longer novices in electronic navigation. Waypoint navigation, range, bearing, speed over the ground, and cross-track error are as commonplace as raising sails and setting anchors.

In response to the increasing demands of a discerning user community, manufacturers have come to realize the importance of delivering sophisticated, easy-to-use mutltifunction receivers. In fact, most manufacturers now assume that the majority of their receivers will be owner installed.

I. Installation

In keeping with the trend toward user-friendly manuals, most installation manuals that accompany today's GPS receivers provide clear concise instructions for installing their product. Often all that is needed are a few basic tools in addition to the specialized parts provided with the unit. Although receivers will vary depending on the manufacturer, installation usually involves four basic parts: the antenna, antenna cable, the main navigator unit or receiver, and the power cable.

The Antenna

Although GPS antennas come in many different shapes, one thing they all have in common is that they are generally much smaller than antennas used with other radionavigation systems. More often than not the housing is larger than it need be, as it is designed to protect the antenna surfaces inside. Most GPS antennas can be easily held in the palm of your hand.

Positioning of the antenna is an important factor in signal reception and basic receiver performance. The position should be relatively accessible for installation, yet the antenna must be kept out of reach near grab rails, life line gates, or boarding ladders where it might be mistaken for a handhold. It should be in a position as close to 90° to the water (straight vertical) as possible when the boat is level.

There are a few areas to avoid in positioning the antenna. The antenna needs line-of-sight with the satellites in order to track them, so it should be kept away from any large obstructions such as a mast or rigging or places where it could be shaded by sections of a large cabin top. Smaller objects will not interfere with reception as long as they shadow only a small part of the antenna. The masthead of a sailboat is not a good place to mount a GPS antenna because motion on top of the mast caused by excessive rolling and pitching will distort speed readings. While most motors and generators do not cause interference problems, the antenna should be isolated from high-power radio frequency sources and out of the beam of radars. This requirement could be a problem for those with powerboats in which a radar might be mounted on a cabin top. If this is the case, an alternative location for the antenna might be high on the stern rail or the bow pulpit. On aluminum or steel boats, the antenna must be at least 1 meter above the deck. (See Figure 5.1.)

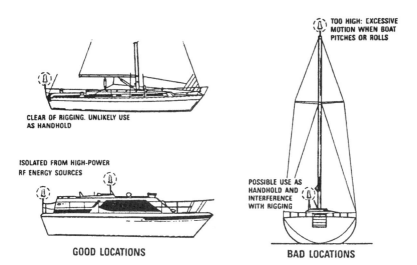

CLEAR OF RIGGING. UNLIKELY USE
AS HANDHOLD

ISOLATED FROM HIGH-POWER
RF ENERGY SOURCES

GOOD LOCATIONS

TOO HIGH: EXCESSIVE
MOTION WHEN BOAT
PITCHES OR ROLLS

POSSIBLE USE AS
HANDHOLD AND
INTERFERENCE
WITH RIGGING

BAD LOCATIONS

Courtesy of Magnavox
Government and Industrial Electronics Company
Torrence, California

Figure 5.1   *Mounting the GPS Antenna*

Once the antenna site is chosen, there are a number of different ways to mount the antenna. Because the size and shape of GPS antennas vary a lot, mounting brackets often are tailor-made to fit the specific antenna. Most often manufacturers will include an antenna mounting bracket with their installation package. Depending on the site chosen, it may be necessary to custom make one's own bracket. A common placement on both powerboats and sailboats is to attach the bracket out of the way and somewhat elevated on a corner of the stern rail. Another option is to use some kind of extension pole on the stern rail. (See Figure 5.2.)

Antenna Cable

Connecting the GPS antenna to the receiver is the antenna cable. It transfers the received satellite signal to the receiver for signal processing. Note that in some receivers, receiver hardware actually accomplishes this task in the antenna, and the resulting data is then transmitted to an external display and control panel. For example, some units are designed to be integrated with other navigation instruments such as Loran-C, radar, or electronic charts through which the GPS data is displayed.

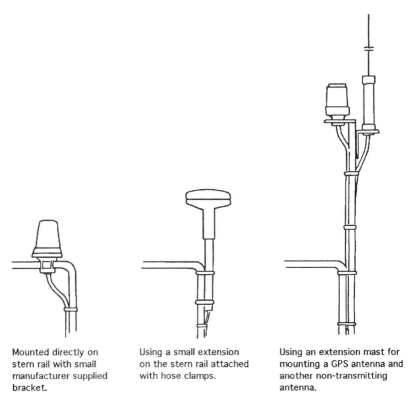

Mounted directly on
stern rail with small
manufacturer supplied
bracket.

Using a small extension
on the stern rail attached
with hose clamps.

Using an extension mast for
mounting a GPS antenna and
another non-transmitting
antenna.

Figure 5.2   Different Methods for Mounting a GPS Antenna

The length of antenna cable provided with a GPS unit is usually more than adequate. However, if more length is required, the cable should not be spliced but special ordered from a dealer. In stringing the cable from the antenna to the main navigation unit, use the shortest length possible to reduce signal loss. However, do not string the cable too tightly or around sharp corners where the protective covering can chafe. Likewise, the cable should not come in contact with hot areas such as those near the engine exhaust, manifolds, or steam pipes. Cable ties can help to hold the cable in place and reduce chafe in crucial areas. If you have to lead the cable through a hole drilled in a bulkhead, sealing the hole with caulking compound after the cable has been strung also reduces chafe.

The Receiver

In mounting the main unit of a GPS receiver, there are a few important considerations. One of the most important factors is that the receiver is positioned so that it is accessible for data input and that the screen can be easily read. It may be advantageous to use a bracket that has some flexibility in tilting the receiver at different angles for different lighting conditions as opposed to a rigid fixed mount. A few manufacturers offer a swivel mount, which lends itself nicely to turning the unit for different viewing angles or lighting conditions. *See Chapter 5 photo #1 for an example.*

If the receiver is not waterproof, it should be installed in a dry area well away from spray, occasional cabin leaks, etc. Even if the unit is advertised as "water-resistant," a dry location is a good precaution. The receiver should also be kept well away from extreme heat such as direct sunlight. Also with some receivers it may be difficult to read the display read-out in bright sunlight.

Most manufacturers provide mounting brackets that accommodate a number of different mounting options. Some alternatives are to mount the unit directly on a bulkhead, hanging from an overhead, on a flat working surface such as a chart table, or in the bridge next to the wheel station. Many manufacturers provide alternate mounting brackets for flush mounting on a bulkhead or in the nav-station. (See Figure 5.3.) *See Chapter 5 photo #2 for an example.*

Another nice option is to install the unit in such a way that it can be used for chartwork down below in the nav-station and then swung out into the companionway for easy viewing from the helm. For this option, unless the receiver is waterproof, some provision must be made to protect the unit from spray using a dodger or protective covering. Sufficient cable lengths (antenna and power) should also be used to allow for movement without cable strain.

Regardless of the type of mount or bracket used, it is important that the receiver be held securely in place and not be vibrated by excessive boat motion. In areas where theft is a consideration, provisions should be made to deter easy removal of the receiver. On the other hand, if the boat is laid up during the winter months, it should be possible to remove and reinstall the receiver without a major effort.

Power Cable & Ground Cable

The power cable connects the main navigator unit to its source of power. There are two basic ways to connect the cable with the ship's power supply. The process can be as simple as just connecting the two

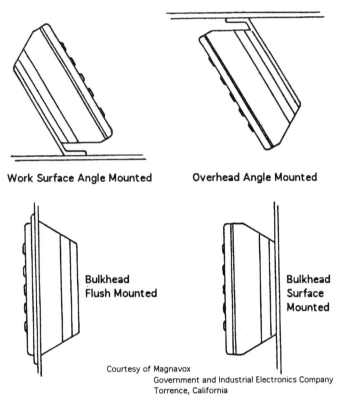

Work Surface Angle Mounted   Overhead Angle Mounted

Bulkhead
Flush Mounted

Bulkhead
Surface
Mounted

Courtesy of Magnavox
Government and Industrial Electronics Company
Torrence, California

Figure 5.3   *Different Ways of Mounting a GPS Receiver*

terminals directly to a battery, as long as care is taken to note the correct leads. A more prudent approach may be to lead these connections through a control panel with circuit breakers or fuses in line. This method has the advantage of keeping any spikes or power surges from entering the receiver. It is also another way of controlling input power to the unit.

In addition to the power cable, a ground cable is usually supplied with most receivers. Grounding is important to ensure reliable performance of the receiver. On metal boats, the ground cable may be connected to a grounding bolt on the hull. On wood or fiberglass boats, there are a number of grounding options. A common ground used in fresh water is the engine block or drive shaft. This method of grounding, however, should be avoided in salt water to prevent serious electrolysis problems. Some boats may have special grounding plates attached to the outside of the hull. Other locations are underwater through-hulls or keel bolts on a sailboat. Attachment of the power cable and ground cable to the receiver varies with manufacturers.

Interfacing with External Sensors

It is possible to interface many GPS receivers with external sensors such as an autopilot, depthsounder, compass, speedlog, and wind instruments. Most receivers are provided with NMEA 0183 or 0180 outputs. However, it is important to check the data sentences for these ports to make sure the specific function required is available. The sentences are a variety of message formats that are used for transmitting special types of information between different kinds of equipment. Having the specific output just means that the GPS receiver conforms to the standard, making it possible for the receiver to communicate with any other piece of equipment that conforms to that standard. Unless the receiver and external sensor send or receive the same messages, they will not interface.

Internal Batteries

One final consideration in receiver installation is that most receivers have internal batteries, which are used to maintain receiver memory when the main source of power is turned off. With most units, these batteries are placed in the unit at the time of installation. Since the life of these batteries varies, it is important to note the date at the time of installation. Typical battery life can vary from 6 months to 5 years.

Portable Units

Even though many of the receivers on the market today are sold as portable units, in the interest of conserving internal batteries, most portables will require some installation, if only to be hooked up with the ship's batteries for external power supply. Quite often this installation is accomplished by using some form of a "hot-shoe," a derivation of the mounting bracket that is connected into the ship's electrical system. All portables have antennas that are directly integrated with the unit either internally or in the form of an external swing antenna. With many portables, there is the option of purchasing another external antenna, which involves the same installation considerations as antennas used with fixed-mount receivers.

II. Getting Started

Once the receiver is installed, the next step is to initiate the first start, sometimes called a "cold start". Depending on the sophistication of the receiver, the first start may simply involve turning the unit on. With some receivers, a few initialization steps may be needed.

First Start/Initialization Procedures

Most GPS receivers are a lot smarter than their earlier Sat Nav cousins, which required a lot of initial input to get to that first fix. Some contemporary GPS receivers require no information at all for a cold start—it's called an "anywhere fix." Others require input of **approximate location** and **approximate time** (within 30 minutes). Location is usually within 50 miles and could be a problem if you have left your receiver off for a long period of time while moving and have no reference points to determine your approximate position. With some receivers, you have to input not only local time, but also the time zone, Standard/Daylight time, day of the week, and the date, month and year. With other receivers, all that is required is to have the correct **time offset** from Universal Time Coordinated (UTC). Many manuals include a world chart showing the different time zones to assist in determining the degree of offset. Note that even though approximate time may be entered initially, once the receiver is tracking satellites, the time read-out will be updated, providing a highly accurate source of time.

If you are navigating in the two-dimensional mode, it is important to enter in the **antenna height** as part of the initialization procedure. With most receivers, there is a choice of using meters or feet. When navigating at sea level, all that is needed is the height of the antenna above the water. However, when you are located in inland waterways or lakes, then the total height of the antenna above sea level is needed. If you are inland and don't know your height above sea level, you can select the three-dimensional mode to determine your altitude and then use this figure to enter into the two-dimensional mode. For mariners, there are decided advantages to navigating in the two-dimensional mode, especially when there is reduced satellite coverage or small satellite crossing angles.

Regardless of the amount of information required to initialize a GPS receiver in a first start, usually a certain amount of time must pass before the first satellite is acquired. This lag occurs because the receiver has no almanac memory to assist it in tracking satellites, and it has to search virtually every satellite in view until it gets a match with a pseudorandom code. Once the first satellite is tracked, the receiver will take approximately 12-15 minutes to collect the almanac.

The cold start **time to first fix** (TTFF) will vary depending on the type of receiver architecture. With sequencing receivers, the process could take 15–30 minutes. Parallel channel receivers, which can use other channels for searching and tracking satellites while the almanac is being collected from the first satellite, will have a much shorter TTFF. Once the almanac is in the receiver memory, subsequent starts, sometimes called "warm starts," can take 1–3 minutes.

Customizing Read-out/Performance Options

Before you start navigating, it is important to note that with most receivers, you have a number of read-out and performance options to choose from. With these options, it is possible to customize the receiver to display data selected for your individual needs. For example, you can select the navigation mode as a great circle or a rhumb line. Great circle navigation involves a constantly changing heading between two way-points. Although it represents a shorter distance between the points, great circle navigation is generally used when traveling large expanses on the open ocean. Rhumb line distance is a little longer than a great circle route, but it is generally used for shorter runs as it employs a constant heading between two points. Unless you are covering large distances, the differences between rhumb line and great circle navigation are usually insignificant. Some other read-out options involve the ways in which the time of day, antenna height, and speed/drift are expressed.

There are two additional read-out options that bear further discussion. One relates to boat speed, which may be displayed as knots or miles/hour, and waypoint range, which may be expressed as nautical miles, statute miles, or kilometers. It might be advantageous to use the statute mile option if you are navigating in a waterway where the track is divided on the chart as specific mile numbers, for example, mile #132. However, with most navigation, it is more convenient to use nautical miles for a couple of reasons. First of all, most navigation instruments (speedos, knotmeters, knotlogs) on the market today are usually calibrated in knots and nautical miles. Another reason is that chartwork lends itself nicely to nautical miles by using the latitude scale on the side of the chart in which one minute of latitude equals one nautical mile.

The other read-out option deals with the manner in which <u>steering directions</u> are stated. Steering directions (COG, waypoint bearing) may be expressed as true or magnetic readings. Using true readings in all your navigation has the advantage of doing all your chartwork without having to add or subtract for magnetic variation. With an external GPS remote displayed near the helm, the vessel is actually steered using GPS headings as opposed to the ship's compass. The compass can still be used by using calculated GPS data to correct a given heading by simply adding or subtracting so many degrees, regardless of the magnetic compass heading. A quick check with continued GPS read-outs will verify if, in fact, the vessel is on the desired course.

In using the automatic magnetic variation option along with entered deviation data, subsequent GPS read-outs will automatically be compensated for these two variables. The advantage is that the ship's compass headings and GPS read-outs will be in close correlation. The disadvantage is that magnetic variation and deviation will then have to be added or subtracted in chartwork. It is important to note that some receivers offer a third option in which the degree of magnetic variation can be entered manually. This option may be useful for those areas in that the variation has changed significantly from the model that has been programmed into the receiver. Which of the three options is used for describing steering directions is a matter of personal preference depending on the particular area being navigated.

A number of performance options may also be customized, for example, the size of the zones for cross-track error, waypoint arrival, danger zones, and anchor watch. With some receivers, it is even possible to set an alarm clock, which may be convenient for watch changes, tuning in for a weather fax transmission, etc. With many receivers, audio alarms can be turned on or off and even adjusted for tone and loudness. Finally, it is important to select the correct chart datum for the charts in

Alarms:	on/off
Antenna height:	meters/feet
Beeper:	on/off
Chart datum:	offerings may vary from 50 - 100
Display:	timeout for viewing secondary function lists different minute options
Navigation mode:	rhumb line, great circle
Range:	nautical miles, statute miles
Speed/drift:	knots, statute miles/hour, kilometers/hour, meters/second
Steering Directions:	true, magnetic
Time:	24 hour, 12 hour AM/PM

Note: These are examples of some customizing functions and are not present on all receivers.

Figure 5.4   Customizing GPS Receiver Options

114

use for the particular area being navigated as there are some variations in datums in different areas of the world. For a summary of some of the customizing options with a GPS receiver, see Figure 5.4.

Simulated Voyage/Demo Mode

Many GPS receivers on the market today have built-in software that will take you through a simulated voyage to demonstrate the different features available when using the unit. This simulation may take a variety of forms. It may be a fictitious voyage from a point of departure through a series of waypoints to a given destination. The waypoints may be pre-entered or you may be required to enter them as part of the learning process. Once initiated, the program will then run through the receiver as a function of time until the last waypoint is "reached." If the receiver has a plotter, it is actually possible to watch your boat advance and turn at each waypoint—again as a function of time.

There are a number of advantages in using a receiver demonstration mode. The most obvious, of course, is becoming acquainted with the receiver functions. The demonstration mode is also a valuable tool for learning how to input and access GPS data. On some units, this function can be used to simulate your own voyages, a handy asset for planning next summer's vacation. Some manufacturers even provide an AC/DC power adapter as an accessory so that this function can be used in the comfort of your home.

III. Using GPS

Of the many applications in using GPS, probably the most basic is just simple position fixing. In fact, in the world of marine navigation, position fixing is the basis of all other navigation. If you do not know your position, you cannot compute the distance to your destination, the course to take, or your estimated time of arrival. In terms of absolute accuracy in determining position, GPS leads all other radionavigation systems—even with the implementation of selective availability.

Plotting Position

GPS position read-outs are usually given as latitude/longitude

(Lat/Lon) coordinates that can be plotted on any chart. Some manufacturers provide the option of formatting the data into different coordinate systems. Examples of these are Universal Transverse Mercator (UTM), Military Grid Reference System (MGRS), or Universal User Defined (UUD). Since the Lat/Lon coordinate system is the one most commonly used, it is the one described in this book.

A GPS fix can be plotted using Lat/Lon coordinates in two different ways. One uses parallel rules; the other uses a pair of dividers. In each case, the coordinates are measured off on the scales printed on the sides or top and bottom of the chart. Latitude values are printed on the sides, longitude values at the top and bottom. These values are divided into degrees and minutes. The minutes are subdivided into fractions of minutes. Sometimes a sample of these subdivided scales will be printed at intervals.

To determine a fix using parallel rules, the rules are first lined up with the nearest latitude or longitude "guide or reference" line, as in Figure 5.5, Step 1. These lines are printed at various intervals (such as every 10 minutes) and extend into the chart. The rules are next opened to the specific latitude (or longitude) reading on the scale (Step 2) and then "walked" across the chart (Steps 3 and 4) into the approximate area of your location. This procedure produces a latitude line of posi-

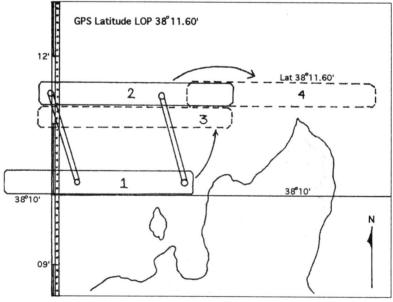

Figure 5.5 *Using Parallel Rules to Establish a GPS Latitude LOP*

tion (LOP), which is drawn parallel to the guideline. To get a position fix, the procedure must be repeated with the GPS longitude reading to get a longitude LOP. One disadvantage of this technique is that a lurch of the boat can make the rules slip and you either have to start over, or worse, plot a fix with an unknown error.

To determine a GPS Lat/Lon fix with a pair of dividers is incredibly simple and the technique preferred by many users. Latitude and longitude are still measured at the edge of the chart—but this time the distance of the specific latitude or longitude is measured with the dividers in reference to the nearest guideline mark. It is this distance that is then transferred into the chart with the dividers and marked off from the reference line in the area being traveled. Again, a line is drawn parallel to the latitude or longitude guideline. (See Figure 5.6.) This method is particularly fast and accurate if you are using the type of dividers that can

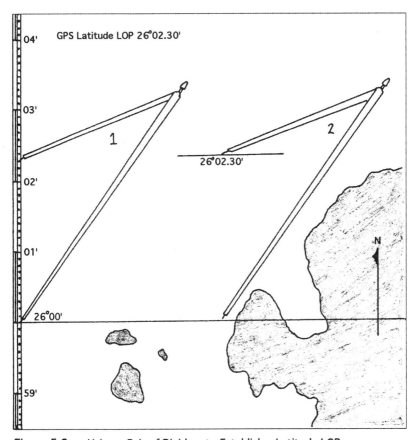

Figure 5.6 *Using a Pair of Dividers to Establish a Latitude LOP*

117

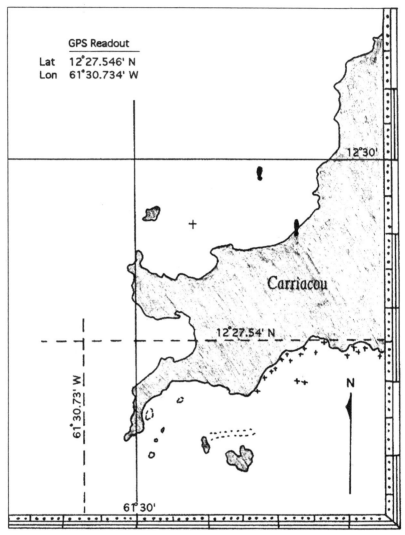

GPS Readout
Lat 12°27.546' N
Lon 61°30.734' W

12°30'

Carriacou

12°27.54' N

61°30.73' W

N

61°30'

Figure 5.7   *Using GPS Latitude/Longitude Coordinates to Plot Position*

be operated with one hand and have sufficient tension to hold a given set as the distance measured is being transferred.

An example of a typical GPS fix is shown in Figure 5.7. Note that although the GPS read-outs are given to the thousandth minute, it is possible to plot each coordinate only to the nearest hundredth minute with any degree of accuracy with either the latitude or longitude scales given.

Degrees	Minutes		Degrees	Minutes	Seconds
12°	18.50'	OR	12°	18'	30"

Figure 5.8   Two Different Ways of Representing Latitude/Longitude

Using Different Chart Scales

At this point, it is important to note that Lat/Lon coordinates can be expressed in two different ways. These are based on the form in which the fractions of a minute are represented: as decimal fractions of a minute or as seconds, with 60 seconds in a minute. (See Figure 5.8.) Most GPS receivers display Lat/Lon by using minute decimal fractions— either to 0.01 or 0.001 minute. These numbers are easily transferred to most charts, which are printed with the minutes divided into 10 equal parts as decimal fractions. However, a number of charts are printed in minutes and seconds, with each minute divided into 60 seconds. Depending on the scale of the chart, the minute seconds can be represented in different ways. One of the most common forms is the division of each minute into six equal parts with each division equal to 10 seconds. Regardless of the form, using charts that display minute seconds can lead to confusion when transferring GPS position read-outs to these charts.

To illustrate this principle of changing from one scale to another, suppose you are trying to plot the latitude of 12° 18.500'N on a chart printed in minutes and decimal fractions of a minute. A quick glance at the latitude scale shows that each minute is divided into 10 parts, and the 0.500 read-out should be plotted on the fifth mark, or 0.5' reading, as in Figure 5.9A. If a chart printed in minutes and seconds is used instead, and the latitude is again plotted on the fifth mark, position will be off. On this new scale, which is divided into six parts, each point represents 10". In this case, the position in error would be at 18'50," the equivalent of 18.83', which would put the charted position approximately 1/3 mile too far north. Since 0.5 minutes is 1/2 minute or 30 seconds, the position should be plotted at the third mark on the minute/second scale. (See Figure 5.9B.)

If you are using a chart in which the fractions of minutes have been expressed as seconds, you will have to convert from hundredths of minutes to seconds to plot position. There are a couple of ways to do this conversion. One is to use a calculator to change minute hundredths to

119

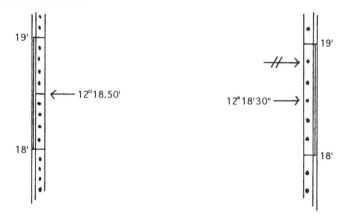

A. Minutes and Decimal
Fractions of Minutes

B. Minutes and Seconds

19'

18'

←— 12°18.50'

19'

18'

12°18'30" —→

Note: ⟶//⟶ would equal 12°18'50" or 12°18.83'

Figure 5.9   Using Different Chart Scales to Plot GPS Latitude

A. To change from hundreths of minutes to seconds:

Seconds = minute hundreths x 60

Example: 0.30 minutes = ? seconds
seconds = 0.30 min x 60 sec = 18
OR 0.30 min = 18 sec

B. To change from seconds to minute hundreths:

Minute hundreths = seconds/60

Example: 45 seconds = ? minute hundreths
minute hundreths = 45 sec/60 = 0.75
OR 45 sec = 0.75 min

Figure 5.10   Minute/Second Conversion

seconds by multiplying the minute fraction by 60. (See Figure 5.10A.) It is also important to be able to convert from seconds back to minute hundredths, for example, when lifting a waypoint off the chart for entry into the receiver. To do this conversion, the seconds are divided by 60. (See Figure 5.10B.)

Another way to convert is to use a conversion table such as the one shown in Figure 5.11. For those values that do not fall exactly on the given numbers, it is possible to roughly interpolate between the given

120

Minute Hundreths	Seconds	Minute Hundreths	Seconds
0.05	3	0.65	39
0.10	6	0.70	42
0.15	9	0.75	45
0.20	12	0.80	48
0.25	15	0.85	51
0.30	18	0.90	54
0.35	21	0.95	57
0.40	24	1.00	60
0.45	27	min	sec
0.50	30	Ex. of Interpolation:	
0.55	33	32° 12.43' = 32° 12'26"	
0.60	36		

Figure 5.11   Conversion Table for Minutes/Seconds

numbers. For example, suppose you have a reading of 32° 12.43' and want to plot it on a chart printed in minutes and seconds. A quick look at the table shows that 0.43' is between 0.40' and 0.45'. Equivalent readings in seconds are 24" and 27", respectively. Interpolation would give 32° 12' 26".

The following example illustrates this technique of changing GPS readings to their minute/second derivatives and plotting them on a chart. Suppose you wish to plot your GPS position on a chart in which the minute subdivisions are in seconds as opposed to tenths and hundredths of a minute, as in Figure 5.12. Using a calculator, you quickly convert the GPS minute decimal fractions to their equivalent seconds. Using each mark, which represents 10 seconds, position can now be plotted on the chart.

These conversions are advantageous in a couple of other situations. One is checking GPS accuracy in which a good method is to plot position on a very large-scale harbor chart. These charts are often found as blown-up insets on regular charts. Unfortunately, their coordinates are often printed as minutes and seconds, so it is necessary to convert from the receiver read-out to chart coordinates. (See Figure 5.13.)

Another example in which conversion calculations would be applicable would be just the reverse situation: lifting coordinates off a chart printed in minutes and seconds to be entered into the receiver as a waypoint. In the interest of accuracy, you may prefer to lift the entrance coordinates of a harbor off a large scale-harbor chart inset as opposed to a smaller scale chart used for navigation. The coordinates are then converted to minute fractions to be entered into the receiver. (See Figure 5.14.)

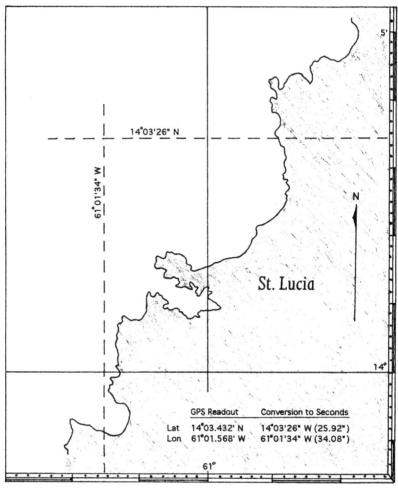

Figure 5.12   Plotting a GPS Fix Using Minutes and Seconds

Using GPS in Anchoring

GPS position read-outs can be used in anchoring in a couple of ways. One is in determining whether the anchor is set or the vessel is dragging while setting anchor. As you are backing down on the anchor, relatively constant position read-outs will verify that the anchor is set, while changing numbers indicate that the boat is still moving and dragging anchor. This information is particularly useful when anchoring in the dark or when there are no close landmarks to use to make reference bearings. A remote GPS read-out near the steering station is very helpful when using this technique.

122

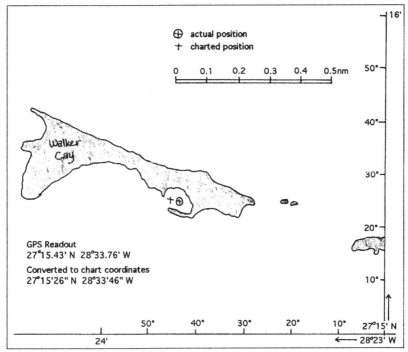

Figure 5.13   Checking GPS Accuracy on a Chart Using Minutes and Seconds

The second way in which GPS position is used in anchoring is by activating an "anchor watch." Receivers vary in how this function is employed. Basically, it involves enabling the anchor alarm, entering the anchored position as a present position, and entering the desired drift range in nautical miles. An imaginary circle will then be "drawn" around the boat, and if it should drag outside the range limit, an alarm will sound.

Man Overboard

Before leaving the topic of plotting position, it is important to note one of the most important functions that many GPS receivers provide. The man overboard function is a special adaptation of position fixing that can be initiated just by the touch of a special key. Position is immediately recorded as a special waypoint along with the date and time of the event. This invaluable information can be relayed to the Coast Guard or other boaters who may be engaged in a man overboard search.

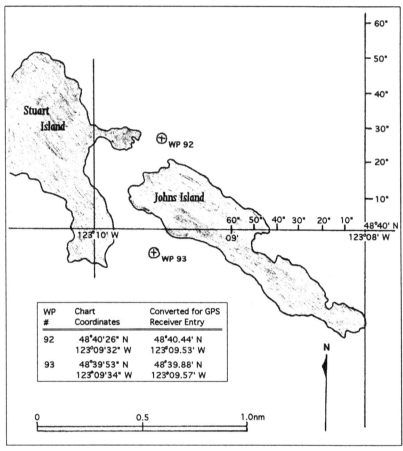

Figure 5.14   Converting from Chart Minutes and Seconds to Receiver Coordinates

Another very important feature of the man overboard function is that the receiver will now display the bearing and distance for guiding the boat back to the overboard position. Those receivers with track plotters will display this information in a graphic display. In using GPS, it is a prudent practice to initiate simulated man overboard drills to become acquainted with the techniques needed to use this function to go back to a specific position.

Using Waypoints

Next to plotting position, the most common use for GPS in the

124

marine environment is waypoint navigation. A waypoint is a specific position that is entered into a GPS receiver for navigation. A waypoint may be the entrance of a harbor, a position outside a favorite anchorage, the location of a lobster pot, or simply a position where a desired course change should be made. (See Figure 5.15.)

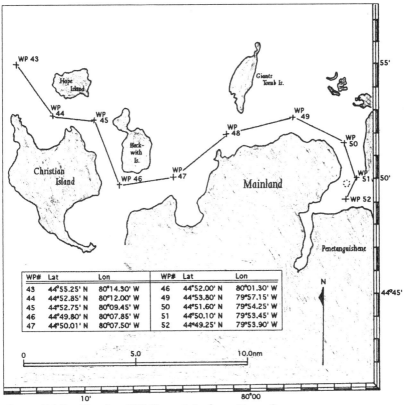

Figure 5.15   Plotting GPS Waypoints for a Given Course

WP#	Lat	Lon	WP#	Lat	Lon
43	44°55.25' N	80°14.30' W	46	44°52.00' N	80°01.30' W
44	44°52.85' N	80°12.00' W	49	44°53.80' N	79°57.15' W
45	44°52.75' N	80°09.45' W	50	44°51.60' N	79°54.25' W
46	44°49.80' N	80°07.85' W	51	44°50.10' N	79°53.45' W
47	44°50.01' N	80°07.50' W	52	44°49.25' N	79°53.90' W

There are a couple of ways to enter a waypoint into a GPS receiver. The simplest way is to press the position save function. The position can be saved when entering or leaving an anchorage, setting a buoy for fishnets, or changing course on a specified track. The position is then recorded as a waypoint in receiver memory for retrieval at a future time.

Another way to enter a waypoint is to lift position coordinates directly off a chart and manually enter them into the receiver. This procedure varies with different units, but basically, it involves assigning the waypoint a number and entering in the latitude/longitude coordinates.

With many receivers, it is also possible to enter in short descriptive names to aid in waypoint identification for retrieval.

Waypoints can be used either by themselves or in a group as the vessel passes from one waypoint to another. A valuable feature with most waypoints is called "waypoint rolling," which automatically switches to the next waypoint in the sequence once a waypoint has been achieved. There are, however, some important considerations for determining what constitutes the size of the waypoint and thus its realization parameters. (For a discussion of these principles, see Chapter 7 on Waypoint Realization.) Frequently used waypoint sequences can be stored into routes that can be retrieved by simply entering one number. Another important way to use waypoints is in waypoint or route reversal in which the course is executed in reverse for the return trip. For example, a lobster fisherman who wants to pull a series of pots set at a previous time could use this function to retrace the route.

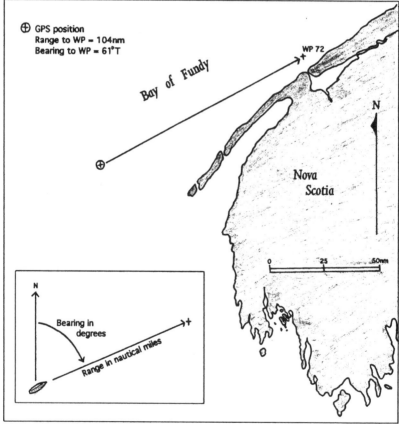

Figure 5.16 Determining GPS Waypoint Range and Bearing

Whether a single waypoint or a series of waypoints is used, waypoint navigation opens up a whole battery of important navigation information based on the waypoint's relation to your changing position. Two key elements are the range and bearing to the waypoint. Range is the distance between your present position and the waypoint. Bearing is the angle between your present position and the waypoint with respect to true north. (See Figure 5.16.)

Other features of waypoint navigation are derivations of waypoint range and bearing. Time to go and estimated time of arrival are continuously computed on the basis of vessel speed and the range to the waypoint. Steering directions and cross-track error are computed on the basis of vessel course and the waypoint bearing. Another function of waypoint navigation is the velocity made good, which tells how fast you are approaching the waypoint in knots. This function is helpful in those areas affected by currents where the speed over the ground may not be a true indication of the actual speed of advance.

Using the Time Function

In addition to position fixing and waypoint navigation, most GPS receivers are incredibly accurate timekeeping devices. This function can be used in a variety of ways from simply resetting the ship's clocks to providing precise time for working on comparative celestial navigation determinations.

One of the most common derivations of the time function is a yacht racing timer, a function that can be used in a couple of ways. One is as a countdown timer to keep track of the time to go to the beginning of a race. This function can be an invaluable asset as boats jockey back and forth in front of the starting line in an attempt to cross just at the right moment and with the best wind advantage. Once the race is begun, some receivers will keep track of the race time in a count-up function. Some may even keep track of the time in individual laps, like a regular stopwatch, which can be recalled at a future time for analysis.

With some receivers, it is possible to integrate the GPS timekeeping function with the alarm function in a variety of applications. As previously described in the section on read-out options, some additional uses for this function might be setting a time to turn on the ship's radio for a special weather report or a time to be ready to receive a pre-scheduled call via ham radio or SSB. If the receiver doesn't provide an alarm clock function, it is possible to produce the same effect by setting the countdown timer for a specific event as one would do for a race.

Using a GPS Receiver as a Computer

With some of the more sophisticated GPS receivers, it is possible to use their computer functions to solve a number of navigation problems. One of these is to use the receiver as a basic calculator that can add, subtract, multiply, and divide. Some applications might be in assisting dead reckoning calculations to compare with GPS read-outs. Others might be in computing fuel consumption or engine running time.

One of the most valuable computer functions is the ability to convert Lat/Lon readings from minute decimal fractions to minutes and seconds and vice versa. It is possible to use conversion tables or to compute the conversions using the equations in the section on "Using Different Chart Scales." However, using the receiver computer functions, if available, is not only quicker but, in some instances, more accurate.

Getting Information

There are a couple of good ways to keep up to date with current information on the GPS system and its application. One way is through the **GPS Information Center** (GPSIC), which is operated and maintained by the U.S. Coast Guard for the Department of Transportation. The center's purpose is to provide GPS information for the civil user. Information is dispensed in a number of ways: through voice recordings, computer bulletin board, and voice/data broadcasts. Other sources dispense information through **WWV/WWVH HF Radio Broadcasts, DMA Weekly Notices to Mariners,** and special **Broadcast Warnings.** For a more thorough discussion of these information sources, see Chapter 2 and Figure 2.11.

One of the most valuable sources of current information is the magazine **GPS World.** This monthly publication is particularly good at keeping abreast of current policy and program development. It features discussions on recent advances in GPS technology and is especially adept at presenting GPS applications in a variety of fields. Also published by the group is a bimonthly newsletter called **GPS World Newsletter.** This publication concentrates more on new products and updates in product technology. It also provides information on new uses and trends in GPS development. For more information on either publication, write:

GPS World
Aster Publishing
P.O. Box 10955
Eugene, OR 97440-9972
USA

IV. Record Keeping

Most GPS receivers provide at least 100 waypoints, and it is not uncommon for some to have in excess of 200 or even 500 waypoints. Most receivers also have the option of creating routes that contain additional waypoints or legs. The number varies from 10 to 20 routes, each of which may contain up to 20 different waypoints. Thus, it becomes necessary to have some efficient means of record keeping to organize waypoints and routes for quick retrieval.

Building A Receiver Data Base

Waypoints are usually kept in receiver memory in numerical order of entry. Often these numbers may not have any meaningful sequence as waypoints may be kept from one season and then more added in another season. Thus, finding a particular waypoint can be difficult, especially if you have to scroll through 200 or more waypoints in the receiver data base.

One way to assist in quick retrieval is to enter the waypoints in specific groups into the receiver. For example, with a receiver that provides 200 waypoints, some can be reserved for those waypoints that are used often in the immediate cruising area, some for waypoints on specific

Waypoint #	Designation
1	Home
2 - 40	Common WPs used in local cruising
41 - 100	Favorite anchorages
101 - 151	Trips
151 - 180	Miscellaneous
181 - 200	Temporary storage/present position
200 WPs	Possible

Figure 5.17   Organization of GPS Waypoint Storage Bank

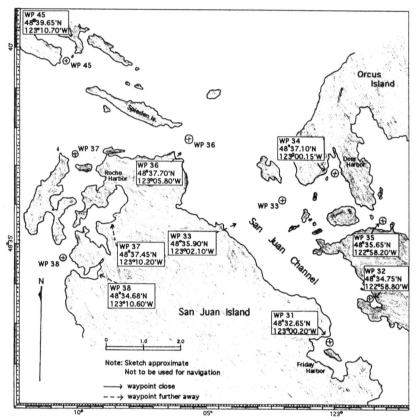

Figure 5.18 Storing Waypoints on a Chart

trips, some for important warning zones, and finally, some for those waypoints that identify entrances to favorite anchorages. Quite often the receiver will intentionally reserve a special group of numbers for those waypoints that are entered either as present position or temporary storage. Once the present position is recorded, it can then be transferred to a more permanent section at a later date. (See Figure 5.17.)

Waypoint Identification and Retrieval

Once a waypoint data base is built into receiver memory, quickly finding and retrieving waypoints may still be difficult, even though they are put in groups. An advantage that most manufacturers provide with their units is additional identification with alpha-numeric names. Yet, since these names often have to be substantially abbreviated, identification may still be difficult. Thus, it is important to have some additional means for waypoint identification and quick retrieval.

One of the easiest ways is to just **mark the waypoint on the chart** at the time the Lat/Lon coordinates are lifted off or present position is recorded. (See Figure 5.18.) The advantage to this method is that whenever you come back to that area, the waypoints are shown along with their identification numbers and positions on the chart ready for use. The disadvantage with this method is that the specific chart has to be out and in use to get the waypoint information. Thus, it is prudent to

Waypoint #	Name/Description	Lat/Lon
#8	Pt. Abbaye Bouy	46° 35.00' N 89° 19.90' W
#14	Perley Rock 2W of Bustard Is	45° 53.01' N 80° 59.00' W
#19	Pilot Cove East end of L.Sup.	47° 54.90' N 85° 34.50' W
#42	Portage Lake, lower end Keweenaw Waterway	47° 02.40' N 88° 28.85' W
#43	Pequaming SW of point	46° 51.00' N 88° 24.80' W
#65	Pancake Shoal SW of buoy	46° 53.80' N 84° 51.00' W
#58	Passage Island East of	48° 14.45' N 88° 19.85' W
#59	Passage Island West of	48° 13.25' N 88° 22.25' W
#102	Pilot Cove N.Channel	45° 59.92' N 83° 29.78' W
#117	Penetanguishing Outside harbor entrance	44° 48.71' N 79° 56.00 W
#129	Parry Sound Just off city dock	45° 20.28' N 80 02.21' W

Figure 5.19   Using a Waypoint Logbook

also have a central source that contains all GPS waypoint information.

To assist navigators in waypoint tabulation, many manufacturers will provide small **books/logs for recording waypoints and routes**. These are often printed with specific entries for each waypoint: number,

Lat/Lon, description, chart number, etc. The disadvantage with using specially prepared log books is that entries are usually printed in numerical order, which can make finding an individual waypoint difficult—especially if there are a large number of waypoints to go through. In this case, a better option may be to obtain a book that has no labeled entries, but is separated into sections by dividers, which are usually alphabetical. Then you can tailor make your own entry format and most importantly file your waypoints alphabetically for quick retrieval. (See Figure 5.19.)

The disadvantage with either method of entering waypoints in a book is that, other than scratching them out, the waypoints are fairly permanent. Should you move to another area or run out of waypoints, you will probably want to replace old waypoint numbers with new position coordinates. Thus, another option is to build **a card file** as you are building your waypoint bank in the receiver. Each time a new waypoint is entered, you make out a new card that also contains other pertinent information such as a description, warning of navigation hazards, points of interest, etc. Those waypoints that you do not want to be erased can be tagged with some kind of a mark like a red star. (See Figure 5.20.) If alphabetical dividers are used, the card file has the advantage that waypoints can be filed for quick retrieval. It also has the advantage that when one waypoint is replaced with another, the card can be simply pulled from the usable section and filed at the back of the box. That information can be retrieved and reentered, should the decision be made to go back to that position at some future time.

Finally, it should be mentioned that the judicious navigator will often plan a day's run in advance while in the quiet of an anchorage where waypoints can be easily entered or chosen rather than struggling to do the chart/receiver work in a boat tossed about in heavy seas. At this time, it is also prudent to check waypoints directly on the chart unless they have withstood the test of repeated use. This is because one of the most common errors in any radionavigation is to incorrectly enter waypoints into a receiver and then blindly rely on receiver output for navigation. This also points out the importance of never relying on any single tool or system for navigation. The discriminating navigator will use all the tools at his or her disposal and use one system as a check on the other.

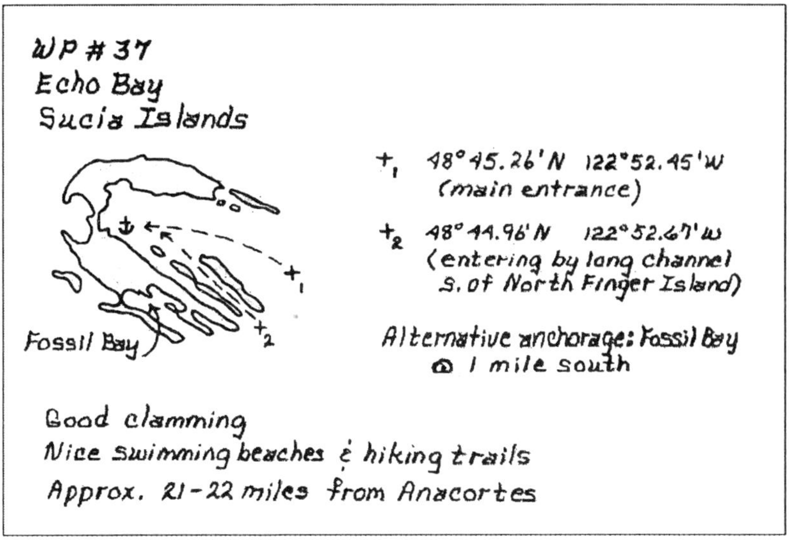

WP #37
Echo Bay
Sucia Islands

+₁ 48°45.26'N 122°52.45'W
    (main entrance)

+₂ 48°44.96'N 122°52.67'W
    (entering by long channel
    S. of North Finger Island)

Alternative anchorage: Fossil Bay
    @ 1 mile south

Fossil Bay

Good clamming
Nice swimming beaches & hiking trails
Approx. 21-22 miles from Anacortes

Figure 5.20   Using a Card File for Storing GPS Waypoints

Photo #1: The Garmin GPS 50 can be used either as a portable with a detachable quadrifilar antenna or with a mounting bracket (shown) which attaches to a swivel surface mount for easy viewing from any angle. Courtesy of Garmin International, Lenexa, KS.

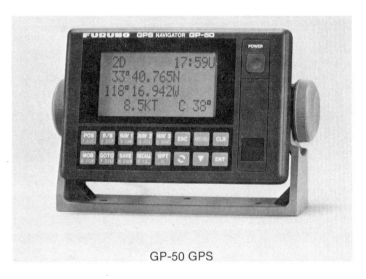

GP-50 GPS

Photo #2: Furuno's GP-50 GPS receiver uses 8 parallel channels to track 8 satellites. It's designed for tabletop, bulk head, or flush-mount installation. Courtesy of Furuno U.S.A., Inc.

CHAPTER SIX

Are You Where You Think You Are: Accuracy

GPS has the promise and potential to become the end all in all areas of navigation and position fixing. It provides a degree of accuracy in terms of position, velocity, and time that has never been seen before. Depending on applications in the user community, GPS is capable of delivering accuracy ranges from a few millimeters up to 100 meters. Within this spread there are many different levels or modes of operation.

The fact that GPS can deliver a wide range of accuracy demonstrates the degree of sophistication with which the system operates and is controlled. Yet, it is in the area of accuracy that there is widespread concern in the user segment, and the degree of GPS accuracy is one of the main topics of discussion in navigation circles.

I. Types of Accuracy

There are three main types of accuracy depending on the basis for the reference position. They are predictable accuracy, repeatable accuracy, and relative accuracy. Two other types of accuracy that may be of concern to the GPS user are velocity accuracy and time accuracy.

Predictable Accuracy

Predictable accuracy (which may also be called absolute or geodetic accuracy) is the accuracy of a radionavigation system's position solution with respect to the charted solution or actual geographic/geodetic coordinates of the earth. The coordinates are most often measured in latitude and longitude but can also be measured with other coordinate systems such as Loran-C TDs.

Predictable accuracy is what you use when homing in on a waypoint lifted off a chart at the entrance of a harbor. Does the waypoint get you to the entrance or does it put you on the rocks 300 feet to the side? Predictable accuracy is also important when trying to find a particular nav-aid such as a buoy from coordinates given on a light list or a chart. A very good way of determining the degree of predictable accuracy is by comparing the GPS coordinate read-outs at a known position with those on the chart. For example, when lying in a particular anchorage, does GPS indicate the position where you are actually anchored or 0.1 mile inland? (See Figure 6.1.)

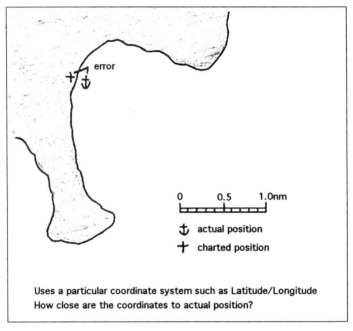

Figure 6.1   Predictable (Geodetic) Accuracy

Depending on the system in use, predictable accuracy can be affected by a number of factors. For example, with Loran-C, it is affected by the fixed bias of land propagation errors (Additional Secondary Factor or ASF). Predictable accuracy is the most relevant form of accuracy for GPS users and is affected by a number of factors including the accuracy of incoming satellite signals available to the user and the ability of the user's receiver to process those signals. These and other factors pertinent to GPS accuracy are more thoroughly discussed in Section III.

136

In GPS use, predictable accuracy for Precise Positioning Service (PPS) users is at least 22 meters for horizontal fixes (95%) and 29 meters for three-dimensional fixes (95%). For Standard Positioning Service (SPS) users, predictable accuracy is 100 meters for two-dimensional fixes (95%) and 140 meters for three-dimensional positioning (95%).

Repeatable Accuracy

Repeatable accuracy is the ability to return to a position using coordinates that have been determined at a previous time with the same navigation system. For example, it is repeatable accuracy that a fisherman uses to retrieve set nets. It is repeatable accuracy that allows us to find the entrance of a favorite anchorage in dense fog if we are using previous coordinates rather than chart values. When actually charted, the coordinates may not position us exactly at the entrance. But as long as we were there once, the coordinates will bring us back to the same position. The main disadvantage with repeatable accuracy is that there always has to be a first time to record the position coordinates. (See Figure 6.2.)

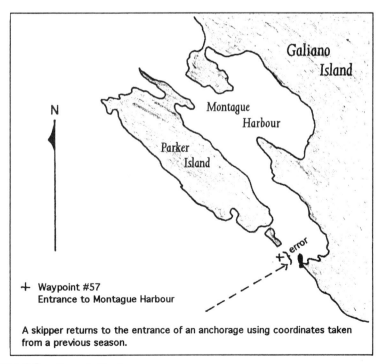

A skipper returns to the entrance of an anchorage using coordinates taken from a previous season.

Figure 6.2   Repeatable Accuracy

137

The loran system really excels with repeatable accuracy. Because land propagation errors are fairly consistent for a given area, it is possible to home in on previous loran coordinates with incredible accuracy—often within 100 feet. In the repeatable mode, Loran-C may often deliver better accuracy than the degraded form of GPS available to nonmilitary users. One reason that good repeatable accuracy (better than 100 meters) really isn't a viable option for GPS users is because of Selective Availability (SA), the induced range errors are inconsistent, varying from one period in time to another. Also there are many error sources that change over time: the satellites used, their position errors, ephemeris errors, and ionospheric errors.

Relative Accuracy

Relative accuracy is the accuracy with which a user can measure positions relative to that of another user on the same navigation system at the same time. A good example of relative accuracy took place in the third BOC single-handed sailboat race around the world. In the third leg of the race 1800 miles off Cape Horn, John Martin on *Allied Bank* was rescued by Bertie Reed on *Grinacker* after Martin sustained a fatal hull fracture from an underwater iceberg. Both sailors were using GPS, which greatly simplified finding each other in the vast expanses of the open ocean. Whatever errors were present in the system were shared by both receivers and thus canceled each other out as Reed homed in on Martin's position.

Relative accuracy may also refer to the accuracy with which position is measured relative to a previous position with the same receiver. For example, say you want to measure the course or distance traveled between two points. With many systems, it doesn't matter if there are any errors in either position as they will cancel each other out. (See Figure 6.3.) However, it is important to note that with GPS, these errors are subject to change as a function of time due to SA, new satellites coming into view, etc. Relative positioning accuracy is good for GPS receivers if they are using the same satellites and computing postion fixes at the same time because the same error in magnitude and direction is being applied to the receivers.

Because GPS accurately determines not only position but also velocity and time, two additional types of accuracy are important in the GPS system.

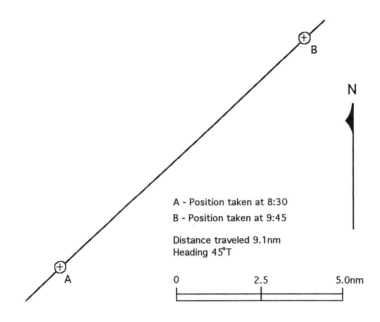

A - Position taken at 8:30
B - Position taken at 9:45

Distance traveled 9.1nm
Heading 45°T

0   2.5   5.0nm

Figure 6.3   Relative Accuracy

Velocity Accuracy

A GPS receiver can calculate velocity by measuring the rate of change in pseudorange, also called the delta range. Depending on the situation, PPS receivers are capable of determining velocity to 0.2 meters/second per axis (50% probability). This accuracy level is the same for SPS receivers when SA is turned off. When SA is implemented, the exact amount of velocity degradation for SPS users is classified, but empirical observations under SA-active conditions indicate 0.5 to 1.0 meters/second.

Time Accuracy

There is also a difference in time accuracy for different levels of GPS use. The stated value for Universal Time Coordinated transfer accuracy for the PPS is 200 nanoseconds (95%). Yet, it is possible for authorized users with a PPS receiver tracking the P code from four satellites to achieve an absolute time accuracy of better than 100 nanoseconds in a stationary or low-dynamic situation. Higher dynamics will increase this

139

time error.

UTC time transfer accuracy for those with SPS receivers is approximately 340 nanoseconds (95%). In static or low-dynamic applications, the time error may be as small as 155 nanoseconds. For a summary of GPS Accuracy Parameters, see Figure 6.4.

	Accuracy (Meters)*		
	Predictable	Repeatable	Relative**
PPS	Horz - 21 Vert - 29 Time - 200ns	Horz - 21 Vert - 29	Horz - 1 Vert 1.5
SPS	Horz - 100 Vert - 140 Time - 340ns	Horz - 100 Vert - 140	Horz - 1 Vert - 1.5

   * Horizontal (2drms); Vertical (98%); Time (95%)
  ** Preliminary estimates

Taken from the 1992 Federal Radionavigation PlanP

Figure 6.4   PPS and SPS Accuracy Parameters

II. Measures of Accuracy

Position accuracy in all types of radionavigation is influenced by a number of factors. Random errors may be induced by instabilities in signal propagation, reference clocks, receiver measurement circuits, etc. The resulting effect is a cluster of points around any given position taken over a period of time.

GPS accuracy can be expressed in a number of different ways. These are expressed as a statistical value along with a probability for that value. The number of dimensions is also expressed or implied in the type of accuracy value.

Circle Error Probable (CEP)

One way to define accuracy is as the radius of the circle that contains 50% of the individual measurements (position fixes) being made. In other words, there is a 50% probability of a measurement/fix occurring inside the circle. There is also a 50% probability of a measure

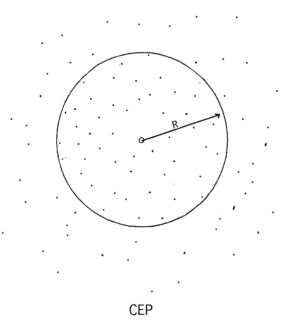

CEP

R = radius of a circle in which 50% of the distribution points fall

Figure 6.5   Circle Error Probable

ment/fix occurring outside of the circle. (See Figure 6.5.) This type of accuracy measurement is applicable only to two-dimensional position fixing. Its counterpart for three-dimensional position fixing is the **Sphere Error Probable (SEP)**, which is the radius of a sphere within which there is a 50% probability of a point (fix) being located.

The main advantage with this type of accuracy measurement is that it is easily understood. It is also a good descriptive measure when the distribution of errors is uniform. Because of these advantages, it is the measure most often used by the military.

One disadvantage with this type of measurement is that the circle (or sphere) is so small that there are just as many distribution points outside of the circle as there are within it. Another disadvantage is that only the <u>number</u> of the points are counted. The <u>degree of errors</u> outside the circle has no effect on the CEP/SEP value. There is no way of recognizing very large errors, and they have the same impact on the final accuracy expression as those errors that are outside the circle, yet still close to it. Thus, a more conservative approach is to use an accuracy

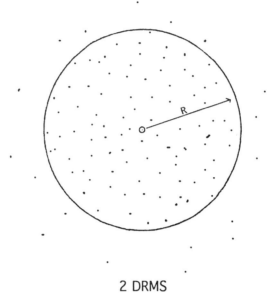

2 DRMS

R = radius of a circle in which 95% to 98% of the distribution points fall.

Figure 6.6   Distance Root Mean Square

measurement that reflects all errors, large and small.

Distance Root Mean Square (drms)

By taking the root-mean-square of the distances of all points from the true location point, the magnitude of all errors is given better representation. The actual measure for position accuracy is called **2 drms**. It involves taking twice the square root of the sum of the squares of all the radial errors surrounding the true point divided by the total number of measurements.

$$2\,drms = 2\sqrt{\overset{N}{\underset{}{\varepsilon}}(X_n^2 + Y_n^2)/N}$$

By squaring each individual error, the overall effect is to reflect even large errors in the 2 drms value. (See Figure 6.6.)

The 2 drms value then is the radius of a circle that contains at least 95% of the fixes that can be obtained with the system at any one place, depending on the degree of ellipticity of the error distribution. For a near-circular distribution, it is closer to 98% probability, whereas it is

142

95% for strongly elliptical distributions.

What the 2 drms value means for the civil GPS user is that fixes have a 95-98% probability of falling within a given circle from the true location at its center. The radius of that circle is dependent on the total error budget and satellite geometry. With selective availability implemented, the radius of the circle is 100 meters for nonmilitary users. Without selective availability, the radius is much less. If the CEP value, which represents a much smaller circle, is given, the confidence level is at 50%. According to the Federal Radionavigation Plan, an approximate relationship between the two values can be expressed as follows:

2 drms = 2.5 x CEP (approx.)

User Equivalent Range Error (UERE)

The above statistical distributions are dependent on two important variables: the equivalent user range error and the position dilution of precision.

User Position Error= Equivalent User Range Error x Position Dilution of Precision

The user equivalent range error or UERE is a calculation of the range measurement error to each satellite as seen by the receiver. It represents errors that are constantly present as normal variations in accuracy.

The UERE basically consists of two parts: the user range accuracy (URA) and the user equipment error (UEE). The URA is an accuracy performance figure, which is given in meters as part of the broadcast ephemeris message of each satellite. It is an important quality control figure indicating the accuracy status of the transmitted signal. The UEE consists of inherent receiver errors resulting from noise, resolution, and multiple signal paths. Taken altogether, the total of these errors results in a system range-error budget, which is affected by many factors.

Dilution of Precision (DOP)

The other parameter that affects the accuracy of the statistical distribution of GPS position fixes is the spatial geometry of those satellites used to determine a fix. (See also next section.) This factor is expressed by yet another accuracy value, the dilution of precision, or DOP. Actually, there are many different kinds of DOP values, but for the

A. Large Crossing Angles   B. Smaller Crossing Angles

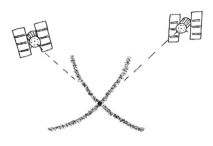 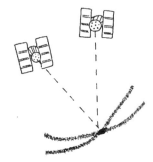

Because satellites are far apart in space, range lines or LOPs cross at large angles producing a small "box" of uncertainty where position occurs. This is measured by a small HDOP.

When satellites are closer together in space, their range lines or LOPs cross at much smaller angles producing a much larger "box" or area of uncertainty where the fix may be. HDOP becomes larger.

Figure 6.7   Effects of Satellite Geometry on Position Fixing Accuracy

marine user, who relies primarily on two-dimensional position fixing, the **horizontal dilution of precision,** or HDOP value, is the one most commonly used. It is the one used here to explain the concept.

Despite the complicated sound of the term, HDOP is not a new concept for mariners, as loran navigators quickly learned the importance of having large crossing angles in the lines of position from two or more master-secondary pairs. The concept is exactly the same with satellite geometry: the closer the range lines cross at right angles, the smaller the box of uncertainty and thus, the more accurate the fix. (See Figure 6.7A) Satellites that are geometrically closer together or in the same plane produce small angles between the range lines, and the box of uncertainty becomes larger. (See Figure 6.7B.) The HDOP is a way of measuring the size of the box with numbers from 1 (in some instances, even less than 1) to 10 and greater. The closer the HDOP is to 1, the smaller the box and the more accurate the fix.

Dependent on user application/requirements, there are a number of different kinds of DOP values. The **GDOP** (geometric dilution of precision) is the most conclusive representing the three coordinates (x,y,z) for three-dimensional position fixing and time. **PDOP** (position dilution of precision) is the same as GDOP minus the time variable. PDOP is most important for aircraft weapons delivery. **HDOP** (horizontal dilution of precision) is used not only for two-dimensional position fixing in land

144

and marine environments, but also in air navigation since enroute aircraft altitude is usually determined by a barometric altimeter. **VDOP** (vertical dilution of precision) values are used by those with specific altitude requirements. **TDOP** (time dilution of precision) is important for those who require time transfer applications. **DDOP** (differential dilution of precision) is for those who use differential GPS. There is even a **EDOP** (easting dilution of precision) and a **NDOP** (northing dilution of

GDOP	Geometric Dilution of Precision	
*PDOP	Position Dilution of Precision	<6.0
*HDOP	Horizontal Dilution of Precision	<4.0
*VDOP	Vertical Dilution of Precision	<4.5
*TDOP	Time Dilution of Precision	<2.0
DDOP	Differential Dilution of Precision	
EDOP	Easting Dilution of Precision	
NDOP	Northing Dilution of Precision	

* The more commonly used DOPs and their accepted accuracy values.

Figure 6.8   The Different DOP Values

precision). Generally accepted "good" values for the more commonly used DOPs are PDOP < 6, HDOP < 4, VDOP < 4.5, and TDOP < 2. For a summary of the different DOPs, see Figure 6.8.

Because of satellite distribution in the GPS constellation, there are a few locations around the world that will experience reduced accuracy for short periods of time due to high PDOP values. These periods will normally be of short duration (a few minutes, the longest 30 minutes) and will normally occur only once per day at the indicated locations. At a few locations, these periods will occur twice every 24 hours. Furthermore, only one to three of these periods can occur at any given time throughout the world. (See Figure 6.9.) It is important to note, however, that these areas of degraded coverage apply only to the three-dimensional users requiring four satellites. For two-dimensional users who know their altitude and have velocity information provided by other sensors, there are no areas of substantial degradation.

DOP values are relative numbers that vary because the satellites are in constant motion and their geometric relationships are continuously changing. Also, due to random satellite failures, end-of-life failures, and the availability of spare satellites, the GPS constellation will not always remain constant. Mathematical models are determined by computer simulation, which represent the GDOP for a given satellite configuration. It is the responsibility of the Control Segment to assure that the

145

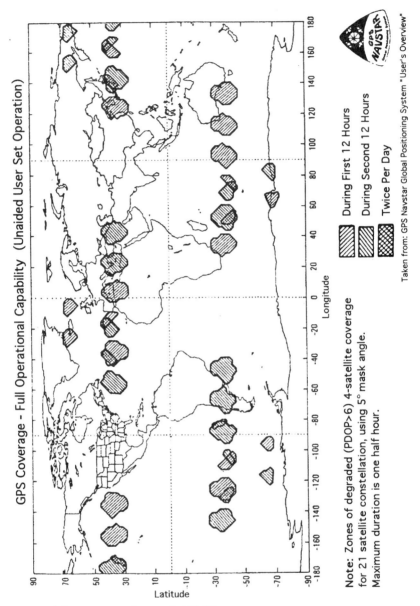

Figure 6.9 *Zones of Degraded PDOP*

GDOP distribution meets the requirements of all users for both Precise Positioning Service and Standard Positioning Service.

III. Factors that Affect Accuracy

There are many factors that affect the accuracy of a GPS fix. Some are common to other radionavigation systems; others are unique aspects of the GPS system. Basically, these errors can be divided into three groups related to signal propagation, user factors, and system control.

Signal Propagation Errors

With GPS signals traveling very fast (at the speed of light), time is of the essence, and anything that affects this transmission time, even to a small degree, will likewise affect the range between the satellite and the user and thus position. As long as the signals travel through particle-free space, there are no problems. But once they hit the earth's ionosphere and atmosphere, they are slowed down by small particles.

Probably the largest source of propagation error is due to **ionospheric delay**. The ionosphere is a band of electrons and charged particles that surrounds the earth approximately 50 to 600 miles above the earth's surface. These particles are formed by ultraviolet radiation from the sun, which in effect splits up normally neutral particles. Radiowaves are bent and slowed down when they encounter these particles, similar to the way light is refracted or bent in a swimming pool. The more particles there are (greater density), the greater the effect on slowing down the radio signals. Since the charged particles tend to recombine and become neutral on the night side of the earth, the density varies depending on the time of the day. This change in density affects the delay error, which can be as much as 20-30 meters during the day and 6 meters or less at night. The positions of the satellites also affects the amount of ionospheric delay. With low elevation satellites, the delay will be greater because the signals are transmitted through the ionosphere at an angle and thus travel a larger distance through the ionosphere than those signals coming from satellites at higher elevations.

There are a couple of ways in which this type of error can be corrected or at least minimized. One way is to program receivers with mathematical models that will automatically make these corrections. Unfortunately, a number of inconsistent variables can affect the particle density such as sun spot activity, time of the year, etc., so it still remains a sizable source of error.

Another correction method, which is much more effective, uses the fact that the amount of delay is inversely proportional to the frequency of the signal: the lower the frequency, the more it gets slowed down. By comparing the arrival times of two GPS signals of different frequencies, it is possible to actually calculate the amount of error caused by ionospheric delay and thus correct for it. It is largely this concept that provides the military its enhanced edge on accuracy by using receivers that can access the P code on the two different carrier frequencies. Finally, it should be noted that this type of error isn't as much of a concern to the mariner who is already at sea level, as the main effect of the error is on the altitude portion of the navigation solution.

Propagation error can also be due to **tropospheric delay**. Here sources of error are dependent on temperature, pressure, and the amount of water vapor in the atmosphere, which, of course, varies from day to day and is difficult to model. The error, however, is directly proportional to the distance the satellite signal travels and can vary from 3 meters for satellites directly overhead to 50 meters for satellites at extremely low elevations (less than 5 degrees) whose signals must travel through more of the troposphere. Receiver programs that eliminate signals from low elevation satellites in the navigation solution reduce this type of error considerably.

Even though the atomic clocks on the satellites are incredibly accurate, they are subject to minor variations. Ground control stations monitor these discrepancies and inject corrections when needed to the satellites. Yet, minute inconsistencies may still exist, and **satellite clock errors** may account for an error of 1 meter or less.

Another very small error is due to inconsistencies in actual satellite location, or **ephemeris error**. Factors that may contribute to these errors include the influence of earth gravitational anomalies and gravitational effects of the moon and sun. Again, corrections are injected into the broadcasted satellite ephemeris from a ground control station so that the error is usually 4 meters or less.

Sometimes the GPS signals are reflected off varying sources, resulting in **multipath errors**, which in effect increase the signal path length and thus the transmission time. Again, the magnitude of these errors is usually small, 1 to 3 meters.

Although these and other errors may seem quite small, when you add them up, together they can have an impact of approximately 27–40 meters (daytime, less in nighttime) in the error budget for the civil user. (See Figure 6.10.)

This combination of errors lends itself to an "area of uncertainty"

Propagation Errors

Ionospheric	20 - 30 meters	3 - 6 meters
	(daytime)	(night time)
Tropospheric	@ 1 - 3 meters	
Satellite Clock	1 meter or less	
Ephemeris	4 meters or less	
Multipath	1 - 3 meters	
Total	@ 27 - 40 meters	

Induced Errors

(SA)	@ 30 meters	

Figure 6.10   GPS Error Budget

so that position can no longer be counted as being on a finely drawn line (as in Figure 6.11A), but rather a thicker fuzzy one directly proportional to the amount of error currently being encountered. (See Figure 6.11B) This area of uncertainty is further influenced by the **satellites' geometry** when a fix is determined by crossing the range lines from two different satellites. As discussed in the previous section, the crossing angles of the ranges from different satellites have a large impact on the

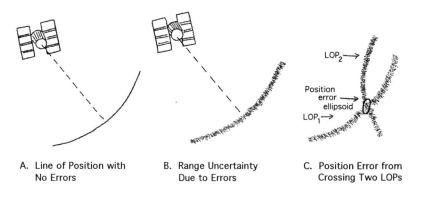

A. Line of Position with No Errors

B. Range Uncertainty Due to Errors

C. Position Error from Crossing Two LOPs

Figure 6.11   Effects of Error Budget on Range and Position Uncertainty

accuracy of the fix. Range LOPs that cross close to right angles are more accurate than those that cross at smaller angles. The area of uncertainty is represented by a small box (or a position error ellipsoid) where the lines cross called the dilution of precision. (See Figure 6.11C.) Numbers are assigned to represent the size of the area of uncertainty— the smaller the number, the more accurate the fix.

For a final assessment of propagation errors in a GPS fix (two-dimensional), multiply the total range error budget times the HDOP. For example, if the range error budget is 30 meters and the HDOP is 1.5, accuracy is at 45 meters. If the HDOP is 3, accuracy is reduced to 90 meters. One way to reduce the HDOP is to track more satellites. Most receivers have programs that assist in identifying and using only those satellites yielding the best crossing angles. Even though you really need only three satellites to determine a two-dimensional fix, the more satellites tracked, the better, as the dilution of precision box becomes smaller and the HDOP approaches 1.

User Factors

Aside from misplotting a fix (which we have all done), there are a few loopholes for the GPS navigator that can introduce error into position fixing. A couple of these loopholes occur when **initializing** the receiver to get it working correctly.

It is possible when initializing a GPS receiver for a "cold start" to introduce errors, which can range from throwing position off by hundreds of feet to actually preventing the receiver from tracking satellites. Depending on the sophistication of the receiver, it may be necessary to inject basic position and time information. If the introduced errors are large enough, they may prevent the receiver from tracking satellites.

It is also possible to introduce an initialization error that allows the receiver to function but introduces errors in the navigation solution. One error is to enter incorrect **antenna height** when operating in a two-dimensional mode. The receiver will still function as though normal, but position accuracy may be severely degraded.

Most receivers have the option of choosing the **mode of operation:** two-dimensional or three-dimensional mode. For mariners who already know their altitude, it is advantageous to operate in the two-dimensional mode in which you enter in your antenna height. One reason is because the three-dimensional mode requires a minimum of four satellites to obtain a fix. If there are less than four satellites available or there is a poor HDOP from one of the satellites in relationship to the others, navigation could be interrupted, thereby reducing accuracy. Operating in the two-dimensional mode gives you that extra edge for position fixing with only three satellites.

The **type of receiver** can also affect accuracy to a degree. In the early days of GPS, there were a number of single channel receivers on the market. These receivers had a disadvantage: they had to stop navigating every so often to collect ephemeris and almanac data, which, of course, affected their accuracy at that time. Multiple channel and multiplex channel receivers solve this problem by providing continuous navigation while tracking many satellites. A number of receivers now on the market advertise carrier-aided tracking in which the GPS carrier signal is used to get a more accurate lock on the pseudorandom code improving the timing measurements and thus position accuracy.

Another factor on the user end that is important to the degree of accuracy is that the **chart datum** used by the receiver in determining a fix is the same or compatible with the datum of the chart on which you are positioning the fix. Different datums in use around the world have been compiled by different techniques of geodetic survey. Notable errors will result if a nautical chart prepared using one datum is used with a fix determined from another datum.

Until 1987, GPS used a datum called the World Geodetic System 1972 (WGS-72). It then changed to the newer WGS 84. Within the United States, the National Oceanic and Atmospheric Administration is changing its charts from the 1927 North American Datum (NAD 27) to NAD 83. For positioning purposes, WGS 84 is equivalent to NAD 83. If you are using old charts or navigating in remote areas of the world, it is important to check the datum of the chart in use. Many receivers provide the option of changing to different chart datums. Some receivers may have over 100 datums to choose from.

System Controls

One of the main attributes of the GPS system (at least from the military point of view) is the incredible control the military has over certain aspects of the system. Not only can the military position the satellites exactly where it wants them, but it also has a firm handle on the level of accuracy it can deliver to GPS users.

To begin with, two distinct levels of accuracy are provided. Standard Positioning Service (SPS) accommodates civil users with a proposed accuracy of 100 meters horizontally (2 drms, 95% probability) and 140 meters vertically (95% probability). The Precise Positioning Service (PPS) is limited to military and authorized users and provides positioning accuracy of least 22 meters horizontally (2 drms) and 27.7 meters vertically. One way in which this accuracy level is achieved is by tracking the P code on both carrier frequencies so that ionospheric errors can be eliminated, as mentioned in the previous section. Another way in that PPS achieves its accuracy is through the use of special **decryptographic keys** to override any error messages that are intentionally induced in the C/A code for SPS users.

The military also has another way of limiting access and thus accuracy of GPS. Through a technique called **anti-spoofing (AS)**, the highly accurate but published P code is replaced with a different secret code called the Y code. Its main purpose is to deny unauthorized users access to PPS accuracy. It also serves to deny enemy access to the possibility of jamming the P code (which because of its complexity is difficult to jam anyway) and to prevent generation of false P code signals for the purpose of "spoofing" receivers. Encrypting of the P code and anti-spoofing have been implemented intermittently through 1992 and will become permanent in the mid-1990's.

It is, however, in the area of **Selective Availability (SA)** that the degree of military control on the GPS system has its greatest impact on the civil user. If land propagation errors (ASF) are the Achille's heel for Loran-C, then without question, SA is the Achilles's heel for the nonmilitary GPS user. It has become one of the most hotly contested issues in radionavigation circles and is the single largest source of error for the civil user.

It was originally intended that the 100-meter degree of accuracy for the civil user would be accomplished by allowing SPS users access to only the C/A code. But one of the surprises in the early days of testing with only 11 operational satellites was that GPS was turning out accuracy values much better than anticipated: precise positioning of 5–15 meters, coarse signal accuracy of 20–40 meters. Thus, another method had to be devised to limit the accuracy of civil use of the system — SA.

SA is implemented in two different ways. One is by adding slight errors to the satellite orbit information (ephemeris) in the navigation message. The other is by "dithering" the satellite clock frequency, which degrades the excellent timekeeping qualities of the atomic clocks. Only Block II satellites are affected by SA; Block I satellites lack this capability. Therefore, position fixing from any of the remaining active Block I's will not suffer SA degradation.

SA was initiated in March 1990. Interestingly, it was turned off during the Persian Gulf crisis (August 1990–June 1991). Because of a lack of sufficient military receivers, the U.S. military was forced to use civilian receivers that could not access the P code. The war provided an impressive testing ground for the undegraded C/A code, which demonstrated such a high degree of accuracy that the military was convinced of the need to reactive SA. SA was turned back on 30 June 1991 (1 July at 0400 UTC or late on the 30th in the U.S.). However, many civil users reported that SA was again substantially reduced a few days later, demonstrating that even though the standard signal degradation is established at 100 meters, it can also be set to 40–50 meters. It should also be noted that in times of national emergency, the C/A signal degradation could even be set as much as 1,000 meters, demonstrating the fine degree of control the military has over the system.

The implementation of SA is one of the most sensitive issues connected with the GPS system. The military strongly feel that in the interest of national security, the precise position-fixing capabilities of GPS must be kept out of the hands of potential aggressive forces. Opponents argue that the really "smart" battlefield doesn't need GPS to be effective and achieve its objectives. Yet, Desert Storm clearly demonstrated that use of GPS gave a battlefield advantage in all applications of position, velocity, and time.

One of the main arguments against SA is the spending of so much money on such a highly accurate position-fixing system, only to withhold its potential capabilities from the largest user community. SA opponents argue that in times of peace, the undegraded form of SPS should be made available and SA could be activated when needed. The military responds by saying that it is important to have the system in operation as it would be during times of national emergency or conflict for training its forces. Without SA implementation, procedures and hardware needed in an SA environment would be neglected.

Probably one of the strongest arguments for SA implementation is that the civil community needs a system that is stable and predictable. SA ensures a constant degree of accuracy that wouldn't be available with an "on-call" SA that allowed users undegraded C/A code access only to be SA degraded in times of national emergency. There are also some concerns about what constitutes a national emergency. Would SA be implemented any time there was even the slightest hint of a threat? Would military advantage be compromised to avoid the "pain" of activating SA? Finally, there are also concerns about undegraded C/A signals being available to and accessed by terrorists.

Despite SA implementation, in actual use GPS still remains a highly accurate position-fixing system even for the civil user. Of course, that accuracy depends on the mode of operation and the specific application. For the mariner on the high seas, 100-meter accuracy may well be sufficient. Accuracy also depends on the scale of the chart in use. Consider

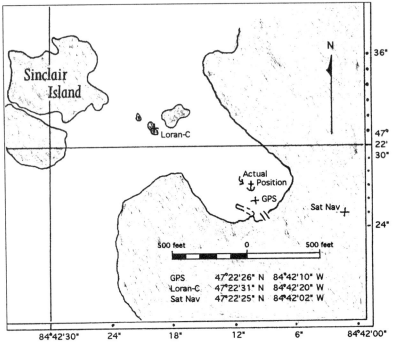

Figure 6.12   Comparing GPS Accuracy with Loran-C and Sat Nav

navigating with a chart that has a scale of 1:120,000. On such a chart, the width of a pencil line is already greater than 50 meters and if GPS gives you position-fixing accuracy that is less than 100 meters; it couldn't be plotted more accurately anyway.

A typical example of GPS position-fixing capabilities not only shows the effects of reduced degradation, but also gives an accuracy comparison with two other radio navigation systems. Positional fix data was taken at a known location in early July 1991 using Loran-C, Sat Nav, and GPS. The Loran-C position was 800 feet off, Sat Nav 650 feet off, and GPS 100 feet or approximately 30 meters. (See Figure 6.12.)

There are two areas, however, where SA degradation really hurts the mariner. One involves navigating in confined areas such as waterways and harbor approaches. According to the 1990 Federal Radionavigation plan, 100-meter accuracy (or even the PPS 17.8-meter accuracy) in these applications is not good enough. To meet these needs, the U.S. Coast Guard is implementing a network of differential stations to provide coverage in the coastal waters of the conterminous United States, Hawaii, and Alaska. (See next section on types of accuracy enhancement.)

The other area of SA implementation that affects the mariner is velocity. SA degradation can really disrupt the velocity component of slow-moving marine vessels, which interferes with accurate speed and heading information. Some manufacturers of GPS receivers advertise units that can display velocity readings to within 0.1 knots and headings within 1 degree. Yet, on a day-to-day basis for the civil user, there may be considerable discrepancies between GPS speed and heading and that information from other instruments. It is not uncommon to have GPS headings off by several degrees or to see speed fluctuations in excess of 1 knot. These errors naturally affect other functions of the GPS receiver in calculating navigational solutions, especially in waypoint navigation such as bearing, time to go, etc. For example, speed fluctuations of just a few tenths of a knot can change predicted arrival time by as much as an hour or more on a particularly long leg. Of course, the closer you come to your destination, the smaller the effects of this type of error produced by speed variations. A good way to see whether SA is activated is to turn on your GPS receiver while tied up to a dock. Heading fluctuations and speed readings of a few tenths of a knot are a sure sign that SA is in effect. Another way is to check the User Range Accuracy (URA) index, if the receiver can display it. (Note that for a stationary user, any error in velocity components will cause large heading errors. Thus, the speed reading is a better test of SA being on or off.)

IV. Accuracy Enhancement (Position Aiding)

A number of different enhancement or aiding techniques can be employed to improve the accuracy of the GPS navigation solution. Aiding refers to any method that contributes additional information to the receiver, easing its computational tasks by reducing the number of unknowns. Some of these techniques were especially useful in extending GPS use before a fully operational constellation was complete. They are also useful in providing missing information for solving the navigation solution in case of limited satellite visibility or poor satellite geometry. Some techniques, such as those employed with Differential GPS, improve the accuracy of a GPS fix considerably. A few of the more commonly used techniques for accuracy enhancement are discussed in this section.

Height Aiding

Height aiding is probably one of the most common types of position aiding and is particularly applicable to the marine environment where the user knows that position is somewhere at sea level. Some receivers require the use of a barometric altimeter to enter height information; others need only antenna height above sea level for input. What height aiding does, in effect, is provide another satellite range with the "satellite" positioned at the center of the earth. Thus, only three satellites are required for navigation, which eases the receiver's computational load, especially in conditions of limited satellite visibility or poor geometry. Another distinct advantage for the two-dimensional user is that height is the weakest element of the navigation solution, so accuracy is enhanced.

Clock Aiding

Clock Aiding isn't as viable for the average civil user because of cost. But it may have some applications for military or research/exploration vessels. This technique requires the use of an additional atomic clock (rubidium), which may cost in excess of $10,000, providing accurate time to the receiver. By monitoring the clock during a four-satellite solution, the clock frequency, phase bias, and drift can be calculated. What this technique does is rule out one of the four unknowns (time) in the navigation solution. It can then be used for short periods of time to extend position fixing, again when thereare limited satellites in view, satellite outages or poor satellite geometry. When clock adding is used in conjunction with height aiding, it is even possible to navigate with only two satellites, but only for short periods of time, as accuracy will deteriorate due to drift of even the rubidium clock.

Carrier-Aided Tracking

By recovering and locking on to the carrier signal in addition to the codes (also called carrier-aided smoothing), it is possible to make range measurements that considerably enhance accuracy. This technique involves observing the rate of change of the carrier frequency (Doppler shift) produced by satellite movement. The effect is to filter out the noise on the pseudorange and measure the phase angle of the carrier to within a few degrees. With a carrier wavelength of 0.2 meter or approximately 20 centimeters (L1 = 0.19m; L2 = 0.24m), these phase measurements can be made to fractions of a wavelength, which helps the receiver get a better lock on the edge of the pseudorandom code and allows

156

more precise timing measurements.

It is possible to use these techniques to track just the carrier (codeless GPS) to produce relative position. With a truly codeless receiver, the Navigation Message and ephemeris data are not accessed and must be supplied by another source. By using pairs of receivers operating in differential mode, a combination of Doppler positioning and phase comparison can be used to determine position. One advantage of codeless GPS is that both the L1 and L2 frequencies can be tracked, thus eliminating the largest source of propagation errors, ionospheric delay. Although these techniques are not generally applicable to marine navigation, they are being used for high-precision surveying applications.

Differential GPS

Differential GPS (DGPS) may well be the ultimate in accuracy enhancement. In fact, the accuracy potential of DGPS is so great that many call it the "second generation GPS."

There are many different forms of DGPS and depending on the mode of operation, incredible accuracy is possible — to less than a centimeter. Even in the basic mode of differential operation, DGPS can provide better accuracy than that achieved with P code access. According to the Federal Radionavigation Plan, accuracy for harbor and harbor approach (HHA) is between 8–20 meters, an accuracy that cannot be met by GPS even when accessing the P code. But by using GPS in the differential mode, this degree of accuracy is easily obtainable—even by the nonmilitary user.

In addition to accuracy enhancement, integrity is also a problem with GPS. Integrity is the ability of a system to provide timely warnings to users when there are system failures and GPS should not be used for navigation. An example might be satellite clock failure, which is 0not quickly discovered so that reliability in the system is reduced. Another example is inconsistent SA degradation. DGPS has the added value of providing confidence in the system, an important element for the civil user.

DGPS is made up of two basic components. The first is the placement of a GPS receiver at a known reference site that has been accurately surveyed to one meter or less. By comparing the GPS position with the known geodetic position, corrections can be computed for both normal signal propagation errors and SA-induced errors. These corrections are then transmitted to the user over a separate communications link, the second component of DGPS.

The receiver at the **reference station** tracks all the satellites in view and measures their pseudoranges. It then computes corrections to the pseudoranges based on knowledge of its own precise geodetic position, the broadcast ephemeris data, and the rate of change to each satellite. These corrections essentially rule out those errors common to all receivers, such as those produced by ionospheric delay, clock error/dithering, and ephemeris errors. Remaining errors are those caused by receiver noise, interchannel biases, and differential station uncertainty.

The accuracy of the corrections is dependent on two factors: their age (temporal decorrelation) and the distance between the user and the reference station (spatial decorrelation). One way in which selective availability introduces error into the pseudorange is by clock dithering. Since dithering takes the form of a slowly varying, unknown delay, it is important that differential corrections are continuously updated. Temporal decorrelation may amount to approximately 2 meters after 30 seconds. Thus, differential corrections should be updated several times per minute.

The spatial decorrelation error budget is affected by many factors. Atmospheric errors are the major contributor to spatial decorrelation and can only be described statistically. Spatial decorrelation is also directly proportional to the distance between the user and the reference station. For example, if the ephemeris error induced by SA is 16 meters and the user is 1,000 km (540 nm) from the reference station, the error of the differential correction would be a little less than 1 meter. If the user is only 200 km (108 nm) from the reference station, this error is reduced to a little more than 0.1 meter. During system development, 1 meter/70 nautical miles was used as an estimate of the total spatial decorrelation error budget.

The differential corrections are applied to the user range measurements (pseudorange differential) as opposed to actual measured position as a latitude/longitude correction (positional differential). The reason for this is that the user and reference station may be using different satellites. For example, the receiver criterion for satellite selection may differ between the two, or the satellites available to the user may not be the same as those available at the reference station. Even with one non-common satellite used in the navigation solution, the position errors could end up being worse than uncorrected GPS if a positional differential were used as opposed to a pseudorange differential.

158

The corrections are transmitted to the user via a **communications link,** or transmitted broadcast message, the second main component of the differential system. The Radio Technical Commission for Maritime Services Special Committee 104 has established a standard data format (RTCM SC104 Version 2.0) for DGPS that has been adopted for general public use. This format is very similar to that used for the GPS navigation message and uses the GPS parity algorithm. The main difference is that the differential format uses variable length messages as opposed to the fixed length navigation message. Although the data link can operate at a number of different frequencies, the primary requirement is that the messages be reliably transmitted at a minimum data rate of 50 bps (continuous transmission). In the private sector, the data message might be encrypted to limit differential service to paying customers.

The message consists of range corrections and a correction rate-of-change. It also includes specific information for each satellite: identification number, health, estimated accuracy, and the age of the data. Because each satellite range is determined within the user's receiver, the range corrections allow the receiver to apply these corrections directly to each range and thus compute a better navigation solution. The rate-of-change correction can be applied to future navigation until a correction update is received from the DGPS broadcast. The differential message can also alert user receivers to occasions when there is so much error in specific satellite data that it should not be used for navigation.

The data can be transmitted to the user in a number of ways. One is to use **geostationary satellites** that illuminate a wide area of use (WADGPS). In a feasibility study in the early 1990's using Inmarsat satellites, the ability to provide real-time accuracy of approximately 10 meters to a wide area of users was demonstrated. An example "wide area" of one of these satellites, which went into operation in May 1992, covers all of North and South America and the western halves of Europe and Africa. Beginning in 1994, Inmarsat III satellites with the ability to transmit GPS integrity data will be launched. If differential corrections are also provided with the transmissions, worldwide differential GPS could become a reality. On a much smaller scale, many local companies in the private sector transmit differential corrections with accuracy values of 1–5 meters to select user communities.

Within the coastal waters of the conterminous U.S., Alaska, and Hawaii, the U.S. Coast Guard has been given the authority and funding to generate differential data via **marine radiobeacons.** Some of the reasons why radiobeacons were chosen over other existing systems such as

1. The radiobeacon broadcast range is compatible with the DGPS accuracy range.

2. Coast Guard owned and operated radiobeacons already exist and will be operational well into the future.

3. The radiobeacon broadcast equipment is reliable, commercially available, and relatively inexpensive.

4. No further changes are necessary in international regulations as provisions are already present for the broadcast of differential information on radiobeacons.

Figure 6.13   *Advantages for Using Radiobeacons for the Differential Broadcast Message.*

Loran-C or satellite transmissions are listed in Figure 6.13.

A very important reason for selecting radiobeacons was that feasibility tests with a DGPS prototype conducted from the Montauk Point, New York, radiobeacon in the late 1980's demonstrated that the accuracy goal of 10 meters or less was possible. Tests continued with the Montauk beacon in the early 1990's, and additional prototypes were added in 1991-1992 in Lake Superior area, on the Texas Gulf Coast, and in the Northeastern U.S.

In addition to the reference station and communications link (broadcast transmitter), other components are an integral part of the DGPS system. One of these is the **integrity monitor**, a separate station that monitors the integrity of the GPS broadcast, the correction data, and the broadcast signal. There are also plans for at least two **control centers** at existing Coast Guard radionavigation facilities, one on each coast, each of which will be capable of managing the entire system in case of an emergency. As reference station equipment comes down in price, it may be feasible to collocate the equipment at all broadcast sites, negating the need for separate reference stations. For an overall picture of DGPS system components, see Figure 6.14.

Although the primary goal for U.S. DGPS is to fulfill the Federal Radionavigation Plan accuracy requirements for Harbor and Harbor Approach Navigation, secondary goals involve meeting the needs of other agencies and programs such as positioning floating aids to navigation (ATON) and assisting NOAA survey vessels. Implementation plans call for a fully differential service to be on line by 1996. (See Figure 6.15.)

One interesting adaptation of DGPS that may be very useful to the aviation community is the use of **pseudolites**. A pseudolite is a ground-based transmitter station that transmits the same signal characteristics as the satellites so that it looks to the user and behaves like another

160

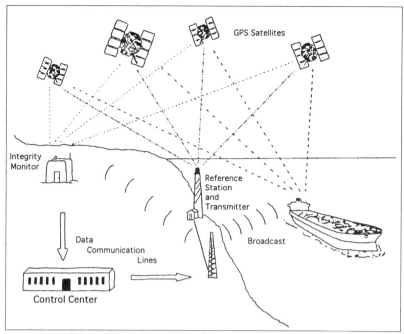

Taken from: "Description of the U.S. Coast Guard Differential GPS Program" April 1992

Figure 6.14   DGPS System Components

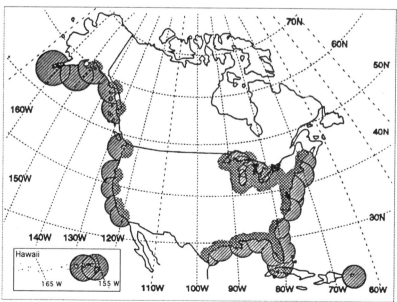

Taken from: "Description of the U.S. Coast Guard Differential GPS Program" April 1992

Figure 6.15   Proposed DGPS Coverage Using Marine Radiobeacons

161

satellite—a pseudosatellite. A pseudolite serves two basic functions. One is to compute pseudorange error in the differential mode by being at a known location and transmitting the error back to the user. The other is that the pseudolite actually delivers another range determined, as any satellite does, by being at a known location. This ability improves system reliability in periods of poor satellite coverage. Another advantage is that a separate communications link is not needed. The pseudolite transmits on the regular GPS L band, so the signal can be processed by hardware already in GPS receivers. One potential disadvantage with the pseudolite technique concerns the dynamic range of signals received by the user. The pseudolite range changes enormously for the user, and therefore, its signal strength also changes, which can overwhelm the receiver front end. Another disadvantage of this technique is that the transmissions are only line-of-sight, limiting its use to local areas. It does, however, hold promise for aviation use in solving the integrity/accuracy problem, especially in airport and runway approaches.

Before leaving the concept of DGPS, it is important to note that a number of varied applications using the differential concept can produce incredible accuracy—in the order of centimeters and even millimeters. Although these applications are used primarily in the static surveying environment, technological advances are providing applications in even low-dynamic environments. The result is that there are now many different accuracy levels, which lend themselves to a large variety of use applications. *See Chapter 6 photo #1 for an example of differential ready receivers.*

V. Levels of Accuracy

Six basic levels of accuracy can be separated into two different groups, depending on the way in which the GPS signal is tracked. The most common way of tracking the signal is by making measurements on the pseudorandom code. Another way, which employs an even higher degree of technological sophistication, is by tracking the phase angle of the carrier. Within each group exist distinct differences in the levels of accuracy.

Using Code Measurements

Four levels of accuracy are possible using the technique of tracking the pseudorandom codes on the GPS signal. The two most common are the two basic services provided by the GPS system: Precise Positioning Service (PPS) and Standard Positioning Service (SPS). PPS tracks the P code (Y code) on both carrier frequencies in addition to the C/A code. SPS tracks only the C/A code on the L1 frequency.

PPS accuracy can be expressed as being at least 9 meters CEP or 22 meters 2 drms (95% confidence). SPS with implementation of Selective Availability provides 100 meters or better, 2 drms 95% with a CEP of a little more than 50 meters. It is important to note that there is a third level of accuracy, SPS in the undegraded form. Without SA, SPS provides accuracy values almost as good as those achieved with PPS. These are on the order of approximately 30 meters 2 drms or slightly under 20 meters CEP.

The fourth level of accuracy in this group is that achieved by the most common form of DGPS, which also uses pseudorandom code tracking to compute satellite range. DGPS can deliver 10-meter accuracy, 2 drms 95% and often well under that.

Using Phase Measurements

By applying the techniques of DGPS to the enhancement technique of tracking the phase angle of the signal carrier, incredible accuracy can be achieved. This technique, which is sometimes called **phase differencing,** has been developed in the surveyor user community.

The principle involves two high-precision multichannel receivers separated by a given distance taking simultaneous observations of the same satellites. By measuring the differences in the phase angle on the L1 carrier wavelength, it is possible to compute position that is accurate

Using Code Measurements

SPS with SA degradation	100 meters or better
SPS without SA	@ 30 meters
PPS	22 meters or better
DGPS	<10 meters

Using Phase Measurements

Survey (moving)	1 - 5 centimeters
Survey (static)	<1 centimeter

Figure 6.16   Levels of GPS Accuracy

to one centimeter or less. In order to get this level of accuracy, data must be collected in a stationary position for 15 to 45 minutes to resolve ambiguities in the carrier phase measurements. One factor that does affect this type of accuracy is that it requires a relatively short base line between receivers. The degree of error is directly proportional to the distance between receivers: approximately 1 part per million of the distance with single frequency receivers, less for dual frequency receivers. For a further discussion of this topic see the section on Surveying in Chapter 8 and Figure 8.4.

Once the ambiguity in the phase measurements is resolved, it is possible to move the survey receiver. This produces slightly lower accuracy, in the order of 5 centimeters or less due to less averaging time allowed at each new location. For a summary of the different levels of GPS accuracy, see Figure 6.16.

Magellan increases GPS accuracy ten-fold with the differential-ready NAV 5000D and NAV 5200D, and the Magellan Differential Beacon Receiver (DBR™).

Examples of fixed-mount and handheld GPS differential receivers. Courtesy of Magellan Systems Corporation.

CHAPTER SEVEN

Navigating With GPS

GPS is quickly becoming the most eagerly embraced navigational tool in the history of navigation. One reason is its potential for highly accurate position fixing. But it is possible to use GPS for more than just position fixing. As with its predecessor, Loran-C, GPS is also a valuable tool for checking against other instruments, solving countless navigation problems, and augmenting other navigation systems. In the realm of navigation, GPS's varied uses are only limited by the ingenuity of the navigator.

I. Checking/Calibrating Other Instruments

One of the most common things to do when you get a new nav-aid on board is to start comparing its read-outs with other navigation instruments on the vessel. It quickly becomes apparent if these instruments are "in sync" or not, and it is possible to verify or discredit their accuracy. It is even possible to extend these comparisons to calibrate one instrument against another. Of course, this calibration depends on the accuracy of the reference instrument. In the case of GPS, the accuracy of read-outs can be degraded by selective availability for the civil user. However, by taking data using relative accuracy, these errors can often be canceled out. The key is to take data on many different occasions so that consistency and confidence are established in the reference system, which, in this case, is GPS.

Compass

Probably one of the most common instruments to check against GPS information is the ship's compass. Unfortunately, SA degradation makes straight comparisons between the compass and GPS heading/course over the ground impractical. The GPS readout will be seen to fluctuate by a few degrees even when the vessel is set on a constant course. It is, however, possible to determine accurate vessel heading by taking a series of position read-outs and plotting them on a chart as Lat/Lon coordinates. For this technique to work, a calm day with no current or seas running is essential.

For example, suppose you are traveling on a course of 45°T after subtracting/adding for magnetic variation. Yet, after taking a number of GPS position readings and plotting them on a chart, you use a protractor to show that the actual course made good is 43°T. Providing there are no currents or seas, as they could produce similar results, you can conclude that the ship's compass (or magnetic deviation) is off with a 2 degree west variation. (See Figure 7.1.) Note that even though the GPS heading read-out may fluctuate and jump around, plotting a series of position fixes will display the true heading. It is important to remember that GPS's strength is its position accuracy and not its ability to give instantaneous velocity or heading readings. Confidence in this information can be achieved by repeated runs in the same direction.

This technique can be extended to include other points on the com-

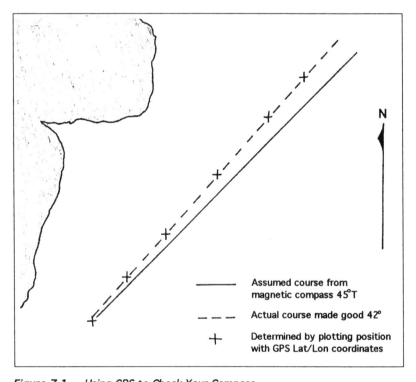

N

——————— Assumed course from magnetic compass 45°T

— — — Actual course made good 42°

+ Determined by plotting position with GPS Lat/Lon coordinates

Figure 7.1   Using GPS to Check Your Compass

pass. With care, data can be collected for all directions, which, in effect, is using GPS to "swing" the compass and produce a deviation card. To build confidence in the results, it is important to collect data over many different occasions because compass deviation depends on heading. An easy practice is to take periodic position coordinates on a day's run while maintaining a constant compass course. Eventually, enough data will be accumulated to produce deviation values for different points on the compass. With more sophisticated GPS receivers, this information can be manually entered into the software to be used for future navigation in which the deviation will be automatically added or subtracted for each course traveled.

Knotmeter

Another instrument that can be checked for accuracy with GPS is the knotmeter. One way is to simply compare the GPS speed over the ground (SOG) with the knotmeter readout. Unfortunately, this method is subject to a number of errors. One reason is that the two instruments determine speed in two different ways. The knotmeter measures speed by measuring the flow of water past a paddle wheel. Depending on the type of receiver, there are two different ways in which GPS is used to determine speed. Sequencing and multiplexing receivers compare GPS positions as a function of time. Continuous tracking (parallel channel) receivers also do that but have the option of computing speed by measuring the Doppler shift in the carrier signal. If Selective Availability is turned off, the Doppler method is more accurate. With SA activated, there is no advantage in using Doppler. Regardless of the method used, the GPS read-out is given as calculated speed over the ground (SOG), which could vary significantly from a paddle wheel-based reading.

If strong seas are encountered, the knotmeter and GPS read-outs will be different. For example, if a boat is getting an extra push by a following sea, the knotmeter will display a reduced reading compared to the GPS reading. This difference between the two readings, however, can be used to advantage. By subtracting the two, a general estimate of the effects of the following sea can be determined and used for further navigation. Because of these two different methods of determining speed, it is again important when comparing GPS with a knotmeter that the data is collected in calm conditions with no sea running.

By far the biggest problem in comparing GPS speed with a knotmeter is the degradation of satellite signals due to SA, which can cause a

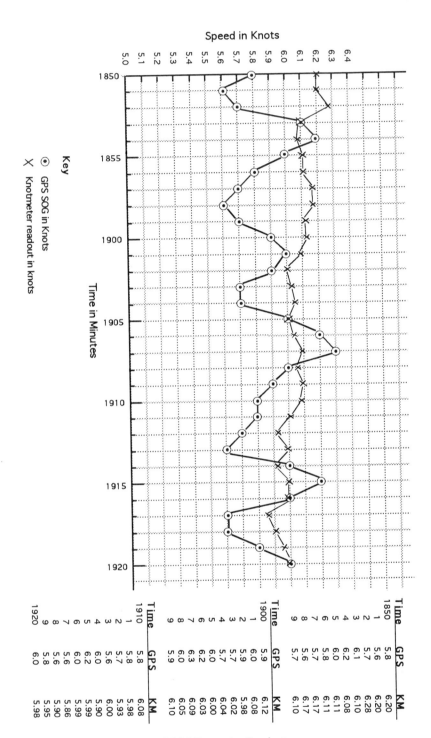

Speed in Knots

Time in Minutes

Time	GPS	KM
1850	5.8	6.20
1	5.6	6.20
2	5.7	6.28
3	6.1	6.10
4	6.2	6.08
5	6.0	6.11
6	5.8	6.11
7	5.7	6.17
8	5.6	6.17
9	5.7	6.10

Time	GPS	KM
1900	5.9	6.12
1	6.0	6.08
2	5.9	5.98
3	5.7	6.02
4	5.7	6.04
5	6.0	6.00
6	6.2	6.03
7	6.3	6.09
8	6.0	6.05
9	5.9	6.10

Time	GPS	KM
1910	5.8	6.08
1	5.8	5.98
2	5.7	5.93
3	5.6	6.00
4	6.0	5.90
5	6.0	5.99
6	6.2	5.99
7	6.0	5.86
8	5.6	5.90
9	5.8	5.95
1920	6.0	5.98

Figure 7.2   Comparing GPS SOG Knotmeter Readouts

variance in the GPS SOG readings. One of the most interesting comparisons of GPS and other ship's instruments is to collect data on the GPS SOG and the knotmeter over a given segment of time. To illustrate this comparison, a set of sample data was collected under relatively calm conditions with the ship's knotmeter set at 6 knots for 30 minutes. (See Figure 7.2.) Shortly after 1900, a little bit of a head wind was encountered, which is seen in the slight reduction of speed of the knotmeter.

Graphing the data not only showed that the knotmeter was running a little higher than the GPS SOG, but also revealed some interesting effects of SA. Note that while the knotmeter curve is reasonably steady, there are decided peaks and troughs in the GPS curve. This wide degree of variance in the GPS SOG clearly demonstrates the results of dithering the satellite clocks in the navigation message. These errors can largely be eliminated by taking the SOG readings over a given segment of time and averaging them. When the knotmeter readings were averaged for the 30-minute period in the example, the knotmeter average was 6.05 knots. The average for the GPS read-outs was 5.67 knots. Subsequent tests, particularly using GPS position read-outs at the beginning and end of a given time segment, did, in fact, show that the knotmeter was running a little high.

Although the example demonstrates the extremes in GPS SOG readings, there is another technique that uses GPS to check on the accuracy of your knotmeter. It involves plotting GPS position coordinates over a given time interval while the boat is running at a constant speed. Plotting GPS position at the beginning and end of this time period and then lifting off the resulting distance and measuring it with a pair of dividers will show whether the knotmeter is correct.

For example, suppose a boat is set to travel at a constant speed of 6 knots. Six knots is a nice speed to use because the math is so much easier: theoretically, a vessel should travel one nautical mile every 10 minutes. If GPS position readings are taken at 1320 and 1350 and then plotted on the chart, the distance between the two positions can be measured by transferring the distance with a pair of dividers to the nautical mile scale printed on the chart or directly to the latitude scale, as one minute of latitude equals one nautical mile. (See Figure 7.3.) In 30 minutes running time, this distance should equal 3.0 nautical miles. If the distance is less, in this case, it is 2.9 nautical miles, the knotmeter is either off, or possibly a head sea is being encountered, which would induce error in the speed of the knotmeter paddle wheel by making it read faster than the actual ship's speed. By dividing the distance covered

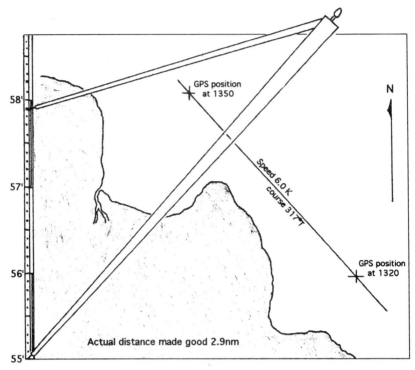

Figure 7.3 *Using GPS Position Fixing to Determine Distance Made Good*

by the running time, a more accurate speed can be determined. (See Figure 7.4.)

Theoretically, the longer the time segment between the plotted positions, the more accurate the results, as the percentage of error is reduced by spreading it out over a larger area. However, because of SA, the differences in the accuracies between the two GPS positions may vary over longer time periods so that the relative accuracy between the two no longer cancels out the induced errors. Therefore, it is again important to collect data on a number of different occasions to gain confidence in the comparison between GPS speed readings and the ship's knotmeter. Obviously, using a large scale chart and differential GPS is the best way to calibrate your knotmeter.

Distance Log

There are a couple of ways in which GPS can be used to check a vessel's distance log. One way is by using the same technique as described

170

Equation:

$$\frac{\text{Distance (nm)}}{\text{Time (hours)}} = \text{Speed (in nm/hr or Kts)}$$

Example:

$$\frac{2.9 \text{ nm}}{0.5 \text{ hours (30 min)}} = 5.8 \text{ Kts}$$

Figure 7.4   Using Distance and Elapsed Time to Determine Speed

Date	GPS Log			Ships Log			Difference	% Error
	End	Begin	Distance	End	Begin	Distance		
4 Sept	3023.7	3013.2	10.5	10.9	0.0	10.9	+0.4	3.6%*
5 Sept	3032.9	3023.7	9.2	20.6	10.9	9.7	+0.5	5.2%
6 Sept	3050.7	3032.9	17.8	38.6	20.6	18.0	+0.2	1.1%
7 Sept	3065.8	3050.7	15.1	53.8	38.6	15.2	+0.1	0.6%
11 Sept	3076.3	3065.8	10.5	64.7	53.8	10.9	+0.4	3.6%*
12 Sept	3087.4	3076.3	11.1	76.3	64.7	11.6	+0.5	4.3%*
13 Sept	3107.0	3087.4	19.6	96.7	76.3	20.4	+0.8	3.9%*
18 Sept	3114.8	3107.0	7.8	104.9	96.7	8.2	+0.4	4.8%*
19 Sept	3129.3	3114.8	14.5	119.9	104.9	15.0	+0.5	3.3%*
20 Sept	3151.5	3129.3	22.2	143.4	119.9	23.5	+1.3	5.5%
25 Sept	3157.5	3151.5	6.0	149.5	143.4	6.1	+0.1	1.6%
26 Sept	3170.6	3157.5	13.1	162.4	149.5	12.9	-0.2	-1.5%
27 Sept	3192.6	3170.6	22.0	184.6	162.4	22.2	+0.2	0.9%
2 Oct	3200.3	3192.6	7.7	192.7	184.6	8.1	+0.4	4.9%*
3 Oct	3215.1	3200.3	14.8	208.0	192.7	15.3	+0.5	3.2%*
4 Oct	3229.8	3215.1	14.7	14.9	0.0	14.9	+0.2	1.4%

All log readings, distances and differences are in nautical miles.
* Results from readings taken in calm conditions.
Average of these readings is 3.95%

To calculate log % error: $\dfrac{\text{difference between readings}}{\text{specific log distance}}$ x 100 = % error

Figure 7.5   Comparing GPS Running Log with Ship's Distance Log

before, in which GPS-plotted position is used to determine distance made good. By simultaneously noting the log read-outs when the positions are taken, the read-outs can be subtracted and compared directly to the distance made good on the chart. Again, it is important to use this technique in calm conditions with no running seas.

Another way to check the distance log is by direct comparison of log read-outs as most GPS receivers keep a running log. Again, it is important to note sea conditions when comparing because the distance log depends on water passing by the keel for its determinations, whereas GPS determines actual distance over the bottom by comparing calculated positions. However, in calm conditions, it is possible to get a fairly good comparison between the two instruments and thus determine the accuracy of the ship's log. This comparison, of course, assumes that the GPS running log is accurate. Also it helps to use read-outs between known reference points, such as two buoys or a harbor entrance and a channel marker where actual distance is known. By comparing the two instruments over a number of different occasions, confidence in the accuracy of each can be achieved.

To illustrate these principles, a set of sample data comparing the GPS log and ship's log is shown in Figure 7.5. Once the difference between the two instruments is known, it is possible to calculate the degree of error. Note the variations on different occasions under supposedly varied conditions. Note also the closer degree of consistency in those readings (*) taken in calm conditions. In this case, the average of those readings is 3.95% error, which again shows that the knotmeter/log is reading too high. Once the degree of error is known, most logs provide the capability of correcting for errors. If it is not possible to actually correct for the error, once the percent error is known, it can be used for future navigation.

II. General Navigating Applications Calculating Magnetic Variation

Even though all charts display a compass rose depicting magnetic variation for an area, in some areas magnetic variation does change over the years. Most GPS receivers have software programs that calculate the magnetic variation for the area of present position along with updated corrections as a function of time. But it is also possible to manually determine magnetic variation with GPS, a nice technique to know especially if old charts are being used. It is also a useful technique for checking on the accuracy of the GPS receiver magnetic variation read-out.

The principle is the same as comparing the ship's compass course with GPS position fixes plotted on a chart. In the case of swinging the compass, magnetic deviation is the unknown, and magnetic variation must be entered into the solution. Now in the case of determining magnetic variation, the deviation has to be known and accounted for.

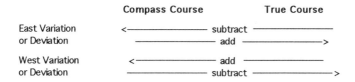

	Compass Course		True Course
East Variation or Deviation	<——————— subtract ———————		
	——————— add ———————>		
West Variation or Deviation	<——————— add ———————		
	——————— subtract ———————>		

Figure 7.6   *Effects of Magnetic Variation/Deviation on Compass Course and True Course*

To illustrate this principle, suppose you are traveling on a course of 90° according to the ship's compass. Magnetic deviation previously determined for this direction is 2° east, so if there are no effects of magnetic variation, the actual course made good would be 92°. (Going from compass course to true course, add east deviation—see Figure 7.6.) Yet, by using GPS to determine periodic positions plotted on a chart, the actual course achieved is 85°. The magnetic variation for the area is then 92° - 85° or 7° west. (See Figure 7.7.) In future navigation in this area, 7° will have to be added to each compass course (+ the specific deviation for that heading) to make good the desired course. In this particular case, if you wanted to make good a course of 90°T, you would add 5° (+7,-2) for a compass course of 95° magnetic.

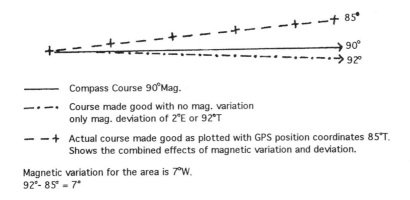

——————— Compass Course 90°Mag.

— • —• Course made good with no mag. variation only mag. deviation of 2°E or 92°T

— — + Actual course made good as plotted with GPS position coordinates 85°T. Shows the combined effects of magnetic variation and deviation.

Magnetic variation for the area is 7°W.
92°- 85° = 7°

Figure 7.7   *Using GPS Position to Determine Magnetic Variation*

Deviation from the Rhumb Line

Unless you are sailing great distances across large expanses of the open ocean, most skippers navigate by sailing on the rhumb line. The rhumb line is the shortest distance between two points that involves sailing on a constant heading. GPS provides many ways of determining whether you have deviated from the rhumb line.

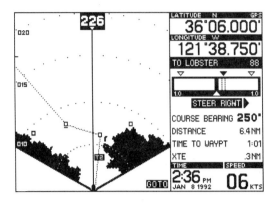

The Hummingbird GPS has two different ways of displaying cross-track error. One is on a large "Forward Looking View" on its built in electronic chart display. The other is expressed on a course deviation display to the right.

Figure 7.8   Displaying Cross-Track Error

Many GPS receivers are equipped with a graphic display that will depict deviation from the rhumb line as cross-track error. The amount of deviation can be expressed either with symbols or numerical values with the outer limits of those values capable of being programmed by the user. (See Figure 7.8.) One easy way to correct for cross-track error is to adjust the vessel's heading as it is displayed on the receiver so that it matches the bearing to the destination or waypoint. It doesn't matter if you are working magnetic or true headings/bearings as long as they are both the same.

On receivers with a track plotter function, there is another way to determine cross-track error. Here the boat's position is displayed relative to a waypoint, which is also pictured. Cross-track error limit lines can be added with the limits established by editing the receiver's software. Then the vessel's course made good can actually be seen as it closes on the waypoint. Plotters also have the capability of zooming in and out to change the scale from a small area to a large one. Additional navigation information is usually displayed such as range/bearing to the waypoint and vessel heading/speed. One of the nicest features of a track plotter is the memory function in which a trip can be stored, then recalled and studied at a later time. This function can be especially useful for sailors who try to analyze the events of a race or calculate tacking angles.

With receivers that do not have a graphic display or a track plotter,

174

it is possible to manually calculate cross-track error by laying a line between the original starting point and the destination and then periodically plotting position from GPS Lat/Lon read-outs. The bearing from your position to the destination can then be lifted directly off the chart. Any deviation of the ship's course from the lay line can be quickly seen and thus corrected. There may be situations, however, when it is not desirable to head directly to the bearing when off the original course.

Such a situation is illustrated in Figure 7.9. Suppose a boat is headed on a course (1) of 45°T to reach a waypoint at the entrance of an

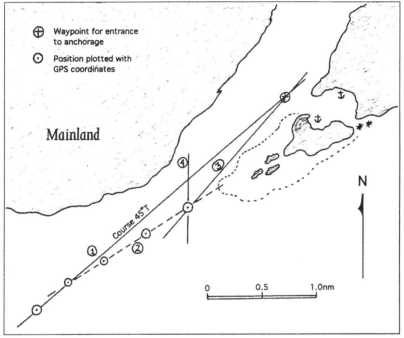

Figure 7.9 *Plotting GPS Position to Determine Deviation from the Rhumb Line*

anchorage. As the mainland is neared, strong winds encountered off the land make the boat drift off course (2). If continued, the course will take the boat into the shoals off the anchorage. If the course is corrected to match the bearing from the waypoint (3), it would still lead dangerously close to the shoal area. This is not a desirable course, particularly since the accuracy of the GPS fixes, may be questionable due to SA degradation. In this case, a more prudent course would be to head directly north for 0.3 nm (4) to get back on the original rhumb line, which could be determined by GPS position, and then continue heading

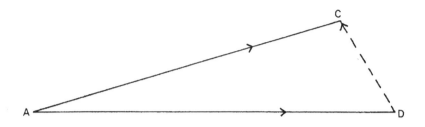

Triangle Part	Determining Actual Current	Navigating with Estimated Current
Point A	Initial position of vessel	Present Position
Point D	DR of vessel at present time	DR position at future time
Point C	Fix at present time	Estimated position at future time
Line AD	Course and speed vector	Course and speed vector
Line AC	Actual CMG and SMG	Track and SOA
Line DC	Actual current encountered	Anticipated/expected current

CMG	Course Made Good - actual course achieved between two points.
SMG	Speed Made Good - actual speed between two points based on time and distance.
Track	Intended/anticipated course taking into consideration current effect
SOA	Intended/anticipated speed taking into consideration current effect

Figure 7.10   The Current Triangle

for the waypoint.

Determining Set and Drift

The techniques described earlier can be used to calculate the actual set and drift of deviation from the rhumb line. Set and drift are the results of currents and tides on a vessel's course made good. They can also result in leeway from a strong wind on a vessel's course. **Set** is the direction of the deviation or the direction toward which the current is flowing. **Drift** is the rate at which the boat departs from the plotted course or the speed of a current as measured in knots.

Set and drift can be determined by using a current triangle. A current triangle is a vector diagram in which one side represents the vessel's course and speed, the second side represents the actual track, and the third side represents the set and drift of the current. There are two different types of current triangles. (See Figure 7.10.) One is used to compute the actual current by comparing position after vessel movement with a predicted dead reckoning (DR) position. The other uses estimated current to predict vessel track, course required to make an intended position, and course and speed required to achieve a given estimated

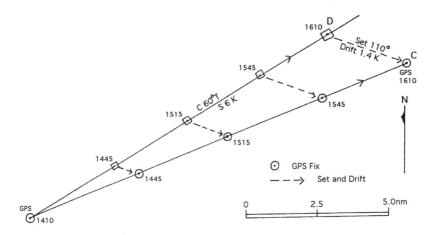

Figure 7.11   Using GPS to Determine Set and Drift

time of arrival (ETA). Whenever any two sides are known, the third can be determined by direct measurement on the chart or by calculation.

To illustrate the first case in which the set and drift of a current is determined, suppose you are traveling on a course of 60°T at 6 knots. (See Figure 7.11) At 1410, you plot your GPS position at Point A on the chart. A line is drawn bearing 60° from that position, and in 2 hours running time, your estimated position by dead reckoning should be at Point D, or 12 nm from Point A. However, at 1610, another GPS position is plotted on the chart at Point C, indicating that the actual course made good has been affected by a current. By comparing these

two positions, the estimated DR position at D and the actual GPS position at C determined for the <u>same time,</u> it is possible to calculate the set and drift of the current. By connecting the two positions with a line (DC), the direction from the DR fix to the GPS fix can be determined using a protractor or compass rose. In this case, it is 110°, which is the

set of the current. The drift is calculated by measuring the distance between the two points, which, in this case, is 2.8 nm, and dividing it by the lapsed time from the first fix taken at 1410, or two hours. The set then is 2.8/2, or 1.4 knots.

Actually, there are a couple of ways that the GPS receiver can be used to indicate that a current is affecting both a vessel's course and speed without determining the specific set or drift. Initial clues may be the lack of agreement between the boat's instruments (compass and

177

knotmeter) and the GPS read-outs for COG and SOG. An increasing discrepancy between the two instruments is a good indicator that a current is being encountered. Since some of these variations could also be due to SA, a better way to determine whether a current is present is to plot periodic GPS positions and compare them with DR positions for the same time on the DR rhumb line. This technique is also illustrated in Figure 7.11.

Once the set and drift are determined, this information can be used for future navigation in the area as long as the current remains constant. With many GPS receivers, it is possible to manually enter in the set and drift, and the software will make the corrections in subsequent read-outs. The danger with this method is that the receiver will continue to make these corrections even when there is no longer a current or the current has changed. It is important, therefore, to keep checking actual GPS positions against a projected DR position.

It is also possible to use computed set and drift information in GPS navigation not by entering it into the receiver, but by constructing the second type of current triangle in which one side represents the vessel's course and speed, a second side is the set and drift of the current, and a third side represents the actual track. Because currents are known to fluctuate and change, GPS can be used as a check on these measurements by taking periodic position fixes and plotting them on the triangle.

For example, suppose you are traveling on a course of 90° at 10 knots in an area that has an estimated current with a set of 215° and a drift of 2 knots. (See Figure 7.12A.) Present position is determined with GPS at Point A. By constructing a vector diagram, you can determine the effects of the current on your course and speed. This is done by laying a line 90° from A using a protractor or compass rose. Speed can be represented using any scale, but it is most convenient to lift it directly off the latitude scale on the side of the chart. In one hour running time, 10 knots would equal 10 nautical miles. This distance is then used to determine Point D. Vector DC is laid off in the direction of the set of the current at 215°. The drift is determined by marking off the equivalent of 2 knots with your speed/distance scale to give Point C, which would be your position in one hour running time without correcting for the current. By connecting Points A and C, the anticipated course of the track and speed of advance can be determined with using a protractor and measuring with the speed/distance scale. Plotting periodic GPS positions will also verify the effects on course and speed of advance (SOA)

178

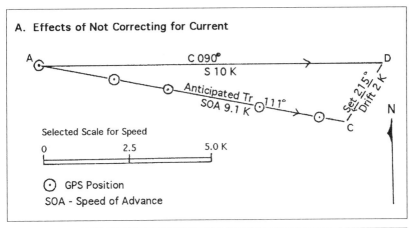

A. Effects of Not Correcting for Current

Selected Scale for Speed

⊙ GPS Position
SOA - Speed of Advance

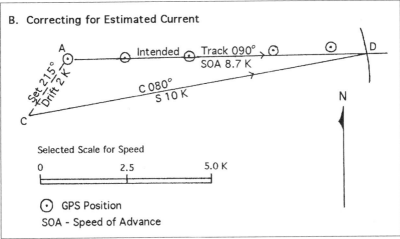

B. Correcting for Estimated Current

Selected Scale for Speed

⊙ GPS Position
SOA - Speed of Advance

Figure 7.12   Correcting for Set and Drift

without correcting for the current.

A reciprocal form of the triangle can be constructed to compute what heading (track) is needed to make good a course of 90°. (See Figure 7.12B.) First plot your GPS present position at Point A. Then lay off a line of indefinite length in the direction of 90°. The current vector is then drawn from A with the direction of the set at 215° and a distance equal to its drift of 2 knots, which establishes Point C. From Point C, swing an arc equal to your boat speed of 10 knots so that it crosses the 90° line extended from Point A. This intersection then becomes Point D of the triangle. The course needed to make good the intended track of 90° can now be measured with a protractor or compass rose as being 80°. It is also possible to determine the speed of advance (SOA) against the current as being 8.7 knots even though the boat speed is set at 10 knots.

GPS can be used as a check to see whether, in fact, you are staying on the intended track of 90° by plotting periodic position fixes on the triangle. For example, suppose that subsequent fixes show that you are actually drifting a little "high" off the intended track. (See again Figure 7.12B.) Possibly the current has changed slightly. The course could then be corrected to 82° or 83° to compensate for the change. Again, use of GPS position fixing will confirm whether or not you are making good the intended track.

Finally, it should be noted that some of the more sophisticated receivers will automatically compute set and drift through the use of external sensors. To do this, the receiver needs to be integrated with an external knotmeter, electronic compass, and wind speed/apparent wind sensor. These sensors open up a whole additional realm of information. Not only are set and drift calculated and used in the navigation solution, but the true wind angle, wind speed, and wind direction are also given. This information is especially helpful to sailboaters and can be used to determine the timing of the next tack and the bearing and wind information on that tack.

III. Using GPS Waypoints in Navigation

Waypoint Realization

Probably the most common use of GPS in the marine environment is waypoint navigation. Once a waypoint has been established, the GPS receiver will deliver a wealth of information: distance to the waypoint (range), direction to the waypoint (bearing), how long it will take to reach the waypoint (time to go), when the waypoint will be reached (estimated time of arrival or ETA). Yet one important factor in waypoint navigation needs to be identified: what constitutes arrival at the waypoint, or **waypoint realization.**

Most GPS receivers have the option to change the size of the area or zone around the waypoint in which the receiver will recognize that the waypoint has been achieved. The area may be a circle around the actual waypoint that has a radius of 0.1 nm, 0.2 nm, 0.5 nm, etc. The size of

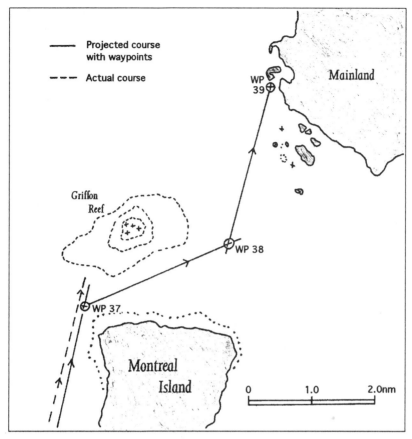

Figure 7.13 *Missing a Waypoint in Which the Limits Have Been Set too Small*

the area used is important and depends on a number of factors. It also has some important implications for the actual arrival accuracy, ability to achieve the waypoint, and navigation to the next waypoint.

In the interest of accuracy, there may be a tendency to pick a waypoint size limit that is too small. For example, unless you are right on course, it is possible to come close to a waypoint but miss it altogether if the realization limits are small and keep going right by it. This has a decided disadvantage if you are using a series of waypoints in a given run. The receiver won't automatically "roll" to the next waypoint until the first has been achieved. If this happens you will have to manually enter the receiver program to delete or skip the missed waypoint in the waypoint series or route so that navigation can continue with the next waypoint.

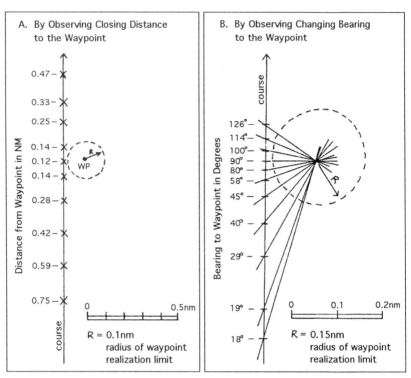

Figure 7.14   Determining if a Waypoint Has Been Missed

For example, suppose a series of waypoints has been lifted off a chart to bypass a reef and area of shoal water, as in Figure 7.13. Suppose also that the realization parameter has been set at 0.1 nm, which is a circle around the waypoint coordinates with a radius of only about 600 feet. Unless you are very close on course, the waypoint could be missed. This miss could have unpleasant consequences if the skipper is not attentive or if the GPS receiver is integrated with an autopilot and driving the boat.

If a waypoint is missed, there are no alarms or indications such as those a receiver gives with waypoint arrival. There are, however, a couple of ways to use the receiver to tell whether the waypoint is being or has been missed. One is to watch the range read-out as you close on the waypoint. It will become less and less the closer you get to the point. If

the waypoint is going to be missed, there will come a time when the distance will remain the same for a short period and then the distance read-out from the waypoint will get larger and larger as the vessel moves away from the waypoint. (See Figure 7.14A.)

Another way to tell whether a waypoint may be missed is by observing the waypoint bearing as you close on it. If you are close to or right on track, the bearing will match closely with the receiver COG read-out and will remain constant. A constantly changing bearing to the waypoint as you near the waypoint, over short segments of time means that you are not heading directly to the waypoint, and depending on the size of the realization limit programmed into the receiver, the waypoint may be missed. (See Figure 7.14B.)

The tendency then may be to set the parameters for waypoint realization larger so that waypoints won't be missed and the receiver will automatically roll to the next waypoint. There are times, however, when a larger size isn't advantageous. Consider navigating in restricted waters where it is necessary to make crucial turns to avoid closely spaced shoals. A larger waypoint realization zone would mean that the receiver acknowledges waypoint arrival before the actual waypoint position has been achieved and starts giving bearing and direction information to the next waypoint before it is needed. In fact, if the new waypoint informa-

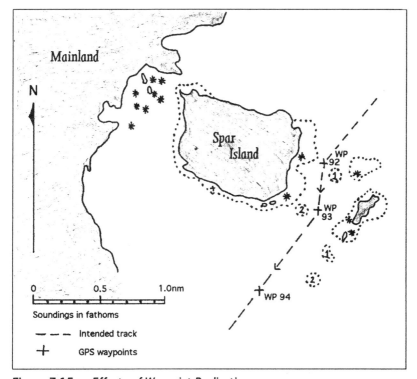

Figure 7.15   Effects of Waypoint Realization

tion is followed before the actual waypoint is reached, it could bring the boat dangerously close to the very shoals you are trying to avoid.

To illustrate this concept, suppose you are navigating in tight quarters to avoid a number of shoals and have defined your intended track with waypoints as in Figure 7.15. With the waypoint radius set at 0.1 nm, the receiver would indicate that you are at Waypoint #92 0.1 nm before you have arrived at the desired position. Should you initiate the turn for Waypoint #93 at this point, your course would come very close to the one-fathom shoal you are trying to avoid.

In this case, a couple of tricks can be used with a GPS receiver to tighten up on the accuracy of realizing the actual waypoint. One is to

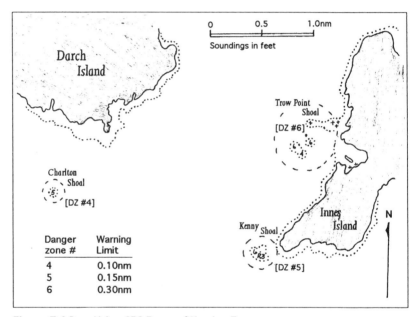

Figure 7.16   Using GPS Danger/Warning Zones

note the size (radius) of the waypoint realization limit that has been programmed into the receiver. In the last example, this limit is 0.1 nm. The trick is to not turn when the receiver tells you but <u>keep on the same heading</u> until 0.1 nm has been covered by noting the read-out on the GPS log (or the ship's log). Another way is to closely watch the changing GPS position Lat/Lon coordinates while staying on the same heading used to reach the outer limits of the first waypoint. When the GPS position read-out (Lat/Lon) is the <u>same as the waypoint position coordinates</u> (Lat/Lon) that were put into the receiver, it is time to turn and start

184

heading for the next waypoint. These techniques, of course, assume that the GPS position read-out is geodetically accurate. The worst case scenario is accuracy within 100 meters (300 feet) due to SA, which is still better than being 900 feet off (approximately 600 feet for 0.1 nm limit + 300 feet accuracy) if the turn were initiated when the waypoint was realized at its outer extremities.

Avoiding Danger Zones

There are a number of ways in which GPS can be used to help you stay away from certain areas or to warn you when getting too close to a specific zone. This function is particularly useful when there are unmarked shoals, sunken wrecks, or other obstructions near the area to be navigated.

Some GPS receivers provide the option of inputting the Lat/Lon of a danger zone as a special kind of a waypoint. The warning area is then defined as a circle around the waypoint with the radius of the circle determined by user input, similar to waypoint realization limit input. If the vessel penetrates this circle, an alarm will sound. For example, supposed you are under sail tacking back and forth in an area between two islands where there are a number of unmarked rocks and shoals.

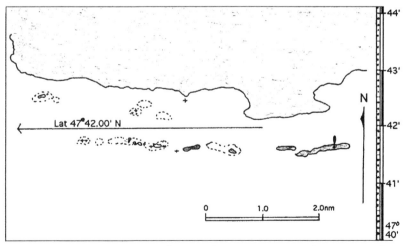

Figure 7.17 *Establishing a Safety LOP by Running a Latitude or Longitude LOP*

Entering these trouble spots as danger zones with realization limits pro

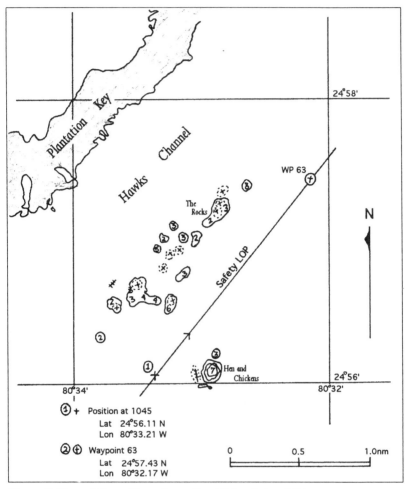

Figure 7.18 *Using a Waypoint to Establish a Safety LOP*

portional to their size can not only ease your mind as the danger zones are approached, but also prevent the boat from coming too close to these areas of concern. (See Figure 7.16.)

If your receiver does not have the warning zone option, there are atleast a couple of ways to accomplish the same task. One is to establish a safety line of position (LOP) by running a specific latitude or longitude. For example, suppose you are leaving an area in which there are visible rocks to port and underwater shoals to starboard restricting the amount of safe navigable water. By looking at a chart, you can see that as long as the course is kept south of a particular latitude, in this case,

186

47° 42.13'N, the shoal water can be avoided. By steering a course that produces a continuous latitude reading of 47° 42.00'N, you can keep well to the south of the shoals. (See Figure 7.17.)

More often than not, the danger zone does not line up nicely with a straight latitude or longitude course. By establishing a waypoint at the extremities of the zone and using cross-track error, you can avoid the zone. This technique is especially useful in areas where there may not be any identifiable landmarks or landforms from which to get bearings.

A good example of this technique could be used in the Florida Keys while motoring in Hawks Channel off Plantation Key where there is a particularly foul area known as The Rocks. Suppose your position is confirmed by GPS as being abeam of the area known as the Hen and Chickens at 1045. To assure that you won't come too close to The Rocks, you can enter a waypoint at a spot well clear of the bad water that will provide a safety LOP to travel from your present position. (See Figure 7.18.)

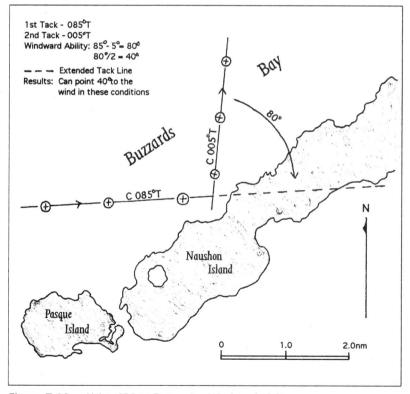

Figure 7.19   Using GPS to Determine Windward Ability

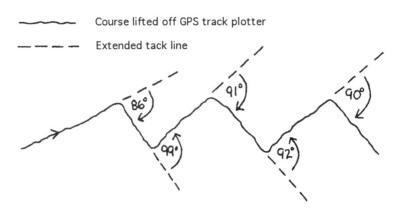

Figure 7.20   Using a Track Plotter to Determine Windward Ability

IV. Sailing Applications

Determining Windward Ability

GPS has numerous special applications for those on sailboats. One is in determining how close to the wind a boat can point, or its windward ability. One common way to determine how close a boat can point is to measure compass headings on two different tacks, subtract them, and divide by two. But since this may necessitate compensation for magnetic deviation on different points of sail and fluctuations due to wind gusts, wave action, etc., it may be difficult to accurately determine windward ability.

A more accurate way is to take a number of GPS position readings on each tack and plot them on a chart. The actual course made good on each tack can be determined with a protractor, and then one heading can be subtracted from the other and divided by two. (See Figure 7.19.) An even easier way to do this without actually determining the heading for each tack is to extend the course from the first tack so that the angle between the two can be measured on the chart and then divide by two. (See again Figure 7.19.)

Many GPS receivers have a couple of features that can be applied to these techniques. One of these is the ability to record "present position" by simply pressing a button. Some receivers have the ability to store up

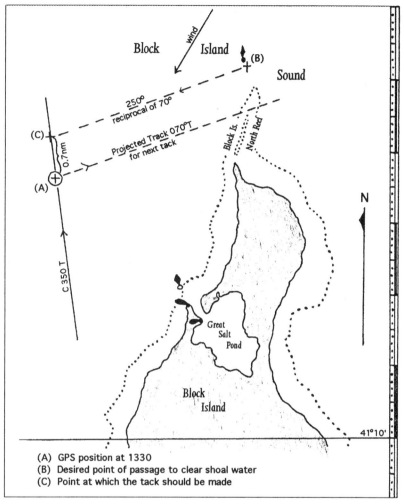

Figure 7.21 *Using GPS to Determine when to Change Tacks*

to 20 of these special waypoints. Thus, a number of GPS positions can be recorded on each tack and stored in the receiver's memory for retrieval at a later time. This function is particularly helpful when you are short-handed or in rough conditions. Vessel track and subsequent tacks can then be plotted in the quiet of an anchorage.

Another receiver function that is quite useful in recording tack angles is a track plotter. By calling up the track plotter memory, the boat's track, which displays each tack, is presented on the screen, and the angles between tacks can then be measured. Since it is rather diffi-

189

cult to measure these angles directly on the screen, one useful trick is to place a piece of clear cellophane tape, which can be written on, over the track. It is then very easy to trace the track directly on the tape, remove the tape and put it on paper so that the tacks can be extended and the angles measured. (See Figure 7.20.)

By measuring tack angles for each tack, it is possible to note wind shifts, as the angles between the tacks will vary proportionately. It is also interesting to measure tack angles for different wind strengths, as it is often possible to sail closer to the wind with increased wind as opposed to sailing in lighter airs. This technique can also be used to determine whether boat performance is better on one tack than another. For example, with a double headstay system in which two headstays are installed side by side, it may actually be possible to point closer to the wind on one tack than on another. By plotting GPS positions on a series of tacks, important information on boat performance can be collected and used for future navigation.

Using GPS to Determine When to Tack

Another useful GPS application for sailors is in determining when to change tacks or come about. Once the tack angle is known, this function can be applied in different situations in deciding when to tack to lay a particular course or make good a specific destination.

For example, suppose you are tacking against a NNE wind in Block Island Sound with the intent of going around the north end of Block Island. You are on a starboard tack with a course heading of 350° and you want to know when you should tack to clear the shoal water off the north end of Block Island. At 1330, you plot your GPS position on the chart. Previous windward performance has shown that you can point 40° to the wind so you double that and subtract from your present course to project a new course of 70° on the next tack (350° - 80° = 70°). Extending a lay line of 70° from your GPS position shows that you won't clear the shoal water off the reef and must still continue on the present tack. (See Figure 7.21.)

In this case, you can even use GPS to determine how much farther you have to go on your present course before coming about to clear the shoal water. One way is to pick a point on the chart that lies in deep water between the shoal and the bell buoy off the north end of Block Island. From this point, extend the reciprocal of 70°, which is 250°, and where this intersects with your present course is where you must be before coming about. By using a pair of dividers, you can determine this distance quickly at the side of the chart on the latitude scale. In this case, you would have to continue another 0.7 nm before coming about on the port tack. Noting the GPS distance log and adding 0.7 miles to it will tell you when it is time to come about for the next tack. Another way would be to confirm your position with another GPS fix before tacking. Extending your 70° tack line from the new position would tell whether you can clear the shoal or not.

There is even an easier way in using GPS to determine when to change tack to make a given lay line or clear a point, obstruction, etc. Enter in your destination that you want to make good on the next tack as a waypoint, leaving the receiver to do the calculations in place of your doing the chart work. The GPS present course heading is then noted, and your doubled angle of windward ability is added or subtract

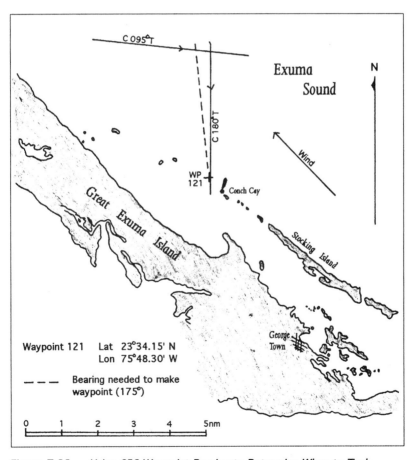

Figure 7.22   Using GPS Waypoint Bearing to Determine When to Tack

ed, as the case may be, to determine your expected track on the next tack. When this expected track is the <u>same as the bearing</u> to the waypoint, it is time to tack. A common practice with this technique is to give yourself a little advantage by adding a little more to windward angle as it is easier to ease off on the next tack than it is to make yet another tack to your destination.

To illustrate this concept, suppose you are tacking against a southeasterly wind down Exuma Sound in the Bahamas with the intent of going into George Town on Great Exuma Island. Your present course is 95o T and you want to make sure you will make Western Channel, which lies NW of Conch Cay, on the next tack. You enter a GPS waypoint for your intended point of entry to the channel and begin watching its bearing to your changing position, which will likewise change as you continue on the present tack (e.g., the bearing may be 152°, 159°, 167°, etc.). You know from previous experience that your windward ability is 40°, so you double that and add it to your present course to determine your course on the next tack. In this case, it would be 175°, or $95^o + 80^o$. When the bearing to your GPS waypoint is 175°, it is time to come about for the next tack. Just to be on the safe side, you decide to give yourself a little leeway and continue on until the waypoint bearing is 180° as you can always ease off the closer you come to the waypoint. (See Figure 7.22.) The beauty of this particular technique is that it can all be done in your head with a minimum of chart work. The reason that either of these techniques for tacking can be used with such confidence is because of the inherent accuracy of the GPS fix.

V. Other Applications

Using GPS With Dead Reckoning

One of the problems with electronic navigation is the tendency for heavy reliance on the particular system in use while disregarding other navigational techniques. Dead reckoning still remains one of the best tools in navigating, if for no other purpose, as a component in a method of checks and balances on your navigation.

When dead reckoning is used simultaneously but independently with GPS, it is possible to gain confidence and hone your technique for future navigation. Often the use of dead reckoning along with GPS is the first clue that set and drift from currents is occurring. Finally, for those few times when intermittent GPS satellite coverage is experienced due to poor satellite geometry or signal/noise ratio in transmitted satellite signals, dead reckoning provides the option of continued navigation.

Using GPS with Other Nav-Aids

Another result of the advances in electronic navigation in recent decades is that use of the **sextant** to solve navigation problems has seen considerable decline. Certainly it can be understood that the advantages of using a fix from Loran-C, Sat Nav, or GPS outweigh a sextant fix in both accuracy and the time it takes to determine a fix. Yet, the sextant remains an important tool in the navigational arsenal, especially for those who sail the high seas.

In learning to use a sextant, it is common practice to take sights at a known position so that you can check on the accuracy of your fix. GPS allows you to work on sextant navigation anywhere by providing an accurate fix for comparison. By using GPS as check on the accuracy of a sextant fix, you can not only improve those skills used in determining a fix with this important navigational tool, but also gain confidence in using this nav-aid for future navigation.

At this point, some may wonder why you would even need to have a sextant on board when you have GPS. Yet, there may be times when the sextant is the only navigational tool present. For example, if you have engine failure, you couldn't charge batteries to run the vessel's electronics, or if the boat were struck by lightning, all navigation instruments would be taken out.

For many years to come, **Loran-C** is going to remain an important nav-aid, particularly for the recreational boater in coastal U.S. waters. It was with Loran-C that many got their radionavigation feet wet, and it is doubtful that users will get rid of their loran receivers just because they have GPS. With the prices of both loran and GPS receivers plummeting, it is not uncommon to have both systems on board. Still the question might be asked, why use loran when you have GPS?

A common practice again is to use both nav-aids independently as a check of one against the other. It is also possible to use one nav-aid to correct the signals of the other or when accuracy of one system is affected by certain factors.

For example, consider using loran in an area that has large signal propagation errors due to Additional Secondary Factor (ASF). GPS position can be manually entered into the loran receiver, which will then determine the amount of correction necessary and use it for correcting future Lat/Lon calculations from the loran signals that still contain the error. There are also times when loran navigation suffers from cycle slip, again producing errors of considerable magnitude. Converting GPS position to its respective loran TDs with the loran receiver calculator functions allows the degree of cycle slip to be identified and corrected for continued loran navigation.

On the other side of the coin, Loran-C can be used for continued navigation for those times when GPS coverage is reduced by poor satellite geometry or satellite signal strength. Loran navigation also has a distinct advantage over GPS in that heading and bearing readings are constant as opposed to those determined with GPS, which suffer from erratic fluctuations due to Selective Availability. In fact, by comparing GPS read-outs with the same loran function, it is possible to get a reasonably good idea of the degree of present error due to SA. Another way of using the two systems simultaneously is to have one receiver that expresses read-outs with magnetic variation included, the other in only true readings. Even with the promise and potential of GPS, Loran-C will remain an important part of the radionavigational mix, and by using both systems, it is possible to use one to enhance the other's performance.

Probably the nav-aid that holds the most promise in conjunction with GPS is the marine **radiobeacon**. For decades, radiobeacons have served a primary function in coastal U.S. waters for position fixing and as homing devices. With the decision to use their signal broadcast as the data link for transmitting corrections for Differential GPS, radiobeacons have gained new importance in solving navigational problems. By providing the accuracy standards necessary for navigating in harbors and waterways, radiobeacons have become an integral part of the GPS system.

CHAPTER EIGHT

GPS Applications and Uses

GPS has the promise and potential of revolutionizing the worlds of navigation and position fixing. Even before the system was fully operational, users from all sectors were quickly adapting GPS to innovative applications. Manufacturers have been quick to recognize the potential of diverse system applications and have invested millions in product development to meet the specialized demands of an ever-growing user community. Modest projections are that the civil user community will well exceed 1 million by the year 2000. Retail sails of GPS receivers and associated equipment are expected to exceed $5 billion by 1996.

Although the system was designed primarily as a military utility, it is expected that worldwide civil use will dwarf all military applications. Initially, the primary emphasis of GPS has been on traditional applications in the marine environment. However, static land applications, particularly in the world of surveying, are also developing very rapidly. Other areas that hold much promise for the use of GPS are in the automotive industry for vehicle tracking and monitoring. As GPS is brought down to earth and more divergent uses are added to the list, it becomes apparent that the uses for precise position fixing, velocity, and timing are expanding into a number of different fields, often with novel and innovative applications.

It is beyond the scope of this book to explore all of the inherent uses and applications possible in utilizing GPS technology. Thus, the following examples are but brief glimpses that illustrate the potentials of GPS use as users strive to exploit system capabilities. Civil applications of GPS can be roughly divided into five major areas: marine, land, aviation, space, and time.

I. Marine Applications

Historically, the marine community has been the largest user of radionavigation systems, and this is likely to continue well into the twenty-first century for GPS. Within this user group, there are four distinct areas in which radionavigation systems are used, each with their own specific requirements and applications. These are:

1. Harbor/harbor approaches.
2. Inland waterways.
3. Coastal navigation.
4. On the high seas with open ocean navigation.

The requirements for **harbor/harbor approaches** and navigation in **inland waterways** are quite similar as both involve navigating in constricted, well-traveled areas, which are often congested with waterway traffic. Because of the need for frequent maneuvering and the greater possibility of collision or grounding, accuracy requirements are most stringent and the need for Differential GPS (DGPS) is greatest in these areas.

Coastal navigation takes place in those areas that are within 50 nm of the coastline or the limit of the continental shelf (200 meters), whichever is greater. Although traffic is reduced in these areas, there is still concern for collision, particularly where traffic patterns parallel the coastline or there is incoming/outgoing commercial shipping into harbors. **Ocean navigation** occurs in those areas beyond the continental shelf where a vessel is more than 50 nm from land. Although the danger of grounding or collision is considerably reduced in these areas, depending on the application, there is often still the need for highly accurate position fixing.

Within in these broad categories of GPS use in the marine environment, there is a great diversity in user applications. These may range from simply finding the entrance to a harbor or an anchorage to dredging operations in waterways, buoy positioning, charting ocean currents, oil and mineral exploration, or charting underwater volcanoes. Present marine applications are but a prelude to full-system capabilities, and it is predicted that more sophisticated uses will be developed as users adapt GPS to individual requirements. (See Figure 8.1.)

Recreational/Small Craft

One of the largest segments in the marine user community is comprised of those with recreational or small craft (under 100 feet). They may include sports fishermen, racing/cruising sailors, powerboaters, live-aboards, and basically anyone who takes to the water in any kind

Recreational Craft	Buoy Positioning/Monitoring
Commercial Boating/Shipping	Dredging/Hydrographic Survey
commercial fishing	Marine Surveying
small merchant vessels	Oceanography
tugs and barges	ocean floor mapping
oil tankers	underwater volcanoes
cargo/container ships	measuring ocean currents
Traffic Management	deep sea mining
Coast Guard/Marine Policing	Oil/gas exploration/production

Figure 8.1   Marine Applications for GPS

of recreational craft. Although most recreational boating occurs within coastal areas, inland waterways, and harbor approaches, sufficient numbers of those in small noncommercial boats now also traverse the open oceans.

Within this user group, use of GPS involves primarily basic position fixing and enroute navigation. For example, bass fishermen have been quick to catch on to the advantages of being able to accurately return to a productive "hole" on an inland lake, whether when competing in a tournament or guiding a fishing charter. In coastal offshore waters, searching for large game fish often 12 to 30 miles offshore, GPS is an invaluable tool where there are no nearby distinguishing landmarks. Whether in the coastal waters off Australia, Hawaii, the Caribbean, or the African Ivory Coast, GPS can be used to enter waypoints every time a billfish is raised or a bait school needs to be relocated after drifting off while fighting or bringing in a prize fish.

Cruising sailors and powerboaters alike are discovering the advantages of pinpoint navigation whether skirting a reef, finding the entrance to an anchorage before nightfall, or returning to a favorite diving spot. Racing sailors use GPS to determine the shortest distance between two points, and those with power cruisers use it to save time and fuel. (For additional applications in the marine environment, see Chapter 7 on Navigating with GPS.)

Commercial Boating/Shipping

Within the commercial sector, using GPS means saving time and money. It is also important in enhancing navigation safety by preventing collisions and groundings. GPS provides the ability to return to productive areas and, at the same time, avoid hazards to navigation.

Commercial fishermen use GPS position fixing in setting and retrieving fishnets, crab pots, or lobster pots. The reverse sequencing of waypoints in a string is very helpful in returning to previous locations. There is a problem, however, with accuracy, and for many, 100-meter accuracy with SA degraded GPS is not good enough, especially when trying to retrieve lobster pots in dense New England fog. As DGPS comes on line, it is expected that more fishermen will be turning to GPS in lieu of more traditional forms of radionavigation such as DECCA and Loran-C in which repeatable accuracy is a decided advantage over GPS.

In addition to regular navigation, offshore fishing fleets use GPS for returning to specific locations. Once a good area is found, GPS has the advantage of interfleet position reporting so that other vessels in the area may quickly close on a shoal for a productive harvest.

Small merchant vessels use GPS to supplement position fixing and navigation with other radionavigation aids basically in coastal waters and in harbor approaches. Tugs and barges, which operate primarily in congested harbors and the constricted areas of waterways, often present their operators with unique maneuvering requirements as they are often larger than many seagoing ships. Those in large seagoing ships use GPS enroute, in harbor/harbor approaches, and sometimes in waterways such as the St. Lawrence Seaway.

In all of these uses, there is concern for GPS accuracy when transiting congested areas where there are hazards of maneuvering in tight quarters to avoid collision or grounding. Within the coastal areas of the continental United States, the accuracy requirements for these uses of GPS are being met by DGPS as implemented through the marine radiobeacon system. One of the earliest examples of this application was initiated in the early 1990's with the transmission of differential GPS signals from the beacon at Whitefish Point at the eastern end of Lake Superior. This beacon serves one of the most congested waterways used for commercial shipping in the world, the St. Marys River, which connects Lakes Superior and Huron.

Outside of the United States, other countries are implementing DGPS to assist with commercial shipping, fishing vessels, and other craft. By the early 1990's, most Scandinavian countries, Iceland, Greenland, Germany, and parts of the United Kingdom had coastal differential systems in place.

Before leaving the area of commercial shipping, it is important to note the special concerns connected with the large super oil tankers and

cargo/container ships that roam the oceans and enter coastal waters. The trend toward increased size to minimize costs has produced vessels that are relatively less powerful and maneuverable than their predecessors. We need only to be reminded of the tragic consequences of the grounding of the *Exxon Valdez* on 29 March 1989, in Prince William Sound in Alaska, to emphasize the importance of precise position fixing in commercial navigation. After rupturing its hull on underwater rocks, the tanker dispersed 11 million gallons of crude oil into the sound, devastating the region's ecology and wildlife for months to come. Using GPS, particularly in the differential mode, can prevent disasters such as this from occurring. In light of this prevention, different subcommittees are preparing legislation for Congress that would make GPS mandatory on ships and oil tankers navigating in U.S. waters that carry hazardous materials or weigh more than 10,000 gross tons. Another incentive for using GPS on large commercial vessels is that it can providing the most efficient Great Circle route, not only reducing transit time, but also providing savings in terms of fuel consumption. It has been estimated that GPS could potentially save $17,000 in a Trans Atlantic passage for a large tanker.

Traffic Management

As commercial shipping increases, there are many areas in the world where waterway management, much like the airspace management practiced in airways and in airport approaches, is a viable application of GPS technology. Not only is there the issue of safety, but there is also an economic penalty if waterways and port facilities are not used efficiently. GPS can be used to expedite port transits, improve harbor throughput, and at the same time enhance navigation safety by reducing the probability of groundings and collisions.

To illustrate this application, we look again to Prince William Sound. In September 1992, the Coast Guard required all tankers licensed to carry crude oil from the Trans-Alaska Pipeline to install a differential GPS receiver and certain specified communications equipment. This equipment is used to determine the tanker's position with an accuracy of 10 meters or less, then broadcast that position along with a unique identification code to a vessel traffic center (VTC) in Valdez, the terminus for the Trans-Alaska Pipeline. Once the information is received at the VTC, it will be integrated onto an electronic chart display where each vessel's progress will be tracked by Coast Guard personnel throughout its transit.

This technology, called **dependent surveillance**, may eventually be employed in other areas where **Vessel Traffic Services** (VTS) now operate. At present, most of the world's VTSs rely on radar for surveillance of the waterway. Dependent surveillance using DGPS can be used to complement other technologies such as electronic charts, radar, and the more traditional means of tracking vessels to enhance navigation safety in the world's busiest ports and waterways.

Similar applications of the technology have already been in use in different waterway and canal systems of the world. For example, traffic in the Suez Canal has been monitored for a number of years via Loran-C with vessel positions being transmitted back to a central control center. It is expected that GPS will have similar applications in other canal or waterway systems such as the Panama Canal and the St. Lawrence Seaway. When used in the differential mode, GPS can provide highly accurate position information for monitoring vessel traffic in these constricted areas.

Coast Guard/Marine Policing

There are a number of areas in which the Coast Guard and law enforcement authorities may use GPS. These may fall into a number of different categories such as monitoring pollution, enforcing customs and excise regulations, protecting fisheries, enforcing offshore security for oil installations, and controlling drug traffic. Precise positioning capability is invaluable in vessel identification and surveillance, and when necessary, vessel interception. *See Chapter 8 photo #1 for an example of a Coast Guard vessel using GPS.*

One of the most important areas in which these agencies become involved is **search and rescue**. In coordinating a search, GPS becomes an important tool in establishing a structured grid pattern and in collision avoidance. In rescue operations, initial positioning with GPS is critical to identify the scene or general locality of the incident. For example, precise positioning information can be transmitted prior to abandoning a ship or ditching an aircraft. Continued monitoring of a position once it is identified is also important. For example, a search helicopter may find and identify a distressed vessel, record the position, and continue to monitor the position until help arrives. GPS position can then be transmitted to and entered into rendezvous vessel receivers as a waypoint to home in on.

Buoy Positioning and Monitoring

In areas covered by winter ice, floating aids to navigation are pulled and then replaced each spring. This is a laborious task often complicated by finding the exact positions for buoy location. Using DGPS not only speeds up the job of buoy positioning, but also improves accuracy in specific buoy location.

An example of the expeditious feature of buoy positioning using GPS occurred in the wake of Hurricane Bob, which devastated the East Coast in August 1991. The damage to the Coast Guard's floating aids systems was so complete that all the waterways in New England were closed as a result. By adding GPS receivers to Coast Guard buoy tenders and using the differential GPS beacon broadcast site at Montauk Point, New York, the waterways and channels were reopened in just over four days. Using conventional methods for positioning and checking aids, the job would have taken over a month.

DGPS can also be used to monitor floating aids to navigation to make sure they do not drift off position but remain precisely on the mark. Monitoring buoy position can also be used to gather important information. For example, in Germany, buoys on inland waterways have been used to gather important data in a GPS sea level project. By installing GPS antennas on top of free-floating buoys, position data has been used to determine sea surface height and movement. When compared with a nearby tidal gauge, the results have been within a few centimeters.

Dredging and Hydrographic Survey

One of the major programs of the U.S. Army Corps of Engineers is the dredging of waterways, ports, and harbors. This is a multimillion-dollar operation (approximately $400 million/year), which operates under contracts to local/state/national contractors. A key element in dredging is the performance of highly accurate hydrographic surveys, which in the past have positioned vessels (horizontally) using electronically measured ranges and angles from transponder stations at known sites. To establish position, it is necessary for two or more of these stations to have a line of sight to the vessel. One disadvantage with this system is that vertical fluctuations (tides, inland lake levels, river variations, etc.) must be referenced to some type of datum such as averaging daily low tides or mean low water. This technology also requires daily calibration to verify its accuracy, which is usually around 3 meters.

The Corps is actively looking at using DGPS to more accurately determine position in the surveying component of its dredging operations. The system involves three basic segments: the vessel receiver and data processing unit, reference stations, and a communications link. It has the advantage that only one reference station with a range of 20 nm is needed for a given fix. There is the possibility that this range can be increased and the number of stations reduced by networking the reference stations. GPS also has the advantage of providing altitude determinations and thus fluctuations of water levels. The accuracy with this system is expected to be in the order of 10 centimeters.

Marine Surveying Applications

Hydrographic surveying has other applications than those connected with dredging operations. These may include **general charting** and the location of shoals and hazards to navigation in which approximately 5-meter accuracy is needed. Other areas that require accurate position fixing are **coastal and channel engineering, harbor design and maintenance**, and **breakwater construction. Revetment construction**, for achieving bank integrity on inland rivers, is another application of DGPS that has been employed by the U.S. Army Corps of Engineers. An example of this technology is found on the lower Mississippi River where DGPS has been used to provide real-time positioning to assist in revetment construction with a savings of over $150,000 per year.

In **offshore surveying,** most positioning services use radio signals transmitted from onshore stations, offshore platforms, or tightly moored buoys. Transit (Sat Nav) and Loran-C have been useful to check the accuracy of real-time position fixes. However, the irregularity of Sat Nav fixes and the location of these surveys are often out of range of terrestrial systems, making these systems incapable of providing real-time position fixing for modern marine surveys. Terrestrial systems, along with buoys and offshore platforms, have additional problems because signals are transmitted along the earth's surface where they may reflect certain distortions. Another disadvantage is that position must be established from multiple transmitters, which have limited range.

GPS in the differential mode solves these problems in a number of ways. It can provide real-time position fixes that are more accurate than most of the systems in use today. It can also perform position fixing over longer ranges and at lower cost. Finally, the survey vessel needs to be in range of only one station or satellite (e.g., Inmarsat — see Section III. Aviation Applications, Possible Solutions to the Problems), which transmits the corrected differential data.

Oceanography Applications

There are a number of areas in which GPS can be employed in oceanography. A few of these are described to illustrate the extent to which GPS can be utilized in improving traditional technology or in exploring new innovations. One of the most important is in using GPS for **mapping the ocean floor**. This data can then be incorporated in navigational charts for future navigation.

Traditionally, bottom contour data has been tabulated by corresponding single beam transponder (echo sounder) data with land-based radio position-fixing coordinates. One disadvantage with this method is that the bottom measurements cover only a small portion of the area that lies along the ship's track. Another is that land-based positioning systems require at least three to four stations as well as significant support personnel.

One of the most aggressive programs in charting the ocean floor has

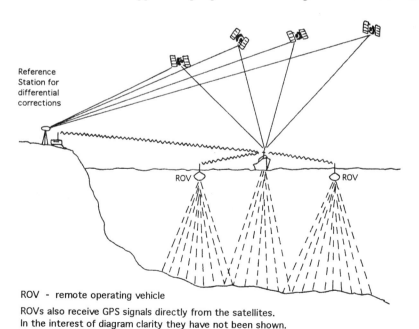

ROV - remote operating vehicle
ROVs also receive GPS signals directly from the satellites.
In the interest of diagram clarity they have not been shown.

Figure 8.2   Using GPS to Map the Ocean Floor

been undertaken by the Canadian government. Employing multibeam acoustic sounding systems, which perpetuate large fan-shaped beams, in several remotely operated vehicles (ROVs), large swaths of the ocean floor can be simultaneously mapped. ROVs are semisubmersible; they travel a few meters beneath the surface unaffected by waves. There are two different ways in which GPS is used with this system. One is to make sure that the mother ship and ROVs follow the intended track (linekeeping). The mother ship and ROVs are also equipped with a GPS receiver and radio antenna, for differential corrections, to reference the sounding data to GPS coordinates as it is collected. This data is then stored in the ship's computer as a data base for a number of different applications. (See Figure 8.2.)

In addition to providing data for hydrographic charts, one of the main applications of GPS is providing data for oil tanker routes. The data can also be used for different types of coastal and offshore engineering projects such as laying pipelines or underwater cables or positioning platforms. Vessel salvage, wildlife management, fishery habitats and exploration for oil and minerals are other areas in which a data base of this nature may provide useful information.

Another example of using GPS is in **the search for underwater volcanoes.** In November 1991, the research vessel, *New Horizon,* boat name conducted a month-long study in the Pacific Ocean south of Mexico along the section of the sea floor known as the East Pacific Rise. GPS was used in a number of ways, one of which was to maintain constant vessel speed despite wind and current fluctuations while towing an underwater sensor/water-sampling package. In addition, position vs. time data was used to construct two-dimensional maps, which integrated data from the sensors that showed the location, intensity, and composition from sea floor hydrothermal vents.

Additional oceanography applications include those technologies associated with **measuring ocean currents, geophysics,** and **marine geology.** In the area of **deep sea mining** for various minerals, GPS is expected to assist in the development of accurate maps of the ocean floor and the precise positioning of drilling platforms.

Oil/Gas Exploration and Production

The industries associated with the exploration and production of fossil fuels make up one of the largest commercial groups that benefit from the precise position-fixing qualities of GPS. Whether it is in exploration, drilling, establishing platform sites, or piloting mammoth tankers, the oil industry spends millions each year on radionavigation systems in some form or other.

As onshore energy supplies are depleted, exploration for fossil fuels and exploitation of deposits tend to branch out farther into the depths of the oceans, intensifying the need for self-location. In order to pinpoint promising oil-bearing geological formations from reflected seismic pulses, it is necessary to correlate these pulses with exact positioning coordinates. Other aspects of exploration and development involve hydrographic surveying, site reconnaissance, well site surveying, rig positioning, and pipeline surveying and inspection.

Accuracy requirements may vary from 10–30 meters for initial site investigations to less than 5 meters for exploration and pipeline surveillance. At all levels of use, 100-meter GPS accuracy in the degraded mode is insufficient. Consequently, the oil industry has been a leader in developing various levels of the differential mode of GPS operation, particularly in the field of exploration. In the private sector, a number of DGPS services have been developed to meet the needs of precise precision fixing for specialized consumers.

GPS and Electronic Charts

A key element in many of the foregoing applications of GPS is the ability to display positioning and navigation data on electronic charts. In fact, the use of electronic charts is in itself yet another application of GPS technology.

Integration of electronic charts with radionavigation systems is not a new concept. For many years, it has been possible to integrate radar, loran, Sat Nav, and now GPS data on electronic chart screen displays. The technology is called Electronic Chart Display and Information Systems (ECDIS).

ECDIS basically involves digitizing each detail from a paper chart, bit by bit, storing it as a data base, and then projecting it on a CRT display. Two different techniques are used. The **raster-scan method** uses electronic scanning methods to scan a paper chart and store every bit of information, producing a very close replica of the chart. The **vector method** defines each point on the display as a point on the end of a vector. These charts are not as exact but provide more flexibility of use. In addition to shorelines and depths, other details such as buoys, beacons, channel boundaries, underwater wrecks, tide depths, and even symbols for protected areas may be presented. The technique has many of the advantages of computer technology as these details are stored in separate files so they can readily be added to or removed from the display. Scale can easily be changed by zooming into or out of a particular location. Depending on the manufacturer, the display may be enhanced with different color overlays, which can present different types of information such as depths at high/low tides, bottom morphology, specific hazards, etc.

When GPS data is entered on an ECDIS, vessel position is displayed relative to surrounding landmasses and objects such as buoys, hazards, etc. Vessel movement can be viewed in real time. There are a number of advantages to using GPS information with ECDIS. One is that if you are moving at high speeds, positioning a vessel on a paper chart may be too time consuming. Or if your course is constantly changing, as in a tight waterway, there are decided advantages to constant position fixing on an electronic display. Waypoints may be selected by simply moving a cursor, which will then produce range and bearing read-outs. On some displays, previous track is recorded so that effects of currents vs. speed and heading can be determined. *See Chapter 8 photo #2 for an example of a ECDIS unit.*

One of the more interesting applications of the technology is to overlay an electronic chart with a radar picture. This produces a direct correlation between the digitized chart and the radar image, which is a good check on the accuracy of GPS positioning. If the GPS position is accurate, the two will "click" into place as radar images of shorelines, buoys, etc. fall directly on top of the same representations on the electronic chart. If GPS position is off, there will be a discrepancy between the two. Manual adjustments can be made to correct any errors and bring the two displays into alignment. When DGPS is used, corrections should not be necessary as there should be very close alignment between the electronic chart and the radar overlay.

When GPS positioning/tracking on electronic charts is integrated with other vessel sensor inputs from autopilots, depth sounders, and fuel use, engine rpm and wind instruments, the applications of the new technology are even more widespread. Use of electronic charts also has applications in other areas, and prototype aeronautical charts are in the process of being digitized. One of the most recent adaptations of this new technology, which is moving ahead rapidly, is the use of digitized charts with GPS positioning in land applications.

In addition to using GPS on the application side of integrating GPS data with an electronic chart display, GPS is also becoming instrumental in producing accurate, up-to-date charts. One problem in using any chart, paper or electronic, is that some of the hydrographic surveys used to construct the chart date back to the 1800's when positioning was established by taking bearings and sextant sights while soundings were determined with leadlines. Unfortunately, when used with precise electronic navigation systems, these charts often fall uncomfortably short of contemporary accuracy requirements.

In its program to resurvey and update charts, the National Oceanic and Atmospheric Administration (NOAA) is using differential GPS positioning coordinates whenever possible. For the formidable task of digitizing all its marine charts for ECDIS, NOAA estimates it should take approximately 5 years. Another problem in applying GPS to either electronic or paper charts is in correlating the chart datum between the two. GPS coordinates use World Geodetic Survey 1984 (WGS84), which for all practical purposes is equitable to North American Datum 1983 (NAD83) chart datum. Older charts are based on NAD27. NOAA is also in the process of converting all its 1,000-plus charts to NAD83.

Projections are that ECDIS will first be used as a supplemental aid to navigation rather than as a replacement of the paper chart. It is expected that ECDIS will achieve legal status in the mid-1990's when the United Nations International Maritime Organization (IMO) publishes performance standards for ECDIS. The Radio Technical Commission for Maritime Services (RTCM) also determines operating standards for using GPS in position fixing with ECDIS, both in the maritime and aviation communities. When combined with the accuracy of DGPS, it is anticipated that ECDIS will become an accepted norm of the twenty-first century.

II. Land Applications

When compared with marine use of radiolocation systems, land applications are a relatively new sector in the expanding world of GPS. Yet, in many respects, this user group could possibly prove to have the largest market potential in GPS applications. For example, it has been estimated that more than 75% of the $4.9 billion in DGPS equipment sales projected through the year 2000 will come from land vehicle use. Although the uses in this group are as diverse as in any other, they fall into two basic categories: vehicular positioning/navigation and surveying.

Vehicular Positioning/Navigation

Land navigation received its impetus when earlier terrestrial systems such as Loran-C were linked to electronic digital displays for position read-outs and navigation information. A number of problems, such as the need to initialize the system at a starting location and the need for dead reckoning during periods of signal loss, prevented these systems from ever developing to their full potential. The ability of GPS to provide absolute position coordinates every second, combined with new advances in digitizing and storing information, have virtually put this new technology back on the map.

The technique of vehicular positioning and navigation goes by a number of different names. Sometimes it is called Automatic Vehicle Location and Navigation (AVLN). In North America, it may also be referred to as Intelligent Vehicle Highway Systems (IVHS), while in Europe, it is known as Road Transport Informatics (RTI). Within these designations, applications can be further broken down into two broad categories of operation. Automatic Vehicle Location (AVL) simply involves showing the vehicle's precise position on a display screen. Automatic Vehicle Monitoring (AVM) uses some form of communications link back to a central dispatch unit for vehicle/fleet monitoring of position and movement. These modes of operation can be further enhanced by providing route information for navigation and guidance.

In addition to GPS input, there are number of key elements in the technology. One is the ability to call up a digitized electronic road map on a display screen in which the vehicle's position is plotted relative to the destination. In many cases, both visual and audio input are employed. The "talker", as it is called, actually tells you what turns to make and when to make them to get to your destination. Additional information displayed on the screen may be local road hazards, construction, or dynamic traffic conditions.

Another element within the technology is the use of a communications link for sending position to a central dispatcher or receiving information for further navigation. This link can take a variety of forms including digital, cellular, UHF/FM radio, paging services, or satellite. An example of a system using a satellite communications link is with Inmarsat's Standard-C data communications system, which has been used to transmit GPS position fixes for delivery trucks and railcars in Europe. By the mid-1990's, this service will be available worldwide with the launching of Inmarsat's third-generation satellites, which will include GPS navigation packages. Another interesting method of dispensing information to users in Europe is through the Radio Data System, which sends digitized traffic information "piggyback" on normal FM broadcasts, which is then decoded by a car radio and displayed on the monitor screen. A number of new car radios have been manufactured with this feature so they are ready to be interfaced with RTI systems.

Accuracy requirements for AVLN vary, depending on the application. If vehicle positioning is needed only for fleet monitoring and management on the open road, 100-meter accuracy is adequate. If navigation in tight roadways or precise positioning on specific streets within city blocks is required, accuracy of 5 to 15 meters is considered necessary. Therefore, many systems are looking at implementing differential technology through their own monitor and correcting stations. However, as differential service in the United States comes on line through the use of marine radiobeacons, many land users within range of the coastal beacons will benefit on the "back side" of the system. For example, Florida because it is surrounded by water on three sides will essentially become a "differential state" in which extremely accurate positioning capabilities will be available for all applications.

The applications of vehicular positioning/navigation are incredibly varied, ranging from personal transportation to trucks involved in interstate commerce and vehicles carrying hazardous materials. For example, Japan has been a leader in installing GPS receivers in cars; by the early 1990's, approximately 200,000 cars were implemented with guidance systems. It is projected that by the mid-1990's, three million Japanese cars will be equipped with GPS receivers. A key element in the progress of this technology has been the ability to digitize all of Japan, a relatively small country, onto electronic charts.

Within the United States, a number of automotive concerns have been incorporating their own vehicular navigation systems, some of which use GPS input. In support of this growing technology, in the early 1990's, Congress passed the Intermodal Surface Transportation Act, which appropriated $660 million for IVHS programs for a period of five years. If the potential of this system is fully developed, it is projected that automobile use of GPS will become a multibillion dollar industry that will outweigh all other uses combined.

Emergency Dispatch Services in Sacramento, CA	25 vehicles
Minuteman Delivery in Los Angeles, CA	35 vehicles
Fire Department, San Diego, CA	113 vehicles
Police Department, Schaumburg, IL (Chicago suburb)	40 cars
Expressit Courier, San Francisco, CA	70 vehicles
Regional Medical System in Alameda and Contra Coasta counties, CA	100 ambulances
Dallas Emergency Medical Service, Dallas, TX	40 vehicles
Emergency Medical Service Authority, Tulsa, OK	70 ambulances
Proposed Fleet Management System for emergency fire, medical and police vehicles, Chicago, IL	over 3,500 vehicles

Taken from *GPS World*, February 1993, pg.16.

Figure 8.3   *Examples of GPS Use in Vehicle Monitoring and Dispatching*

GPS also holds a lot of promise for systems that dispatch and monitor fleets of vehicles. These may involve bus, taxi and truck fleets; armored car companies; fire and police forces; emergency care units; and even trains. (See Figure 8.3.) Some advantages in fleet monitoring are minimal routing, reduction of fuel costs, and schedule improvement. In the **trucking industry**, a number of mobile satellite companies now integrate GPS data with their services. One example is the American Mobile Satellite Corporation which leases spare Inmarsat channels for dispatching interim mobile data in the United States. Other examples are Telesat Mobile in Canada which provides data service to approximately 1,000 trucks, and TRANSTRACS, an electronic vehicle-monitoring system that operates in Australia. Qualcomm, a very large San Diego-based service, plans to use GPS in its foreign markets in Mexico, Brazil, and Japan. By monitoring truck progress in the field, dispatchers can trace cargo movements, predict delivery times, and determine when it is advantageous to pick up additional cargo enroute.

In tracking buses in **city transit systems**, integration with GPS improves fleet management, route guidance, and even customer information. An example of this type of system is the Denver Regional Transit District, which has equipped its buses and supervisory vehicles with Trimble six-channel receivers. Continuous location information about the fleet is received at an operations center where it is displayed on a video screen that shows bus routes. The information is also displayed at bus stops and other intermodal transportation sites for passenger use in determining bus location and time of arrival.

One of the most important applications of AVM is with **emergency care units** where saving transit time translates into saving lives. GPS not only expedites arrival time at a disaster or stress site, but also dispenses location information for site reconnaissance for the evacuation of victims. For example, in the rural areas of southeastern Virginia where there are few distinguishing landmarks, ambulance rescue squads use GPS latitude and longitude coordinates when radioing into a dispatch center to request helicopter evacuation of severely injured trauma patients. Once in flight with the injured victim, the GPS speed over the ground feature is used to determine the time of arrival to the nearest medical facility, which can be radioed ahead. *See Chapter 8 photo #3 for an example of use.*

This technology can even be transferred to search-and-rescue squads traveling on foot with handheld units. For example, GPS has been used in rescue missions in rugged areas of New Mexico and in southern California's mountainous terrain and deserts. Linking the unit to a radio transmits signals back to a computer at a base camp where a team's progress is recorded automatically. Rescue site coordinates can then be radioed to helicopters and other resources for speedy evacuation. *See Chapter 8 photo #4 for an example of a handheld unit.*

Surveying

There are a number of different surveying techniques used by surveyors to determine the coordinates of a point. Some of these include inertial positioning, analytical photogrammetry, electronic distance measurement (EDM), and satellite ranging. Using satellites in surveying is not new; for years, surveyors have used the Transit (Sat Nav) system to determine position. One advantage in using Transit is that its equipment is easy to use and less expensive than that used by some other surveying systems. Disadvantages are lack of speed and, in some instances, Transit doesn't meet certain accuracy requirements. Even before system completion, GPS has proven to be competitive with Transit in terms of availability, speed, and accuracy. It is also competitive with more traditional methods, such as EDM, in that it is faster and less labor intensive. As costs of GPS surveying equipment drop, it is expected that use of GPS will challenge traditional surveying techniques, and the surveying community will become one of the largest GPS user groups. *See Chapter 8 photo #5 for an example of a surveying unit.*

As with any user community, the accuracy requirements of different surveying projects vary. However, because many surveying applications require centimeter accuracy, the surveying community has long been a forerunner in establishing different types of differential techniques. One technique uses standard differential operation in which a receiver stationed at a precisely surveyed location transmits error corrections to another receiver in the position to be surveyed with accuracies of one meter or less.

Another technique, which is one of the most accurate, involves **phase differencing** of the carrier wavelength. By having GPS receivers at two different locations make simultaneous measurements from the same satellites, the overall effect is to eliminate the unpredictable errors from the satellite and ground clocks, which are one of the main sources of error. (See Figure 8.4.) Centimeter precision can be achieved with this technique by measuring the phase angle of the L1 wavelength, which is 19 cm. Ionospheric errors can be removed by making phase measurements on both the L1 and L2 carriers with dual frequency receivers. The advantage of this technique is that you don't have to have P code access, and yet you can achieve the same effect of negating ionospheric errors as though the P code were tracked on both frequencies. Initially, these methods were developed for static applications. However, it is now possible to use these techniques in kinematic (moving) applications, once a benchmark or reference point has been established.

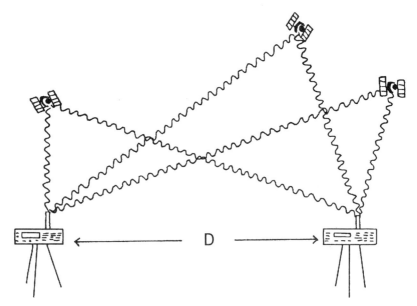

D = Baseline between receivers
   Degree of error is directly proportional to the baseline with shorter baselines having smaller errors.

Figure 8.4 *Using the Technique of Phase Differencing*

212

One variation of carrier phase differencing is to use **interferometric techniques**. In this method, two different antennas are used to sample the GPS signal wavefront at two different locations. The antennas are connected to a single amplifier and mixer (interferometer), and phase difference observations are made. This technique is especially useful in determining attitude parameters on roll stabilized platforms such as ships, aircraft, orbiting space vehicles, and missiles.

One of the biggest advantages in using GPS in surveying is the time element. Projects that used to take months can be completed in half the time, and that translates into cutting costs. GPS is being used in the traditional survey modes such as surveying for land boundaries, highway routes, and construction sites and in various geophysical surveys. It is also being used in some interesting surveying applications around the globe. For example, GPS has been used to develop a high-precision survey network between the southern tip of South America and Antarctica to assist scientists in studying plate tectonics, volcanic activity, and other geodynamics of the Antarctic.

Another example of using GPS is in the continuous monitoring of the crustal deformation of geologic faults. This has been done in California in certain zones of the San Andreas Fault and in Japan in an area that spans three different plate segments. As data is collected, it will contribute to our understanding of the earthquake cycle and possibly assist in more precise predictions of future earthquakes and their locations. Additional examples of some innovative uses of GPS in the world of surveying are found in Figure 8.5.

GPS has been used in the following areas to:

map roads in Pupua, New Guinea
determine the coordinates of radar towers in the North Sea
map the burn area of a forest fire in the Heilongjiang Province of China
map 40,000 square kilometers of the Bangladesh coastal area for development
construct GPS survey networks in Jerusalem and Tel Aviv-Jaffa
topographically map Egypt's Eastern Desert and Nile Valley
update the hydrographic atlas of the lower Mekong River basin in Thailand, Laos, and Vietnam
develop a reconnaissance model for preclassic and classic Mayan archeological sites

Figure 8.5   Examples of Using GPS in Surveying Applications

III. Aviation Applications

213

It is estimated that global air traffic will double by the year 2000 and then double again by the year 2015. It is expected that the resulting demands will far exceed present navigation systems. GPS, as a part of a global navigation system, is looked to as a possible answer to augment and eventually replace existing technologies. However, there are a number of problems in using GPS to meet the requirements of the aviation community. To better understand these problems, it is helpful to take a brief look at the different levels of air navigation.

There are two basic categories of air navigation: enroute and approach/landing. These two can be further divided into subgroups. The **enroute** category consists of five different groups that vary in the amount of air traffic density. They are oceanic enroute (low traffic density); domestic enroute (moderate to high traffic density); terminal, which consists of converging routes and transitions in altitude (moderate to high traffic densities); remote areas (low traffic density); and flight between ground level and 5,000 feet with helicopter and some fixed wing aircraft (increasing traffic density). The **approach/landing** category can be divided into two separate groups: nonprecision approach and precision approach and landing. (See Figure 8.6.) These different levels of air traffic use are mentioned because they have different requirements, which have an impact on the degree and type of GPS used as an aid to air traffic navigation. *See Chapter 8 photos #6,7 for examples of fixed-mount and handheld units.*

System Requirements/Performance Standards

GPS system requirements are different for the high dynamics of the aviation environment as opposed to those for the low dynamics of the marine community or the static dynamics of the surveying user group. Because of this difference, the Federal Aviation Administration (FAA) imposes tough performance standards on any navigation system used. There is also concern on the international level, and the International Civil Aviation Organization (ICAO) is working with the FAA to integrate U.S. systems into a global satellite-based navigation system of which GPS is a major constituent. Basically, the problems with using

I. En Route/Terminal
  a. Oceanic En Route
  b. Domestic En Route
  c. Terminal
  d. Remote Areas
  e. Flight Between Ground Level and 5,000 feet

II. Approach/Landing
  a. Nonprecision approach
  b. Precision approach and landing

Figure 8.6   Different Categories of Air Navigation

GPS in aviation applications fall into three different areas: reliability/availability, accuracy, and integrity.

Reliability/availability. There is concern in the foreign sector about heavy reliance on a U.S. military-controlled system that could be withdrawn or could impose a high user fee. Although the Department of Defense (DOD) has pledged 10 years of free civil service, many would feel more comfortable with a guarantee of a minimum of 15 years of service such as that announced by Glonass. It has also been suggested that the DOD should provide at least a 5-year advance notice of any change in availability of GPS to civil users.

Accuracy. The Standard Positioning Service (SPS) with 100-meter accuracy (2 drms) 95% of the time is sufficient for enroute navigation (both ocean and domestic) and nonprecision flight operations. However, there is concern by users over the possibility that in times of national emergency, this accuracy level could be even further degraded beyond 100 meters. For precision approaches, higher accuracy standards are necessary than those that are available with SPS.

Integrity. One of the biggest problems in using GPS in aviation applications is in solving the integrity issue. Integrity is the ability to detect system failures and present users with timely warnings when specific GPS satellites should not be used for navigation. In the present system, the Master Control Station detects anomalies, which are then uploaded to the satellites to be transmitted in the Navigation Message, a process that may take a couple of hours. Again, because of the high dynamics of aviation use, the integrity requirements are quite severe. Warnings for enroute (ocean or domestic) navigation are less critical, with 30 seconds being acceptable. However, with terminal navigation and different types of approaches, the requirements become more stringent, requiring 10 seconds or less depending on the precision of the approach.

Possible Solutions to the Problems

A number of task force groups have been working to address the issues of integrating GPS use in national and international airspace navigation. On the national level, as part of the FAA Satellite Navigation Program Plan, the FAA has initiated Special Committee 159 of the RTCA, Inc. (used to stand for Radio Technical Commission for Aeronautics, now just called RTCA, Inc.) to draft Minimum Operational Performance Standards (MOPS) for GPS as the sole means of navigation in nonprecision approaches for civil aviation including integrity monitoring. The FAA has delegated the Flight Standards Service, of which the Satellite Operational Implementation Team (SOIT) is a subgroup, to determine operational standards, limitations, and ways of implementing authorization for GPS. The FAA is also working closely with the ICAO Future Air Navigation Systems (FANS) for global integration of systems for air navigation, of which GPS is an integral part.

Short-range plans are for integrating GPS to supplement current onboard inertial navigation systems or other navigational aids presently in use. It is expected that GPS will be approved and in use as a supplemental navigation aid for four categories of flight (oceanic enroute, domestic enroute, terminal use, and nonprecision approaches) by the mid-1990's. Long-range plans call **for a Global Navigation Satellite System (GNSS)**, which has been approved by the ICAO and is under serious study by the FAA/RTCA. This is a satellite-based system of which GPS is the main constituent, possibly supplemented by Glonass. With full constellations of GPS and Glonass satellites supplemented by Inmarsat satellites, it will be possible to track up to 20 in-view satellites at one time. This system is expected to eventually replace many of the present ground-based air traffic systems and become the sole means of navigation for enroute and nonprecision and precision approaches and landings. To meet these goals, a number of different approaches are being considered to augment GPS signals to satisfy requirement standards.

One of the most viable options for improving accuracy is through the use of **DGPS**, particularly if the reference stations transmit the corrections as pseudolites. In addition to transmitting error corrections, a pseudolite also transmits the same signal characteristics as a GPS satellite so that it can be used for ranging, providing another "satellite" for the navigation solution. Another possibility is developing **kinematic carrier-phase tracking**, which would extend the proven accuracy technology used in the static surveying environment to the high dynamics of the airways. Other ways to augment GPS signals are **to use signals from other sources** such as inertial reference systems, Loran-C, or Glonass. To date, there are a number of manufacturers working on combined GPS/Glonass receivers.

To solve the integrity problem, one recommendation by SOIT is the use of "smart receivers." This built-in receiver function allows a receiver to detect satellite failure and is called **receiver autonomous integrity**

monitoring (RAIM). Depending on the unit, it can either warn the user of unreliable data or negate the affected satellite from the navigation solution, which will provide the level of integrity required for many flight phases. One disadvantage with this system is that depending on the number of satellites in view and satellite geometry, it may be effective only 60–80% of the time.

One option that holds more potential is a proposal from **Inmarsat.** Inmarsat is a 65-nation consortium established in the mid-1970's to provide improved maritime public correspondence and radiodetermination capabilities. In 1992, it proposed the use of a built-in receiver, **GPS Integrity Channel** (GIC), in which GPS integrity data is sent from ground monitoring stations to Inmarsat satellites. The updates are then transmitted to GPS receivers on a signal similar to that transmitted by GPS satellites. In addition to an integrity service, Inmarsat also proposed a ranging signal overlay to enhance GPS accuracy. *See Chapter 8 photo #8 for an example of an Inmarsat system.*

There are a number of advantages to this system. One is that the wideband integrity channel will use the same L-band frequencies that are electrically similar to GPS signals (same code family and spread-spectrum modulation) so that only small software changes will have to be made on the receiver end to accept the data. Another is that integrity data will be broadcast every 6 seconds for as many as 50 GPS-type satellites, which will satisfy the stringent requirements of even precision approaches for aircraft.

As with pseudolites, the Inmarsat satellites can also transmit ranging data of their own, which in essence provides additional satellites in the navigation solution. Because Inmarsat satellites are geostationary, there are no "holes" in the system or problems with geometry, so that coverage/availability is good all the time. Accuracy is also improved because these satellite transmissions do not suffer SA degradation. Finally, if differential corrections are provided in addition to integrity and ranging data, accuracy expectations may well be in the 2–5 meter range providing a worldwide "space-based" differential system. The proposal is scheduled for implementation in 1994-95 when Inmarsat will include GPS and Glonass navigation packages in its third-generation satellites. *See Chapter 8 photo #9 for an example of an Inmarsat satellite.*

Despite the problems with accuracy and integrity, GPS has been tested and used in many applications that demonstrate the potential for its use in the aviation sector. For example, in Desert Storm, GPS was an integral part of aircraft navigation and reconnaissance. Both the FAA and the civil aviation community conducted tests in the early 1990's primarily to explore the accuracy capabilities of using GPS. Northwest Airlines and Honeywell conducted tests using GPS without SA degradation in which they found that GPS accuracy approached the accuracy that could be achieved with DGPS, provided ionospheric delay errors were low. Northwest and Honeywell have also worked on the production of a GPS/Glonass prototype receiver.

A primary implementation goal of the RTCA GNSS Task Force is to achieve an initial operational capability for precision approaches under Category I conditions by the mid-1990's. (Category I conditions are 200 ft. decision height with 1/2 mile visibility.) Tests performed to determine the possibility of using DGPS in these conditions found that the lateral accuracy levels achieved were equivalent to those obtained with instrument landing system (ILS). Although additional work is required in vertical guidance and in the standardization of the differential corrections data link, initial tests demonstrate the potential of using GPS in air navigation.

One of the most innovative aviation applications of GPS is found in Sweden. Beginning in the late 1980's, a Swedish research and development program explored a comprehensive solution to the combined problems of air navigation, communications, surveillance, and traffic control. At the heart of the system is a GPS transponder that consists of three parts: a high-precision, multichannel GPS receiver; communication processors; and a transmitter/receiver. An optional component is a navigation processor and ECDIS integrated with the transponder. Via satellites the GPS transponder determines its position, which is then transmitted along with an identification number to all other transponder-equipped units such as other aircraft, ground vehicles, and land-based stations within signal range. When operating in the automatic dependent surveillance mode (ADS), the system can determine the identification and position of other aircraft in the area. When approaching airports, incoming aircraft will be able to monitor other aircraft in the vicinity and also vehicles on the ground. When the airport's control tower is equipped with ECDIS, air traffic control can accurately monitor every moving vehicle on the ground as well as in the air.

In the United States, there are currently some 17,000 civil and privately operated airports, seaports, and heliports. Whereas larger airports are equipped with a number of navigation aids including instrument landing system (ILS) or microwave landing system (MLS), smaller airports often have few, if any, navigation aids. Just as Loran-C and other radionavigation aids have been used for nonprecision approaches in the past, the use of GPS will literally open up thousands of airports for the civil small aircraft user. GPS has also been shown to adequately meet the demands of enroute navigation which in the past have been met by a variety of systems. Particularly in remote areas of the world where other systems are not available, GPS provides an invaluable aid in aircraft navigation. When combined with the possibilities of enroute surveillance, GPS can not only be instrumental in preventing air collisions, it can also be used to reduce the corridor limits for enroute navigation, which translates into reduction of fuel cost. It can supplement on-ground navigation which traditionally has been provided by directions from a tower controller. Whether GPS is used in the cockpit or on the ground, it is projected to revolutionize navigation in the airways and those applications that are dependent on utilizing aircraft of all types.

IV. Space Applications

There are a number of different space applications possible for GPS. Many of these are currently under testing and evaluation by different NASA programs and are still in the experimental stage.

Control and Navigation of Space Missions

One of the potential space applications is the guidance and positioning of launch vehicles by incorporating GPS on the next generation of space shuttles. In the past, GPS was not used on shuttle flights for many reasons, including an incomplete constellation of GPS satellites, the high cost of receivers, extensive modifications to incorporate GPS with existing on-board systems, and the presence of a navigation system that was performing well. Recent developments, including the eventual obsolescence of TACTAN ground stations, have led to initial testing for implementation of GPS to be used first to supplement and then replace current systems. When fully operational, GPS will be used in all phases of shuttle flight including precise trajectory and orbit determinations, relative tracking, time referencing, attitude, re-entry, and landing applications.

Another example of using GPS with a space transportation vehicle is

Japan's H-II orbiting plane (HOPE) scheduled for launch towards the end of the 1990's. The National Space Development Agency is planning on using a GPS sensor for HOPE guidance during different stages of flight, including space station rendezvous and re-entry.

In the future, GPS may also be used for interplanetary or lunar spacecraft returning to earth orbit or rendezvousing with a platform such as the Space Station. In the case of returning space craft, it is expected that GPS will be instrumental in providing precise navigation for the new technologies of aerobraking for re-entry into the earth's atmosphere.

Positioning Space Platforms

Orbiting the earth there are a number of space platforms presently used in a wide variety of scientific studies. Many additional projects are scheduled throughout the 1990's. It is expected that GPS will be able to provide real-time or post-flight position data which not only is valuable for tracking the spacecraft, but may also be a crucial segment of the telemetered data stream for individual studies.

These space platforms can be divided into two broad categories: high-Earth orbiting satellites and low-Earth orbiting satellites. Examples of high-Earth orbiting satellites are orbiting radio telescope platforms such as the Japanese Very Long Baseline Interferometry (VLBI) Space Observatory Platform, which is scheduled for launch in the mid-1990's. Another example is the International VLBI Satellite, which is scheduled for launch in the late 1990's. In both cases, it is proposed that the space vehicles will carry GPS flight receivers for position and velocity determinations.

Low-Earth orbiting platforms are presently using and are expected to use GPS for orbital data. Examples of these projects are TOPEX/POSEIDON launched in 1992 and ARISTOTELES and EOS, which are proposed for 1996 and the late 1990's, respectively. The TOPEX/POSEIDON project is an interesting program that is already well underway. It is a joint project sponsored by NASA and the French Space Agency, CNES (Center National d'Etudes Spatiale). TOPEX (The Ocean Topography Experiment) is a 2–4 year, $350 million project, which along with POSEIDON, its French counterpart, is engaged in accurately mapping the surface of the oceans. The TOPEX/POSEIDON satellite is equipped with a precision radio altimeter, which accurately determines the sea surface relative to the center of the earth. It is also equipped with a GPS flight receiver that precisely locates the satellite's position in orbit. The data is transmitted to six different ground stations where it is processed, yielding surface heights with decimeter accuracy above the geoid. Possible applications of the project are in charting the El Niño current, which has a reputation for adversely affecting global weather patterns.

Another low-Earth orbit project, the proposed Earth Observing System (EOS), consists of six satellites scheduled for launches starting in 1998. Each satellite will be equipped with two GPS PPS receivers, which will be capable of reporting orbital data accurate to several centimeters. The project is part of the "Mission to Planet Earth" campaign, one of the main U.S. space programs extending into the twenty-first century.

The GPS satellites themselves have also become important platforms for scientific study, particularly of the earth's ionosphere. A number of different agencies around the globe have used GPS signals to study the varying effects of the earth's ionosphere to calibrate the ionospheric delay for other satellites and other space-based systems. A better understanding of the ionosphere may help GPS users avoid problems related to ionospheric effects or diagnose system anomalies. Through these studies, it may also be possible to build better ionospheric models, particularly regional ones, which, if programmed into GPS receiver software, could improve accuracy and even possibly eliminate the need for dual frequency receivers for some uses.

V. Time Applications

Although GPS is used primarily for navigation, it has yet another area of application: using its highly accurate time standard, which is used in the ranging method to determine location. Thus, another user group is emerging for whom precise time determinations are important for different applications. Although these are found primarily in the scientific community, there are also a number of military and civil applications.

GPS provides an important source of precise time for those users who require time references on the nanosecond level. Before the implementation of SA, users could count on an absolute accuracy of 50–100 nanoseconds. Through SA, initiated by clock dithering, the timing error for a given satellite will randomly oscillate between 100

To determine the origins of lightning.

In ionospheric wave propagation tests, to prevent disruptions in network communications.

To analyze the auroral electrojet, which causes the northern lights, to develop a communication system with submarines.

In industry, to accurately monitor with sensors equipment conditions as a function of time.

To accurately correlate time of financial transactions between different institutions.

As a timing reference to accurately determine (within one centimeter) the distance between points thousands of miles away.

Figure 8.7   Examples of Using GPS Timing

and 300 nanoseconds. However, by viewing the same satellite from two different sites remotely stationed from each other, these errors and others can be almost entirely eliminated, producing incredible timing accuracies and stabilities.

As with any user group, the applications of precise time dissemination will vary. Some of these may be the simultaneous observations of heavenly bodies or space objects from observatories. Other applications may be used by national standards laboratories or in the development and calibration of frequency standards. Taking advantage of the long-term stability of GPS time, GPS may be used to drive or discipline a low-cost oscillator. To illustrate this last example, in the late 1980's, AT&T used GPS-referenced timing to bring Hawaii into sync with the rest of the national network. The results were so successful that today all of AT&T's telephone system is timed by clocks referenced to and monitored by GPS. Additional examples of how GPS timing functions can be or are being used are illustrated in Figure 8.7.

Even before the GPS system was fully operational, it soon became apparent that accuracy was, and still is, the prime concern for many GPS users. To quote a popular trade magazine, "GPS users are showing an insatiable appetite for ever more precise data — give them a mile and they want an inch." (GPS World, October 1991) Today, real-time DGPS is being regarded as the second generation of GPS, which will dominate the industry well into the twenty-first century. In three out of four GPS applications, the accuracy requirements are for 10 meters or less. Yet it is still important to remember that not all applications require the precise positioning qualities of DGPS.

As new markets keep opening up and expanding, additional and diverse applications will continue to be added, subject only to the latest that technology, human imagination, and ingenuity can produce. In addition to being used on small marine pleasure craft, GPS is found on the automated bridges of ships, in the cockpits of aircraft, on the dashboards of luxury cars, in the cabs of trucks, in the backpacks of surveyors and field engineers, and on the space platforms circling the globe.

With new trends in microelectronics producing smaller, quicker, better display and greater accuracy-enhanced units, it is not impossible to foresee small wristwatch-sized GPS receivers. Yet, this is only the beginning. GPS is very good and promises to get even better. It may, however, be but the forerunner to new systems in radiolocation and navigation that are waiting just around the corner, products of the twenty-first century.

Photo #1: Redwood. Courtesy of the U.S. Coast Guard.

Photo #2: The Hummingbird GPS receiver is a completely self-contained unit which combines GPS positioning with ECDIS. No external discs or cartridges are required. A single memory chip smaller than a dime provides built-in maps of the coastal U.S. including Nova Scotia to the Caribbean, Vancouver Island to Baja California and island waterways. Photo courtesy of Hummingbird GPS Navigation Systems, Eufaula, AL.

Photo #3: Using GPS for emergency vehicle tracking. Photo courtesy of Eastern Land Navigation Systems Inc., Richmond, VA.

Photo #4: Magellan's 5 channel NAV 5000 Pro uses carrier-phase measurements for sub-meter accuracy in land-based applications. Courtesy of Magellan Systems Corp.

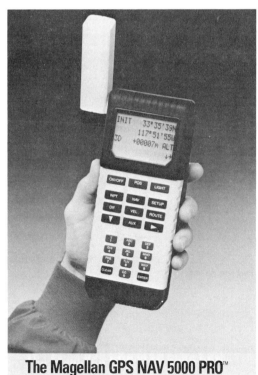

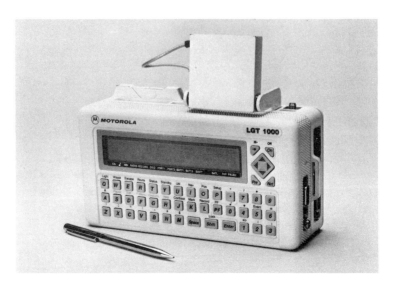

Photo #5: Motorola's LGT 1000 (TM) Lightweight GPS/GIS Terminal enables users to quickly and accurately record position and attribute data for animate and inanimate objects. Courtesy of Position and Navigation Systems, Motorola, Inc.

Photo #6: Magellan's Avionic GPS receiver uses 4 parallel channels to track 4 satellites for a 3-D fix and a 5th channel to track all other satellites in view. Features a world-wide Jeppesen database that identifies airports over 1000 feet in length, VORs and NDBs. Magellan.

Photo #7: Garmin's portable GPS receiver for avionics. Provides a built-in Jeppesen database for easy access to airports and VORs. External quadrifilar antenna detaches for easy temporary window mounting. Courtesy of Garmin International, Lenexa, KS.

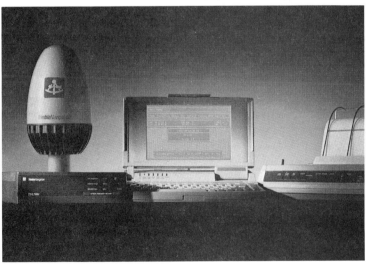

Photo #8: Trimble's Inmarsat-C GPS combines the power of Inmarsat-C 2-way text messaging with the precision of GPS in a single unit with a shared common antenna. Courtesy of Trimble Navigation, Ltd.

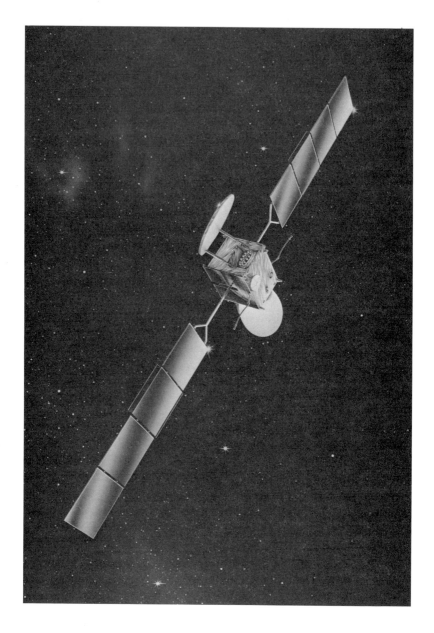

Photo #9: An Inmarsat 3 Spacecraft. Courtesy of GE Astro Space.

APPENDIX

Abbreviations & Acronyms

Because this book contains many abbreviations and acronyms, it may be helpful to consult the following list for their meanings.

ADF - Automatic Direction Finder

ADS - Automatic Dependent Surveillance

AFB - Air Force Base

A/J - Anti-jamming

AM - Amplitude Modulation

AS - Anti-spoofing

ASF - Additional Secondary Factor (Loran-C)

ATC - Air Traffic Control

ATON - Aids to Nagivation

AVL - Automatic Vehicle Location

AVLN - Automatic Vehicle Location and Navigation

AVM - Automatic Vehicle Monitoring

BPSK - Binary Phase Shift Keying

C/A - Course Acquisition

CCW - Coded Continuous Wave

CCZ - Coastal and Confluence Zone

CEP - Circle Error Probable

CNES - Center National d'Etudes Spatiale

COG - Course Over the Ground

COP - Circle Of Position

CONUS - Continental United States

CS - Control Segment

CW - Continuous Wave

DGPS - Differential Global Positioning System
DMA - Defense Mapping Agency
DME - Distance Measuring Equipment
DOD - Department of Defense
DOP - Dilution of Precision
DOT - Department of Transportation
DR - Dead Reckoning
DRMS - Distance Root Mean Square

ECDIS - Electronic Chart Display and Information Systems
EDM - Electronic Distance Measurement
EOS - Earth Orbiting System
EHF - Extremely High Frequency
ETA - Estimated Time of Arrival

FAA - Federal Aviation Administration
FANS - Future Air Navigation Systems
FM - Frequency Modulation
FOC - Full Operational Capability
FRP - Federal Radionavigation Plan

GDOP - Geometric Dilution of Precision
GIC - GPS Integrity Channel
GIS - Geographic Information Systems
Glonass - GLObal NAvigation Satellite System
GMT - Greenwich Mean Time
GPS - Global Positioning System
GPSIC - GPS Information Center

HDOP - Horizontal Dilution of Precision
HF - High Frequency
HHA - Harbor and Harbor Approach
HOPE - H-II Orbiting Plane (Japan)

HOW - Hand Over Word

Hz - Hertz

IALA - International Association of Lighthouse Authorities

ICAO - International Civil Aviation Organization

ICS - Interim Control Segment

IFR - Instrument Flight Rules

ILS - Instrument Landing System

IMO - International Maritime Organization

INS - Inertial Navigation System

IOC - Initial Operational Capability

ION - Institute of Navigation

IVHS - Intelligent Vehicle Highway Systems

JPO - Joint Program Office

kHZ - Kilohertz

km - Kilometer

L1 - GPS carrier frequency, 1575.42 MHz

L2 - GPS carrier frequency, 1227.6 MHz

Lat - Latitude

Lat/Lon - Latitude/Longitude

LCD - Liquid Crystal Display

LED - Light Emitting Diode

LF - Low Frequency

Lon - Longitude

LOP - Line Of Position

Loran - Long Range Navigation

MCS - Master Control Station

MEP - Midcontinent Expansion Plan

MF - Medium Frequency

MGRS - Military Grid Reference System

MHz - Megahertz

MLS - Microwave Landing System

NAD - North American Datum

NAS - National Airspace System

NASA - National Aeronautics and Space Administration

NATO - North Atlantic Treaty Organization

NAV-msg - Navigation Message

Nav Star GPS - NAVigation Satellite Timing And Ranging Global Positioning System

nm - nautical mile

NMEA - National Marine Electronics Association

NNSS - Navy Navigation Satellite System (Transit)

NOAA - National Oceanic and Atmospheric Administration

NOCUS - North Central U.S. Chain (Loran-C)

NOS - National Ocean Survey

NRL - Naval Research Laboratoryns - nanosecond

OAB - Operational Advisory Broadcasts

OCS - Operational Control Segment/System

P-Code - Precision/Protected Code

PDOP - Positional Dilution of Precision

PPS - Precise Positioning Service

PR - Pseudorange

PRN - Pseudo Random Noise

PVT - Position Velocity and Time

R&D - Research and Development

RAIM - Receiver Autonomous Integrity Monitoring

RDF - Radio Direction Finder

RDSS - Radio Determination Satellite Systems

RF - Radio Frequency

RFI - Radio Frequency Interference

RMS - Root Mean Square

ROV - Remotely Operated Vehicle

RTI - Road Transport Informatics

RTCA - Radio Technical Commission for Aeronautics

RTCM - Radio Technical Commission for Maritime Services

SA - Selective Availability

Sat Nav - Satellite Navigation (Transit System)

SEP - Sphere Error Probable

SHF - Super High Frequency

SNR - Signal to Noise Ratio

SOCUS - South Central U.S. Chain (Loran-C)

SOIT - Satellite Operational Implementation Team

SOA - Speed Of Advance

SOG - Speed Over the Ground

SPS - Standard Positioning Service

SV - Space Vehicle

SVN - Space Vehicle NAVSTAR, also known as Space Vehicle Number

TACAN - Tactical Air Navigation

TAI - International Atomic Time

TD - Time Difference

TDOP - Time Dilution of Precision

TOA - Time Of Arrival

TOPEX - The Ocean Topography Experiment

TTFF - Time To First Fix

UE - User Equipment

UEE - User Equipment Error

UERE - User Equivalent Range Error

UHF - Ultra High Frequency

URA - User Range Accuracy

URE - User Range Error

US - User Segment

USAF - United States Air Force

USCG - United States Coast Guard

UT - Universal Time

UTC - Universal Time Coordinated

UTM - Universal Transverse Mercator

UUD - Universal User Defined

VDOP - Vertical Dilution of Precision

VHF - Very High Frequency

VLBI - Very Long Baseline Interferometry

VLF - Very Low Frequency

VLM - Vehicle Location Monitoring

VOR - VHF Omni-directional Range

VORTAC - Collocated VOR and TACAN

VTC - Vessel Traffic Center

VTS - Vessel Traffic Services

WADGPS - Wide Area Differential Global Positioning System

WGD - World Geodetic System

WGD-84 - World Geodetic System - 1984

GLOSSARY

Absolute Accuracy - *See* predictable accuracy.

Accuracy - How close a fix comes to actual position.

Acquisition - The ability to find and lock on to satellite signals for ranging.

Additional Secondary Factor (ASF) - Error in propagation time causedby radiowaves slowing down as they pass over different terrain. It is in addition to the slowing down as radiowaves pass over sea-water (Application with Loran-C.)

Algorithm - Special method used to solve a certain kind of mathematical problem.

Almanac - The description of GPS satellite orbital data used to determine approximate satellite position as a function of time.

Amplitude - Height of a radiowave as measured from an imaginary center line to a peak of a wave.

Amplitude Modulation (AM) - A method of encoding a message on the carrier signal by altering the height of the signal while keeping the frequency constant.

Anti-spoofing - The technique of replacing the P-code with a secret Y-code to prevent jamming and the generation of false P-code signals.

ASF - *See* additional secondary factor.

Automatic Vehicle Location (AVL) - The technique of using a navigation system to determine a vehicle's position.

Automatic Vehicle Monitoring (AVM) - The technique of using a navigation system to determine a vehicle's position, which is then transmitted back to a central dispatch unit for monitoring position and movement.

Bearing - The angle between two different points on the earth's surface with respect to true north.

Bandwidth - That range of frequencies that compose a signal.

Bit - The smallest piece of information in a computer system. A bit has two values, 0 and 1.

C/A code - Coarse Acquisition code. The short (1023 bits) GPS pseudorandom code available on only the L1 band and to civil users.

Carrier - A signal that is used to "carry" other lower bandwidth signals from transmitter to receiver.

Carrier-Aided Tracking - A technique to improve accuracy by using the GPS carrier signal to get a more exact lock on the pseudo-random code.

Chayka - The Russian equivalent of Loran-C.

Circle Error Probable - The radius of a circle within which there is a 50% probability of a point (fix) occurring.

Circle of Position (CEP)* - Same as a line of position, except that position is now somewhere on a prescribed circle.

Clock Aiding - An accuracy enhancement technique in which an additional atomic clock (rubidium) provides accurate time to the receiver for calculating satellite clock frequency, phase bias, and clock drift.

Coastal Confluence Zone - That area from a harbor entrance extending 50 nautical miles seaward or to the edge of the continental shelf (100 fathom curve), whichever is greater.

Cold Start - The ability of a GPS receiver to start navigating without the assistance of any almanac information stored in its memory.

Conterminous U.S. - The 48 adjoining states and the District of Columbia.

Control Segment - That segment of the GPS system that consists of a Master Control Station, Monitor Stations, and Ground Antennas, which monitor and update satellite signals and upload correction data to the satellites.

Course Over The Ground (COG) - The track of a vessel over the bottom as measured in degrees.

Crossing Angle - The angle between two lines or circles of position.

Cross Track Error - The difference between a vessel's actual position and desired position on a given heading. Is usually measured as a range error in nautical miles, but may also be expressed graphically with symbols.

Datum - The coordinate system used to define position on the earth's surface.

Dead Reckoning - The technique of determining position by computing distance traveled on a given course. Distance traveled is determined by multiplying speed times elapsed time.

Demodulation - Separating coded information from the carrier signal.

Differential - The technique of improving accuracy of a radionavigation system by measuring position errors at a known location andtransmitting the error between the known positon and mea sured position to users of the same radionavigation system in the area.

Dilution of Precision (DOP) - The sum effect of all combined error sources on accuracy when crossing two or more lines of position.

Distance Root Mean Square (drms) - A measurement used to describe the accuracy of a fix. It is twice the square root of the sum of the squares of all radial errors surrounding a true point divided by the total number of measurements.

Dithering - Introducing errors into the satellite clock read-out on GPS signals for the purpose of degrading GPS position accuracy for civil users.

Doppler Aiding - The technique of measuring Doppler shift to assist a GPS receiver in tracking a satellite signal. Sometimes called "carrier-aided smoothing."

Doppler Shift - The apparent shift in the frequency of radio or sound waves as a function of the changing distance or relative velocity between the source of the signal and the receiver.

Drift - The rate of a vessel's departure from a given course as measured in knots. The speed of a current as measured in knots.

Electromagnetic Spectrum - The continuous distribution of energy in the form of electromagnetic waves, which are arranged in order of their frequencies or wavelengths.

Enroute - Navigation between the point of departure and the point of arrival.

Ephemeris (pl., ephemerides) - A description of a GPS satellite's position in space as a function of time.

Epoch - A given segment of time; recurring periods of time.

Error Budget - The total number of errors that may affect the accuracy of a fix.

Estimated Time of Arrival (ETA) - The approximate arrival time at a given destination based on a specific speed made good and the distance from current position to destination.

Federal Radionavigation Plan (FRP) - The official Federal Government document that states radionavigation planning and policy. Is published biennially.

Fix - Defining position as determined by one or more navigational aids or techniques, e.g., where two lines of position such as latitude and longitude cross.

Frequency - The number of waves passing a specific point within a unit period of time, expressed as hertz.

Frequency Modulation - A method of encoding information on a carrier signal by altering the frequency (amplitude remains constant).

Geodesy - The branch of applied mathematics that deals with the measurement, curvature, and shape of the earth.

Geodetic - Geographic, pertaining to geodesy. Latitude and longitude readings are geodetic coordinates.

Geodetic Accuracy - *See* predictable accuracy.

Geoid - An imaginary surface that coincides with mean sea level in the ocean and its extension through the continents. The geometric figure formed by this surface as an ellipsiod that is flattened at the poles.

Geometric Dilution of Precision (GDOP) - The effects of the combined errors of four variables (latitude, longitude, altitude, time) on the accuracy of a three-dimensional fix.

Geostationary Satellites - Those satellites positioned in a constant position relative to a given area of the globe with the purpose of maintaining constant coverage of that area.

Glonass - GLObal NAvigation Satellite System. The Russian counterpart to GPS.

Great Circle - The shortest distance between any two points on the surface of the earth. To achieve this, heading is constantly changing making a different angle at each meridian that is crossed.

Ground Wave - A radiowave that travels along the earth's surface.

Handover Word (HOW) - That part of the GPS navigation message that tells P code users where to "jump-in" to access the week-long segment of the P code. Is measured in 1.5 second intervals called "Z counts."

Height Aiding - An accuracy enhancement technique in which the known height of the receiver is entered into the navigation solution, which in effect provides another "satellite" range.

Hertz - Unit used to measure a wave's frequency, one cycle per second.

Horizontal Dilution of Precision (HDOP) - The effects on accuracy of the combined errors in a two-dimensional fix obtained from crossing two lines of position.

Inclination - "One of the orbital parameters that describes the orientation of an orbit. It is the angle between the orbital plane and a reference plane, the plane of the celestial equator for geocentric orbits and ecliptic for heliocentric orbits." (1990 FRP)

Initialization - Entering data into a receiver (cold start, no almanac) to assist it in finding and tracking satellites, e.g., time, time off-set, date, approximate position, antenna height.

Inmarsat - A 65-nation consortium chartered in the mid-1970's to provide improved maritime public correspondence and radio determination capabilities.

Integrity - The ability of a system to supply timely warnings in the event of loss of navigation solution, excessive noise, or other fac tors affecting measured position.

Interference - Same as noise. Any distortion of the transmitted signal that impedes the reception of the signal at the receiver.

Ion - An electrically charged particle formed by either adding or taking away electrons from neutral particles.

Ionization - The process by which atoms form electrically charged particles called ions.

Ionosphere - That layer of the atmosphere that contains electrically charged particles (ions). It lies approximately 30-300 miles above the earth's surface. These charged particles interfere with or distort transmissions of electromagnetic signals through the layer.

Ionospheric Delay - The retardation of radio signals as they pass through the ionosphere. Is inversely proportional to the frequency of the signals: the higher the frequency, the less the signals are slowed down.

Interferometric Differencing - A variation of phase differencing in which two different antennas sample the GPS signal wavefront at two locations and then feed the information into a single amplifier and mixer (interferometer) in which phase difference observations are made.

Kilohertz (kHz) - A radio signal that has 1000 cycles per second.

Kinematic - Pertaining to motion or moving objects.

Kinematic Positioning - Positioning a continuous moving platform by using GPS carrier-phase data while operating in a differential mode.

L1 Band - The GPS carrier frequency of 1575.42 MHz that transmits both the C/A code and P code.

L2 Band - The GPS carrier frequency of 1227.60 MHz that transmits only the P code.

Latitude - A line of parallel. The distance north or south of the equator measured in degrees. One degree of latitude equals 60 nautical miles/one minute of latitude equals one nautical mile.

Line of Position (LOP) - Location somewhere on a single line. A fix is determined by crossing two LOPs.

Longitude - A meridian. The distance east or west from the prime meridian measured in degrees. At the equator, one degree of longitude equals 60 nautical miles with each degree getting smaller the closer one is to either of the poles.

Loran-C - LOng RAnge Navigation system which determines position by comparing the arrival times of radio signals from two or more master/secondary station pairs.

Magnetic Deviation - The error in a magnetic compass reading caused by onboard magnetic influences.

Magnetic Variation - The error in a magnetic compass reading caused by the difference between the true north pole and the magnetic north pole.

Megahertz (MHz) - A radio signal of one million cycles.

Microsecond (s) - One millionth of a second.

Millisecond (ms) - One thousandth of a second.

Modulation - A method of encoding a message signal on top of a carrier, which can be decoded at a later time.

Multipath Error - Interference error caused by a signal that has taken two or more different paths and then is received by a receiver. Is usually caused by one path being reflected or bounced.

Multiplexing - The technique of using a single fast switching channel in a GPS receiver that rapidly sequences (at least 50 times/sec) through the satellites under track to obtain ranging data and the navigation message.

Nanosecond (ns) - One billionth of a second.

Nautical Mile (nm) - The unit of distance used in most maritime navigation. It is 1.15 times longer than a statute mile, or 6076.1 feet.

Navigation Message - Information included in the GPS signal that gives the health of the satellite and parameters for computing its position in space as a function of time (ephemeris). Also includes time information, specifications for P code access, and health/position information (almanac) of other satellites in the system.

Noise - A distortion of a signal as it travels from transmitter to receiver due to ions, objects, and electromagnetic fields in its path.

Oscillator - A device that generates a signal of a given frequency.

Parity - An extra bit at the end of a string of bits that tells whether the number of 1s is odd or even. Used in error detection.

P code - The very long (267 days) GPS code used for more precise position fixing, which is restricted to only authorized users. It is located on both the L1 and L2 bands.

Period - The time from one point on a wave to the same point on the next cycle.

Phase Angle - The time difference between the same point on two different waves. Usually measured in fractions of a cycle (radians or degrees).

Phase Differencing - The technique of using two GPS receivers at different locations to measure the phase angles of the carrier signal from the same satellite, which are compared by a communications link between the two locations.

Phase Modulation - Encoding information on a carrier signal by changing the phase so that some segments of the carrier are out of phase while others are in phase. With GPS, only two phase angles are used, 0 and 180, representing the two values, 1 or 0.

Positional Decorrelation - *See* Spacial Decorrelation.

Positional Differential - Corrections that are applied to actual mea sured position as a latitude/longitude correction.

Position Dilution of Precision (PDOP) - The effects of the combined errors of crossing three lines of position (latitude, longitude, altitude) on the accuracy of a three-dimensional fix. Is the same as GDOP minus the time element.

Precise Positioning Service (PPS) - The positioning accuracy level using GPS available to military and authorized users.

Precision - The degree of accuracy or exactness.

Predictable Accuracy - "The accuracy of a radionavigation system's position solution with respect to the charted solution. Both the position solution and the chart must be based on the same geodetic datum." (1992 FRP)

Prime Meridian - The meridian passing through Greenwich, England. Zero degrees longitude.

Pseudolite - A GPS ground-based transmitter station that transmits the same signal characteristics as GPS satellites so that it looks and behaves like another satellite. Can be used in providing differential corrections in addition to another range for computing position.

Pseudorandom Code - The modulation of a GPS satellite signal that appears to be random noise but in actuality consists of a complicated pattern of 1's and 0's. The C/A code is an example of a pseudorandom code. See also pseudorandom noise.

Pseudorandom Noise (PRN) - The modulation pattern on each GPS satellite signal that identifies it from other satellite signals.

Pseudorange - The calculated range between a receiver and a GPS satellite that contains errors due to clock differences and propagation delays.

Pseudorange Differential - The type of corrections that are used in differential GPS. They are applied to the pseudorange determinations as opposed to a latitude/longitude correction (positional differential).

Radio Direction Finder (RDF) - A radio receiver that has a directional antenna and a visual null indicator. It is used to determine LOPs from radiobeacons at known positions.

Radionavigation - The use of the signal characteristics of radiowaves and transmitters at known locations to determine position.

Ranging - The technique of determining a line of position by calculating the distance beween a receiver and a known point of reference.

Reference Station - A ground station at a known location used in differential GPS in which a receiver tracks all satellites in view, computes their pseudoranges, corrects these for errors, and transmits the corrections to users.

Relative Accuracy - "The accuracy with which a user can measure position relative to that of another user on the same navigation system at the same time." 1992 FRP.

Reliability - The ability to perform a specified function without failure under specified conditions for a given length of time.

Repeatable Accuracy - "The accuracy with which a user can return to a position having coordinates that have been measured previously with the same navigation system." (1992 FRP)

Rhumb Line - The distance between two points, which involves sailing on a constant heading. A line that crosses each meridan at the same angle.

Satellite Constellation - The configuration/arrangement of satellites in a given system in space.

Satellite Geometry - The position of satellites in space with respect to each other and the receiver.

Sat Nav - *See* Transit.

Selective Availability (SA) - The degradation of GPS signal accuracy by clock dithering and introducing errors into satellite ephemerides.

Set - The angle between a vessel's charted course and actual course made good. The direction toward which a current is flowing.

Signal to Noise Ratio (SNR) - The ratio of incoming signal strength to the amount of interferring noise. Measured on a logarithmic scale in decibels (dB).

Space Segment - All the satellites in the GPS constellation.

Spacial Decorrelation - The distance between the user and reference station in differential GPS. The greater the distance between the two, the greater the error of the differential correction.

Sphere Error Probable (SEP) - The radius of a sphere within which there is a 50% probability of a point (fix) being located.

Spread Spectrum - A technique used for transmitting radio signals in which the transmitted signal is spread over a wider frequency bandwidth than the minimum bandwidth needed to transmit that particular information. This is done for increased noise immunity and protection against jamming.

Standard Positioning Service (SPS) - The GPS service that provides civilian access to the C/A code on the L1 band. Accuracy is usually degraded by the implementation of selective availability (SA).

Surveillance - "The observation of an area or a space for the purpose of determining the position and movements of craft or vehicles in that area or space." (1988 FRP)

Temporal Decorrelation - The age or time lapse in corrections used in differential GPS. The longer the time lapse between corrections, the less accurate the corrections. Differential corrections should be updated several times per second.

Terminal - That phase of navigation that involves operations to end a planned mission or function. Used primarily in navigation in the airways.

Transit - The satellite-based system that measures successive Doppler (frequency) shifts of signals transmitted from satellites in polar orbits to determine position.

Tropospheric Delay - Retardation of GPS signals caused by elements in the troposphere such as temperature, air pressure, and water vapor.

Tsicada - The Russian equivalent of Transit (Sat Nav).

User Equipment Error (UEE) - Residual errors after compensation for atmospheric delay and the inherent receiver errors of noise, resolution, and multipath.

User Equivalent Range Error (UERE) - The calculation of the range measurement error to each GPS satellite as seen by the receiver.

User Range Accuracy (URA) - A statistical indicator of the ranging accuracies obtainable with a specific satellite. Includes all errors for which the Space and Control Segments are responsible but not those introduced in the user set or transmission media.

User Range Error (URE) - A performance figure that is given in meters as part of the broadcast ephemeris message of each GPS satellite.

User Segment - All those users of the GPS system: marine, land, air, space, and time.

Warm Start - The ability of a GPS receiver to begin navigating with retained almanac information stored in its memory from previous use.

Wavelength - The distance, in meters, from one part of a wave to its corresponding part on the next wave. It is usually measured from wave crest to wave crest or wave trough to wave trough.

Waypoint - A destination. The coordinates of locations on the desired path at the end of a run or points along the way. Is usually measured in geographic coordinates of latitude and longitude.

World Geodetic System (WGS) - "A consistent set of parameters describing the size and shape of the Earth, the positions of a net work of points with respect to the center of mass of the Earth, transformations from major geodetic datums, and the potential of the Earth (usually in terms of harmonic coefficients). FRP

Y-code - The encrypted form of the P code that is used to prevent jamming or the generation of false P code signals.

Z count - The 1.5-second intervals beginning at midnight each Saturday that tell P code users where to access the week-long segment of the P code. Is found in the Navigation Message as the Hand-over Word (HOW).

INDEX

BIBLIOGRAPHY

Ackroyd, Neil; Lorimer, Robert. *Global Navigation: A GPS User's Guide*, London, New York, Hamburg, Hong Kong: Lloyd's of London Press Ltd., 1990.

Askenazi, Vidal; Hill, Christopher J. *"Wide Area Differential GPS: A Performance Study."* Proceedings of ION GPS-92: Fifth International Technical Meeting of the Satellite Division of The Institute of Navigation, Albuquerque, NM, Sept 1992.

Beser, Dr. Jacuques. *"GPS and GLONASS Visibility Characteristics and Performance Data of the 3S Navigation R-100 Integrated GPS/GLONASS Receiver."* Proceedings of ION GPS-92: Fifth International Technical Meeting of the Satellite Division of The Institute of Navigation, Albuquerque, NM, Sept 1992.

Braasch, Soo Y. *"Realtime Identification and Mitigation of GPS SA Errors Using LORAN-C."* Proceedings of ION GPS-92: Fifth International Technical Meeting of the Satellite Division of The Institute of Navigation, Albuquerque, NM, Sept 1992.

Brogdon, Bill. *"More Than Channels"*. OCEAN NAVIGATOR, Portland, ME, June 1992.

Brown, Dr. Alison K. *"A GPS Precision Approach and Landing System."* Proceedings of ION GPS-92: Fifth International Technical Meeting of the Satellite Division of The Institute of Navigation, Albuquerque, NM, Sept 1992.

Dahl, Bonnie. *"Sailing With Sat Nav: Part I."* CRUISING WORLD, Newport, RI, Feb 1986.

Dahl, Bonnie. *"Sailing With Sat Nav: Part II."* CRUISING WORLD, Newport, RI, Mar. 1986.

Dahl Bonnie. *"Selecting A GPS Receiver."* CRUISING WORLD, Newport, RI, June 1991.

Dahl, Bonnie. *"The Big Three."* CRUISING WORLD, Newport, RI, May 1991.

Dahl, Bonnie. *The Loran-C Users Guide*. Second Edition, Evanston, IL: Richardsons' Marine Publishing Inc., 1991

Dahl, Bonnie. *"Understanding Loran: Part I."* GREAT LAKE SAILOR, Cleveland, OH, Sept. 1991.

Dahl, Bonnie. *"Understanding Loran: Part II."* GREAT LAKES SAILOR, Cleveland, OH, Oct. 1991.

Daly, P.; Riley, Stuart; Raby, R. *"GLONASS Status an Intial C/A and P Code Ranging Tests."* Proceedings of ION GPS-92: Fifth International Technical Meeting of the Satellite Division of The Institute of Navigation, Albuquerque, NM, Sept. 1992.

Description of the U.S. Coast Guard Differential GPS Program. USCG Headquarters Office of Navigation Safety and Waterway Services Radionavigation Division, Washington, DC, updated Apr. 1992.

Enge, Per K.; Kalafus, Rudolph M.; Ruane, Michael F. *Differential Operation of the Global Positioning System,* IEEE Communications Magazine, Vol. 26, No. 7, July 1988.

Federal Aviation Administration. *"Loran/GPS Interoperability: Aviation Considerations"* (Video). A Report To The Secretary of Transportation In Response To Public Law 100-223. Research and Special Programs Administration, Department of Transportation.

Federal Radionavigation Plan 1990, U.S. Department of Defense, DOD-4650.4 and U.S. Department of Transportation, DOT-TSC-RSPA-90-3, National technical Information Service, Springfield, VA, Jan. 1990.

Federal Radionavigation Plan 1992, U.S. Department of Defense, DOD-4650.5 and U.S. Department of Transportation, DOT-VNTSC-RSPA-92-3, National Technical Information Service, Springfield, VA, Jan. 1992.

"Final Pick in Handheld GPS Wars." PRACTICL SAILOR. Greenwich, CT., Vol.19, No. 1, Jan. 1, 1993.

Gibbons, Glen, Editor. *GPS World Newsletter,* Eugene, OR, June 19, 1992.

"GPS Navigation." (Video). BENNET MARINE VIDEO, Marina del Rey, CA.

GPS World SHOWCASE, Eugene, OR: GPS World Corporation, Dec. 1992.

GPS World News and Applications of the Global Positioning System. Eugene, OR, Jan. 1991, Feb. 1991, Mar. 1991, Apr. 1992, May 1991, June 1991, July/Aug. 1991, Sept. 1991, Oct. 1991, Nov./Dec. 1991, Jan. 1992, Feb. 1992, Mar. 1992, Apr. 1992, May 1992, June 1992, July/Aug. 1992, Sept. 1992, Oct. 1992, Nov. 1992, Jan. 1993, Feb. 1993.

Graviss, Col. Lawrence P. *"GPS Program Status."* Proceedings of ION GPS-92: Fifth International Technical Meeting of the Satellite Division of The Institute of Navigation, Albuquerque, NM, Sept. 1992.

Hern, Jeff. *GPS: A Guide To The Next Utility.* Sunnyvale, CA: Trimble Navigation Ltd., 1989.

Howell, Jack. *"Inside the FAA."* Proceedings of ION GPS-92: Fifth International Technical Meeting of the Satellite Division of The Institute of Navigation, Albuquerque, NM, Sept. 1992.

"How To Use Loran-C and GPS." (Video). AZURE SOFT, San Jose, CA.

Hundly, Warren; Rowson, Stephen; Courtney, Glenn. *"Flight Evaluation of a Basic C/A Code Differential GPS for Category I Precision Approach."* Proceedings of ION GPS-92: Fifth International Technical Meeting of the Satellite Division of The Institute of Navigation, Albuquerque, NM, Sept. 1992.

Husick, Chuck. *"Getting it Back: Differential GPS."* OCEAN NAVIGATOR, Portland, ME, June 1992.

Irving, Robert. *"Satellite Navigation."* OCEAN NAVIGATOR, Portland, ME, July/Aug. 1987.

Kazantxev, V.N.; Reshetnev, M.F.; Kozlov, A.G.; Cheremisin, V.F. *"Current Status, Development Program and Performance of the GLONASS System."* Proceedings of ION GPS-92: Fifth International Technical Meeting of the Satellite Division of The Institute of Navigation, Albuquerque, NM, Sept. 1992.

Loh, Robert; Wullschleger, Victor; Crowing, Jim. *"FAA/Honeywell/Northwest GPS Flight Test Program; Summary of Results and Their Implications."* Proceedings of ION GPS-92: Fifth International Technical Meeting of the Satellite Division of The Institute of Navigation, Albuquerque, NM, Sept, 1992.

Madden, Charlene; Lee, Samuel; Tran, Hung. *"Near Term GPS Applications for Shuttle."* Proceedings of ION GPS-92: Fifth International Technical Meeting of the Satellite Division of The Institute of Navigation, Albuquerque, NM, Sept. 1992.

Maloney, Elbert S. *Chapman Piloting Seamanship & Small Boat Handling.* New York: Hearst Marine Books. 56th edition, 1983.

Maloney, Elbert S. *Dutton's Navigation & Piloting.* Annapolis, MD: Naval Institute Press, 1978.

Mauney, Dr. Thad. *"GPS/GIS Integration: State-of-the-Art."* Proceedings of ION GPS-92: Fifth International Technical Meeting of the Satellite Division of The Institute of Navigation, Albuquerque, NM, Sept. 1992.

Milliken, R.J.; Zoller, C.J. *Pringciple of Operation of NAVSTAR and System Characteristics.* Papers published in NAVIGATION, Washington, DC: reprinted by The Institute of Navigation, no date.

Munjal, Dr. Prem; Feess, William; Ananda, Dr. Mohan. *"A Review of Spaceborne Applications of GPS."* Proceedings of ION GPS-92: Fifth International Technical Meeting of the Satellite Division of The Institute of Navigation, Albuquerque, NM, Sept. 1992.

NATO-TEAM, U.S. Air Force Space Systems Division. *NAVSTAR GPS USER EQUIPMENT*, Los Angeles Air Force Base, CA: NAVSTAR-GPS Joint Program Office, updated 1991.

Nickolson, Nick. *"GPS Update: Expanding Coverage, Crashing Prices,"* PRACTICAL SAILOR, Greenwich, CT, Vol. 17 & 18, September 1992.

Pike, Dag. *"Europeans Look To Loran."* OCEAN NAVIGATOR, Portland, ME, Sept./Oct. 1987.

Queeny, T.E. *"Electronic Charts."* OCEAN NAVIGATOR, Portland, ME, Nov./Dec. 1989.

Queeny, T.E. *"Navigation Receivers."* OCEAN VOYAGER, Portland, ME, 1991.

Queeny, T.E. *"The Next Wave of Electronic Charts."* OCEAN NAVIGATOR, Portland, ME, Sept./Oct. 1987.

Radio Navigation Bulletin. Washington DC, U.S. Coast Guard, Department of Transportation, No. 22, March 1988; No. 23, Spring 1990; No. 24, Fall 1991.

Recommended Standards for Differential GPS Service, Version 2.0, Radio Technical Commission for Maritime Services Special Committee 104, Washington, DC, Jan. 1990.

"Round II - Nine-Way GPS Test." PRACTICAL SAILOR, Greenwich, CT., Vol. 18, No. 5, Mar. 1992.

Stansell, Thomas A. Jr. *"GPS Perspectives."* Paper presented at International Navigation Congress, Sydney, Australia, Feb. 1988. Reprinted with permission of Magnavox Co., Torrance, CA.

The Global Positioning System. (Booklet explaining system characteristics, types of receivers & products), Torrence, CA:

Magnavox Advanced Products and Systems Company, no date.

The Goose Gazette. Newsletter of the Wild Goose Association. Beford, MA, Winter 1989; Vol. 90-3, Summer 1990; Vol. 90-5, Fall, 1990; Vol. 91-1, Winter 1991; Vol. 92-1, Winter 1992; Vol. 92-2, Spring 1992; Vol. 92-3, Summer, 1992.

"Trimble Engsign Takes on Magellan and Garmin," PRACTICAL SAILOR, Greenwich, CT, Vol. 17 & 18, Sept. 1992.

U.S. Department of Transportation/United States Coast Guard. *GPS Information Center Users Manual 1990 Edition*, Washington, DC, U.S. Government Printing Office, 1991.

USER'S OVERVIEW: GPS NAVSTAR Global Positioning System, Los Angeles, CA, Deputy for Space Navigation Systems, NAVSTAR Global Positioning System, Joint Program Office, Sept. 1986.

Van Dierendonck, Dr. A.J.; Nagle, Jim; Hua, Quyen D.; Wescott, David C. *"Testing Ranging GNSS Integrity Channel (RGIC) and Wide Area Differential GNSS (WADGNSS)."* Proceedings of ION GPS-92: Fifth International Technical Meeting of the Satellite Division of The Institute of Navigation, Albuquerque, NM, Sept. 1992.

Walters, Harvey. *"GPS: Great Portable Selection."* CRUISING WORLD, Newport, RI, November, 1992.

Walter, Harvey. *"The GPS Buyers' Guide".* CRUISING WORLD, Newport, RI, July 1991.

West, Gordon. *"GPS Anytime, Anywhere."* LAKELAND BOATING, Evanston, IL, Jan. 1991.

West, Gordon. *"Handheld LORAN versus GPS."* LAKELAND BOATING, Evanston, IL, Jan. 1992.

West, Gordon. *"It's a Bird, It's a Plane, It's a Satellite?."* LAKELAND BOATING, Evanston, IL, June 1992.

West, Gordon. *"Ten-fold GPS: What Can Differential GPS Do For You?."* LAKELAND BOATING, Evanston, IL, Jan. 1993.

Zachmann, George W. *"GPS Accuracy For Civil Marine Navigation."* Paper presented at National Marine Electronics Association, Boston, MA, Oct. 1988. Reprinted with permission of Magnavox Co., Torrance, CA.

TAKING GOD TO WORK
the keys to ultimate success

Taking God to Work: *The Keys to Ultimate Success*
© 2018
DAVIWIN Publishing

Printed in the United States of America by DAVIWIN Publishing
First Printing
Print book: ISBN-978-0-9977747-7-1

Cover: JD&J Design, LLC
Interior: Gary Jenkins

Contents

Introduction

Epilogue

Praise for **TAKING GOD TO WORK**

"Steve Reynolds has written a much needed book. For years I've looked for just the perfect book to give to business people in our church, regardless of their faith level. This is that book! I'll be using it as both an individual gift and in our small groups. Highly recommend!"

Nelson Searcy, Founding / Teaching Pastor, The Journey Church NYC and founder, ChurchLeaderInsights.com

"When I see the names on this book I know I can expect excellent writing, a passion to help others change, and inspiration on a timely and timeless topic. This one delivers."

Carole Lewis, First Place 4 Health Director, Emeritus
Author, *Give God A Year* and *Change Your Life Forever*

"Almighty God has given some men the gift to speak into the lives of other men. Steve Reynolds has that gift and his heart is to steward this gift and help build men that would advance the Kingdom of God. We love every opportunity Steve has to speak at an Iron Sharpens Iron Equipping Conference!"

Brian Doyle, Founder and President Iron Sharpens Iron

"Regardless of your age or time in the workforce, this book is an excellent resource aimed at equipping you to share your faith at work. This work by co-authors David Winters and Pastor Steve Reynolds provides valuable biblical work insights from two men that served well in their chosen fields. Weaved within these pages are transparent stories of individuals from a variety of backgrounds in positions that also will inspire you to excellence with character qualities pleasing to God."

Valerie Caraotta, Book Reviewer

Introduction

The co-authors of this book—a pastor of a medium-size church in the Washington, DC, suburbs, and a career-long federal employee and manager—believe strongly in the power of ordinary Christians to transform their jobs, their co-workers, and their employers. This book offers advice and insights on how you can travel the path for lasting success, both in business and in your spiritual walk. Although an unashamedly Christian book, the advice is timeless, and you will find it helpful regardless of where you are on your spiritual journey.

This book features numerous spotlight stories about real people who are taking God to work each day and reaping the rewards of sharing their faith with those around them. The stories include people from all walks of life—from store clerks to leaders of industry and government. Several entrepreneurs also share their secrets for honoring God in their businesses and using His principles to improve the quality of their goods and services. By conquering temptations and traps, real people have found the way to lasting happiness on the job and at home. You can too.

Although you could easily read this book from cover to cover, we have provided study questions and prayers at the end of each chapter, if you wish to go deeper. Substantial portions of the material have been used in a highly successful Christian growth campaign at Capital Baptist Church in Annandale, Virginia, and many of the questions have been tested in Growth Groups to further involve church members. However, as with any study, it will have greater impact if you embrace the ideas and implement the practical how-to suggestions that are offered. All Scripture references come from the New King James Version of the Bible.

When relating anecdotes about the workplace, the co-authors use the terms "I" and "me" to refer to either Pastor Steve Reynolds or David L. Winters. Because Steve has been a pastor all his adult life, and David has worked as a government manager for most of his career, we believe you will easily be able to differentiate the stories told from a manager's experience and those from a pastor's perspective.

We hope this book will help you learn how to maximize your faith at work and grasp hold of lasting success—spiritually, physically, mentally, and financially. Our purpose in writing it was to equip you to make the most of your work life and help create long-term success for you based on biblical principles. We also hope it will help you to gather courage, understand God's tactics, and find your unique mission to bring God's Kingdom to those you meet every day through your job or business.

Applying God's principles to your work will likely lead to many successes and help you overcome challenges as well. The Lord will use your difficulties to build your character and refine your personality to be more like Jesus. To this end, we have devoted much of this book to unpacking the complications of workplace relationships and showing you how to apply biblical wisdom to help you succeed at work. We offer specific strategies to respond to life's challenges, including what to do when you make a major mistake at work, how to handle the feeling you've been forgotten, what to do when you are stabbed in the back by a co-worker, and how to handle sexual temptation when it comes knocking. We will also go into detail in the chapters ahead about how to deal with various stressors.

We believe that with humility and the ideas presented in this book, you will be equipped to share your faith at work while maintaining your professionalism and enhancing your relationships. Your calling is to use your work to care for God's world and the people in it. While no one does this perfectly, most of us wish we could do it better, and this book will show you how to effectively bring God into your workplace.

So, come with us on the journey to recognize these opportunities and make the most of them for eternity.

Steve Reynolds and *David L. Winters*

God's Plan For Your Work Life

1

Does God Fit In My Briefcase?

And whatever you do, do it heartily,
as to the Lord and not to men.
Colossians 3:23

THE DAY STARTED LIKE ANY OTHER on my way to the Department of Homeland Security. After another too-hot summer, the first cool breezes of fall were filling up my Impala as I cruised past Georgetown on the George Washington Parkway. The Christian radio station I was playing laid down peaceful tracks in the background, and I marveled at the beauty of the large trees lining the historic road. Soon my journey to work would take me across the Potomac River and past several of the iconic landmarks of our nation's capital. The Lincoln Memorial, Washington Monument, and the White House stood stoically along Constitution Avenue.

The trip from the outside world to my desk at the Department of Homeland Security included many layers of security. Badges, keycards, chips, frowning guards, and even old-fashioned keys comprised the security measures that had been employed to get me into my small office with a view of the back alley. Once I was seated behind my computer, more chips and passwords stood between me and logging onto the computer system, retrieving emails, and checking out the latest management reports.

Before I had a chance to read the first message, an employee of mine named Martin burst into my office and began ranting about the unreasonable demands of a program manager and his team. "We told them the deadline for the fiscal year was three weeks ago. Last night, they called me into their scientific director's office and demanded that I get this contract out by next week. They don't even have a statement of work!"

I looked over at Martin and tried to calm him with my expression. It had the opposite effect. He became more agitated, because I seemingly had failed to rise to his level of warble. "Martin," I said, "this happens all the time. Have a seat. Let's talk. We either can do it, or we can't. There is no reason to get so upset. Think about your blood pressure."

Not to mention my blood pressure, I said to myself.

Martin sat down, but my gentle rebuke soon triggered a new tirade from him about management being unsupportive and how our mutual boss kept turning up the pressure by over-promising to our customers. At that point, Martin rose from his seat and stood on his chair. He began yelling something perverse as he tried to make me see his level of hysteria.

I quickly lifted up a silent prayer. God gave me some defusing words, and Martin climbed back down from his chair. That's when things got *really* interesting.

"Martin," I said, "you have to look at the big picture here. We are only on this planet for a relatively short time. There is no reason to get this upset. Think about our higher purpose."

"Don't give me that God stuff!" he snapped. "Never talk to me about that again!"

He stomped away from my office, leaving me feeling shaken and alone. Although I had barely alluded to a "higher purpose," he had clearly taken offense. Would he file an Equal Employment Opportunity complaint or just hold a continuously simmering resentment toward me? All I knew at that point was that God needed to be a much bigger part of my daily life at the office. Challenges like this exceeded the shallow faith I had brought along to my work life. While solid in my belief in Christ, perhaps I had separated faith from my work.

Why and How Do You Take God to Work?

Obviously, the first step to taking God anywhere is to ask Him into your life—not just to be your Savior, but also your LORD. The Bible is the story of His love for mankind, and you in particular. If you are not yet a believer, please do come along. I'm praying that by the end of this book, you would like to join millions of others who take God to work each day.

God never intended you to function in this world on a solo basis. He wants to be actively engaged in all parts of your life. Believers have the Holy Spirit as a resident within them, but God wants to be your President. He wants to tear down the wall of partition between your work life and your spiritual life. Not only can you consult with Him at work, but you can also co-labor with Him. If you accept His challenge, He will help you to be your best and make the most of every opportunity. Will you take the challenge to influence your workplace in a positive way for Christ?

If you already believe in Jesus as your LORD and Savior, the next step is to make the leap from believer to follower. It takes a leap of faith to believe in God, but it takes a leap of the will to become a disciple of Jesus. At a time in history when forces are shouting at believers to sit down, will you have the courage and skills to practice your faith on the job? Will you follow Jesus to the very end of your career—let alone your life?

God Created Work Before the Fall

Like every life-giving thing, God created work. In Genesis 2:5, we read that there existed "no man to till the ground." So, God created men and women to work in the Garden and take care of the world. God wants to have fellowship with mankind as we enjoy and use all aspects of His creation, including work. From the earliest times until now, the primary purpose of work has been for men and women to take care of God's world and each other. Whether our current role is to clean hotel rooms or manage a Fortune 500 company, our efforts care for our fellow travelers here.

Work is fundamentally a good thing. It brings purpose to our lives. It brings structure to meeting our basic and most complex needs. God introduced work before mankind first disobeyed Him (which is known as the Fall of mankind.) God's intention has always been that we will find something worthwhile to do with our energy, brain power, and love for others. When we combine our vocation with our spiritual mission, it produces supernatural dynamite that moves mountains and clears the way for great accomplishments.

Work is also good for us mentally and physically. Sadly, in life we lose those things we don't use, exercise, or develop. Our unused talent atrophies and sometimes leaves us forever. Working is human-life exercise that builds character, defines our motives, and teaches us valuable lessons.

If we accept the premise that work is intrinsically good, then as Christians our labors should be specially blessed. In Colossians 3:23, Paul directs us to do our work with dedication, as if we work for the LORD directly instead of merely working for a human boss. If you ever lack motivation, think about the King of the Universe looking on as you do your job. He notices when you review that important document for the second time to ensure the quality, even if your earthly boss won't notice. The LORD knows, and He will reward you accordingly somewhere down the road—if not on earth, then in heaven.

Working as unto the LORD has a potentially world-changing side effect. Your co-workers may see your extra effort and realize there is something different about you. Jesus said, "Let your light so shine before men, that they may see your good works and glorify your Father in heaven" (Matthew 5:16). Enthusiasm, a good attitude, and even exhibiting joy in spite of tough times will draw attention to you in a good way. Working unto God doesn't mean you have the license to ignore your earthly boss, but this principle will instill an extra motivator to keep you working diligently when no one is looking.

Your Boss Is a Gift from God

While you may think your boss came straight from the pit of hell, he or she actually became an authority in the world with God's approval. Isn't that a mind-blowing thought? With all of your boss's idiosyncrasies, character flaws, and physical imperfections, God has approved him or her (at least tacitly) to be in your life for this season. Although the passage of Scripture that supports this idea deals specifically with governmental leaders, the same principle is true about the authorities at your work:

> Let every soul be subject to the governing authorities. For there is no authority except from God, and the authorities that exist are appointed by God. Therefore whoever resists the authority resists the ordinance of God, and those who resist will bring judgment on themselves. For rulers are not a terror to good works, but to evil. Do you want to be unafraid of the authority? Do what is good, and you will have praise from the same. For he is God's minister to you for good (Romans 13:1–4).

What an amazing idea. Your leader, supervisor, or foreman acts on God's behalf during the time he or she is your boss to bring order to your world. As you try to do good things and accomplish the mission of your company or organization, your boss will be a blessing to you. If you do good things and contribute to success in the workplace, you will earn praise that is sent from

God. Your boss can become a minister to you for good to keep you on the right track.

The challenge is that if you resist your boss's authority, you could well be resisting God's authority over your life. Opposing or trying to circumvent authority at work is actually the opposite of accepting God's will. The penalties of opposing your boss's authority is further explained in the next few verses of this passage in Romans:

> But if you do evil, be afraid; for he does not bear the sword in vain; for he is God's minister, an avenger to execute wrath on him who practices evil. Therefore you must be subject, not only because of wrath but also for conscience' sake. For because of this you also pay taxes, for they are God's ministers attending continually to this very thing. Render therefore to all their due: taxes to whom taxes are due, customs to whom customs, fear to whom fear, honor to whom honor (Romans 13:4–7).

The secret is to look beyond your earthly boss and see the Father as your employer. Think of God as the Chief Executive Officer (CEO) of all employers. He wants you to follow the instructions of your day-to-day manager, but He is above that person on the organization chart. He is your friend and always available, with His office door open. You can come to God at any time and talk over all situations with Him. No appointment is needed.

This principle has played out many times during the course of my thirty-three-year work life. When I represented my earthly leaders well and worked hard for their agenda, amazing blessings flowed my way. Promotions, bonuses, and awards piled up as I worked as unto God for my bosses. Conversely, when I got on the wrong side of my boss, everything seemed out of whack. I'm not talking about short-term disagreements over the right path ahead, but times when my attitude became less than supportive of my management. When this happened, something had to give. Thankfully, each time God helped me transition to a different job relatively quickly, or He moved the leader onto his or her next challenge. Either way, I learned a lesson about authority from each of these encounters.

No doubt, someone out there is thinking about Hitler or another evil boss. Did God allow Hitler to be someone's boss? The answer is yes, even Hitler. "The LORD has made all for Himself, yes, even the wicked for the day of doom" (Proverbs 16:4). Remember that Paul penned Romans 13 when the Roman Emperor Nero ruled. Even with this despot on the throne, Paul charged believers to respect the ruling authorities. There are times when you may find yourself with terrible, evil supervisors. In those cases, God may use you to respectfully speak into their lives. You can pray for them and do your best to influence them for good. But if they don't turn around, God is able to transition you away from bad leaders. God did it for me multiple times.

Life and Work Are Difficult

Although our boss is a gift from God and work is a good thing, it became difficult after sin entered the picture. In Genesis 3:17–19, we read how God cursed the ground:

> Cursed is the ground for your sake; in toil you shall eat of it all the days of your life. Both thorns and thistles it shall bring forth for you, and you shall eat the herb of the field. In the sweat of your face you shall eat bread till you return to the ground, for out of it you were taken; for dust you are, and to dust you shall return.

Understanding that work can, at times, be difficult and challenging should have the positive effect of changing our expectations. If we presume that being redeemed will make every moment of our work lives easy, we are sorely mistaken. "Man who is born of woman is of few days and full of trouble" (Job 14:1). There will be trouble in this fallen world. We, as Christians, will experience our share, but Jesus will see us through the storms if we build our foundation on Him. Without this understanding, each problem or obstacle will seem exaggerated in size and scope. We need to recognize that work includes difficult challenges and

be prepared to tackle each problem as a hill to climb over, not
a brick wall to halt our progress.

The good news of the gospel includes God's comfort. He
promises to bring relief to our souls when we are troubled. Just
look, for example, at how Paul was comforted:

> I am filled with comfort. I am exceedingly joyful in all our trib-
> ulation. For indeed, when we came to Macedonia, our bodies
> had no rest, but we were troubled on every side. Outside were
> conflicts, inside were fears. Nevertheless God, who comforts the
> downcast, comforted us (2 Corinthians 7:4–6).

God wants to comfort us as well with peace inside.

With our redemption, bought by Christ on the cross, we will
experience the blessing of God's help, but it will not necessarily
make our labor easy or without effort. However, we have a friend
"who sticks closer than a brother" (Proverbs 18:24), helping us
navigate the waters of our workplace. So, how does God help
us at work? His Word teaches us principles that lead to success.
He often answers our specific prayers to overcome obstacles,
bless specific meetings or projects, apply wisdom to difficult
problems, and give us joy in hard times. As we walk in God's
promises and obey His commands, our work will bear fruit, and
we will be blessed. God promises to direct our paths and show
favor to His children.

The Secret to Getting Paid

God's plan for work remains solid today. If we work at something that is valued by people, either individually or collectively,
we get paid. If that work is valuable to God, we will also get a
spiritual reward in heaven. Any legitimate work that involves
caring for people and doesn't involve sin is part of God's plan
to care for the world. The key for us as Christians is to connect
our earthly work to God's value system.

God's eternal plan for work is that our productive efforts
will take care of His world. He uses our nine-to-five jobs or

our businesses to feed, clothe, house, warm, and provide for His creation. When we partner with God in this exercise, He makes our work easier, more productive, and more satisfying. The Holy Spirit leads us to the truly valuable experiences of life. Beyond our direct efforts to care for others through our work, earning a paycheck enables us to support God's work locally and all around the world. What an incredible opportunity! Paying tithes and giving offerings multiplies our effectiveness beyond the physical touch of our direct efforts to people throughout our community and around the globe.

Heavenly Repayment

As you've added eternal value at your workplace, a reward has been accruing for you in heaven. This eternal currency is different from earthly money, because it doesn't rust, doesn't suffer the effects of inflation, and it won't get stolen. Whether you work in an office, retail establishment, or at home, you will likely get the amazing opportunity to come into contact with others through in-person exchanges, phone calls, emails, or other communications.

God is a worker, and He created us in His image. As Paul wrote, "For by Him all things were created that are in heaven and that are on earth, visible and invisible, whether thrones or dominions or principalities or powers. All things were created through Him and for Him. And He is before all things, and in Him all things consist" (Colossians 1:16–17).

Jesus worked throughout His adult life, first as a carpenter and later as a minister. God meant for us to be workers, whether we work at a job, by volunteering, or at home in the family. God judges our work and will reward us based on our efforts. This isn't to say our salvation is determined by our works—that is by faith alone—but we have the promise that if we work diligently, "knowing that whatever good anyone does, he will receive the same from the LORD" (Ephesians 6:8). When we decide to work for God at our workplace, He becomes our employer.

Given that work is good and believers will be rewarded for their diligence, it might sound like smooth sailing for us. If only that were the case. For those of us who have actually worked at a job, we know that dangers, toils, and snares lurk around many corners of the office or other work environment. Relationships with people can get very complicated.

God's Love At Work

One of the most powerful tools in the Christian's toolbox is love. When we take love with us to work, more than any other trait, it will set us apart. Loving or demonstrating acts of kindness toward our co-workers, supervisors, and customers is a major opportunity and a rich benefit of work. Christians are to "love one another, for love is of God; and everyone who loves is born of God and knows God. He who does not love does not know God, for God is love" (1 John 4:7–8).

Even in the midst of the death, decay, and discouragement of today's world, love shines outward. Love cannot be faked for very long. If we exhibit *agape* love—self-sacrificing love—on the job, people will feel it. Love is the light that shines from the Christian soul walking in the Spirit. Because work is already a way of taking care of people, love is a natural motivator to keep us performing when our patience, energy, or selfish motives run out.

Rest

In a high-pressure environment, the stress battle sometimes begins during the commute to work. Angry drivers, unruly subway passengers, or day-dreaming homeless people may stress our frayed nerves. Then we arrive at the office or job site, just in time to beat the clock and figure out what's on our plate for the new day. A mountain of unread emails greets us and gives us the uncomfortable feeling we are already behind. But God has an answer to all these pressures. If we are in need of intensive care for stress, we can take this gentle advice as a start: *do your best work each day, and then give it a rest.*

As we've already discussed, God instituted a system of work, but He also created a system of regular rest. In Genesis 2, we read how God rested from His labors. After six days of work creating the universe, He took a day off. We should do the same. The ability to continue walking in love is dependent on our ability to renew and refresh ourselves along the way. Days off and vacations give us the replenishment we need to meet the challenges ahead. Daily times of prayer and Bible study, like a mini-retreat, fill us up spiritually. Prayer gives us the renewal to keep the right attitude at our workplace and at home. We need these times of refreshing from the LORD to handle all the responsibilities of our modem world.

Resting has many purposes, but three are particularly important. First, *rest refocuses our spirit.* Our eternal spirit can be drawn this way and that by our circumstances and the people around us. Resting, particularly with worship, allows us to refocus on God. "And [God] said to them, 'The Sabbath was made for man, and not man for the Sabbath'" (Mark 2:27). God knew we needed to rest and reset at regular intervals. He programmed in the whole waking and sleep cycle. We sleep every night and are resurrected each morning. It is all part of our body's resetting process and a picture of God's ability to eventually resurrect us from death.

Second, *rest recharges our emotions.* Life would be really boring without emotions. Highs and lows are normal. Love, hate, joy, and sadness are just some of the many emotions that are part of the game of life. Sometimes, we can overdose on emotions. We need to settle down and calm down at regular intervals. In 1 Thessalonians 5:11, Paul encouraged the believers to pause for the refreshment of fellowship: "Therefore comfort each other and edify one another, just as you also are doing."

Third, *rest replenishes our bodies.* Aside from all its other functions, rest allows our body to heal itself. Every system in our body benefits from the sleep cycle. Exercise and moving around is important, but exercise only benefits us if it is followed by rest. "And [Jesus] said to them, 'Come aside by yourselves to a deserted place and rest a while.' For there were many coming and going, and they did not even have time to eat" (Mark 6:31).

Taking God to a Fallen World of Work

The workplace, like all facets of our fallen world, is a battlefield between good and evil. Christians must be wise about the environment in which they find themselves.

For the past forty years, a seismic shift has been occurring in attitudes about morality. It began during the turmoil of the 1970s and grew, slowly at first, into a movement that no longer supports biblical principles about sexuality, marriage, authority, or even the importance of human life. Whereas forty years ago most people and employers promoted marriage, current attitudes lean more toward an "anything goes" morality—if it is consensual and everyone is happy, let the good times roll. In government, as in most companies, progressive forces have pushed the envelope in an attempt to win society's approval of their morality.

In addition to not supporting biblical values, many workplaces now prohibit Christians from saying even a word of opposition about non-biblical relationships or living arrangements. *Sin* is not a term that is welcome in most workplaces, and Christians often wonder how far the pendulum will eventually swing. Is there ever going to be a point when godliness will again be valued at work? Furthermore, how can Christians live out their faith without fear of reprisal? We know that following God's principles produces a happier life than ignoring His scriptural warnings, but we may be hesitant to tell our co-workers about the benefits out of fear.

At times, it seems as if it is open season on Christians. Evil schemes are at work to keep us quiet and promote spiritual decay across the globe. If we do speak out about Jesus in the workplace, the consequences could result in anything from mild ostracizing by co-workers to formal disciplinary action from supervisory managers. As a result, many of us have retreated into a shell. We avoid conflict at almost any cost—in spite of the biblical admonition to "sanctify the Lord God in your hearts, and always be ready to give a defense to everyone who asks you a reason for the hope that is in you, with meekness and fear" (1 Peter 3:15).

Did you hear the last part of that verse? It provides a major clue about how we can share our faith without ruffling feathers unnecessarily. Humility, while it sometimes seems a rarely practiced discipline, opens doors. Timing and self-awareness are the keys.

Summary
God created work before the Fall of mankind and intended work for our good. His purposes for our work include taking care of His creation and using our unique gifts to meet the needs of others. By connecting our earthly job to God's purposes, we can please God and earn rewards in heaven. God's system of work includes a plan for rest, which recharges us and makes us more effective for future work. Though work is essentially good, it can be difficult in our fallen world.

Spotlight Feature
Jonathan Tack

Jonathan Tack, a chief pilot for a small aircraft services firm, considers his current position his "dream job." His firm began when a few of his friends decided to create a business that would be run on Christian values. Working with friends who are also respected colleagues has yielded several advantages in his life.

"This is definitely the best job I've ever had," Jonathan says. "I know everyone who works here and respect them. This Midland, Texas, company is committed to godly values and to missions." A Christian, for-profit company, the employees and owners meet together and draft goals for missions giving, which come out of the company's profits. In 2017, they met their giving goals by July. Beyond just donating money, they are working with authorities in a central African country, trying to leverage their business relationship with a pre-positioned mission organization there. If it all works out, the officials at Jonathan's company intend to bring general aviation into new places as an economic opportunity and conduit for the gospel.

"The whole culture of the company is Christian," Jonathan says. "We are committed to showing excellence in every regard as a witness to those we serve." Employees conduct themselves and live in a way that reflects Christ's love to their customers.

For Jonathan, a typical day involves first going to the plane he will be flying for that day. Sometimes, this is locally in Fort Worth, but at other times it is a plane parked in another city. The planes that Jonathan flies are owned by other companies or private individuals who need a pilot for a single flight or a longer trip. Jonathan's employer ensures required flight plans are filed and maintenance and/or warranty logs are updated. As the pilot, Jonathan then flies the plane to the chosen destination. Depending on the length of time the client will be in the other city, Jonathan will either stay in that city or return to Midland.

According to Jonathan, faith has been a big part of getting their company off the ground. God helps them each day in response to their prayers. He has sent customers at the right times and in the right quantities to keep the company from being overwhelmed or over-extended. Going forward, they plan to continue depending on God as they grow and expand.

Although working as a pilot in a Christian environment is Jonathan's dream job, he admits God uses challenges and dilemmas there to help him grow. Benefits so far have included developing patience, proving God's faithfulness, and testing the limits of his integrity. Jonathan also finds that he spends more time praying and interceding. His plans include humbly confessing God's sovereignty and trusting Him to bring the company more business so they can expand their mission's contributions around the world.

Jonathan recently attended a Christian businessmen's conference and resonated with the speaker's message that the gospel has always been spread by business people. Original missionaries had jobs. Church planters took the gospel with them on their business travels. They brought seeds of faith along with their spices, textiles, and other products. Just as Jonathan's company has high ideals, he seeks to pursue excellence every day. "I want to demonstrate an unusual loyalty and commitment to customer service," he says, "along with a strong work ethic."

Over the years, Jonathan has learned it is not smart to have separation between his work persona and his Christian persona. He encourages others to be stellar colleagues and businesspeople—to make themselves valuable and do the best they can, for getting recognized as a child of Christ depends on it. To Jonathan, being excellent is a major way to stay relevant to the culture and those he serves.

Spotlight Questions

What could you identify with in Jonathan's story?
What action steps occurred to you about taking God to work?

Study Questions

1 *Read Colossians 3:23 and Romans 13:1.* Paul encourages believers to do their jobs as unto the Lord. Do you know a person who lives (or lived) up to this admonition?

2 What resulted from that believer's commitment to serve God through his or her work? How did it effect that person's life and the lives of his or her co-workers?

3 How does knowing that God has set authorities in your life change your attitude toward your earthly bosses and leaders?

4 What are the advantages of praying for your supervisor or leader?

5 *Read Colossians 1:16–17.* We know that God created the world and everything in it. What impact should this knowledge have on your work?

6 The Bible says we have been created by God and for God. How should this set you apart in your work?

7   Do you have any personal experiences regarding sharing faith in the workplace? How did you share it? How was it received—positively or negatively?

8   *Read Mark 2:27 and 6:31.* Why do you think God emphasizes rest after working?

9   How do you relax on the weekends after a hard week at work?

10 Read 1 Peter 3:15. When was a time you took this advice and shared the hope in your heart with a co-worker?

11 Peter admonishes us to "always be ready to give testimony." How can you make sure you are ready to do this?

12 What do you hope to get out of reading this book and/or discussing it with others?

Prayer

Lord, as You resurrect me each morning this week, teach me how to fulfill my purpose of caring for the world. Please accept my praise and offerings for the new day. Multiply Your love to my supervisors, co-workers, and clients/customers. Teach me about Your loving kindness and how You care for me each day of the week. Grant me satisfaction with the results of my labor and my salary earned. Grant me and my family safety and peace as we travel to and from work. As I thankfully end each day, enable me to sleep well each night, knowing that You are faithful to fill in for those tasks that I missed or didn't get done. Finally, please grant me and my co-laborers joy for our journey, a smile for each stranger, and contentment in abundant measure. In the name of Jesus, Amen.

What will you do to take God to work this week?

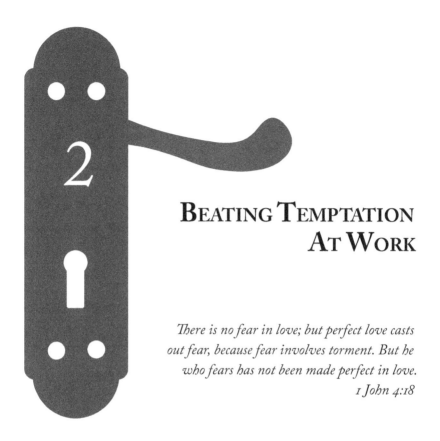

BEATING TEMPTATION AT WORK

There is no fear in love; but perfect love casts out fear, because fear involves torment. But he who fears has not been made perfect in love.
1 John 4:18

AS SENIOR PASTOR of Capital Baptist Church in Annandale, Virginia, I minister to an eclectic congregation representing dozens of countries and almost every work background common to the region. The members occupy jobs at every station of life, from high-ranking government officials to cashiers at the local fast food restaurant. Located just outside Washington, DC, the church is a medium-size congregation, with about 800 in attendance on Sunday mornings. In anticipation of writing this book, I asked this congregation, "What is your number one temptation at work?" Including Facebook comments, I received more than 200 responses to that question.

The following represent the dirty dozen work temptations in reverse order.

Top Twelve Temptations At Work

12. FEAR

Human beings are prone to fear. In fact, it is perhaps one of the major drivers that energizes the world of business. Whether it is fear we will lose our job or fear the company will cease to exist, it motivates so much of what happens within the four walls of an office. Government organizations are far from exempt. Without the profit motive, they thrive on survival instincts. *Take no chances. Don't get into trouble. Avoid anything remotely risky.*

Heaven's economy is the opposite of our earthly fear-based ones. It is faith-based. Jesus put it this way: "Now if God so clothes the grass of the field, which today is, and tomorrow is thrown into the oven, will He not much more clothe you, O you of little faith?" (Matthew 6:30). If we want to follow Jesus at work, we have to conquer our fears. Sure, this is easier said than done, but it is not impossible with God.

The key to avoiding a fear mentality is love. "There is no fear in love; but perfect love casts out fear, because fear involves torment. But he who fears has not been made perfect in love" (1 John 4:18). We have to think about, meditate on, and immerse ourselves in God's love for us. The Creator of the whole universe loves *you*. He is always thinking about you, your life, your problems, and your workplace.

Could any thought be more awesome? No matter where you go or what you do, God is watching over you. He loves you. In the end, you will not be defeated as long as you trust in the Lord.

11. COMPROMISING BELIEFS

Biblical standards are much higher than the standards held by most people and companies, and Christians can feel pressured at times to compromise their beliefs. However, we have to

remember that God keeps His covenant with us and His love
will constrain us, if we allow it to do so. Remembering all that
God has done and continues to do for us will make it difficult, if
not impossible, for us to compromise our faith. "Therefore know
that the LORD your God, He is God, the faithful God who keeps
covenant and mercy for a thousand generations with those who
love Him and keep His commandments" (Deuteronomy 7:9).

10. STEALING FROM THE COMPANY

Although it may sound surprising, many Christians are tempted
to steal from their company in both small and large ways.
Whether it is pilfering pens or stealing time by surfing the
Internet instead of working, all stealing is wrong. We are paid
to do our job. "Let him who stole steal no longer, but rather let
him labor, working with his hands what is good, that he may
have something to give him who has need" (Ephesians 4:28).

9. LYING

Lying is a dangerous game, because before long it can become a
habit. Eventually, if we keep on lying, our conscience becomes
seared to the point we can no longer be honest even with ourselves. Some have bought into the lie that their job requires
"fudging the truth" at times, but the reality is that lying is part
of our "old man" behavior. "Do not lie to one another, since you
have put off the old man with his deeds" (Colossians 3:9).

8. OVEREATING OR EATING UNHEALTHY FOODS

One of the most nurturing acts a human can perform is to provide food to another person. It speaks life and encouragement
to the soul on a deep level. Unfortunately, symbolic confusion
results when the food provided is grossly unhealthy. We find this
in many offices today, where traditions include serving unhealthy
foods from donuts to rich desserts at certain functions.

For Christians who are trying to become or stay healthy, this
can be a temptation. "Do you not know that your body is the
temple of the Holy Spirit who is in you, whom you have from

God, and you are not your own? For you were bought at a price; therefore glorify God in your body and in your spirit, which are God's" (1 Corinthians 6:19–20). When it is our turn to bring food into the office, we can turn around some of these unhealthy traditions. We can be creative and thoughtful in making an effort to bring food and beverages that are healthy *and* taste good. When others bring in highly caloric or unhealthy treats, we can set an example by thanking them for their thoughtfulness while abstaining. Usually, one or two sentences about "watching our weight" is all that is needed. Before long, they won't even ask us to engage in eating the unhealthy foods they have brought into the office.

7. COMPLAINING

Everyone has likes and dislikes. At work, certain tasks invoke great pleasure while others are arduous. One way to quickly set ourselves apart is to avoid complaining. While it is fine to scope out a new project and explain the obstacles that have to be overcome, it is important to immediately follow this up with a *solution*. Generally, everyone can see the negatives—we don't have to be the first to point them out. So, if you do find it necessary to bring up a problem, be sure to focus on the fix or solution. Otherwise, you will soon be labeled as the office complainer. "Do all things without complaining and disputing" (Philippians 2:14).

6. ANGER

Anger in and of itself is not always wrong. A word study of the Old or New Testament yields examples of God becoming angry with various kinds of bad behaviors. Paul, under the inspiration of the Holy Spirit, wrote, "'Be angry, and do not sin:' do not let the sun go down on your wrath" (Ephesians 4:26). This verse speaks of righteous anger, which includes expressing anger at sin and its consequences. Yet even then, we are told to express anger only in a controlled manner (see James 1:19–20).

Often, we will be tempted to express unrighteous anger when we feel our personal rights have been violated. We then strike back in anger as an act of vengeance, which is sin (see Romans 12:19–21). In business, however, getting angry—regardless of whether it is righteous or unrighteous—is almost always the wrong move. When we lose control of our emotions, we seldom win arguments or friends.

If you feel anger starting to rise up at work, call on the Holy Spirit to bring peace into the situation. "An angry man stirs up strife, and a furious man abounds in transgression" (Proverbs 29:22). Believers should never be the ones stirring the pot or making trouble over minor issues. Rather, they should be peacemakers whenever possible.

5. LAZINESS

Everyone has an off day now and then. People are not machines— and who among us has not been distracted by problems with a loved one or a car in need of repair? Laziness, however, is a regular pattern of just doing the minimum. It can cause many problems for a company or organization, because productivity is the key to profits and success.

Planes have fallen from the sky because someone didn't keep up with the required maintenance. Car brakes have failed because an auto worker decided to goof off on a Friday afternoon. "He who is slothful in his work is a brother to him who is a great destroyer" (Proverbs 18:9). When you remember that your work is God's hand extended to take care of the world, it becomes much easier to stay motivated. "Not lagging in diligence, fervent in spirit, serving the LORD" (Romans 12:11).

4. CURSING/SWEARING

As Christians, our witness may be the only example of Jesus that some people see on a regular basis. We don't want to be an excuse for anyone not to believe. Using foul language is never necessary, and often it is just a bad habit. If this is a problem for you, team up with the Holy Spirit and obey His voice when He reminds you to clean up your speech. "Let no corrupt word proceed out of your mouth, but what is good for necessary edification, that it may impart grace to the hearers" (Ephesians 4:29).

3. MISUSING TECHNOLOGY

One would have to be living under a rock to not notice that technology has dramatically changed during the past thirty years, and it will continue to rapidly evolve the way we work and the tasks we perform. Technology can open up incredible possibilities for Christians to be salt and light at their workplace. However, like most tools, it can also be used for evil, for with great opportunities come great temptations. Almost daily, one hears of another scandal about a public figure who misused technology at work or among co-workers. Many times, these indiscretions lead to firing, disgrace, or worse.

Although most employees today know enough to not use work computers for pornography, many still spend too much time browsing the Internet. There is a plethora of ways to misuse technology, but almost all of them involve wasting time. (See "laziness" above.) We are paid for a full day's work, and we should be focusing on work, regardless of the location.

Christians have a great opportunity to shine the light of Christ and be an example at our jobs. As in every other aspect of life, someone is watching us. Our greatest power as Christian employees is our motivation to work as unto the LORD regardless of whether other people see our efforts or don't see them. This witness is stronger than any words we could speak. For example, many businesses and government offices encourage employees to work from home, which can test our self-discipline and diligence on a daily basis. Does our productivity go up when we work from home? Are we watching game shows on television when we are supposed to be creating a presentation? Or does our efficiency increase because we are not having to deal with all the interruptions that define our office life?

2. GOSSIPING

Conversations can quickly turn to gossip if they have negative connotations and the person being discussed isn't there to defend himself or herself. The most outlandish rumors are exchanged by those who have trained their minds to enjoy spreading gossip. "And besides they learn to be idle, wandering about from house to house, and not only idle but also gossips and busybodies, saying things which they ought not" (1 Timothy 5:13). The best way to avoid gossip is to avoid those who spread it. If that isn't an option, a quick word about checking with the subject of the rumor is usually enough to shut down inappropriate talk (at least in your presence). "A perverse man sows strife, and a whisperer separates the best of friends" (Proverbs 16:28).

1. SEXUAL MISCONDUCT/ROMANCE

Office romances have sunk many careers. While they seldom last, employees may spend years feeling awkward around the former object of their affection. For the Christian, engaging in sexual activity with another outside of marriage is sin and can have the unintended consequence of badly damaging our witness to non-believers. It also negatively impacts our relationship with God. Some sources suggest as high as seventy percent of all adulterous affairs begin at work. Many marriages have failed because one partner or another became involved with a co-worker. "Therefore put to death your members which are on the earth: fornication, uncleanness, passion, evil desire, and covetousness, which is idolatry" (Colossians 3:5).

One of the most famous stories about sexual temptation in the Bible involves the patriarch Joseph and his boss's wife. As told in Genesis 39:1–12, Joseph experienced God's favor and became successful in Egypt. An officer of Pharaoh named Potiphar trusted Joseph and made him overseer of his house. Under Joseph's care, the whole house prospered, and everything went well at first. But in this environment of success, temptation soon reared its ugly head. Potiphar's wife became attracted to Joseph, because she found him "handsome in form and appearance." She looked at him with longing and said, "Lie with me" (verses 6–7).

Joseph maintained his integrity, cited his loyalty to Potiphar, and pleaded with her not to pursue him in this way. Finally, he said, "There is no one greater in this house than I, nor has he kept back anything from me but you, because you are his wife. How then can I do this great wickedness, and sin against God?" (verse 9). None of this slowed her down. Day after day, she kept after him. Finally, she grabbed him by his garment, and he had to run away without it to escape her intentions. Sometimes, you have to do the same thing. Is a job more important than your marriage? Is flirting with a co-worker more important than your reputation?

All sin begins as an inside problem. "For from within, out of the heart of men, proceed evil thoughts, adulteries, fornications, murders, thefts, covetousness, wickedness, deceit, lewdness, an evil eye, blasphemy, pride, foolishness" (Mark 7:21–22). The origin also leads to the cure. Changes must happen in your inner being. When you lack the capability to make those changes on your own, God is there is to help.

Three Remedies to Help You Resist Temptation

Whether it is in the secretary's office of a cabinet-level governmental department or a Verizon call center, employees can see their workplace as either a well-defined mission field or an intimidating minefield. Overwhelmingly, my church members expressed a desire to overcome temptations and model Christ to their co-workers. So, what are some ways to resist these temptations that often stand in the way of us doing this?

• *Remember the presence of God is always there for you.* As a believer, God promised never to leave you or forsake you (see Hebrews 13:5). His Holy Spirit wants to lead you into all truth and be the answer to your temptation. Pray and ask for that wisdom.

- *Recognize the larger plan that only God fully knows and controls.* Ask how you can help Him accomplish His purposes for your company or organization. God will show you the next right thing to do.
- *Rely on God's power to fight spiritual battles.* "I will lift up my eyes to the hills—from whence comes my help? My help comes from the LORD, who made heaven and earth" (Psalm 121:1–2). God will fight any spiritual forces that are unseen to you. With one word, He can change an entire situation. He wants to do that for you, right where you work.

Over the years, I have heard it all—from members who gave in to sexual sin at work to church guests who felt too ashamed of their sinful past to join Christian fellowship. Yet we need to remember the gospel message brings hope. We can repent of past transgressions and find new mercy in the light of the cross. God has compassion for us, regardless of the extent of our sinful past.

Opportunity In Diversity

American society is becoming ever more inclusive of people of every race and ethnic background. Capital Baptist Church looks a lot like the U.S., with people of many races, ethnicities, and backgrounds represented. God loves all of His creation, in its entirety and with its diversity, and Christians are called to do the same. Differences of language, thought, and culture can make our institutions stronger by inviting innovation, offering new ideas, and compelling employees to share new learning methods or styles.

Diversity has many advantages, and Christians should be at the forefront of promoting them. We have nothing to fear in learning about other cultures, because we already know the right spiritual path, the real Creator of the universe, and His guidebook, the Bible. We know there is no other way to the Father except through His Son, Jesus Christ. "I am the way, the truth and the life. No one comes to the Father except through Me" (John 14:6).

As long as we stay in God's Word and continue in fellowship with Bible-believing Christians, we can remain confident about staying on track spiritually. As Jesus taught, "I am the vine, you are the branches. He who abides in Me, and I in him, bears much fruit; for without Me you can do nothing" (John 15:5). That connected posture gives us our strength, our joy, and the right attitudes at work.

Ideas Come In Three Flavors

Of course, diversity of race and ethnicity is different from diversity of thought. All people are equally important in God's sight, but not all ideologies are equally valid. Some thoughts are not from God, and some ideas can lead many people astray from the truth and the right path.

Ideas come in three categories: (1) they are neutral, (2) they oppose the truth, or (3) they line up with the truth. An example of something in the *neutral* category is that you may prefer red while another person prefers green. Both are fine colors, and neither position is right or wrong. Ideas can be like colors, neutral to the truth.

However, some ideas *oppose the truth,* or are patently false. For example, you may have the idea to jump from the roof of your three-story house because you believe you will not be harmed. This assertion is likely to be proven wrong when you jump onto the sidewalk below.

Other ideas *line up with the truth*. These ideas are true and may be demonstrated as such. For example, if you subject pure water to temperatures below thirty-two degrees Fahrenheit for a long enough time, the water will freeze and solidify. This is a constant law of nature, and it can be proven to be true.

Discerning Truth

There is also a difference between *natural* truth and *spiritual* truth. For the Christian, spiritual truth is proclaimed in the Bible. "All Scripture is given by inspiration of God, and is profitable

for doctrine, for reproof, for correction, for instruction in righteousness" (2 Timothy 3:16). Ideas that oppose God's Word are
therefore not true. Societies will, for periods of time, wholly
attest to spiritual falsehoods. A good example of this is that for
a period of time in the past, many people believed the earth
was flat. Conventional wisdom indicated that sailing too far
west would lead a boat to the edge of the world and put it in
danger of falling off.

In the name of progress and diversity, some governments,
businesses, secular organizations, and even churches have
marched toward accepting various spiritually false ideas. During
the last thirty to forty years, immorality in sexual relationships,
confusion about gender identity, and disrespect for human life
have been institutionalized into laws, regulations, and corporate
policies. While the heart behind some of these changes appears
to be good, the reality is that sin eventually ends in death. Sin
damages the soul and pollutes the mind.

In an attempt to end legitimate evils, like bullying and discrimination, the powers that be may select cures that are worse
than the disease. Some of these philosophies of men are backing
Christians into a corner by compelling them to accept and even
promote sin. Christians have choices about how to respond.
Remember the famous quote from Edmund Burke: "The only
thing necessary for the triumph of evil is for good men to do
nothing."

Temptations When Facing False Ideas

When we are confronted with evil ideas, we may be tempted
to remain quiet and do nothing. It is often easier to get along
by going along—and we have scriptural instruction to respect
the authority of those over us in our jobs and in government.
But what should we do when authorities choose an evil path?
The first thing we must do is remember that we are not warring
against people. "For we do not wrestle against flesh and blood,

but against principalities, against powers, against the rulers of the darkness of this age, against spiritual hosts of wickedness in the heavenly places" (Ephesians 6:12).

Once we get that perspective, it should bring us to our knees in prayer. There is no way to win a spiritual war exclusively in the flesh. Our calling is to bring God's light, His Word, and His power into the conflict by praying Jesus into every situation. We don't act recklessly but bring the matter to the LORD and ask Him what we can say or do that might delay or prevent ungodly ideas from being institutionalized.

Another temptation we might face when confronted with false ideas is to fight against those who are championing the immoral causes. However, this kind of personal animosity will only lead down an unproductive path and hinder our mission to lead our enemies to Christ. As Paul noted in the passage above, it isn't primarily *people* who we are fighting against. We love people, notice their amazing qualities and God-created humanity, care about them personally, and pray for them. But we also need to oppose, with the shrewdness of a snake, their wicked schemes. We can't concentrate on the personalities but, in prayer, on the evil scheme.

The final temptation we might face is to get confused about compassion. Some followers of Christ believe the best way to love people is to accept their sin and help them continue in it. God knows this strategy doesn't work for believers—or we would not have repented from our sin—and sinful living won't work for others either. The only way to deal with sin is to label it, repent of it, and accept God's free gift of forgiveness. Other people's sin should not be the number one thing on our minds, but we have to be careful not to let their wrong choices become a stumbling block for us. In other words, we have to maintain a sharp edge in recognizing sin compared to purity and God's standard.

What Can We Do About Company Policies?

As Christians, we do not control all policies, rules, and decisions of our superiors. However, as long as we willingly choose to work within the infrastructure of our employer, it is our obligation not to discriminate, ostracize, or otherwise try to harm people whom we feel are not living up to biblical standards. This doesn't mean we necessarily agree with or embrace all our employer's policies or all the behaviors of our co-workers. We can push back when policies are in the developmental stage and tell our colleagues about our moral code, which, in a nutshell, is following the teachings of the Bible as a way to happiness and fulfillment.

We are entitled to opinions, and God may put us in specific places to make a difference at a key moment. For this reason, we must pray, stay humble, and be willing to speak up when the Spirit directs us to do so. Furthermore, when we are asked to participate in workplace activities that conflict with our faith, we can do the following:

- *Start with prayer.* Talk over the situation with God.
- *Study the Bible.* We need to make sure we understand why the activity conflicts with God's Word.
- *Consult with other Christians.* We can talk the situation over with our pastor or another mature Christian whom we respect.
- *Talk with our employer.* Depending on the situation, we may be able to ask our employer for a reasonable accommodation related to our beliefs.

There may ultimately come a day when the choice comes down to doing something that goes against our faith or quitting our job. In such situations when an employer's culture conflicts with our beliefs, God will call us to seek new employment. For example, one Capital Baptist member felt boxed into a corner when his employer required certain New Age training that encouraged occult practices. He eventually quit his job to avoid participating. Other obvious examples include if our employer asks us to do something illegal or even immoral, such as promoting products or services that prematurely end human life (which would conflict with the biblical commandment not to kill).

In such cases, after praying about the situation, checking with our pastor, and asking for a different assignment, our Holy Spirit-filled consciences may force us to transition to another job. When this occurs, we can be sure the Holy Spirit will be our guide and will work with us in the timing of such a change. Following God's will is always the right move to make.

Is Chip Technology a Precursor to the End Times?

Christian scholars have long theorized about the meaning of Revelation 13, which talks about the Mark of the Beast. With the proliferation of computers and technology, it is easy to envision scenarios in which the government or employers will one day require us to have an implanted chip or device. For the Christian, accepting a mark on our hand or forehead is untenable. We can't do it. Yet for believers, this might become the ultimate temptation in the future—especially if the chip is required to purchase key items like food and gasoline.

In the past few years, the U.S. government and many companies have adopted chip technology for identifying people, keeping track of medical records, and other purposes. Before I left the Department of Homeland Security, all employees needed to use chip technology and a reader to access their computers. One could not log onto the computer system without the chip. Likewise, entry into many Homeland Security buildings also required use of the chip. A few companies have gone even further, offering employees a chance to embed chips in their hands. While this certainly is convenient, it is an unacceptable measure for students of the Bible.

The question of exactly how the Mark of the Beast will play out is an open question. However, Christians would be well advised to avoid taking any mark, chip, or other permanent designation embedded in their hands or foreheads. It is just too close to the imagery John discusses in the following passages: "He [the beast] causes all, both small and great, rich and poor, free and slave, to receive a mark on their right hand or on their foreheads. And that no one may buy or sell except one who has the mark or the name of the beast, or the number of his name" (Revelation 13:16–17).

How to Overcome Temptations From Within

So far, we have talked about temptations of an *external* nature. But now we turn to temptations that come from our own *internal* fallen nature or fleshly desires. As a pastor, few things are as heartbreaking as when I see marriages in my congregation fail. Time and again, I hear the same story of how one partner or the other succumbed to temptation at work and entered into an adulterous affair. While there are many different pitfalls, the formation of inappropriate physical and/or emotional attachments are among the most damaging.

At work, we seek to look our best, smell our best, and act on our best behavior. Co-workers spend hours together, sometimes toiling on interesting and even exciting projects. We may accomplish great things as a team and weather difficult circumstances. Bonds are formed and friendships grow. This is normal and meets basic needs such as respect, companionship, and even nurturing. But it can also lead to dangers.

So, how can we work closely with others but avoid taking our relationships in an unhealthy area? Here find some ideas.

Bring God Into the Workplace

If you regularly practice God's presence, temptation will head in the other direction. So, begin your day with prayer. You can do this silently at your workstation. Read a short devotion. Play worship music (if it is permitted). Invite God's presence into your workspace. Ask Him to take an active part in your day. Taking God to work (mentally and spiritually) is for your benefit.

Also recognize that God is with you and sees it all. He is not bound by your actions or inactions. He is everywhere. "There is no creature hidden from His sight, but all things are naked and open to the eyes of Him to whom we must give account" (Hebrews 4:13). Your spouse, parents, or pastor may not be with you at work, but God definitely sees you and your behavior. "Do you not know that your bodies are members of Christ? Shall I then take the members of Christ and make them members of a harlot? Certainly not!" (1 Corinthians 6:15). With God's help, you can walk worthy of His calling on your life.

Recognize God's Plan

God sent the gift of work for your sanctification, to support yourself, to help take care of others in your life, and to learn more about Him. "For this is the will of God, your sanctification: that you should abstain from sexual immorality; that each of you should know how to possess his own vessel in sanctification and honor" (1 Thessalonians 4:3–4). Getting waylaid in a sexual relationship at work is not only likely to mess up your career but also your spiritual life and your relationships at home. It is about not letting down those who love you the most.

"Marriage is honorable among all, and the bed undefiled; but fornicators and adulterers God will judge" (Hebrews 13:4). Beyond the earthly consequences of sexual trysts, God will eventually judge those who participate in sexual sin. You may repent and find your sin covered by the blood of Christ, but your partner in the affair may not come to that same place of repentance. As a believer in Christ, you do not want to have a part in their undoing. Even if you are single, the wages of sin are always death on some level.

Control What You Say

Affairs seldom start with a single glance. It may begin with a few innocent words that come out the wrong way. The book of Proverbs warns, "My son, pay attention to my wisdom; lend your ear to my understanding, that you may preserve discretion, and your lips may keep knowledge. For the lips of an immoral woman drip honey, and her mouth is smoother than oil" (Proverbs 5:1–3). Don't ever tell someone you are attracted to him or her, as this can be interpreted as a way of letting the person know you are available to take the relationship further.

Limit the Use Of Touch

In addition to enticing words, you have to steer clear of inappropriate physical closeness and touching. If you find yourself attracted to someone at work, make sure you keep a respectful distance from him or her physically. Just standing close can be taken as a signal that more contact is desired. Generally, it is not professional to touch co-workers. There are exceptions, such as an introductory handshake or a hug if someone is leaving the company or recently lost a loved one. Otherwise, there is seldom a good reason to physically touch other employees.

Commit to Purity

Scripture encourages you to flee youthful lusts. Just as Joseph fled from Potiphar's wife, you sometimes may have to take drastic measures to avoid ruining your life. This may include transferring away from an object of desire or volunteering for a different project that leads you away from the temptation. What is your goal? What are your priorities? It goes to the heart motive. "But I say to you that whoever looks at a woman to lust for her has already committed adultery with her in his heart" (Matthew 5:28).

Not all of our temptations at work will be sexual. As many sins as plague mankind, there are that many things that can tempt us at work. We walk in freedom with God, but we don't use our freedom as an excuse for sin. Each of us must do our best to walk in a way that is honoring to our Creator. God will lead us as we let Him into our thoughts and invite Him to direct our steps.

Religious Discrimination

Religious discrimination is prohibited by Title VII of the Civil Rights Act of 1964. According to the Equal Employment Opportunity Commission (EEOC), religious discrimination is "treating a person (an applicant or employee) unfavorably because of his or her religious beliefs. The law protects not only people who belong to traditional, organized religions, such as Buddhism, Christianity, Hinduism, Islam, and Judaism, but also others who have sincerely held religious, ethical or moral beliefs. Religious discrimination can also involve treating someone differently because that person is married to (or associated with) an individual of a particular religion." [1]

As stated above, Title VII protects employees from employment discrimination based on race, color, religion, sex, national origin, or protected activity. The EEOC has responsibility for administering the Act by promulgating regulations and policy associated with related matters. As Christians, we may be tempted to look the other way if we see religious discrimination in our workplace, but we have to remember that rules opposing free religious practice could one day be used against us. For this reason, we should all visit www.eeoc.gov and review the section about religious discrimination. The EEOC website provides valuable information concerning religious freedoms and responsibility to those of other faiths.

In addition to the law itself, the EEOC compliance manual gives specific guidance to employers on balancing the needs of individuals in a diverse religious climate. Much can be learned about the dividing line between acceptable and unacceptable religious behavior in the workplace.

Such prohibited conduct includes (1) treating applicants or employees differently based on their religious beliefs or practices, (2) engaging in harassment because of religious beliefs or practices (or lack thereof), (3) denying reasonable accommodation for sincerely held religious beliefs or practices, and

(4) retaliating against employees who participate in protected religious activities.

As employees within a company or organization, we have the responsibility to treat all people equally, whether or not they adhere to our belief system. It is fine to share our religious beliefs with a colleague or co-worker, provided we respect their reaction to our overtures and stop sharing if they ask us to do so. Continuing to hound someone who rebuffs our proselytizing could be viewed as unlawful religious harassment. The golden rule that Jesus taught should reign over our conduct in this area: "Therefore, whatever you want men to do to you, do also to them, for this is the Law and the Prophets" (Matthew 7:12).

Avoid Harassment

In no situation should Christians ever harass co-workers or employees for their religious beliefs or lack thereof. We also need to be careful not to criticize or tease others in regard to their religious beliefs. Many EEOC complaints begin with one party doing what they consider harmless or gentle prodding in a sensitive area. People take their religious faith, or decision not to believe, very seriously. Lack of respect for the other person's beliefs is a sure-fire way to run afoul of our employers at some point.

However, inviting co-workers to religious events (such as a Christmas play or church festival) is generally allowed. It is considered a protected area of religious speech, to the extent the employer allows others to invite and advertise non-religious events. If a work bulletin board is used for all sorts of employee-generated information, it should be acceptable to post a flyer about a church activity as well.

Interactions with customers can get tricky. Courts have allowed employees who work with the public to use the phrase "have a blessed day" when saying goodbye. However, the circumstances depend on the type of business, customer reaction, and the role of the employee. One example posted on the EEOC

website includes a couple who received a poster at church pro-
claiming, "Jesus Saves!" The couple's pastor urged everyone to
display the posters prominently, so the husband, who worked
as a security guard, displayed the poster at the reception desk
in the lobby of the building. His wife, who worked in the same
building—but didn't interact with customers or the public—
displayed the poster in her workspace.

The EEOC suggests the company would probably be on
safe ground if it required the security guard to take down his
poster. His location at the busy reception desk could imply the
company supported the message of the poster. However, the
company would have trouble proving the wife's poster caused
undue hardship. She should be allowed to leave it up, because
outsiders would not see her poster, and her co-workers would
likely understand this represented her own belief and not the
company's position.

Generally, and according to the EEOC website, companies
may display Christmas trees and wreaths around the holidays
without putting up decorations to accommodate the beliefs of
other religions. The EEOC's stated opinion is that Title VII does
not require a company to remove such decorations or put up
holiday decorations to accommodate other religions.

The guidance provided in this section comes primarily from
the EEOC website. However, it is not intended as a substitute for
legal advice. If you have a sensitive issue at your workplace, we
urge you to seek competent legal counsel before taking action.

Summary

In this chapter, we examined twelve of the most common temptations in the modern workplace. We saw how three remedies
that help us fight temptation are (1) remembering the presence
of God, (2) remembering God's larger plan for our lives, and
(3) remembering to rely on God's power to fight our spiritual
battles. We looked at external and internal temptations.

We saw how prayer, Scripture, and wise counsel can help us understand temptations that come at us from the outside and how to address them. For those issues that run afoul of our religious discrimination rights, we saw how under the law we can request a reasonable accommodation from our employer. We also discussed how to use God's presence and plan for us to combat internal temptations. We also must limit touch and, with God's help, commit to purity.

Spotlight Feature
Heather Halverson

Heather Halverson works for a global leader in the insurance and risk management field as a business resiliency manager. In this role, she helps develop the company's disaster preparedness plans and works to activate them when trouble strikes. In 2017, this meant considerable overtime for her, as one hurricane after another devastated several different states and countries. The firm's many clients urgently needed help, even as the company's employees recovered from their own losses.

This tense situation became worse when management increased the demands on Heather and others on the response team. The team's personal styles sometimes conflicted, causing several employees to consider bailing out on the company. However, Heather decided to put her faith to work in addressing the sometimes ultra-high-pressure environment and encouraging her colleagues. "I start each day with getting myself in the right place with God," she relates. "I pray and ask Him to direct my steps. I read the Bible or a devotional book, and I commit the day to Him. Everything that happens is no surprise to God."

By trusting her Savior, Heather knows God will not give her more than she can handle. Heather tries to pass that calm assurance on to others, including those who are under fire by difficult circumstances or demanding supervisors. Whether it involves assuring co-workers that she sees their tireless efforts or telling someone she is praying for him or her, God plays a major part in helping Heather deal with supervisors and co-workers alike. "You can't control other people," she states. "The Bible tells us how to behave. Check yourself and recognize what's going on. Don't get sucked into gossip."

One time, when a manager seemed to be nitpicking everyone on staff, Heather felt the Holy Spirit cautioning her not to get involved with talking about the manager. Instead, she turned the situation over to God in prayer. "Spreading gossip doesn't make the situation better," she says. "It takes a lot of practice to hold your tongue, but sometimes silence speaks louder than words."

On another occasion, when a high-ranking company official pressed her on a small omission that she deemed inconsequential, God used it to help her grow. "I had worked thirteen hours straight," she states. "After a difficult phone call, he told me to 'get some rest.' All I could manage to verbalize was 'thanks,' in not the most loving tone, and hang up the phone." Later, Heather realized she needed to apologize even for her muted response. "God used the situation to make me stronger."

Heather appreciates her job and the company where she works. "It allows me to do so much," she says. She credits her job and her supportive husband with enabling her family to adopt two children from China and support four other children around the world through various Christian organizations. "My job allows me to tithe and give to church as well," she adds. The leave policy at her job has permitted Heather and her family to travel and support other Christian works, both as short-term missionaries and just as encouragers.

A key verse that keeps her going is Colossians 3:23–24: "And whatever you do, do it heartily, as to the LORD and not to men, knowing that from the LORD you will receive the reward of the inheritance; for you serve the LORD Christ."

Spotlight Questions

In what ways can you identify with Heather's story?
What action steps occurred to you about taking God to work
as you read her story?

Study Questions

1   *Read 1 John 4:18.* When and where have you seen examples
    of fear in your workplace?

2   When have you seen examples of the promise found in
    this verse, that perfect love casts out fear? Describe a time
    you have seen that promise fulfilled.

3   When was a time at work that you applied the principal
    of using love to dispel fear?

4   *Read Matthew 6:30.* In what ways has God taken care of
    you at work?

5   What specific situations require the most faith at your
    workplace?

6   How can faith help you conquer fears that hinder your
    performance on the job?

7   *Read John 14:6.* How should knowing that Jesus is the Way,
    the Truth, and the Life impact the role of the Christian
    believer at work?

8   In this verse, Jesus states that "no one comes to the father
    except through me." What does that say about other
    religions?

9   How can Christians show respect for the beliefs of others
    without compromising their own beliefs about Jesus?

10 *Read John 15:5.* Abiding in Christ is the key to producing
    spiritual fruit at work. In what ways do you prepare yourself
    to abide in Christ at work?

11 How can abiding in Christ help you deal with temptations
    at work?

12 What are your biggest temptations at work?

13 *Read Psalm 121:1–2.* When do you most sense God's presence in your workplace?

14 When you lift up your eyes to heaven, how have you seen God's larger plan for you and your workplace?

15 The Bible says that God will fight your battles for you. How have you seen His power win battles at your workplace?

Prayer

Gracious LORD, *please free me from fear. Instill in my heart respect for and faith in Your power, Your love, and Your gift of a sound mind in Christ. Show me Your care for me at work and throughout the hours of my life. Bring me to repentance for those things I have done wrong and teach me to be holy by walking with Your Holy Spirit. I rely on You only for my salvation, my livelihood, and my well-being. The only identity that matters is my identity in Jesus Christ. Continue to inform and guide my decision-making at work. Clothe me in humility and right understanding for those I work with each day. Fight my battles for me as I yield each situation to You. In the name of Jesus, amen.*

What will you do to take God to work this week?

What God Thinks About You and Your Work

In this the love of God was manifested toward us, that God has sent His only begotten Son into the world, that we might live through Him.

1 John 4:9

HAVE YOU EVER KNOWN A PERSON whose every movement and action captivated your attention? Someone whose words were the equivalent of honey dripping into your ears? Could you spend hours watching that person do the simplest task? That's how God feels about you. He proved it by sending Jesus to the cross. We are infinitely fascinating to Him—so much so that He desires to have a personal relationship with us, even though we are infinitely lesser beings.

Put on God's glasses for a moment and look into the mirror. Imagine the one who created you. He looks at you like a new father looks at his first child; like a new mother fascinated with the little hands and feet of her first baby. Picture God's loving eyes staring back at you. Like a parent watching his or her child's first steps, He sees you as He created you: beautifully conceived and perfectly formed. You are exactly as He intended—unique and created for specific missions to love and care for others.

You have assignments in God's heavenly log book. Today, He sent you to smile at the older lady waiting for the bus or to help the harried mom round up her escaped Jack Russell terrier. He meant for you to care for and love these people He put in your path. Jesus taught, "A new commandment I give to you, that you love one another; as I have loved you, that you also love one another. By this all will know that you are My disciples, if you have love for one another" (John 13:34–35). Every morning when you leave your house for work, the Father will put people in your path who need just what the "redeemed" version of you can deliver.

Perhaps nothing indicates love more than a willingness to spend time, emotions, and resources on another. The God of the universe not only had time to come in human form to our planet but also stoops down individually to woo us to Himself. He takes time to hear and accept our prayers of repentance. He listens to us each day as we pray and include Him in our daily lives. That is a mind-blowing thought! The God of the universe gives us His attention and answers our prayers with His time, emotions, and resources.

Love is the test of your faith. The apostle John wrote, "Let us love one another, for love is of God; and everyone who loves is born of God and knows God" (1 John 4:7). If you accept God as your LORD, you can model His example of walking in love. It's a lifestyle choice. That means you give your time, emotions, and resources to others—not just to your friends and family but also to total strangers who can do nothing for you.

God's love is a challenge. Can you look through the lens of love at this sin-sick world, at your troubled co-workers, or at your harsh boss? Leave on those goggles of love that you used to look at yourself in the morning. See below the surface of the amazing creatures that God has placed all around you. They are fully human and completely fallible. Realize that a perfect being fashioned them in His likeness for a redeemed purpose. With His help, you can show God's supernatural love, every day, through your actions and responses to each situation.

Once you make up your mind to live this challenging Christian lifestyle, you must focus on the "how" of showing God's love. Your test—at work and everywhere else—is to keep God's commandments. "By this we know that we love the children of God, when we love God and keep His commandments. For this is the love of God, that we keep His commandments. And His commandments are not burdensome" (1 John 5:2–3).

You will not be up to this challenge of spreading God's love if you operate only in your own strength and within your own humanity. It will take a lot of prayer and a ton of practice. The good news is that God Himself wants nothing more than to have an all-day, every day, relationship with you. Talking it over with the Almighty will bring the guidance you need to handle any situation. He will show you how to be a sower of love. "Trust in the LORD with all your heart and lean not on your own understanding; in all your ways acknowledge Him, and He shall direct your paths" (Proverbs 3:5–6). God wants to show you the right way.

Serve God Through Your Work

God is a worker, and He created us in His worker image. "In the beginning God created the heavens and the earth" (Genesis 1:1). As workers, we find a sense of satisfaction and gratification through work that only it can provide. Whether it comes from mowing the lawn, tending a garden, or negotiating a successful business deal, our human DNA is wired to glean fulfillment from work.

From the beginning, God's vision for the earth included men and women who would care for the land, the animals, and other people. "Then God said, 'Let Us make man in Our image, according to Our likeness; let them have dominion over the fish of the sea, over the birds of the air, and over the cattle, over all the earth and over every creeping thing that creeps on the earth.'" (Genesis 1:26).

Is Work the Result Of the Curse For Sin?

Work is not the penalty for mankind's sin. Work pre-dates sin. God worked in creating the universe. He created Adam, and He intended for him to work as well. "Then the Lord God took the man and put him in the garden of Eden to tend and keep it" (Genesis 2:15). Adam and Eve had *jobs*. They cared for that first garden, dressed it, weeded it, and harvested its produce. God gave them this assignment before they sinned and before they incurred the penalties for sin.

However, even though work itself is not part of the curse, Scripture indicates the difficulty of life and work stems from that first sin:

> Then to Adam He said, "Because you have heeded the voice of your wife, and have eaten from the tree of which I commanded you, saying, 'You shall not eat of it': 'Cursed is the ground for your sake; in toil you shall eat of it all the days of your life. Both thorns and thistles it shall bring forth for you, and you shall eat the herb of the field. In the sweat of your face you shall eat bread till you return to the ground, for out of it you were taken; for dust you are, and to dust you shall return'" (Genesis 3:17–19).

Keeping the right perspective is essential to holding onto our joy about our work. Work is not a *curse* from God but is a *gift* from God. He cursed the ground, not the people. He made the environment of work more challenging, but He also promised to bless His people as they worked. "I know that nothing is better for them than to rejoice, and to do good in their lives, and also that every man should eat and drink and enjoy the good of all his labor—it is the gift of God" (Ecclesiastes 3:12–13).

The New Testament Model: Everybody Works

The New Testament church began with great unity. The believers realized the Kingdom of Heaven had visited them on earth. Jesus, and His way of salvation, had turned their thinking upside down—to the point they started sharing their belongings freely with each other. But as time went along, some in the early church began to take advantage of the situation. Instead of working, they went from house to house spreading gossip and stirring up strife. This happened so frequently that Paul sent an epistle urging people to work and not take advantage of others:

> For even when we were with you, we commanded you this: If anyone will not work, neither shall he eat. For we hear that there are some who walk among you in a disorderly manner, not working at all, but are busybodies. Now those who are such we command and exhort through our LORD Jesus Christ that they work in quietness and eat their own bread (2 Thessalonians 3:10–12).

Lest we think work is an old-fashioned notion whose purpose has passed us by, the Bible reminds us that work, in and of itself, remains core to God's intention for us. We don't "have to" work. We "get to" work. God made a world where each of us is intended to use our unique talents to make a contribution. Each of us has a strategic part to play in God's plan. In our youth, our purpose may have included mowing the lawn for the older folks down the block. During college, it may have been to bring light and joy into a fast-food restaurant (hopefully one that served salads). As adults, our work may bless hundreds of people or a single person struggling with a serious illness or other major challenge. Embracing God's value system means letting go of our human view of the importance of one task over another.

Meeting Needs Through Your Work

There are several reasons we work. First, we work *to meet our own needs*. Although this may seem like an elementary thought, it holds the value proposition of all work. The company or organization has something of value the worker desires, and in exchange for toil—sometimes even in great difficulty—the worker receives wages to support his or her own needs.

If you want to have shelter, good food to eat, nice clothes to wear, and transportation, you work. Even if there is no one else in your household, you owe it to yourself to work. There is often joy in work, even if that lies in fellowship with co-workers and customers. Every form of work has tasks that are less enjoyable than other tasks, but that just comes with the territory.

You may not need a lot of money to live. You may be financially set thanks to a comfortable retirement income or large inheritance. However, you still have work to do. In this latter case, your work may be of the volunteer variety or take the form of an unpaid ministry. Your retirement status may open up endless volunteer possibilities. Regardless of your age or handicap, someone out there needs something you can offer.

A second reason we work is *to meet our family's needs*. "But if anyone does not provide for his own, and especially for those of his household, he has denied the faith and is worse than an unbeliever" (1 Timothy 5:8). This verse sounds harsh, because it demands action. According to God's Word, allowing your spouse or children to go without when it is within your power to provide for them doesn't cut it. Unless we are too infirm in body or mind, we must work and take care of our own.

The third reason we work is *to meet our neighbor's needs*. At times, everyone needs a helping hand. Some people do not have family that are capable of helping them. In these instances, God may provide you with a surplus and put it on your mind to help a neighbor.

Work Facilitates Giving

As a pastor, I once spent a few months studying every passage in the Bible related to giving. As a result, I developed the following definition of obedient giving: *Obedient giving means to give at least the first ten percent or more of your total gross income to God through the local church in a cheerful manner.* You would be wise to make this a goal as you work and give. "And you shall remember the LORD your God, for it is He who gives you power to get wealth, that He may establish His covenant which He swore to your fathers, as it is this day" (Deuteronomy 8:18).

We give our offerings and pay our tithes to God. The first ten percent of our earnings always belongs to Him. The prophet Malachi illustrates this in the following passage:

> Will a man rob God? Yet you have robbed Me! But you say, "In what way have we robbed You?" In tithes and offerings. You are cursed with a curse, for you have robbed Me, even this whole nation. Bring all the tithes into the storehouse, that there may be food in My house, and try Me now in this," says the LORD of hosts, "If I will not open for you the windows of heaven and pour out for you such blessing that there will not be room enough to receive it" (Malachi 3:8–10).

God continues to show His generosity to us each day. He provides for us in hundreds of ways, not the least of which are the huge spiritual blessings He pours over us. "Blessed be the God and Father of our LORD Jesus Christ, who has blessed us with every spiritual blessing in the heavenly places in Christ" (Ephesians 1:3). In light of His generosity to us, how can we be less than extravagant with our giving?

One of the great joys of working is to be able to give. Whether it is providing for the short-term needs of a family who has suffered great loss or supporting missionary work on a distant shore, nothing connects a believer more tightly to God than giving when prompted by the Spirit. "Let him who stole steal no longer, but rather let him labor, working with his hands what is good, that he may have something to give him who has need" (Ephesians 4:28).

Secular vs. Sacred

In the modern secular world, the conventional wisdom is that enemies are to be ridiculed, defamed, and trampled underfoot. From presidential candidates to talk show hosts, bad behavior is modeled for the masses and quickly adopted as the norm. In the not-too-distant past, those who aspired to top positions in government, industry, or entertainment were expected to comport themselves with dignity and prove themselves worthy of respect. Increasingly, in recent years we've seen the opposite.

In God's view, the believer's whole life is a sacred gift. There is no secular and sacred. All ground that we walk upon is sacred because we carry with us God's Holy Spirit inside. The biggest heart for service wins the day. Our work is a reflection of the love God shows to us, and the humble among us will receive the most honor from Him. Christians who find the balance between being diligent in business and demonstrating love for others are the heroes in God's Book of Life. Those who choose to give away their possessions rate much higher in God's economy than those who die with the most toys. Speed boats and sports cars won't be of much use to us in heaven when consecrated spirits move at the speed of light to do the will of the Father.

Summary

In this chapter, we looked at God's love for us and how that empowers us to love others through our work. The purposes of work include taking care of our needs, our family's needs, and our neighbors' needs. Our salary also supports the work of our church through our tithes and offerings. For believers, every aspect of life, including our work, becomes sacred when we choose to yield to God's will.

Spotlight Feature

John McKinley

As a husband and father of five, John McKinley has worked in managerial accounting for almost thirty years, including twelve years in telecom and the rest in government. After giving into his fleshly side as a young adult, he eventually consecrated his life to Christ and found the zeal that many on-fire believers experience. His Bible became his constant companion, but in the early days of walking with the LORD, he didn't read it or study it in detail. That's when a co-worker stopped him in his tracks by asking him about the meaning of Genesis 4:9: "Then the LORD said to Cain, 'Where is Abel your brother?' He said, 'I do not know. Am I my brother's keeper?'"

From that time forward, John realized the importance of learning the Bible and being able to apply it to everyday situations. He found a Bible study near his office on Capitol Hill and soaked up the concise teachings. Over time, he went from listener to active participant and eventually to Bible teacher. John now leads a growth group at Capital Baptist Church.

Over the years, God positioned John in a work environment where he could do the most good for the Kingdom. He advanced in his career and several times changed jobs and offices within the same organization. With each transition, John kept his ears open for other believers and looked for opportunities to start a Bible study at his workplace

It hasn't always gone smoothly. In one instance, the Bible study grew organically as John and a co-worker studied Scripture over lunch. Eventually, a third man joined them, and it became a regular thing. But then management became aware of the informal meeting, and they asked the men to move their study off work property "to avoid offending anyone." This setback didn't stop the proliferation of God's Word. Through a Facebook friend, John found a way to move the Bible study down the street to a cupcake company. Sweet!

In another instance, John and a few employees started a Bible study at their government office. When they went to schedule a conference room, management approved the request to reserve it, but they told John and the others the entry must be recorded as an untitled "meeting." The rationale, again, was to avoid offending anyone.

Since that time, John has found it best to work under the radar in these situations. Although he talks freely about his faith and church activities, and though most of his co-workers know he is a Christian, he doesn't fight with management over the finer points of scheduling Bible studies. He saves his concerns for more important matters. This low-key approach makes him available should the Holy Spirit draw a co-worker in need to him.

Recently, a close colleague of John's experienced a serious health challenge, and John asked if he could pray with him. Even though the co-worker declined prayer at that moment, he told John to pray for him later and to have others do the same. John brought the man's health struggle to the attention of his small group at church. Periodically, John updated the co-worker about the prayers and well wishes of his class. Eventually, the man became receptive to one-on-one prayer. John has since seen noticeable changes in his colleague as they have talked about God, prayer, and the importance of family.

As John has spent time studying God's Word at work, at home, and at church, he has discovered that, in many respects, he really is his brother's keeper. It is a role he now gladly embraces as a follower of Jesus.

Spotlight Questions

What could you identify with in John's story?

What action steps occurred to you about taking God to work?

Study Questions

1   *Read John 13:4–5.* Who is a person in your life who has demonstrated love through his or her actions?

2   What are some of the ways God demonstrates love for you?

3   How have you demonstrated the love described in this passage through your work?

4   *Read Genesis 1:26–31 and 2:8–15.* What do these passages tell you about work?

5   How should knowing that God created work before the Fall impact your view of work and its importance in your life?

6   After the Fall, life—including work—became more difficult. What are some of the difficulties you have experienced in working?

7   *Read 2 Thessalonians 3:6–12.* Think about your first full-time job. How did it make you feel to be able to provide for your own needs?

8   If God created you in His image, and He is a worker, what does that tell you about your nature?

9   Why do you think this passage challenges Christians to take care of themselves and their families?

10   *Read Psalm 103:13 and Read Ephesians 1:3–8.* In what ways has God been generous to you?

11 Why do you suppose God commands you to be a cheerful giver?

12 This verse describes God as a compassionate father. What does this imply about your struggles at work?

13 What are some of the spiritual blessings God has given to you?

14 How should wisdom and prudence guide you at work?

Prayer

Dear heavenly Father, thank You for the love gift of Your Son, Jesus Christ. Thank You for caring about me even before I was born. Thank You for the many gifts of love demonstrated throughout my career, including Your provision for myself and my family through the salary and other benefits of working. Thank You for molding and shaping my character through the challenges of working and the occasional difficulties with other people. Continue to form me into a vessel that You can work through to accomplish Your pure and holy plans.

Thank You also for the generosity of the Holy Spirit and favor that You have bestowed on me as I study and practice the wise principles of Your Word. Thank You for Your friendship and counsel as I walk daily with You at work. Protect me and hold me close, all the more so when troubles come my way. With each success, remind me through Your Spirit to maintain an attitude of thankfulness. With each failure, call me to rest in Your wisdom, counsel, and comforting words. Show me how to take You to work each day. In the name of Jesus, amen.

What will you do to take God to work this week?

How to Succeed On the Job

FINDING A JOB
YOU CAN LOVE

*As for every man to whom God has given
riches and wealth, and given him power to
eat of it, to receive his heritage and rejoice
in his labor—this is a gift of God.*
Ecclesiastes 5:19

AFTER GRADUATING FROM OHIO STATE with a degree in jour-
nalism, I searched for job prospects near my small Ohio town
and the larger cities nearby. Hundreds of resumes and inquiries
into every applicable job opening resulted in frustration and no
success. At one point, my father even drove me 1,000 miles to
Texas to test the employment opportunities there. My disappointment grew as the weeks turned into months. I had spent
years learning, and now the world seemed closed to me. Finally,
at my mother's suggestion, I took a government service exam
and threw my hat into the ring—or my automated application
in this case—for a myriad of federal jobs.

The months passed by as I dutifully answered ad after ad and
went on interviews whenever they were offered to me. The low
point came when one manager said, "We really didn't expect to
hire a recent college grad, but we wanted to stay in touch with
the college scene. That's why we invited you for an interview." It
took everything within my barely sanctified body not to jump
across the desk and shake that woman silly. How could anyone
have such callous disregard for someone trying to break into the
job market? I wanted to shout, "People have feelings!"

I had almost forgotten about the government job test by
this point, and I was holding on to only a sliver of faith. I spent
hours in my room, listening to music and muttering to God.
I tried not to act depressed that year when my family sat down
for Thanksgiving dinner. My siblings sensed my embarrassment
and tried not to discuss anything about jobs or employment. Six
months had elapsed since graduation, and I was no closer to
getting my first job in my field.

Nights of prayer and crying out to God seemed to lead only
to more frustration. When would God hear me from heaven and
open the right door? *He* surely knew where I could find a job. As
I played with the turkey and dressing on the plate, my brother
recounted amusing story after amusing story, and everyone else
laughed heartily. Then, in an instant, my world changed.

The phone rang. I was sitting closest to the land line and
jumped up to answer it. A female voice on the other end indicated she wanted to talk to me about a job interview. My scores
on the government service exam had evidently qualified me as
a top applicant for a job in Chicago with the Social Security
Administration. The woman on the phone said she doubted
I would want to come all that way at my own expense, but she
wanted to offer me the opportunity. Needless to say, I immediately accepted the interview!

A week later, I grabbed a friend for moral support and headed
to the Midwest's largest city. In my naivete, I got off the highway

in south Chicago, near the housing projects, and made my way through a dangerous neighborhood to the downtown area known as "the loop." The man who interviewed me looked a bit nefarious, and the zip code of the building lurked at 60606, but I accepted the job as soon as he offered it. I saw it as God's provision. My first government position, a GS-5 Benefit Authorizer, paid just under $13,000 per year. I could not have cared less where it was located—whether that was in downtown Chicago or on the moon, for that matter. The job offered me a start, and I became super excited about it.

At the beginning of the new year, I began a months-long training class. The gloom that had descended on my life evaporated and everything became new. Good feelings filled the room as fifteen (mostly young) people began their new lives in the big city. Our world in the training course was a cocoon, though I didn't realize it right away. The only things expected of us were showing up on time, learning the material, and passing the weekly tests. The course called for mostly open-book quizzes and tests, so only a few people struggled with them.

After four months, a manager came to our class with big news. Trainees had been assigned to modules (work areas) within the large facility. As new benefit authorizers, we would soon begin plying our trade for real. In the mornings we would still come to class, but in the afternoon the case work would begin. At first, I couldn't have been happier. The academic setting had become tedious and being cooped up in a basement classroom with the same people had gotten old. Now a whole building of adventure awaited. Soon we would be analyzing the paper social security records of real people.

Enter other co-workers. My mentor—a tall, serious smoker—spoke in short sentences with a deep, husky voice. Management labeled him the cream of the crop in Module 7, which made me lucky to be assigned to him as my trainer. To my young adult mind, he seemed overly grim and humorless. As it turns out, he would prove to be one of my more cheerful co-workers. His mission became to teach me how to make accurate changes to social security payments using the agency's then-antiquated computer system.

In retrospect, and after enjoying a thirty-three-year government career, I have to say my colleagues at the Social Security Administration rank as some of the strangest and most dysfunctional folks I have ever encountered on my work-life journey. In those days, the powers-that-be permitted smoking in the office, and several folks took full advantage of the opportunity. Alcohol may have been a no-no, but the ladies of our module brought in their locally infamous twelve-days-of-Christmas punch and imbibed liberally for two weeks around Christmas and New Year's. I abstained, fearing I would be terminated for being under the influence at work. Gossip became a way of life for several of the other benefit authorizers, and I served as fresh meat for their stories and speculation. Overall, it fell well short of a pleasant environment for a Christian.

America's second-largest city felt chock full of characters, and several of them worked just a few feet from me. In the restroom, I met my first obsessive-compulsive employee. He would wash his face and then dry it with fifteen to twenty paper towels, one after the other. Somehow, it reminded me of a sad cartoon. I had none of the spiritual training that might have given me a chance to help him.

We worked in a building called the Great Lakes Program Service Center. My experiences there stretched my faith and taught me many lessons about depending on God at work. The experience included my first glimpse at the positive and negative behaviors of co-workers that I would continue to witness throughout my career. Several people showed genuine concern for me and tried their best to help me succeed. Others were rude, used foul language, and tried to sabotage me. Fortunately, my first boss rated as one of the best of my entire career. She looked out for me in every way imaginable. She even had the district office phone moved away from my desk, as she didn't want me to be disturbed too frequently while I learned my new job.

After only eighteen months with the Social Security Administration, I heard about a much better paying job with the Air Force. So, I bid farewell to this collection of odd co-workers and beloved former training classmates and headed off to Oklahoma for more adventures in the world of work.

What Makes People Love Their Jobs?

Most of us plod along at our jobs, either liking or disliking them, and giving little thought as to why we do or don't enjoy our work. However, by studying job satisfaction, we can gain clues about our own situation and the best path forward. The following list of why people like or love their jobs is not a comprehensive list, but it includes a synthesis of input from twenty websites:

- *Enjoying co-workers.* Liking the people we work with is an often-repeated reason for job satisfaction.
- *Ability to make a significant impact.* We all want meaningful work. Having a job where we can have a significant impact on the lives of others is a top consideration for job satisfaction.
- *Feeling valued or recognized.* We all want to feel important to the organization's success. When we do something noteworthy, it helps if the organization recognizes our performance or accomplishment.
- *Alignment between our goals and those of the company.* Over the long-term, we will be satisfied as employees if we buy into the mission of our employer. That's easier to do when our beliefs align with the goals of the company.
- *Personal development and growth.* We all want to feel we are learning something and growing as a result of our job. This could be the job itself or the willingness of an employer to fund training or additional education.

- *Being well paid.* Although this is not the primary factor in job satisfaction on most lists, compensation does matter. If the job doesn't pay enough to meet our needs and those of our families (and include benefits like health insurance), our job satisfaction will eventually wane.

- *Makes use of our skills and experience.* Few of us like to feel underemployed. Having a job that calls on us to use our abilities and experiences tends to promote satisfaction in the workplace.

- *Having a good boss.* Who we work for matters a lot in keeping us happy at work. Does our boss promote harmony in the office or keep everything in a state of uproar? Does he or she support work-life balance or demand unnecessary and uncompensated overtime to meet unrealistic deadlines based on staffing levels?

- *Enjoying working with customers.* In some jobs, our satisfaction may be driven by those who depend on the services we provide. If customers are appreciative and easy to serve, their attitudes can make the job easier and more pleasant for us.

- *Projects are interesting or exciting.* If the projects we are working on are interesting and fulfilling, we will have greater satisfaction at work. Some employees even list specific projects as the reason for their job satisfaction.

- *Time off.* Benefits may be more important to some of us than to others. If a prior job demanded us to work extra hours and penalized us from taking our earned vacation time, a new job in which we are encouraged to take our vacation time can represent a big step up in job satisfaction.

- *Opportunities for advancement.* Some of us are motivated the most by opportunities to get ahead. If advancement is our primary motivation, it will be important for us to understand the amount of change within an organization and the likelihood that promotions will come up regularly.

Signs It Is Time to Move On

One of the most challenging parts of working is deciding when it is time to change jobs. No one, other than God, cares more about your career and work life than you, and no one else knows more about you. Although almost a cliché at this point, you are the CEO of your career. If you experience long-term unhappiness at work, it is your responsibility to fix it (with God's help). The following are ten signs it may be time to prayerfully consider a job hunt.

1 You feel your potential is much greater than the demands of your job.

2 Your talents are going unused in your current role and are likely to be unused in future positions within the company or organization.

3 You sense a leading away from your current company due to their hostility toward Christians and Christianity. (Be careful, though, as God may be calling you to stay and initiate change. Every time a Christian becomes uncomfortable we should not automatically take it as a definite word from above to run away.)

4 Your employer expects you or pressures you to do things that are immoral, illegal, or unethical.

5 Your witness has been compromised due to mistakes of the past. (Sometimes a fresh start is the best way to leave behind past mistakes. God forgives you and moving on may be part of self-forgiveness.)

6 A new opportunity offers career advancement. (Remember that as a part of God's family, you are not ruled by your career. You shouldn't make life decisions exclusively to gain a little more money or more influence within your organization. You also need to consider God's will and the effects a new position will have on your family, church life, and so forth.)

7 A new opportunity offers a challenge and personal growth. (I moved from a comfortable job with Navy to the more hectic Department of Homeland Security for the challenge, adventure, and personal growth.)

8 A new opportunity offers the chance to work with outstanding people.

9 A new opportunity offers a much better quality of life for your family. (Some decisions come down to family. If two jobs are roughly equal in pay and responsibilities, a chance to cut sixty minutes from a round-trip commute may be reason enough to change jobs.)

10 A new opportunity offers ministry possibilities that are not present at your current job.

Any and all of these reasons could legitimately prompt a job change. There are many other reasons as well, such as the likelihood your current employer's business is failing, changes in leadership that have taken the business in the wrong direction, and external forces that are shrinking an entire industry.

Before accepting a new job, learn all you can about your potential future employer. Get a feel for their corporate culture and understand their expectations. Seek God and bring Him into all phases of your decision to change jobs. Pray through until you find His will regarding the job change. Ask if He has specific advice about the potential new employer or your role there.

The Holy Spirit will tip you off about potential issues and challenges ahead. This happened to me when I moved from the Navy to the Department of Homeland Security. In times of prayer, God let me know the switch to the new agency would come with some difficulties. I didn't interpret the warning as a sign not to make the change but a heads-up the new challenges would come with a price. Once the difficulties began popping up, I didn't feel ambushed. I found the rewards and impact I had at Homeland Security worth the trouble.

Look Before Leaping

When you feel God is leading you to make a job change, it is important to *look up, look back, look inward,* and *look around* before leaping into a new position.

Look Up: Ask God What He Wants You to Do

Your main focus is to follow Jesus. God knows everything about you and His intention for your life. From an early age, Jesus went about His Father's business (see Luke 2:49). You should have the same mentality. If you feel your current job does not make use of your gifts, ask God for wisdom. "If any of you lacks wisdom, let him ask of God, who gives to all liberally and without reproach, and it will be given to him" (James 1:5). God wants to give you this understanding.

Look Back: Consider What You Have Enjoyed Learning and Doing

While the past is not always a perfect predictor, it can give you clues on how to move forward. Can you remember a special assignment you particularly enjoyed that used a different skill set than your normal tasks? Do you interact with people in jobs that seem more suited to your talents and gifts? "But let each one examine his own work, and then he will have rejoicing in himself alone, and not in another" (Galatians 6:4). God is honored when you tailor your career to your unique abilities and talents.

Look Inward: Consider Who You Are

Take a *SELFIE*/self-assessment:

Spiritual Gifts: "As each one has received a gift, minister it to one another, as good stewards of the manifold grace of God" (1 Peter 4:10). What are you gifted to do? If you don't know, there are many self-assessment tools available online that can help you. Some of these tests focus on personality type, while others focus on spiritual gifts or calling. By understanding yourself better, you can find the work and career that best suits you.

Expertise: "Then the LORD spoke to Moses, saying: 'See,
I have called by name Bezalel the son of Uri, the son of Hur,
of the tribe of Judah. And I have filled him with the Spirit
of God, in wisdom, in understanding, in knowledge, and in
all manner of workmanship, to design artistic works, to work
in gold, in silver, in bronze, in cutting jewels for setting, in
carving wood, and to work in all manner of workmanship'"
(Exodus 31:1–5). Even in biblical times, some people were more
skilled than others at specific jobs. What are your particular
skills? If you've learned them through your work experience,
note them on your resume or work profile.

Likes and Dislikes: "Delight yourself also in the LORD, and He
shall give you the desires of your heart" (Psalm 37:4). What
do you love to do? God will give you latitude to find a career
that interests you. Think about what you've enjoyed doing
in the past as an indicator of where you might fit in well in
the future.

Family: "But he who is married cares about the things of
the world—how he may please his wife. There is a difference
between a wife and a virgin. The unmarried woman cares
about the things of the LORD, that she may be holy both
in body and in spirit. But she who is married cares about
the things of the world—how she may please her husband"
(1 Corinthians 7:33–34). What are your family's needs? You
may enjoy playing video games, but if you can't make a living
at it, it may not work for your family. Perhaps you can take
your passion and work in a related field, such as designing
video games.

Identity: What is your personality? If you are an extreme
extrovert, you will not be happy spending the day alone in
your office or at your job site. Think about different aspects
of your personality and how they provide clues to the right
type of job for you.

Environment: "Now Abel was a keeper of sheep, but Cain was a tiller of the ground" (Genesis 4:2). What places and people fit you best? Do you like to be outdoors? If sitting behind a desk is not for you, explore careers where you can be out and about. If you like a lot of activity, you may be happier working in a hospital than a quiet retail establishment.

Look Around: Consider What Opportunities Are Available

Paul wrote to the Corinthians, "For a great and effective door has opened to me, and there are many adversaries" (1 Corinthians 16:9). Sometimes, open doors provide opportunities, but they also come with obstacles. It is important to use your network and look at the possibilities. You may hold a secret desire to be a movie star, but with no training and no contacts, landing a job would be a true miracle. For the time being, God may provide a job more in keeping with your skills and abilities. Don't abandon your dreams, but be open to taking some training, volunteering at local theaters, and getting some experience before heading off to Hollywood.

You can find a great resource for understanding yourself and selecting the right career path at www.careerdirectionline.org. Many people at Capital Baptist Church have used the Career Direct assessment to better understand themselves and find the types of jobs that suit them best.

Get Feedback From Those Who Know

A woman named Julie felt beyond frustrated. After pouring five years into her job at a well-known accounting firm and even going back to school for an MBA, she wasn't included in the latest round of promotions. As she stared at her computer screen, she considered drafting a snippy email to her boss. After all, he probably gave the promotion panel negative information that caused her to be passed over again. This has to be his fault, she thought.

When she looked at the list of people who had recently been promoted to entry-level management, none of them impressed her. Sure, Jacob had a reputation for being a tough negotiator, but he only had three years of experience—and she had five. Then there was Rene. Upper management always seemed to favor her. They had just handed her a big deal with Boeing without asking who else wanted the high-impact assignment. She got tons of visibility and even won an award from her procurement customer. Julie wondered why Rene got that opportunity while she plodded away on assignments of lesser importance.

Julie reread the promotion announcement and noticed an invitation for a feedback interview. Although she knew it would be embarrassing to hear about her shortcomings, she thought she might learn something that would help her in the future. A few days later, she requested a panel follow-up briefing and met with Mr. Vlasic, the manager who ran the interviews. In addition to his role on the panel, he supervised the largest accounting section within their 300-person division. He sat across from Julie, smiling and without the least bit of nervousness. His calm demeanor allowed her to relax as well.

"Julie," he said, "thanks so much for requesting this debriefing. I think it helps employees better understand promotion decisions, and it will help you be better qualified when future vacancies occur. Let's get down to it. I can't talk about other employees or compare your performance to anyone specifically, but I can tell you what areas the panel labeled as strengths and weaknesses for your candidacy. Is that understood?"

"Yes," Julie said. "I'm just wanting feedback to know why I didn't get selected. My performance appraisals have been excellent, and I even obtained an advanced degree."

"That's true," Mr. Vlasic replied. "Your educational background is strong, and your performance appraisals are indeed excellent. Overall, you are a credible candidate. I can see you being promoted in the near future, assuming your work remains good and the interview goes well. What's lacking on your resume is depth of experience. While you have done many routine accounting transactions, there isn't a lot of complexity in the actions you've completed. In addition to that missing item on your resume, this inexperience showed up in your answers to the mandatory questions we asked each of the candidates."

Julie scratched her head and adjusted her wire-rimmed glasses. "I understand, but my section only receives certain types of accounting work. How can I get the needed experience on more complex opportunities?"

"You are on the right track," Mr. Vlasic responded cheerfully. "You need to volunteer for one of the large projects that come up from time to time. Go see the deputy director and tell him you want to be considered for future projects that are more complex in nature. He keeps a list of people who show the extra initiative and want more challenging assignments."

The interview lasted for several more minutes, but Julie already had the answer to her question. Her current job didn't provide the depth of experience she needed. She hadn't known about the deputy director's list of people who asked for more heavy-duty experience, so the debriefing interview proved well worth her time. Also, while she would follow Mr. Vlasic's recommended advice, she would also do some job hunting with organizations that could give her the needed experience.

A Word Of Hope

Remember the value of contentment in your work and be thankful for those times when your work is going well and you feel that contentment. "I know that nothing is better for them than to rejoice, and to do good in their lives, and also that every man should eat and drink and enjoy the good of all his labor—it is the gift of God" (Ecclesiastes 3:12–13).

In an annual survey conducted by The Conference Board, almost fifty percent of workers reported they were dissatisfied with their jobs.[2] They spend forty or more hours each week in a bad environment or doing tasks they find unrewarding.

While work is work and recreation is recreation, God intends your job to give you some level of gratification and a measure of fulfillment. One of the keys to that satisfaction lies in tying your efforts to a critical mission of your employer.

What do you view as an important job in the world? To those who depend on your products or services, your job may be *the* most important one to them on any given day. At the Department of Homeland Security, lives literally hung in the balance each day. The goods and services purchased helped border patrol agents detect firearms or other contraband. Transportation Security Administration officials uncovered nuclear threats and explosives in airports. And Federal Emergency Management Agency personnel located, rescued, and helped disaster victims. The importance of our mission energized most of us to complete even the most mundane tasks well. As long as you connect the tasks that comprise your job with the ultimate desired outcomes, it will be easy to stay motivated.

Keys to Find the Right Job

Let's look at several keys to finding the right job—or at least the right job for right now.

Involve God

It all begins with involving God in your job search. If you ask, you will receive. God wants to give you wisdom about your vocation. He will even let you know if your timing is right for changing jobs. But remember, He will also give you choices. He will guide you, warn you about potential traps, and may delay the timing of job changes, but He will not make the decision for you. Nothing pleases Him more than when you align your will to His principles.

At one point in my late forties, things had definitely not been going my way. I had accepted a job expecting one thing, but it turned out to be something totally opposite: different duties, a different supervisor, and different work environment. Although

I prayed for two months and sent out feelers, no other job offers (or even interviews) came my way.

When I felt that I couldn't handle any more of my current situation, I cried out to God again. He quickly arranged a short informal meeting with a powerful leader at Homeland Security. This woman went on to serve as the deputy secretary of the department and even filled in as the Secretary of Homeland Security some years later. As a result of this God-arranged meeting, my resume got on the desks of many decision-makers in the department. Before I eventually accepted a new position, I received seven offers of employment from the agency's headquarters and various sub-agencies.

Although not everyone will experience this same kind of blessing, God is well able to help you when you sincerely reach out to Him for help.

Check Your Attitude

Before you change jobs or accept a first job, begin with an attitude check. Remember that as a Christ-follower, you are called to a life of service:

> But Jesus called them to Himself and said to them, "You know that those who are considered rulers over the Gentiles lord it over them, and their great ones exercise authority over them. Yet it shall not be so among you; but whoever desires to become great among you shall be your servant. And whoever of you desires to be first shall be slave of all. For even the Son of Man did not come to be served, but to serve, and to give His life a ransom for many" (Mark 10:42–45).

This has implications for your job search. You defer to God's will. Your purpose becomes finding the position where you can serve the best, not necessarily be pampered the most. The right career move may not be the job that is the cushiest, provides the most salary, or commands the most respect. Remember that you are "His workmanship, created in Christ Jesus for good works, which God prepared beforehand" (Ephesians 2:10). Discovering your gifts and the right work for you may take a lifetime, but the journey can be ultimately rewarding as you walk each day in relationship with the Ruler of the Universe.

Evaluate Yourself

Evaluate yourself honestly and with the help of the Holy Spirit. "For I say, through the grace given unto me, to every man that is among you, not to think of himself more highly than he ought to think, but to think soberly, according as God hath dealt to every man the measure of faith" (Romans 12:3). There is nothing wrong with trying to move ahead in your profession or even changing fields entirely. But some strategies require preparation. Do you have the education, experience, abilities, temperament, and wisdom to succeed at the next level? Ask God to equip you for the opportunities that will come your way. God will lead you into the right relationships and places where you can be the most effective for His kingdom.

Realistic Job Preview

Historically, the process for hiring involves applicants providing input about their experience and education. The best-qualified applicants are then chosen to come in for one or more interviews before hiring decisions are made. Unfortunately, this process can omit a key factor in retaining new hires: the recruits need to know as much as possible about the job itself. If the would-be employee doesn't understand the day-to-day activities of the job, discrepancies can arise between expectations and the reality of working for the employer. This happened to me.

Some of these problems can be avoided if the applicant receives a realistic job preview. The employee can gather this information from personal research and by asking the right questions at the interviews. Wise employers will clearly explain expectations, the type of work that will be required, the challenges associated with the job or customers, and other demands. Getting the big picture of the job also includes understanding the positives of the work environment. Before leaping to a new job, it's important to weigh all aspects of the new position. Understand if the job change will likely fix major areas of dissatisfaction with your present position.

Confirming the Job Change and the Timing

One of the greatest difficulties in your walk of faith can be ascertaining whether it is God's timing to make major changes in your life. God knows what you need and when you need it, and your job is to trust the Spirit's gentle nudging and confirm your feelings biblically. The following are some ways that will help you do this.

Read the Bible

Every Christian should have daily alone time with the Lord. This is Christianity 101. On many occasions when I've faced big career decisions, God has confirmed the right path during these quiet times. His Word is perfect, and it contains acres of wisdom. God will lead you through the words of the Bible in miraculous ways. It is a living document. Often, His guidance will seem to jump off the pages of His written Word. "For the word of God is living and powerful, and sharper than any two-edged sword, piercing even to the division of soul and spirit, and of joints and marrow, and is a discerner of the thoughts and intents of the heart" (Hebrews 4:12).

Pray

One of the habits that separates believers from nonbelievers is prayer. We know God hears us as we talk to Him. "For the eyes of the Lord are on the righteous, and His ears are open to their prayers; but the face of the Lord is against those who do evil" (1 Peter 3:12). Don't forget to pause and listen. Prayer is a two-way street, and God wants to speak with His still, small voice.

God's character is good, and He is not going to respond to your prayer for guidance in an evil way. He will not forget you or ignore your questions. His response may not seem readily apparent at first, but you can rest in the fact that He will answer in the right time. "If you then, being evil, know how to give good gifts to your children, how much more will your Father who is in heaven give good things to those who ask Him" (Matthew 7:11). Don't lose heart if the answer takes longer than expected—but also don't be surprised if you hear back quickly.

Listen to the Holy Spirit

God is a triune being, made up of three parts: the Father, the Son, and the Holy Spirit. God places His Spirit within you to lead you on your journey and comfort you during difficult times. He guides you to the extent you learn to discern His voice and follow His leading. Take time to get to know Him, so that when you face major decisions, you can hear His input. Once you get to know Him, you will never be the same. If a job change is right, He will bring peace into the situation. If you feel a lot of anxiety, either the opportunity or the timing is probably not right.

Listen to Other Believers

While God wants a direct relationship with you, He will sometimes use your pastor, your Bible study group, or other strong Christians to help you hear His voice. "A wise man will hear and increase learning, and a man of understanding will attain wise counsel" (Proverbs 1:5). You should never be afraid to talk over a potential job change with a trusted Christian confidante, but you should also check that person's advice against what you are hearing in the Word of God and from your prayer times with Jesus.

What Are Your Circumstances Saying?

Once you've done all the above, God may use circumstances to make the right path apparent. Perhaps after a significant amount of prayer, you interview for a new job but someone else is selected. This may be God telling you the time isn't right to change jobs. Conversely, you may be offered a promotion to a much more challenging job, but at the same time your spouse is diagnosed with a serious disease that will require a lot of attention over the coming months and years. This may be a signal the time isn't right to accept the promotion. Circumstances aren't everything, but God gave you a sound mind to think these things through.

Carrying Your Cross

The tricky part of the Christian life is knowing when to hang tough in the face of adversity or bail out for something better. God certainly wants us to have joy. "Go your way, eat the fat, drink the sweet, and send portions to those for whom nothing is prepared; for this day is holy to our Lord. Do not sorrow, for the joy of the Lord is your strength" (Nehemiah 8:10).

> My brethren, count it all joy when you fall into various trials, knowing that the testing of your faith produces patience. But let patience have its perfect work, that you may be perfect and complete, lacking nothing. If any of you lacks wisdom, let him ask of God, who gives to all liberally and without reproach, and it will be given to him (James 1:2–5).

So, how do we get to the place of contentment even if things aren't going our way? Paul gives us the secret in Philippians 4:11: "Not that I speak in regard to need, for I have learned in whatever state I am, to be content." We learn to accept our present circumstances, regardless of whether they are easy or difficult, knowing that God is using our life for His purposes. In the Bible, we see that Jesus looked beyond temporary earthly happiness to the great purpose His Father had commissioned for Him to fulfill. He kept His eye on the cross and the work that His Father had laid out before Him to do.

We can do the same by examining our situations at work. Are the difficulties extreme? Are the effects damaging ourselves or our most important relationships. With prayer and Bible study, we can know if it is time to quietly carry our cross a bit further. We can know if God is freeing us to move on to greener pastures where our work life can further take off. Remember that the ministry of our work goes far beyond sharing the gospel with a co-worker. Our love for others is reflected in each customer we serve, each co-worker we encourage, and each time we care for the least of God's little ones.

To the rich young ruler whose whole life lay wrapped up in his possessions, Jesus said, "One thing you lack: Go your way, sell whatever you have and give to the poor, and you will have treasure in heaven; and come, take up the cross, and follow Me" (Mark 10:21). Likewise, we will find the most happiness when we look past the temporal to the eternal value of our work.

What Is Loving Your Job?

How much thought have you given about your "dream job" or dream life? Perhaps you tend to see possibilities in many different ideas and it is difficult to choose just one. Or perhaps you see the negative possibilities before seeing the rewards and benefits. Either way, you will do yourself a service if you stop and think in detail about what you hope to get out of your ideal job. How does it differ from the status quo?

Pray through the possibilities and talk them over with God. If you are married and your children are young, your dream job may look different than if you are single. If you like frequent travel and excitement, your dream job may include several nights per month out of town. If you like routine, your dream job may take place in the same office on the same schedule every day.

Obvious things to think about when analyzing your dream job opportunity include:

- Work duties
- Salary
- Time off
- Health and life Insurance
- Personality of your new boss
- Commute
- Work travel

Not so obvious things to think about include:
- Teammates at the new job (including volume of human contact)
- Work hours (flextime?)
- Responsibilities
- Your place in the organizational chart (will you get the support you need?)
- How much the job will enable you to give
- Who you will be able to love through your job

You should also analyze job opportunities in terms of career path. Will this new position benefit the trajectory of your career for the long term? Accepting certain jobs may look right at the moment but offer little professional growth for the future. Put another way, you have to consider whether the job—even if it is a promotion—will strengthen your resume or weaken it.

Pleasing God

An old saying goes, "If you please God, it doesn't matter who you displease. If you displease God, it doesn't matter who you please." I would add that if you follow God's plan, you will ride your share of dreams in this present lifetime. God has adventures planned for you that you can't even imagine.

Growing up, I admired comedians such as Lucille Ball, Johnny Carson, Mel Brooks, and others. What an amazing gift it is to bring laughter to others. Although I'm sure each of these funny people failed to live up to God's best in one way or another, their gift of laughter must have made God smile a lot. Do the same. Find that special thing only you can do and do it well. That's an amazing gift worth mining and searching for.

Summary

By examining the factors that cause people to love their jobs, we can reverse-engineer the process of finding a job we can love. Factors such as enjoying co-workers, making an impact, feeling valued, and having opportunities for growth may overshadow salary in importance to us. Some job changes are all about quality of life issues, such as dramatically shortening a commute or reducing the stress associated with being a supervisor.

Many factors go into finding a pleasant work life and avoiding a job we dread. Having a great boss can definitely make all the difference. We need to look carefully before leaping from one opportunity to the next. This includes taking a S E L F I E to examine our Spiritual gifts, Expertise, Likes/dislikes, Family needs, Identity, and Environment. The ten ways to know it may be time to change jobs should also be helpful. If we have a specific job in mind, we should get a realistic job preview. It all comes down to finding a place where we can love others and please God.

Spotlight Feature

Stacy Vickers

Stacy Vickers, a fifth-grade science teacher working in an affluent Washington, DC, suburb, has a job she loves. Each day represents another opportunity for her to let God's love shine to her students and co-workers. She doesn't just work for the paycheck but finds her divine mission in caring for the world by teaching science.

Growing up, Stacy recalls three science teachers who were instrumental to her decision to pursue a career in that field. Their encouragement and even-handed presentation of scientific facts gave her the drive to succeed at doing the same thing. Her love of education and passion to glorify God through teaching keeps her motivated during the many weeks that require more than forty hours of effort.

While Stacy doesn't necessarily agree with everything written in current textbooks, she has never felt pressured to teach theories as facts or dissuade students from their faith. "God is very present in school," she says. She sees evidence of His working just about every day.

Stacy teaches her students Christian values such as caring for each other, the importance of the family, and knowing the limitations of scientific knowledge. Occasionally, a parent will see Stacy's faith shining through, like the mother who point-blank asked her, "Are you a Christian?" When Stacy replied that she believed in Jesus, the parent teared up and told her how much she had prayed for her child to have Christian teachers.

"Public schools need to be free of religious bias," Stacy asserts. She is actually glad that proselytizing is prohibited, because she wouldn't want a teacher of another religion trying to influence her children into a different faith. "I believe public schools are not the primary place for children to learn about God and the Bible," she says. "Parents need to be teaching their own children about God and bringing them to church." Her one piece of advice is for parents is to talk to their kids about Jesus and let them see their struggles and successes as Christians. "If you don't teach them about God," she states, "how will they know?"

Fellow believers have asked Stacy whether her Christian beliefs put her at odds with the science curriculum, but fortunately this is not the case. While there are isolated issues, most of the curriculum Stacy teaches is agnostic to religion. She is also one of several voices who provides input into setting up the science curriculum. "When students ask me what I feel about evolution or creation science," she says, "I first send them back to their parents—as the school district suggests." If the student persists in knowing Stacy's opinion, she answers the child's question within her legal right.

Scripture and prayer are Stacy's primary weapons at school. She keeps Scripture cards on her desk for a special boost and to remind her of her primary purpose. She prays often for her students and co-workers.

Stacy's story should be an encouragement to each of us to find a job we can love and do well. Nothing is a better witness than a Christian who does excellent work and treats people well while he or she is doing it. Our work is a way to praise God, if we do it with excellence.

Spotlight Questions

What could you identify with in Stacy's story?

What action steps occurred to you about taking God to work?

Study Questions

1   *Read Ecclesiastes 5:19 and Ephesians 2:10.* What aspects of your current or previous jobs have you enjoyed?

2   Do you have any unfulfilled dreams about work?

3   Paul states in Ephesians 2:10 that God created you for good works. Do you know (or at least have an inkling) of what some of those good works might be in your life?

4   *Read Matthew 7:11, Luke 2:49, and 1 Peter 4:10.* Where can you go to get wisdom concerning a possible job change?

5   In the list of ten signs you may need to prayerfully consider before seeking new employment, do any of the indicators resonate with your current situation?

6   What assurance do you have from Scripture that God is on your side in finding a job you can love?

7   *Read Philippians 4:11 and James 1:2–8.* There are at least two sides to look at related to finding the right position. One side is to look for a job that better matches your experience, knowledge, skills, abilities, and passions. The other side is to learn to love the job you already have. Which side better describes your current situation?

8   As a believer, how can you discern if current difficulties represent God's refining work on your character or are a sign that you need to leave the situation?

9   Why do you think God calls you His workmanship?

10   What hint does Paul provide in Ephesians 4:29 about how to become part of the solution at your job instead of being part of the problem?

11   *Read Ecclesiastes 3:12–13.* This passage states it is a gift from above to be able to work and enjoy the results of your

labor. In what ways have you been blessed by working and earning a living?

12   How can forgiveness play a part in learning to love the job you currently hold?

Prayer

LORD, *thank You for providing employment that I can love. Whether this is the job I currently have or one I will find in the future, help me to see Your hand. Allow me to recognize the many opportunities You give me daily to love others through my work. Grant me contentment with my employment and with the compensation provided from You through my employer. Equip me with the self-discipline and mental strength to excel even in challenging times. Thank You for the opportunity to partner with You in the adventure of working around me. In the name of Jesus, amen.*

What will you do to take God to work this week?

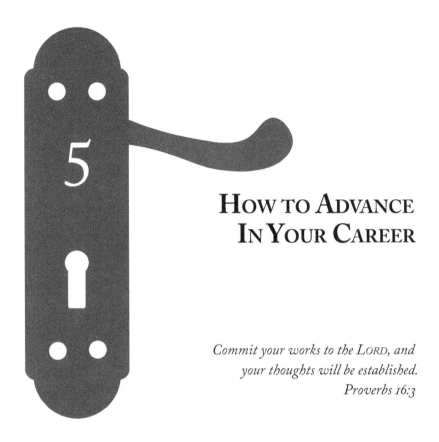

5

How to Advance
In Your Career

*Commit your works to the LORD, and
your thoughts will be established.
Proverbs 16:3*

AFTER GETTING A START IN MY career by surviving eighteen months with the Social Security Administration, I continued my civilian employment with the United States Air Force as an aircraft parts buyer. For some reason, back then in 1984, the Air Force mandated that all new employees had to get a physical from their crack staff of doctors and corpsmen.

I duly reported for said physical and quickly found out a little of what I had missed by not enlisting in the military. They divided us up by sex, male and female, and herded us around like animals. The first stop was filling out a mountain of paperwork, and then we took turns getting blood drawn by a young man who didn't look older than eighteen. This young man's gifts did not include the art of phlebotomy, but he eventually found a vein. The next stop for me—along with the fifty or sixty other male cattle, still woozy from having our blood drawn by the teenager—was to receive a plastic cup and directions to a too-small-at-any-size restroom.

We were then examined by a barely-understandable doctor, who may have had a previous life behind the Iron Curtain. *All this for a higher paying job, I* thought. At the end of the exam, I was judged fit enough to sit behind a desk for eight hours a day. Whew.

After three months of training in my new field of procurement, our large class of 300 eager young professionals departed for various locations around the country. As a result of the interview phase, the Oklahoma Air Logistics Center staff wanted me more than the other available locations. When I heard the cost of living compared favorably to the planet Saturn, I eagerly headed to the oil patch for phase two of my government career.

My flexibility and willingness to move to Oklahoma transported me from an almost dead-end job in Chicago to one with more promotion potential. As I look back, I realize that God wants us to succeed in our dreams and maximize our potential, but He may require some sacrifices for us to grasp that brass ring. God plants dreams in our hearts, but He also gives us discretion about the options along the way. His success meter isn't the same as ours, but we might be surprised at how much He approves of our desires to expand our influence and opportunities. Of course, this is provided we plan to use our position to care for His world.

Six Ways to Excel in Your Career

1. Write Out Your Goals

Knowing where you are going is essential to getting there. Hope will keep you going and lead you toward your goals. It will massage your inner being after a grueling task or set of tasks. Winners write out their goals. "Then the LORD answered me and said: 'Write the vision and make it plain on tablets, that he may run who reads it'" (Habakkuk 2:2). Be specific and include measurable results. Stop at regular intervals, such as quarterly, to determine if you are on track.

While it may be possible to show up for work each day without a vision of where you are headed, it will be impossible for you to bring energy and sustained excellence without hope your life will improve. The Bible puts it this way: "Where there is no revelation, the people cast off restraint; but happy is he who keeps the law" (Proverbs 29:18). We all want to be successful at work. But how are you defining success?

Know what you value and be specific about it. You need a clear roadmap (at least for the near future), and goals can help you frame the picture of your dreams. Generalities are not motivating, so write down specific, measurable goals with deadlines to solidify their importance in your mind. By posting them where you can see them, you will give yourself hope that achieving them is possible. By revisiting and adjusting them occasionally, you will apply faith to your vision of the future. "The plans of the diligent lead surely to plenty, but those of everyone who is hasty, surely to poverty" (Proverbs 21:5). Stay diligent about reaching your goals.

2. Insist On Integrity

Dictionary.com defines integrity as "adherence to moral and ethical principles; soundness of moral character, honesty." Several of the major twelve-step programs rely on the truism that many people, even those with mental illnesses, can recover if they are able to be honest with themselves. There is a bentness to the unsanctified human character that sometimes leads people toward an easier path in life, to excuses for poor performance instead of accountability, and even to self-deception instead of honesty.

Sanctification comes by the washing of God's Word over your life. It will lead you to enduring truth—to the bedrock that can faithfully support a successful life. For this reason, you must insist on integrity from yourself and hold fast to the moral code espoused in the Bible. "He who walks with integrity walks securely, but he who perverts his ways will become known" (Proverbs 10:9). The Internet age makes these words all the more accurate.

Working in a fallen world among morally compromised people can easily lead you astray. You must remind yourself frequently that God's way is the only way. Sin leads to death, and treasure obtained inappropriately holds no lasting gain. Solomon memorialized this thought during his reign when he wrote, "Getting treasures by a lying tongue is the fleeting fantasy of those who seek death" (Proverbs 21:6). Holding fast to the integrity that comes from your heart relationship with Jesus can and will lead to completion of the Father's work in you.

3. Resist Laziness

As we mentioned in the chapter on temptations, diligence is required for success. Just about every get-rich-quick scheme implies or flatly claims its followers will soon be rich if they just do a couple of simple things. Truthfully, the only sure way to financial stability is to make smart decisions again and again.

Realize that work is good and thank God for each day you have a job. Do your work with diligence and never be lazy. The book of Proverbs puts it this way: "The soul of a lazy man desires, and has nothing; but the soul of the diligent shall be made rich" (Proverbs 13:4). God wants to increase your net worth, but it isn't the only thing on His mind. He wants to teach you His principles, and then He wants to show others around you the blessings that result when a life is surrendered to Him.

Don't get caught in the trap of being all talk and no action. Any plan is only as good as its execution. You earn by doing.

Planning is good, but a lot of hard work will also be necessary for you to be successful. Have you met people who are all talk and no action? We all have known them. This personality type existed long ago in the time of King Solomon. "In all labor there is profit, but idle chatter leads only to poverty" (Proverbs 14:23).

Lazy people come up with all kinds of excuses and often shift the blame. If you find your conditions are never right to get to work, you may be suffering from perpetual laziness. "The lazy man says, 'There is a lion in the road! A fierce lion is in the streets!' As a door turns on its hinges, so does the lazy man on his bed" (Proverbs 26:13–14).

4. Never Stop Growing

Lifelong learning is one of those buzz phrases that may or may not excite you, but the wisdom behind it is timeless. Truthfully, those of us who read God's Word knew this truism years before corporate America started talking about it. "The heart of him who has understanding seeks knowledge, but the mouth of fools feeds on foolishness" (Proverbs 15:14). Think about solutions to your company's issues, not just the problems. Potential solutions will guide you to more learning. If you are willing to find the right solution, you will be rewarded.

Perhaps you've known some older folks who seemed to go from vibrant to irrelevant. Although they had no diagnosed diminished mental capabilities, they just didn't seem to be engaged in life. If you try to talk to them about anything, they have nothing to say. If you query their opinion, they indicate they just don't know. I've left some visits with older relatives and friends feeling sad, because it was obvious they had ceased to learn or care about current events, new technologies, or new ways to help others.

Keep learning. Keep growing. Keep finding new ways to help your fellow man. "The heart of the prudent acquires knowledge, and the ear of the wise seeks knowledge" (Proverbs 18:15). Here are some ways you can continue to grow:

- *Grow through the Bible.* "He who despises the word will be destroyed, but he who fears the commandment will be rewarded" (Proverbs 13:13). The Bible contains thousands of lessons that will help you at work.
- *Grow through mentors.* "Without counsel, plans go awry, but in the multitude of counselors they are established" (Proverbs 15:22). Walking with smart people in your life will give you the benefit of their experience.
- *Grow through adversity.* "If you faint in the day of adversity, your strength is small" (Proverbs 24:10). Embrace challenges and recognize they are making you stronger.
- *Grow through critics.* "Poverty and shame will come to him who disdains correction, but he who regards a rebuke will be honored" (Proverbs 13:18). People who learn from criticism get better at their jobs.
- *Grow through mistakes.* "He who covers his sins will not prosper, but whoever confesses and forsakes them will have mercy." (Proverbs 28:13). We all fail at times. Learn the lessons from your failures and move forward.

5. Use Your Time Effectively

Although life can seem long at times, the truth is we all are a vapor and grass quickly fading. For this reason, it is important to figure out how to most effectively use your time. "So teach us to number our days, that we may gain a heart of wisdom" (Psalm 90:12). By budgeting your time, you will become intentional about how you spend it.

Winners closely manage their time. "Trust in the LORD with all your heart, and lean not on your own understanding; in all your ways acknowledge Him, and He shall direct your paths" (Proverbs 3:5–6). God will help you make decisions about your time management. It is a sin to waste your time, because to waste your time is to waste your life. "He who is slothful in his work Is a brother to him who is a great destroyer" (Proverbs 18:9).

6. Resist the Temptation to Quit

God wants you to make it to the end, and He will help you every day to do your best. He will find ways to rejuvenate you. You just have to remain open to trying new things. One of the big secrets of success is to keep trying no matter what obstacles get in your way.

Nick Foles, a perennial backup quarterback, lived out this lesson on national television when he led the Philadelphia Eagles to a win in the 2018 Super Bowl. Foles had spent his career moving from team to team, and he considered quitting several times. But by hanging in there, he put himself in a position to succeed during the 2017–2018 season.

Foles was promoted to starting quarterback when Carson Wentz suffered an injury at the end of the regular season. Foles earned a storybook ending to his year when he played well enough in the playoffs to make it to the Super Bowl and win the biggest prize in football. However, more important than his success on the field, he played a major part in the spiritual revival that swept through the Eagles' locker room. Several players accepted Christ and were baptized during the course of the season. Their witness on television and in print spoke volumes during their playoff run and eventual Super Bowl win.

Everyone falls down. Everyone makes mistakes. And most of us lose our way sometimes. "For a righteous man may fall seven times and rise again, but the wicked shall fall by calamity" (Proverbs 24:16). But the key is to never quit. With God's help, those who pay the price and keep paying it will eventually break through to a measure of success. So, when you fall down, get up and dust yourself off. Remember that others have survived what you are facing, and God can—and will—make you successful if you don't give up.

Winners are not perfect, but they are persistent. "The lazy man does not roast what he took in hunting, but diligence is man's precious possession" (Proverbs 12:27).

Long-term Success

Time and again the Bible teaches about the value of sustained effort. Your career is more like a marathon than a 100-meter dash. Get-rich-quick schemes seldom succeed, but by investing in your education, experience, and character, you increase the likelihood you will achieve your career goals. Sustained excellence won't come exclusively from your God-given gifts and experience. However, it will come as you refine those gifts and learn to bring along the Master Teacher as you practice your profession or skill.

Do the Right Thing For God

Do the right things at work because you respect God and trust His reward system. Believe it or not, others are looking to you for spiritual leadership. They stand by, hoping you are for real and your morality is based on a compass that doesn't fail. Demonstrate God's love and care in all that you do at work. People will judge your character not by the image you portray but by the actions you demonstrate.

God looks on the inside, beyond the façade, and knows your true character. He sees your thoughts and understands your motives. He told Samuel, "The LORD does not see as man sees; for man looks at the outward appearance, but the LORD looks at the heart" (1 Samuel 16:7). As you take God to work, you will conform your inward man and your outward actions to His Word as revealed in the Bible.

Invest In People

Getting to know, understand, and help other people is rarely a waste of time. Relationships lead to results. Every action you take to help someone is a deposit into your relationship bank. Someday, you may need a job recommendation, a tip on a job opening, or support for a promotion. Putting time and energy into others always pays off, even if it only helps the other person. The gold of life is knowing you've helped someone else, and it's a deposit you never need to worry about. Other investments may turn south or evaporate with inflation, but partnership with your colleagues and bosses will always be safe in the bank of goodwill.

When you look back at your career, you should have a lot of people to thank. None of us made it all on our own. Remember to practice gratitude for those who contributed to the tapestry of your career—the boss who recognized your potential, the colleague who comforted you when you made a mistake, or the customer who gave you a chance by placing a large order.

God Is Okay With Happiness

Time invested in figuring out what career or job best suits you will be time well spent. The investment will lead to your happiness, and your contentment, in turn, will lead to creativity, ambition, and commitment. If you love your job and the rewards it brings, you will be more likely to give it your all. Sometimes, Christians feel that piety requires an arms-length relationship with happiness. If you like anything too much, it must not be God's will. The opposite is actually true. Joy is invigorating and strength-producing. While the Bible espouses the benefits of delayed gratification, it also indicates tremendous blessings lie in store for those who consistently follow God's principles.

When Success Seems Slow In Coming

At times, we all feel overlooked at work. Advancement seems to come for one person or another but always seems to pass us by. Even though we are doing the right things and working as unto the LORD, the promotion goes to someone else. This is the exact hour to call out to the LORD in prayer.

Several times during my government career, I almost gave in to envying a co-worker who seemed to be finding more favor than me. Then I went into the House of the LORD, either literally (church) or figuratively (prayer). God often responded with a question, just as He does in the Bible. Here are some of the questions God asked me when I didn't get the promotion

I was hoping to get. See if any of God's simple questions to me apply to your situations relating to a co-worker moving up to a higher position.

- Did you work as hard as your co-worker?
- Would you want to deal with the manager (or customer) who came with that promotion?
- Could it be your time to be picked hasn't arrived yet?
- Is it possible that I (God) have something much better waiting for you?
- Is it okay with you that I chose to bless your co-worker with this promotion?

On the occasions I felt passed over, God brought answers to my questions. The recurring theme in all my gentle rebuffs from the LORD was that He knew what was best for me and the opportunity did not fit that description. I believe the Father shared His heart with me partly because I asked Him to do so but also because I stayed in His Word and studied the Bible. This gave Him an avenue to speak back to me.

By the end of my career, I didn't even apply for promotions until I had thoroughly prayed through about the cost of each move up and God's plan for me personally. God had taught me over the years to more accurately assess my own readiness and willingness to accept additional responsibilities. As it existed, my job by that point required me to be involved in or review the largest procurements in the Department of Homeland Security, which spent upward of six billion dollars each year. My division alone often spent more than a billion dollars a year. My jobs as division director and, eventually, chief of staff gave me plenty of challenges, chances to love people, and opportunities to be in the spotlight.

When Things Are Going Well

Life for believers should not be one big struggle. Each of us goes through periods of success where God blesses us, we get the promotion, or we receive a bonus. The bills are all paid, and we have money to spare. Things are going well at work, everyone is thriving at home, and even the family dog seems to be behaving himself. In these happy times, make sure to stay in God's Word and pray during the times of peace and quiet. Remember to be thankful for all the blessings that come your way.

Part of the road to advancement is being able to handle success. Once you get the promotion, redouble your efforts to serve and love everyone through the added responsibilities. Our freedom in Christ is an amazing gift. "For you, brethren, have been called to liberty; only do not use liberty as an opportunity for the flesh, but through love serve one another" (Galatians 5:13). Once you get ahead, don't let down your guard and get off track. Many good men and women have swelled with pride following a big promotion, and these same people have taken tremendous falls as a result.

Poise Looks Good On Everyone

Reactions to a promotion say a lot about you and your maturity level. Do it right, and even your enemies will cheer for you. Do it wrong, and even the one who promotes you will regret it. As always, a humble spirit looks good on everyone. Keep in mind that your boss promoted you because he or she deemed you able to handle additional responsibilities with poise. In biblical parlance, that means being a servant with broader responsibilities. More people to serve. More responsibilities under your ownership.

Internalize the good feelings of being the one selected. Celebrate and be thankful. But realize that while your number came up this time, next time you may be the one congratulating someone else. As you accept new responsibilities, remember that some of your co-workers may feel stuck in their careers. Your advancement may bring up certain feelings for them, such as resentment and jealousy.

Likewise, react well to your rivals and colleagues when they are promoted and when they face difficult times. "Do not rejoice when your enemy falls, and do not let your heart be glad when he stumbles" (Proverbs 24:17). When one of my co-workers faced demotion, I hurried in to offer her a job in my division. Although she chose a different opportunity, I made a friend for life. People remember how you treat them in good times, but they remember it more when they are facing tough times. Give people a soft landing place when it is their turn to fall. They just might do the same for you later.

When You Feel Stuck

From time to time, it may feel as if you are stuck at a certain level in your career. God wants to hear all of your thoughts, and it's perfectly fine to bring this concern to Him. "The wise shall inherit glory: but shame shall be the legacy of fools" (Proverbs 3:35). While it makes no sense to throw away a perfectly good job that provides for you and/or your family, it's worth taking time to examine why you feel dissatisfied. Is it repetitive tasks? Is it a lack of promotion potential in your field? Is it unpleasant aspects of your job? Beyond staying in faith that God is watching out for you, it may be helpful to look inside during those times. Here are five ways you can do this when you feel stuck in your career.

1. Determine Your Level Of Interest

Determine if you are passionate about your current job, company, or work environment. Most of us find it difficult to succeed if we really don't like what we do, so ask yourself whether the daily tasks are consistent with your personality. For instance, if you hate conflict, you shouldn't be in a position where negotiating contentious issues between the union and management is a major part of your job. In addition, consider whether the mission of your company or organization is consistent with your values and interests. For example, if you don't think plastic bags are good for the environment and that is something you care about deeply, you shouldn't be working for company that makes plastic bags.

2. Get Real With Yourself

Get real with yourself about your level of knowledge, skill, and ability. Ask God to show you what you might be lacking to move ahead, and then pay attention. God will bring up situations and conversations that will help you know what areas to work on, whether it is more experience, training, education, or people skills. Research what credentials are important at the next level in your field and ask yourself if you possess that degree, certification, or experience.

3. Ask Your Boss For Feedback

Ask your boss for feedback about your performance—and don't be thin-skinned about the answers. Most organizations have a regular performance review process, so use it to your advantage. Probe deeper. Don't settle for platitudes such as, "Oh, you're doing okay." Ask what things you could do to increase your chances of being considered for a promotion. How can you improve? Are there special projects that could prepare you for promotion down the line?

4. Test the Marketplace

If you believe there is a better job out there for you, test the marketplace. Whether you find another job or not, it will give you a better understanding of the possibilities out there given your current qualifications. (Of course, if at all possible, be sure to secure the next job before quitting your current one.) As a manager, it used to drive me mildly crazy when employees had an exaggerated sense of their own salary potential. The market is seldom wrong. So, get out there and apply for other jobs if you think you are sorely underpaid. If you don't get offers, try to follow up and find out anything that is missing from your background.

5. **Do Your Best Every Day**

Until you get promoted or find a new job, do your best every day. Managers are not impressed by words; it's all about action. If you start consistently doing excellent work, on time and under budget, opportunities for advancement should eventually come your way.

Give Your Career to God

Previously, I mentioned that in my search for career advancement, I took a job with the Air Force in Oklahoma in 1984. Being raised in Ohio, and coming from Chicago at the time, the move to oil country came with a great deal of culture shock. While all people have things in common, the Oklahoma mindset of that day took some getting used to.

For example, pick-up trucks populated every parking lot. Not a *few* pick-up trucks, but many, many, pick-up trucks. This often led me to park in tight quarters between two behemoth vehicles. I would have to squeeze out of my compact car while trying not bump the extended-cab truck next to me for fear a gun-toting Okie might open fire before I could make it safely into the store. (I exaggerate only slightly.)

Another example of the differences was that my neighbor in the apartment building where I lived had a live wolf as a pet. Not a small, hybrid dog/wolf, but a real, big wolf with fangs and a menacing attitude. My neighbor brought it over to my apartment to show me once, complete with a heavy chain around the animal's neck. I have trouble relating to people with pets that could devour me.

Apart from the broad cultural differences, the Air Force work environment felt different than the one at the Social Security Administration. Several of the long-time Air Force employees worried that all the new trainees from our hiring class would get promoted ahead of them, even though they had more seniority. This led some of the trainers to be less than hospitable.

The biggest issue with my Oklahoma job turned out to be the work itself, as the negotiations required in the position didn't fit well with my personality. I don't like conflict. My job with the Air Force involved negotiating prices on aircraft parts. In most cases, the government did not own the rights to the drawings for these particular aircraft parts, and the defense contractors who owned the proprietary rights did not prove eager to give price breaks.

The companies, like Boeing and General Electric, knew they were the only authorized supplier and the only ones legally permitted to produce and sell the parts. This gave them the upper hand in negotiations. So, my job involved calling people who didn't want to hear from me and argue with them in an attempt to get cheaper prices.

Turning My Work Life Over to God

Finally, I came to the end of myself and cried out to the LORD. I prayed that God would take over my career and show me the right way to go. My best efforts had left me miserable, unfulfilled, and sitting in a large aircraft hangar in Oklahoma. It proved to be an emotional bottom for me. Coming to the end of myself and asking God to take over became the smartest decision I ever made. I realized that just being a Christian wasn't enough. If I didn't let God control my life, I would give up many of the benefits of my relationship with the Ruler of the Universe.

This amounted to a watershed moment. From that time on, God took over the control of my career. Within a few months, a friend told me about an opportunity in Chicago with the Navy. I didn't have to completely change fields or leave procurement, but I was able to go from difficult negotiations with large companies to administering research contracts and grants with universities. The position in Chicago had greater promotion potential than in Oklahoma, and it put me within driving distance of my parents in Ohio. This allowed me to buzz home for an occasional weekend visit, which proved increasingly precious as my dad's health deteriorated.

"Commit your works to the LORD, and your thoughts will be established" (Proverbs 16:3). I certainly found this to be true in my life. While there were still challenges and periods of difficulty, overall the intense struggles subsided when I turned my work life over to God. The last twenty-eight years of my career unfolded much easier than the first five years. All I had to do was commit the whole thing to God and let Him lead me. Try it and see if God is indeed good.

Summary

In this chapter, we examined six ways you can emulate the way God works and move ahead in your career: (1) write out your goals, (2) insist on walking in integrity, (3) never be lazy, (4) never stop growing, (5) manage your time well, and (6) resist the temptation to quit. Avoid stagnating in your career and life by continually seeking out new challenges. We also examined long-term strategies for success, such as avoiding the quest to get ahead just for appearances, investing in people, and not fearing the prospects of happiness.

When success seems slow in coming or you feel stuck, seek to understand the differences between the requirements needed for a promotion you are seeking and your education and experience. Figure out if your company or organization stirs your passion to do excellent work. Get feedback from your boss and, if necessary, prayerfully consider testing the job market to see if another employer might be willing to pay you more or offer more responsibility than your current job. Most importantly, turn your career and work life over to God. Let Him be in charge, because He loves you and wants the best for you.

Spotlight Feature

Ken Matos

Ken Matos faced a major challenge in December 2008 when his employer suddenly terminated him. Just two months before, he had left a secure job as the controller of a different company, so a pink slip was the last thing he expected. The experience jolted him and caused him to assess what had gone wrong. As he reflected, he noticed an ad for government accountants.

Several applications and several months later, Ken landed a job at the Department of Housing and Urban Development in Washington, DC. At the time he and his wife had children in school in New Jersey, so they decided he should get a studio apartment near his job and commute home for the weekends. Ken's four-day work week with ten-hour days facilitated the plan, and everything went well at first. Ken even landed a second job as a part-time accounting instructor at the University of Maryland University College. His key verse during this process became, "Trust in the LORD with all your heart, and lean not on your own understanding; in all your ways acknowledge Him, and He shall direct your paths" (Proverbs 3:5–6).

While Ken had always been open about his faith, opportunities presented themselves frequently at his new job, and he shared the gospel freely with co-workers. After a year in Washington, Ken received a promotion. Weeks turned into years, and before he knew it, he received another promotion. However, this new role required him to transfer to the Bureau of Indian Affairs in the Virginia suburbs of our nation's capital.

Although everything was progressing well with his job, the commute to New Jersey on the weekends eventually wore him down. Enter some not-so-helpful church friends, who started speaking doubts into the ear of Ken's wife. They suggested a young husband alone in another city spelled potential disaster. Ken's wife knew he was a devoted family man and committed believer, so she didn't believe the idle chatter. She knew Ken had put his faith in the LORD and would not stray. Even so, this period in their lives became a trying time for Ken as he commuted weekly almost six hours each way to be with his family.

When Ken's eldest daughter graduated from high school, he and his wife began to arrange for the rest of the family to move to Virginia during the summer of 2014. Thanks to the LORD's leading and advice from a friend at work, Ken discovered lower-priced homes in nearby West Virginia. The location was just over an hour from his job in Reston, Virginia, and he and his wife decided to build their dream house there. The family reunited after five years of long-distance marriage in a brand-new home. Ken and his family had done what they needed to do for him to support them, and he can now see God's hand leading them throughout the process.

Ken credits God for all the gifts he has received, including the promotions at work, the opportunities to live out his faith, and the preservation of his marriage. His five years in the crucible led to amazing ministry opportunities for Ken in West Virginia. He founded a dynamic men's ministry called Kingdom Men, and under his leadership, the group has grown astronomically in numbers. They are doing much today for their church and community.

Throughout Ken's trials and temptations, he held fast to Ephesians 6:13, which tells us to put on spiritual armor. Even today, he mentally puts on the whole armor of God each day and remains rooted in God's Word. This is what being a Kingdom Man is all about.

Spotlight Questions

What could you identify with in Ken's story?

What action steps occurred to you about taking God to work?

Study Questions

1. *Read Proverbs 16:3.* Have you committed your work to the LORD? If so, what are some practical ways you have yielded to His plan for your work life?

2. In what ways has God established your thoughts?

3. *Read Proverbs 29:18.* Do you have written goals related to your work? What are they?

4. In what ways have you bought into the vision or plan at your workplace?

5. How does a lack of vision feed into lawlessness at work and beyond?

6. *Read Ecclesiastes 3:12–13 and James 1:2–8.* God's Word calls it a gift from above to be able to enjoy the fruit of your labor. In what ways do you feel blessed by your work?

7. What is the relationship between contentment and overspending?

8. How are you demonstrating patience and faith when it comes to workplace issues?

9. *Read Proverbs 10:9 and 21:6.* What are some ways employees walk in integrity at work?

10. Why do some people make a habit of lying at work?

11. What are the rewards of walking in integrity versus giving into deceptive shortcuts at work?

12   *Read Proverbs 15:14, 18:15, and 24:16.* What steps have you taken to increase your knowledge of your duties or chosen field?

13   How is acquiring knowledge a sign of prudence?

14   Righteous people are known for getting up after a fall. Why do you think people of faith have more staying power?

Prayer

Dear Father, we know that You lift up leaders and take them down, in accordance with Your great plans. I ask that You make me the best Christian possible, so that I can be used for Your purposes. Grant me a right view of myself and my work. Let me not be lifted up with pride or stooped down by false humility. Show me the way of diligence, patience, and commitment related to my duties. Help me, through Your Holy Spirit, to walk in integrity, eschew evil, and embrace good. Fill me with knowledge and wisdom, so I may be prepared for advancement if that is the best course of action for myself and for Your plan. Finally, let me turn to You in times of great success and in times of failure, knowing You are my source and my protector. In the name of Jesus, amen.

What will you do to take God to work this week?

6

PURSING EXCELLENCE IN A MEDIOCRE WORLD

Inasmuch as an excellent spirit, knowledge, understanding, interpreting dreams, solving riddles, and explaining enigmas were found in this Daniel, whom the king named Belteshazzar, now let Daniel be called, and he will give the interpretation.

Daniel 5:12

DANIEL HAD EVERY RIGHT to shut down emotionally. His homeland had been conquered, and he was living in exile in a foreign capital. His life had been turned upside down, and everything about his outward circumstances had changed for the worse. If anyone could have felt entitled to phone in his performance, it was Daniel. He could have lived out his life a disgruntled prisoner, doing the minimum for his captors. Instead, he kept praying three times a day, kept believing God remained in control, and kept using his gifts to help others. Over the years in Babylon, he developed a reputation among his captors for sustained excellence.

Many of us face similar challenges and similar opportunities for disillusionment. Perhaps we spent a lot of time building a strong track record with our boss, only to see that boss accept another job at a different company. Or perhaps our years of service seemingly became meaningless when our corporation got taken over by a competitor.

Daniel made his mark as a government worker. Even though his adopted country did not honor the LORD God, Daniel still found favor. At times, his faith put him at odds with the powers that be, but that didn't change his perspective of pleasing God first. His diligence proved the saying true that "those who do an excellent job will never lack for work."

Doing the best job possible is never wasted effort. A strong reputation endures in good times and bad. Everyone wants the best performer on his or her team. A persons' reputation spreads—whether it is positive or negative—and excellent workers are always in demand. According to Dictionary.com, "excellence" means superiority or eminence. A person with excellence surpasses others in some respect or area. They do their jobs well. They find creative solutions, document thoroughly, follow up, close the loop, adhere to laws, accomplish the goal, and meet deadlines.

Temporary ups and downs happen to everyone. However, while circumstances may be out of our control, winners find a way to do excellent work even in difficult situations. Excellence has a lot to do with dogged determination and tireless attention to detail. The best employees reread emails *before* they hit send. Preeminent managers carefully gather facts *before* steering their organizations in one direction or another.

Mediocrity Is the World's Standard

Many workers do just enough to get by. If they can get away with a shoddy job and play on their computers all afternoon, they take that path. Instead of double-checking their work or improving a first draft, they pass the work product along to the next person. If no one complains, they consider it a good day.

Mediocrity includes work that is of poor quality and brings about second-rate results. We often recognize unexceptional service as we see it—such as when we order coffee but aren't offered a refill or warm up. Indifferent attitudes spell trouble in customer service jobs. How long can a business last if the employees don't care whether customers are pleased?

As Christians, we are called to a higher standard and a different way of life. Our efforts should reflect the glory of God in everything we do. There is nothing glorious about a document that has several typos or a building with crooked walls. Not everyone may be an artist, but we can all do our best at whatever job is in front of us.

Have you ever spent a day feeling underwhelmed by the undistinguished products and services you receive? Perhaps you go to a fast-food restaurant for breakfast. As you pull onto the highway, you anticipate that first intoxicating drink of diet soda, only to take a disappointing gulp. They gave you regular soda instead of diet! Although it was a minor mistake, it begins your day on the wrong note. There's no time to go back and get it fixed. Perhaps you can't drink regular soda, so you pour it out, wasting your two dollars. With nothing to drink, your breakfast gets cold as you wait to eat it until you get to the office.

After a busy morning, you decide to hike two blocks to pick up your suit from the dry cleaner. They quickly locate the clothes assigned to your ticket and charge you substantially more than you expected. When you get back to your office and hang the suit on the back of your door, you notice the stain on your suit lapel is still there. The cleaners didn't get the Grand Marnier sauce out of it, and it is unwearable. You have a meeting in fifteen minutes, and there is no time to take it back to the cleaners right then.

Finally, your work day is over, and you want to head home. However, before you retrieve your car, you have to return the suit to the dry cleaner for another try. Traffic is more snarled than usual, because the construction crew reopened a couple of freeway lanes later than they should have. It is a minor mistake, but it costs you (and thousands of other commuters) an extra twenty minutes to navigate the resulting traffic jam.

You finally arrive home and retrieve your mail from the box. You absentmindedly open the electric bill, and your eyes nearly bug out of your head when you see the monthly charge: $1,342,567.14. You know it's an error, but the prospect of the time it will take on the phone to straighten it out does not improve the trajectory of your day.

All these mistakes are small matters that reflect less than excellent performance. In some way, each foul-up represents someone's failure to take care of God's world and His creation. That's why it is important for us to always try our best and take pride in our jobs, regardless of whether the world considers them important or not. Mistakes happen, but we can reduce the number of errors by applying our best effort and pushing ourselves just a bit.

Why Should Believers Strive to Do Excellent Work?

The first reason we work as unto God is because He will be our ultimate judge. Although Jesus paid the price for our sin through His death, burial, and resurrection, the things we accomplish with our talents will be subject to God's review. He will use His own value system to test the quality of our work.

> Each one's work will become clear; for the Day will declare it, because it will be revealed by fire; and the fire will test each one's work, of what sort it is. If anyone's work which he has built on *it* endures, he will receive a reward. If anyone's work is burned, he will suffer loss; but he himself will be saved, yet so as through fire (1 Corinthians 3:13–15).

A second reason we work as unto God is because it serves as a testimony to others. We don't do good just to please God but because people need what we have to offer. Not only do they need it, but they also need to know about the God who lies behind our motivations. "Let your light so shine before men, that they may see your good works and glorify your Father in heaven" (Matthew 5:16). We need to testify by our actions and commitment to propriety.

How Do We Demonstrate Excellence?

There are many ingredients to excellence, some of which we must demonstrate as a regular part of who we are and what we hope to become.

Excellence Through Our Character

Regardless of the ethical challenges of our workplace or industry, God expects us to stand up for what is right. Just because "everyone else is doing it" doesn't mean we should also partake. "But Daniel purposed in his heart that he would not defile himself with the portion of the king's delicacies, nor with the wine which he drank; therefore, he requested of the chief of the eunuchs that he might not defile himself" (Daniel 1:8).

Excellence Through Our Skills and Wisdom

Everything we do makes an impression. We have to go beyond just being average and shoot for excellence. We have to get that extra training, take time to watch that video about how to do our job better, study up on the competition, and ensure that our skills far exceed the minimum expected proficiency.

> Then Daniel was brought in before the king. The king spoke, and said to Daniel, "Are you that Daniel who is one of the captives from Judah, whom my father the king brought from Judah? I have heard of you, that the Spirit of God is in you, and that light and understanding and excellent wisdom are found in you" (Daniel 5:13–14).

Having all the training and skills in the world won't accomplish much if you don't have wisdom. So, pray for God to develop the wisdom needed for the challenges ahead of you. He will respond. True excellence is dependent on making wise choices.

Excellence Through Our Dedication

We have to stay committed to doing our best. Others may try to bring us down, but with God's help, we can stay focused on the mission. We can prove our character by steering clear of disloyalty to our boss and our company. "Then this Daniel distinguished himself above the governors and satraps, because an excellent spirit was in him; and the king gave thought to setting him over the whole realm" (Daniel 6:3).

It's important for us to dedicate ourselves to each of the responsibilities that come our way. We can't assume that whatever effort we usually expend will be enough for the new challenge. We have to pray and dedicate ourselves to successfully accomplishing that new project. "Whatever your hand finds to do, do it with your might; for there is no work or device or knowledge or wisdom in the grave where you are going" (Ecclesiastes 9:10). Our time on earth is limited, so we have to give it our all while we can.

Excellence Through Our Enthusiasm

Staying positive shows our enthusiasm. "Not lagging in diligence, fervent in spirit, serving the LORD" (Romans 12:11). It's one thing to accept an assignment politely, but it's another to look for the good in a project and show our excitement about being involved with it.

Excellence Through Sharpening Our Skills

Over time skills can deteriorate, particularly those we don't use often, so we need to keep accepting challenges that build our skills. "If the ax is dull, and one does not sharpen the edge, then he must use more strength; but wisdom brings success" (Ecclesiastes 10:10). We shouldn't run away from *all* conflict, as healthy debate about the right approach can often strengthen the final product and those who participate in creating it. "As iron sharpens iron, so a man sharpens the countenance of his friend" (Proverbs 27:17).

Excellence Through Keeping Our Word
We need to think carefully when signing up for a deadline. Nothing will erode others' confidence in us more quickly than not living up to our word. Over time, it should become easier for us to estimate the hours needed to perform the functions of our job. Until then, we should seek help from more experienced workers so we can understand the spoken and unspoken deadlines associated with it. "Most men will proclaim each his own goodness, but who can find a faithful man?" (Proverbs 20:6). We need to strive to live up to our promises.

Excellence Through Our Positive Attitude
At work, as in other endeavors, people will more likely forgive those who keep a positive attitude. Looking on the bright side will distinguish us from many of our co-workers. The apostle Paul instructs, "Do all things without complaining and disputing, that you may become blameless and harmless, children of God without fault in the midst of a crooked and perverse generation, among whom you shine as lights in the world" (Philippians 2:14–15).

Excellence Through Doing More Than Asked
We shouldn't be disappointed when our boss expects more of us than the average worker. The best employees always receive more assignments and successfully handle them. Jesus taught, "Whoever compels you to go one mile, go with him two" (Matthew 5:41). In the Bible, we read how Rebecca went the second mile when she was asked to give a drink of water. "And she made haste and let her pitcher down from her shoulder, and said, 'Drink, and I will give your camels a drink also.' So I drank, and she gave the camels a drink also" (Genesis 24:46).

What to Expect When You Do Excellent Work

Although it doesn't make sense, human nature will cause some people to resent your efficiency, effectiveness, and effort. Even those who barely try will resent you if you finish your assignments and win the boss's praise. The same thing happened to Daniel. "Then these men said, 'We shall not find any charge against this Daniel unless we find it against him concerning the law of his God'" (Daniel 6:5).

However, while certain co-workers may not appreciate your excellence, you can rest assured God will reward you. "So this Daniel prospered in the reign of Darius and in the reign of Cyrus the Persian" (Daniel 6:28).

The best performers find the spotlight, even if they don't seek it. God has great things in store for those who use their gifts to the fullest. Just when you think no one is looking, God may focus attention clearly on you. "Do you see a man who excels in his work? He will stand before kings; he will not stand before unknown men" (Proverbs 22:29).

Ways to Stay Motivated Toward Excellence

For many people, when it comes to excellence, the issue is not availability or capability but *motivation*. At the beginning of this chapter, we learned that Daniel had a spirit of excellence within him. Each of us must likewise do what it takes to develop a spirit of excellence and learn what helps us stay motivated to always do our best. This could include prayer and even an occasional pep talk. Developing a spirit of excellence is part discipline, part psychology, and part operant conditioning. The more we shoot for the pinnacle, the closer we are likely to come. Let's take a look at some of the components of motivation.

Discipline

Everyone enjoys the accolades that come with superior performance, but not everyone has trained themselves to require excellence. Habits come from repetition. If part of your job involves paperwork, discipline may begin with a checklist. ("Excellent paperwork includes *x, y,* and *z.*") By continually using the checklist, the right answers will begin appearing on the paperwork the first time. A checklist will help you avoid mistakes of omission and commission. Also, excellence involves the habit of double- or even triple-checking your work. Don't just stare at the words but ask yourself if the information is correct. Check it with source documents and make *sure* it is correct. Use spellcheck and other tools to assist you.

Psychology

Doing excellent work requires you to know how your mind works and to use it effectively. Understand your strengths and weaknesses. If you need a co-worker to help you cover your weak spots, don't be afraid to ask him or her to lend a second set of eyes to an important project. Do the same for your co-worker. If your issues occur with people, ask a trusted teammate or your boss for strategies on how to deal effectively with that temperamental customer. Most of all, understand what motivates you. Tap into your inner motivation for excellence.

Operant Conditioning

B.F. Skinner, a famous psychologist and researcher, wrote that learning happens through a series of stimuli and rewards. Some of us believe that God, not Skinner, actually invented operant conditioning. Life tends to reward us for doing certain behaviors and punish us for doing certain others. Following God's laws will make your life better, while disobeying God's laws will lead to consequences. The same is true at work. Promotions, raises, and other rewards come to those who model excellence. Purposefully train your mind to enjoy the rewards so you will put in the hard work to achieve excellence. This trait will serve you well throughout your lifetime.

Examples Of Excellence

Learning to excel in your work will require you to become a student of excellence in your field. You don't want to model your work after the unsuccessful or those who are barely getting by. Instead, choose to emulate the wildly successful. Regardless of the field, some company is known as the "best in class" at what you do. The leader in quality service or superior products is doing something right—and probably many things right.

Find out what those best practices are and learn from them. Try to implement them in your world. This doesn't mean your company or organization will necessarily go along with everything the best-in-class company does, but you should be able to use the lessons learned to improve your own performance. Instead of wasting hours watching television or playing video games, take time to study excellence within your company, your industry, and beyond.

Study successful people. Understand why they have found success. Ask God to show you things about these leaders that made them the best. Learn from their wise counsel, and don't embrace any of their bad habits. Be willing to change when you find a better way of doing things. Set aside those parts of your performance that have been less than stellar.

Uphold righteousness in your work. One important difference between the Christian and those who follow self is the believer's love of righteousness. Make sure your practices in work or business align with your Christian belief system. "The wicked man does deceptive work, but he who sows righteousness will have a sure reward" (Proverbs 11:18).

Are You Stuck in a Rut?

Perhaps you began this study feeling as if your life is just humming along on autopilot. You need your job in order to survive. Your family depends on your income. Maybe you don't see any reasonable alternatives to hanging in there, right where you are, until retirement. The purpose of this study is not to create unneeded discontent or cavalierly suggesting that you abandon your current employment. But if you feel dissatisfied, the LORD may be arranging circumstances to bring you to a higher level of effectiveness for Him and His kingdom.

Like so many parts of the Christian life, the answer begins on your knees. "But you, when you pray, go into your room, and when you have shut your door, pray to your Father who is in the secret place; and your Father who sees in secret will reward you openly" (Matthew 6:6).

Recognizing God's Excellence

God's excellence begins with generosity. Everywhere we look, it's easy to see examples of God's overflowing generosity to mankind: beauty, abundant natural resources, adventurous terrain, and endless varieties of plants and animals. God knows everything we need and even all the things we want. He won't keep any good thing from us, but He might have a different timetable for us than we expect. Trust me, His timing is much better than our own. His power to overwhelm us with His generosity far exceeds anything we might imagine.

The following story represents just one example of God's generosity in my life. When I first came to Washington, I visited Wolf Trap, America's only national park for the performing arts. This beautiful concert venue includes a large covered seating area and an even larger lawn area just behind the pavilion. Acres of beautiful Virginia countryside surround the concert venue. At that first concert, I went with friends and thoroughly enjoyed the night air and the pop music. We had little money for extravagances, so we sat on blankets in the cheaper grassy area behind the pavilion. As the concert progressed, my back started to hurt, and the general lack of comfort sitting on the hard ground started to take away from the experience. While I didn't complain, my mind drifted from enjoyment to pain.

With no understanding of how the seating worked, I prayed that someday, just once, God would allow me to get tickets near the front of the big outdoor venue. Nearly thirty years and approximately 150 shows later, I have literally sat all over that venue, including up front near the stage, many times. Although some would view my prayer as frivolous, God listened. God cared enough to hear my request and make it come true—extravagantly true. He's listening to you too. He hears your secret desires and will generously answer your prayers.

Mirroring God's Excellence

God's excellence is rooted in generosity, and ours should be rooted in the same. Although it is easier to do the minimum for our boss, our colleagues, and our customers, God challenges us to do our best. We reflect God's highest character when we give of ourselves generously to those around us and lavish care on those who depend on it. By asking for the Father's help to provide our best efforts, we open up portals of power from above. By bringing the Holy Spirit with us to work, we become partners with the Almighty to lavish love upon unwitting recipients.

Motives Matter

When we consider our future, many thoughts and ideas may come to mind. God wants us to dream—He created us to dream and imagine. In fact, sanctified imagination is one of His greatest gifts. Moving beyond a mediocre mentality requires courage and vulnerability on our part. Courage allows us to risk, while vulnerability comes from the possibility we will be misunderstood. Saying, "I want more" could be rooted in vain ambition, but if sanctified, it can be rooted in a genuine desire to accomplish more with the talents God has given us.

God is on our side. He knew us before our birth. He loves us. He didn't give us so many talents and abilities without any hope we would use them. Connecting our imagination to God's dream for our potential is the secret to our success. He made us for a purpose, and He wants us to find our place among His many creations. God desires for us to maximize the incredible potential that He placed inside us.

As you consider possible dreams to pursue, let God into your thinking process. Let the dream form. Let God wash the motives around that dream. Are you getting excited because of greed, power, or other wrong motives? Pray it through. Give God your dream and ask for His blessing. He will help you find excellence beyond your imagination.

The next question ahead becomes how much work is the right amount? In other words, how should the believer who wants a well-ordered and balanced life set boundaries to manage his or his career and everything else?

Summary

In this chapter, we looked at excellence from a biblical perspective. While there is a great deal of mediocrity in the world, God wants us to pursue excellence in everything we do. Eventually, He will judge our work. Exhibiting excellence serves as a light to others that might show them our love of God. Excellence says a lot about our character, skill, and dedication. Some ways we can show excellence include demonstrating enthusiasm, sharpening our skills on a regular basis, keeping our word, maintaining a positive attitude, and doing more than asked. If we continually pursue excellence, we can expect jealousy from our co-workers and prosperity from God. We can stay motivated for excellence by practicing discipline, understanding psychological factors (personal motivators), and using operant conditioning (rewarding ourselves for excellence). As believers, we should seek to mirror God's excellence that we find all around us.

Spotlight Feature

Susanne Harrod

Susanne Harrod pursues excellence with a government research and development contractor near Dayton, Ohio. As a security manager, her job is to create, follow, and disseminate security requirements to her company to protect the interests of the United States and further the mission that her company supports.

Susanne was raised in a small-town church. She experienced God from an early age and saw faith demonstrated regularly by her mother and father. In many ways, their lives apart from the church served as a reflection of their relationship with the LORD. Susanne's mother encouraged excellence in the chores she designated to each child. Cleaning, baking, gardening, and canning made up an integral part of Susanne's everyday life. As a teenager, her father owned an ice-cream store, where his excellence in customer service, cleanliness of the workplace, and stocking supplies became the proving ground that eventually served Susanne well in the business world.

In her career, Susanne has worked for both small and large defense contractors. Her drive for excellence has led her to receive numerous awards and accolades for her employers and herself. Like most jobs, there are certain times when life is more stressful than others. Leading up to a big inspection, she might find herself working long hours and feeling the pressure to get everything right.

Susanne's quest for excellence is a natural part of her witness. She tries to demonstrate her faith through her commitment to implement security measures the right way. She tries to shine the light of Christ wherever she works by maintaining the highest level of ethical standards and personal character. She also respectfully tells her co-workers about her faith and church activities. "I talk a lot," she says, "like all the time. Any time I see God working, I mention it to my co-workers. Sometimes my words begin with 'I am not sure you believe, but…' and then I describe what happened. I also talk about my church and our activities in the community, such as the food pantry and clothes ministry, as well as invite co-workers to our Easter egg hunt, festivals, and breakfast with Santa." Susanne uses each opportunity to shine her light.

Over the years, her job demands have included substantial travel to other cities, particularly when she was trying to set up new facilities and install needed security protocols. This area has been a particular stretch for Susanne because of responsibilities with her son, Andrew, who has cerebral palsy. Fortunately, her husband, Jim, has been able to take up the slack and support Susanne in her career. "Without Jim, I couldn't do it," she says.

Susanne offers these words to encourage others toward excellence: "I have been blessed to work with people I love and respect. There is no doubt the world sees things as 'what can I get out of it' instead of 'what can I put into it,' but I work with highly skilled and motivated people who care about others. I have watched believers go through challenges, and I have climbed some pretty steep mountains myself, but we have a light that just cannot be put out. I have been told by others, many times, that they do not understand how I can smile through it all. We know it is because there is always a light of hope for those who believe—and for those who do not."

Susanne's hope is that others can witness the light through her and someday may want to follow Jesus for themselves.

Spotlight Questions

What could you identify with in Susanne's story?
What action steps occurred to you about taking God to work?

Study Questions

1   *Read Daniel 6:3 and 1 Corinthians 13:15.* In what ways do you strive for excellence in your job?

2   From a spiritual perspective, why should you strive for excellence in your work?

3   *Read Matthew 5:16 and 1 Thessalonians 4:9–12.* How is your testimony affected by your work ethic?

4   What did Paul write to the Thessalonians about the role of work in lacking nothing?

5   *Read Daniel 1:8 and 5:12–14.* How did Daniel's discipline bring attention to himself and God?

6   What special talents did God give Daniel to use in making a point with the king?

7   When has God used your talents or personality to help someone at work?

8   *Read Ecclesiastes 9:10, Daniel 6:3–4, and Romans 12:11.* How can the spirit of excellence lead to promotion?

9   What is the relationship between being diligent and being talented?

10 *Read Proverbs 22:29 and Daniel 6:5.* When have you experienced jealousy in the workplace? How did this impact your pursuit of excellence?

11 God's favor includes rewarding excellence in this present
time. When was an instance where you or a co-worker
received a special honor or award?

Prayer

LORD, *bless me with a spirit of excellence so others may see my witness
and turn to You. Show me how to do my daily tasks with excellence
and humility. Teach me to demonstrate a strong work ethic, staying
with tasks until they are completed. Help me to develop self-discipline
so I will not be found wanting by You. On those occasions when I am
noticed or rewarded for excellent work, remind me of the constant
help from Your Holy Spirit and His role in my successes. Steel my
spirit against any jealousy that may arise among my peers. Help
me to show graciousness, whether it is my turn for recognition or
my turn to congratulate a colleague or rival. Finally, show me Your
excellence all around me, and let it inspire me to do excellent work
in response. In the name of Jesus, amen.*

What will you do to take God to work this week?

BALANCING LIFE AND WORK

And on the seventh day God ended His work which He had done, and He rested on the seventh day from all His work which He had done.

Genesis 2:2

THOUSANDS OF YEARS before the first business consultant uttered the term, "work-life balance," God provided the blueprint for such a life. God didn't get tired after creating the universe. The Creator of everything worked, then rested. He didn't need a break. He rested on the seventh day so we would understand how He intended our world to work. He rested to show us how to live our lives.

It all starts with placing Jesus at the center of our being. After all, He is the embodiment of the law and the prophets. Having respect for God and His laws puts us on a track for fulfillment. On our own, we can't keep the letter (or even the spirit) of these rules. However, with Jesus as our guide, we find doing the right thing comes more naturally. He gives us the love and joy we need to be new creatures at work and at home. His Holy Spirit indwells us with wisdom to know when we should crash on a key project at work or leave early for our son's soccer game. "If you then, being evil, know how to give good gifts to your children, how much more will your heavenly Father give the Holy Spirit to those who ask Him" (Luke 11:13).

Some of us know we've been on the wrong track with work. Perhaps we've overemphasized our jobs to the exclusion of spending time with loved ones or taking care of our own health. It may be time to admit our mistakes and embrace the One who has the power to forgive us and make things right. "Repent therefore and be converted, that your sins may be blotted out, so that times of refreshing may come from the presence of the LORD" (Acts 3:19).

Costs Of Working Too Much

One of the more profound challenges in life is understanding the paradox of work and rest. Laziness may lead to destruction but overdoing it at work can lead to the same place. There is a point where more work only leads to frustration. Tiredness gnaws at the mind and erodes productivity. Many well-intentioned souls have put too much of their life's blood into their career or business. Instead of reaping great rewards, the harvest included failed marriages, wayward children, and poor physical health. Riches come and go, but our family should remain. They should be the ones who support us when everyone else forgets our name.

God instructed us to rest one day each week. From the beginning, His plan included rest. Every week, we need down time from work to worship the LORD, focus on our loved ones, and recharge our batteries. Getting enough rest isn't about rigidly following rules one day of the week or another. It's about balancing work and maximizing activities we find restful. If our jobs have busy times, we may need more than just a day to recover from the busiest seasons.

As a former government contracts manager, the end of the fiscal year usually came with an aircraft carrier's worth of stress. Most government appropriations expire at the end of the fiscal year, which is September 30. Depending on the dollar value and other factors, a lot of time and effort went into soliciting requirements, evaluating bids, negotiating prices, and preparing paperwork associated with contracts. Some parts of the process were out of the control of the contracting officer, such as the technical evaluation of proposals and the contractor's own review processes. When the clock struck midnight on September 30, many funding streams evaporated, and the funds couldn't be spent after that time.

Momentum built for months as everyone worked anxiously toward the award of each contract and brought in the required pieces before the money expired. By midnight on September 30, most contracting employees (both on the government side and the contractor side) were exhausted from the long hours and negotiations. That last week of September was commonly referred to as the "thirteenth month," because we felt as though we had squeezed a month's worth of work into those seven to ten days. Most contracting people took at least a week off after the end of the fiscal year. That time of rest helped buyers and contracting officers regain their equilibrium and erase some of the built-up tiredness from the months of extra hours and stress.

Ten Values That Help Build a Balanced Life

The Ten Commandments, as provided in Exodus 20, clearly explain principles that, if we follow wholeheartedly, will lead us in the direction of peace with God and our fellow man. By finding this balance, prioritizing work and home will become much easier for us.

REVERENCE FOR GOD

As we remember the transcendence of God and revere Him as our Creator, we find that life's ups and downs become more manageable. The knowledge of God is a blessing in everything we do. Thus, the first step in finding a balanced life is to acknowledge God and the value of His advice. Commandments 1 to 4 deal with this relationship we have with God:

- *Commandment 1: "You shall have no other gods before Me" (verse 3).*
- *Commandment 2: "You shall not make for yourself a carved image—any likeness of anything" (verse 4).*
- *Commandment 3: "You shall not take the name of the* Lord *your God in vain, for the* Lord *will not hold him guiltless who takes His name in vain" (verse 7).*
- *Commandment 4: "Remember the Sabbath day, to keep it holy. Six days you shall labor and do all your work, but the seventh day is the Sabbath of the* Lord *your God" (verses 8–9).*

RESPECT FOR OUR FELLOW MAN

The second step to living a balanced life is learning to respect others or making a conscious decision to do so. Beginning with our relationship with our parents, a fruitful life flows from respecting others. Disrespect leads to all kinds of trouble. When people feel disrespected by our words or our actions, they will respond negatively to us. Given the proper respect, even our most ardent detractors will see a difference in us that is worth emulating.

So, how do we respect others? We do so by showing them honor where it is due and respecting their lives, their loved ones, their possessions, their reputations, and their work. Commandments 5 to 10 deal with our relationships with our fellow man:

- *Commandment 5: "Honor your father and your mother, that your days may be long upon the land which the* Lord *your God is giving you" (verse 12).*

- *Commandment 6: "You shall not murder" (verse 13).*
- *Commandment 7: "You shall not commit adultery" (verse 14).*
- *Commandment 8: "You shall not steal" (verse 15).*
- *Commandment 9: "You shall not bear false witness against your neighbor" (verse 16).*
- *Commandment 10: "You shall not covet your neighbor's house; you shall not covet your neighbor's wife, nor his male servant, nor his female servant, nor his ox, nor his donkey, nor anything that is your neighbor's" (verse 17).*

How to Find Balance in Your Life
Determine Your Purpose
"Therefore do not be unwise, but understand what the will of the LORD is" (Ephesians 5:17). Your unique purpose in life is to discover your God-given talents and use them. Without purpose in life, you will flail along and live without direction. However, once you know your purpose, it will become easier for you to discern God's will.

God formed each of us in our mother's womb with specific purposes in mind. His plans transcend our mistakes, problems, and delays. In fact, He uses our wandering to our eventual good, if we let Him. Searching and finding your gifts will allow you to apply them to take care of God's world. Your love for others, and their responses to you, will fill up your life. God's immense intellect knows the traps into which you are most likely to fall. He not only knows how to free you but also how to keep you out of trouble in the first place.

If you consult God before making decisions, He will lead you down fruitful paths. Every person receives the breath of life from God, and He is eager to see you succeed at the things that really matter. Earthly fame or popularity is not His primary desire for you—and it shouldn't be yours, either. His mission is so much greater. If you fulfill your appointed mission to bring His kingdom to life for others, your life will blossom like a garden.

It will be difficult for you to feel you are leading a balanced life if you are also feeling you've missed your calling. If you're stuck in the wrong job or the wrong town or the wrong country, you will constantly feel as if you are missing out. Sometimes, God will let your dreams build inside you before He provides the outlet. Active waiting is the way to bridge your present life to your future dreams.

For instance, if you long to be a writer, take a writing course at the local college while you stick with the job that is paying the bills. If you eventually want to go on mission trips in another country, start learning the language from an app on your phone. If your dream is to help inner city children, volunteer to be a tutor for a few hours a week. These bridge activities will serve as outlets for your gifts. They can bring you from dissatisfaction to fulfillment, because they will prove your commitment to get where you are supposed to be going.

Get Control Of Your Time

It's hard to know if your life is out of balance without under-standing how you spend your time. If you don't already do so, spend one month tracking your work and non-work time on a calendar. You may be surprised at how much time you spend commuting, shopping, eating, and the like. Once you know how you're spending your time, make subtle adjustments so that your schedule looks more like your ideal. Make changes first to those items that are most important to you. Cut your commute time. Increase time with your family. Allocate a few hours per week to a volunteer project. Get intentional about how you use your time.

Foil Time Thieves

Set up boundaries against activities that steal your time without yielding results. Leisure activities are fine and needed stress-re-lievers but consider whether you are overdoing it with the time you spend watching television, enjoying social media, looking through internet sites, or constantly checking email. Here it's all about priorities. Decompressing is good, but mindlessly wasting hours every day may be sabotaging your best life.

Do Self-Care and Family-Care

A balanced life includes the health and well-being of yourself and your family. If you are overly busy, it may require extra planning to exercise, eat right, and even get enough sleep. Organize family activities that include movement, even if it's just a bike ride around the neighborhood. Make preparing meals for the week a family togetherness time by buying a bunch of disposable containers and putting together healthy lunches.

Widen Your Circle

Whether you are single or living in a family, balance your life by adding to your social contacts. Adopt people from church or other areas of your life and invite them occasionally to join your family meals, participate in a family game night, or attend a concert or movie. Sometimes, your world may tend to fold in on itself because you lack outside contact. Just getting to know that new couple at church can be a big help to them and to you.

Whom Do We Serve?

Ultimately, we serve God. But on a daily basis, we accomplish this by serving the people in our lives. This should be the crux of our purpose for each day. Tomorrow, it may be a different set of people. Next year, our job or our family might take us to another part of the world. But our purpose will remain the same: to serve those around us with the talents and gifts God has placed within us.

For example, God may have given you the gift of hospitality. You may have a welcoming personality that is endlessly fascinated with other people, which makes it easy for you to go to great lengths to make others feel at home. You can fully operate in your gift by asking a new family at church to come to your house for dinner. It seems simple, but that hospitality could be the door that unlocks church fellowship to these new friends. If hospitality is your gift, your service in making a meal, serving it, and cleaning up afterward may be the best thing you could possibly do for God this week.

King David blessed those who knew him and those who lived in his day. "For David, after he had served his own generation by the will of God, fell asleep" (Acts 13:36). Your calling has great potential to serve your generation as well. Jesus lived this life of a servant. He knew His purpose for living and focused on fulfilling that purpose each day. "For the Son of Man has come to seek and to save that which is lost" (Luke 19:10). I doubt He found service boring. It probably energized Him most days, though the circumstances often proved difficult.

Although Jesus didn't enter formal ministry until He was thirty years old, He spent time doing the Father's will. Just as God had His Son work at a secular job in preparation for ministry, He may have a similar plan for you. Jesus also realized the lateness of the hour. "I must work the works of Him who sent Me while it is day; the night is coming when no one can work" (John 9:4). Likewise, we need to understand the finite span of our service. At some point in the not-too-distant future, each of us will be called home to spend eternity in the presence of God. This should add new excitement to our walk with the LORD.

Having Enough Time

The first words of Jesus recorded in the Bible are, "Why did you seek Me? Did you not know that I must be about My Father's business?" (Luke 2:49). Jesus' last words on the cross were, "It is finished!" (John 19:30). These statements indicate the way Jesus operated while on earth. He remained diligent and cognizant that the clock was running, but He also realized that God directed His path each day.

Remember, there is always enough time to do God's will. If you "can't get it all done," it either means you are doing things

God never intended you to do, or you are doing the right things in the wrong ways (in your own strength). Both of these deserve consideration.

You needn't be weighed down with stress or worry. If you know there is no way to do everything on your calendar, maybe God didn't *intend* for you to do some of the things on the list. Perhaps you need to ask for help. Perhaps part of the to-do list can wait until tomorrow. The other possibility is that God wants to lead you in more efficient ways to accomplish some of your tasks. He may want you to learn new ways to work.

A Balanced Life Includes Certain Disciplines

To be an effective follower of Christ, you have to install certain disciplines. Set aside time for things that matter. Schedule time to pray, read God's Word, exercise, rest, prepare healthy food, and fellowship regularly with other believers. These things will energize you to be more effective for God.

Beginning each day with a time of prayer will allow God to organize your efforts and bring into focus those activities that will make you most effective and productive. Martin Luther put it this way: "I have so much to do that I shall spend the first three hours in prayer." Reading the Bible allows God to speak into your life and will help you focus on what's most important. Taking care of your body is essential to performing your mission for God. While He may not call you to run a marathon, He can't call you to do anything if you are stuck in bed with the myriad of maladies that come from lack of mobility and excessive weight gain.

Discern Your Priorities

You cannot allow the urgent things of life to crowd out the most important priorities. "Let all things be done decently and in order" (1 Corinthians 14:40).

Imagine there is a healthy-sized fishbowl in front of you that can hold forty gallons of water. Also imagine two large bags in front of you. One contains sand and the other rocks. Finally, picture a timer and a lengthy instruction book. A loud horn sounds, and the timer begins counting down a relatively short time, say five minutes. A voice shouts, "Fill up the fishbowl!"

The sand is easier to manage, so you pour all of it into your fishbowl, filling it up to the top. You level it off, being careful not to spill any. The time expires, and another loud horn marks the end of the challenge. As you are waiting for someone to come and judge your success, you read the instruction book. Now you find out that the rocks in the bag are actually unprocessed diamonds. If you had filled the tank with rocks, you would have been rich. But now, your fishbowl is so full of sand it doesn't matter. There is no room for the diamonds.

In life, thank goodness, you still have time to read the instruction manual, the Bible. It is not too late to figure out what activities are diamonds and which ones are sand. Think about what is important in terms of the "big rocks" in your life.

BIG ROCK 1: GOD

Schedule time for private worship. "And Jesus answered and said to her, 'Martha, Martha, you are worried and troubled about many things. But one thing is needed, and Mary has chosen that good part, which will not be taken away from her'" (Luke 10:41–42). The story of Martha and Mary reminds us there is a time for everything. Sometimes, the most productive thing you can do is to stop and get alone with God. This will free your mind of stress and distractions. You may get answers to your problems during such private times of worship, or you may be more productive once you've cleared your mind of the things that are hindering you.

Schedule time for public worship. "Not forsaking the assembling of ourselves together, as is the manner of some, but exhorting one another, and so much the more as you see the Day approaching" (Hebrews 10:25). Although private worship is important, each of us needs fellowship with other believers. By coming together to worship, you will learn new ways to praise God, new songs to keep your experience fresh, and new reasons to glorify God.

Big Rock 2: Family

Schedule time for your spouse. "Live joyfully with the wife whom you love" (Ecclesiastes 9:9). Bringing joy to any relationship involves going beyond the drudgery of life's chores. Take time to delight your spouse regularly. Devise ways to make him or her happy.

   Schedule time for your children. "You shall love the LORD your God with all your heart, with all your soul, and with all your strength. And these words which I command you today shall be in your heart. You shall teach them diligently to your children, and shall talk of them when you sit in your house, when you walk by the way, when you lie down, and when you rise up" (Deuteronomy 6:5–7). Most lessons will be *caught* rather than *taught* by our children. Being around you will allow them to internalize your values, your beliefs, and your love for them. Working to build an empire for your children won't matter much if they despise you while you're away making your second million dollars.

   Schedule time for your parents. "Honor your father and your mother, that your days may be long upon the land which the LORD your God is giving you" (Exodus 20:12). Parents sacrifice so much for their children. Once out of the house, children need to plan time with them. It says, "I care about you for more than just what you can provide."

Big Rock 3: Job/School

"For even when we were with you, we commanded you this: If anyone will not work, neither shall he eat" (2 Thessalonians 3:10). Some people treat their jobs as if it is a big interference with their personal lives. Your work is important. People depend on you to complete tasks, take care of customers, and maintain a diligent attitude. God uses your work to look after His world.

Big Rock 4: Ministry

"As each one has received a gift, minister it to one another, as good stewards of the manifold grace of God" (1 Peter 4:10). Every believer should have one or more ways to minister to others. Your spiritual and practical gifts are an outgrowth of your faith. You show others you love God by lavishing your gifts on them—whether that is through preaching, teaching, picking up trash around the building, or whatever else. All of us have something we can do to help the body of Christ.

Big Rock 5: Self Care

"And He said to them, 'Come aside by yourselves to a deserted place and rest a while.' For there were many coming and going, and they did not even have time to eat" (Mark 6:31). If you do all the other big rocks but forget to take care of your health, your effectiveness will wane too soon. Be a good steward of yourself by taking walks, buying and preparing healthy food, and getting regular medical check-ups.

Develop Your Plan For Balanced Life

The first step in creating a balanced life is to recognize that you need a plan. A balanced life doesn't just happen; it takes thought, prayer, and planning. From time to time, it may require reallocating time to one activity or another. "And Jesus increased in wisdom and stature, and in favor with God and men" (Luke 2:52).

Next, establish your goals. Setting goals is important if you want to be successful. Even with time, you need a plan to know if you are hitting the mark. "Therefore I run thus: not with uncertainty. Thus I fight: not as one who beats the air" (1 Corinthians 9:26).

Finally, harmonize your calendar. Often, it is easy to understand what your priorities are by looking at how you spend your most precious resource. Take control and be more disciplined. Plan your time by integrating time for work, family, self-care, ministry, and rest. By careful planning, the quality of family activities can also improve. "So teach us to number our days, that we may gain a heart of wisdom" (Psalm 90:12).

Remember the Most Important Thing

Although success in business can do many positive things for yourself and your family, it is vitally important for you to keep your most important priority in focus. Honoring God and getting your family to heaven trumps all other priorities. "For what profit is it to a man if he gains the whole world, and loses his own soul? Or what will a man give in exchange for his soul?" (Matthew 16:26).

If you've been reading this book but have never made Jesus Christ the Lord of your life, don't wait another minute. Just accept His free gift of salvation. Realize that He died on the cross for your sins, was buried, and rose again on the third day. He conquered death to save you from an eternity separated from God. Invite Him into your life, and He will surely come in. Put Him in charge of every aspect of your life, including your work. You will never regret it.

Summary

A balanced life includes many rewards, just as an unbalanced one is fraught with pitfalls. The Ten Commandments provide a framework for understanding how to maintain a proper relationship with God and with others. Specific behaviors that will help us lead a balanced life include determining our purpose, getting control of our time, outsmarting time thieves, caring for ourselves and our families, and widening our circle to include others. As Christians, our lives are meant to revolve around God and our service to other people, but we shouldn't feel rushed or hurried beyond measure.

If we are getting stressed out, chances are we are doing things God didn't intend for us to do or we are doing the right things in our own strength. Living a balanced life requires embracing certain disciplines, one of which is defining priorities. We can think of these like big rocks and little rocks. If we fill up on little rocks, we may occupy all our time with less important things and not be able to accommodate the most important issues of life. The big rocks, in order, are God, family, job/school, others, and self-care. Finally, we need to commit to prayer and planning to find balance. By setting goals for each big rock, we can harmonize our calendars and allocate the right amount of time for everything, including rest.

Spotlight Feature
Sarah Reynolds Oji

The terms "Christian" and "real estate agent/team leader" used together may sound to some like an oxymoron. Sarah Oji Reynolds is both. For those who have bought and sold multiple properties, they count themselves blessed if they never run into an unscrupulous seller, buyer, or agent. In an industry where large amounts of money are exchanged, it can prove too much temptation for some who lack a steady moral compass.

At Keller Williams Realty, Sarah and her mother, Debbie Reynolds, take their ethical responsibilities seriously because of their relationship with Christ and their witness to customers, industry colleagues, and staff. Long ago, the Reynolds team made the decision to do things the right way. Sarah, the daughter of a Baptist pastor (book co-author Steve Reynolds), and her mom like to say they focus on earthly real estate while her dad handles the heavenly real estate.

As the primary day-to-day manager of one of the largest and most successful real estate teams in Virginia, Sarah supervises many eager real estate agents from all kinds of backgrounds. Many do not profess to be Christians, either coming from another religious background or none at all. From time to time,

Sarah's employees recommend paths of action that are inconsistent with the company's values. At such times, Sarah reins them in and tells them in no uncertain terms, "That's not how we do business." She knows that treating everyone right is the key to repeat business and to maintaining a solid reputation in the community.

In addition to running one of the largest real estate teams in her company, Sarah excels at being a wife and mother. Family times are important to Sarah, and she ensures there are plenty of them. By maintaining boundaries and sharing leadership responsibilities with her mother, Sarah makes her husband and her children her top priority. Time management and careful scheduling help her avoid most conflicts.

Faith and pedigree aside, Sarah admits she has made some mistakes over the years. At one point, she caught herself speaking less than favorably about someone to her team. The Lord convicted her of her actions, and she publicly apologized and asked for the forgiveness of her employees. It became a teaching moment—and a humbling one.

To keep her team on the right track, Sarah and her mother employ a lot of prayer and Christian music, which plays in the background at their office. "I try my best to be an example to them," Sarah says. Treating others the way she would want to be treated is the key to her Christian business principles.

From time to time, doors open for Sarah and her Christian staff members to share Christ. Her grandfather proved to be one of her best on-the-job evangelists. "My grandpa was a Christian who effectively took his faith to work," she says. "He shared the gospel to *everyone* he ran into, and every day he would talk about Jesus coming back. He worked assisting a realtor in my office, and it opened up the door for me to share the gospel because of the example he set. He was extremely open about his faith and wanted to make sure anyone whom God put in his path would hear the gospel."

The *Taking God to Work* message is a generational blessing for Sarah; one that she hopes to pass along to her own children someday.

Spotlight Questions

What can you identify with in Sarah's story?

What action steps occurred to you about taking God to work?

Study Questions

1   *Read Genesis 2:2.* What is your favorite leisure time activity?

2   Time is your most valuable resource. In what ways do you attempt to be a good steward of your time?

3   *Read Acts 13:36 and Ephesians 5:17.* Balancing requires scheduling time for important things. What are some important things that should be on your schedule?

4   What is an example of how you try to keep your priorities in order between work and the rest of your life?

5   Families need more than just leisure time together. What are some service activities that have brought your family closer together?

6   *Read Luke 19:10 and John 9:4.* What part does determining your purpose play in balancing your life?

7   How do you keep the focus on what's really important when so many things jockey for your time?

8   *Read Luke 10:41–42 and Hebrews 10:25.* In what way did Mary discern the moment with Jesus better than Martha?

9   Why is private worship time important as a balance to work time?

10 *Read Deuteronomy 6:5–7 and Ecclesiastes 9:9.* What times do you schedule to do special activities with your family?

11 How is loving your children an extension of loving God?

Prayer

Heavenly Father, grant me rest from my work. Provide and arrange such times that will feed my spirit and quiet my soul before You. Lead me in the way of righteousness. Help me discern the needs of my family and friends and to balance those needs against those of my job and my employer. Lest my work become an idol, I proclaim that You provided my job, and I am willing to move on from it at any time as You direct. Nothing is more important than You, LORD. Teach me to properly prioritize the important areas of my life, neglecting no vital relationship or obligation. When I fail to give appropriate time or weight to anything, please pick up the slack for me and show me how to do better. In all these things, I thank You and trust You. My whole life is in Your hands. As I co-labor with You, I believe You will make it better than I could have imagined. In the name of Jesus, amen.

What will you do to take God to work this week?

Beating Stress and Discovering Joy At Work

SURVIVING INCOMPETENCE AND BAD BEHAVIOR

Who is wise and understanding among you?
Let him show by good conduct that his works
are done in the meekness of wisdom.
James 3:13

MORE THAN ANY OTHER CHAPTER IN THIS BOOK, this one is about your experience and how to redeem it for God's kingdom on earth. Maybe up to this point in your work life, you thought things just "happened" to you. Good bosses came and went. Bad bosses came and went. Some co-workers became treasured friends. Others drove you up the wall. You may not have seen any rhyme or reason to the parade of people walking through your work life.

From this day forward, we want you to see everyone in your world differently. The people in your work life are a gift from God whom He has entrusted to you so you can make them better—better co-workers, better supervisors, better human beings. You do this not by giving them advice but by exposing them to God's love and care. By showing them how to do every aspect of living in a work family better. By modeling goodness, patience, kindness, diligence, and all the other characteristics of your heavenly Father.

Most Work Problems Are People Problems

Whether your co-workers are as colorful as those I encountered in Chicago during the 1980s, they no doubt pose certain challenges. Unfortunately, some of these co-worker behaviors can damage your career and steal your peace. Given this, we will look at ways to coax colleagues away from bad behaviors and lead them to healthier ways of working together.

The biggest work problems are people problems. In fact, most people change jobs because of relationship issues. However, before running from people problems, it is important to give some thought about whether God has placed that person or group of people in your life for a reason. Difficult circumstances with people can be like sandpaper God uses to smooth out your rough edges and make you more like Jesus.

Just think about the work environment for a moment. Human beings who may have little in common are thrown together, told to work to accomplish one or more goals, and to do it without too many problems. The incentive of continuing to receive a paycheck goes a long way toward motivating people, but it doesn't solve all conflicts. If you are in a place where your co-workers are driving you to distraction, first remember the blessing it is just to have a job. Difficult people, in all their pain and glory, come with the blessing of employment.

Avoid labeling people, because labels can rob them of their freedom to change. The devil is an accuser, but that isn't who you want to align with on life's journey. Your duty is to join the redeeming work of Jesus. Just as the Holy Spirit leads you away from bad behaviors, so you can reinforce healthy behaviors among the people in your office or other workplace.

Nine Cranky Co-worker Behaviors

The following is a list of nine negative co-worker behaviors that may prove to be a challenge to you during your career.

1. The Megaphone

Have you ever had a day, maybe right before a big holiday, when you would rather talk than work? We have all had those kinds of days. But the co-worker who exhibits the megaphone behavior represents something different. He or she has gotten into the bad habit of talking constantly to anyone who will listen. This person's excessive talking drains energy from fellow co-workers who wander into his or her lair. Pity the person who shares a cubicle wall with the constant talker! Gossips come and go from the workstation of the megaphone.

Remedy: Although one person is unlikely to change the megaphone's behavior, you need not get cornered for a long conversation. The first time the megaphone comes up for air, or even before, mention that you have to return to an important task. Then walk away.

2. The Faultfinder

Have you ever met a person who can quickly discern the cloud in every silver lining? One of the least likely people to get promoted in an organization is the one who constantly expresses negative reactions. If you handed this co-worker a bag with one million dollars in it, he or she might reply, "This thing is really heavy." What's worse, this person will tend to find fault with other people, day and night. Like most bad behaviors, finding and expressing the negative side of things is a habit. If you've developed this trait, break it.

Remedy: Help the faultfinders in your organization look at the positive possibilities instead of the inevitable doom ahead.

If criticism comes to mind, ask them to hold onto it until the entire idea is expressed. Then give them an opportunity to turn the potential flaw upside down by suggesting an improvement that fixes the problem and improves the product. This will confirm that they are trying to help—not just being faultfinders.

3. The Volcano

Do you know a co-worker who blows up regularly or with tremendous velocity? This can even be a manager with the patience of a two-year-old. No need to sacrifice yourself (or an unblemished goat) at the hands of this angry tyrant.

Remedy: "A soft answer turns away wrath, but a harsh word stirs up anger" (Proverbs 15:1). Understand that volcanoes need energy to erupt and that it's usually difficult for them to produce that power by themselves. If you refuse to feed into their negative energy cycle, it is possible for them to vent their volcanic personality without you getting burned by their lava.

4. The Bulldozer

It is good to be passionate about your projects. But the bulldozer goes overboard, mowing down anything and anyone that stands between him or her and the completion of the assigned task. Most often, this behavior exhibits itself in a disregard for the importance of everyone else's work. The bulldozer insists co-workers drop everything and help with his or her vital task at hand. No thinking about it . . . just "do as I say."

Remedy: Bulldozers usually cannot be stopped once they have built up a huge head of steam, but they can be slowed down or diverted. If you are genuinely busy with a more important task, let these co-workers know about your priority. Assure them that you will get to their request but ask when they really need it. Give them a realistic timeframe when you can get back to them. Then point them in a direction that does not involve you or your work.

5. *The Victim*

Have you encountered that co-worker who has trouble getting down to work because conditions are never right? This behavior is all about the perceived pain and suffering of the victim. Bosses like employees who show up, do their work, and find ways to solve their own problems. As President Theodore Roosevelt put it, "Complaining about a problem without proposing a solution is called whining." Noting every microscopic impediment—from the stale candy in the vending machines to the color of the office décor—is not helpful or appreciated. Blaming mistakes on everything and everyone but themselves doesn't promote team unity. The victim's attitude eventually causes resentment in co-workers and frustration in his or her manager. Complaints should be like silver bullets: used annually at most, and less frequently if possible.

Remedy: Help the victims at your work know you found a workaround to whatever problem they name. If their martyrdom is able to stump even you, suggest they do something else productive while they wait for their difficult problem to get fixed.

6. *The Snake In the Grass*

Beware the co-worker who lies to you or about you! He or she is likely to throw anyone and everyone under the bus to avoid taking responsibility for mistakes. Subversion not only affects the specific employees involved but is also a cancer that eats away at the morale of the whole work unit. Snakes will bite. Once you are sure a person has lied to you, be careful about trusting him or her in the future.

Remedy: If you catch a co-worker in an untruth that negatively affects you, confront him or her with the facts in a non-emotional manner. If the person is spreading untruths about you or your work, make sure to pray before taking action. God may guide you to speak to the employee directly or to provide the alternate set of facts to your supervisor, without specifically accusing your colleague of lying. If you have your facts in order, chances are your boss will figure out what really happened without your accusations against a co-worker. Finally, forgive your co-worker. Building up a resentment against him or her won't help anything.

7. The Microscope

The microscope criticizes even the most minute of details. The truism "pick your battles" seems to be a foreign concept to the person, and his or her nitpicking saps energy and erodes confidence. When co-workers who demonstrate these traits bring up an issue, they do not think about its relative importance to the overall project. Perhaps the microscope in your office is a boss who majors in looking at every detail of a project, second-guessing seemingly inconsequential steps you took to get to the right answer.

Remedy: If you have a boss or co-worker who engages in a high level of scrutiny over the little things, pray for a critical eye in self-editing your own work products. Once you know the level of scrutiny, it is easier to respond with a satisfactory work product. Understand the microscope's importance of attention to detail. Don't allow the urge to finish a task quickly prevent you from going over the finer points with care.

8. The Space Cadet

Everyone forgets tasks, but the space cadet has trouble finding anything on his or her desk. This person has trouble remembering and executing even basic organization skills. Such habitual absentmindedness destroys confidence among his or her co-workers that the job will get done.

Remedy: If you have co-workers who exhibit space cadet tendencies, make a point to follow up with them well before their tasks are due. Help them become better by staying organized enough yourself to help them be on time. Encourage them to write down easily forgotten subtasks and refer to a to-do list often. "Close the loop" on your responsibilities with these teammates by letting them know a task is completed or will be due soon.

9. The Gossiper

The gossiper loves to spread negativity in the workplace. There is an old truism that if a co-worker is talking to you about everyone else in the office, he or she is talking to everyone in the office about you.

Remedy: Shut down gossips by suggesting you go to the person who is the subject of the gossip and ask him or her firsthand about the situation, as suggested in Matthew 18.

Love Your Co-workers Through Their Bad Behavior

As you take time to care about your co-workers and supervisors, even in their bad behavior, you change your own thinking about the situation. Instead of playing the victim, you become partners with God in recreating your work environment. Obviously, your role does not include assuming responsibility for the bad behaviors of others. You can't control those to whom God gave free will, but you know that love makes up for a multitude of sins. The New Testament is full of admonitions to love one another, such as this one: "And above all things have fervent love for one another, for 'love will cover a multitude of sins'" (1 Peter 4:8).

Leaders Are Human Too

If an alien landed a spaceship in your front yard, sci-fi movies suggest his or her early communications would include the well-known phrase, "Take me to your leader." Your reaction may include a cringe and a pained expression. Your temptation might be to suggest the alien talk to someone more genial and wise, like your second-in-command.

"You don't know my boss," you might say sincerely to this being from another world. "Wouldn't you rather meet the assistant manager or maybe my favorite female vocalist?"

"No, really, take me to your leader," the alien would reply with a hint of irritation in his or her almost monotone, electronic voice.

While we are often able to excuse shortcomings (sometimes major ones) in ourselves, we like perfection in our leaders. At work, part of this double standard may stem from the difference in salary. We know the boss gets paid more, so shouldn't he or she be substantially better at everything than us? Or maybe it is an experience issue. After all these years, shouldn't the boss know how to handle a particular situation? After all, the boss has been at it a lot longer than we have … and he or she gets paid the "big bucks."

The truth is few supervisors even approach perfect. They have good days and bad days, just like us. They have strengths, weaknesses, and blind spots. Over the course of twenty years in management, I received a lot of praise from both my employees and bosses. But they criticized me too. Sometimes it was justified, and sometimes not.

The important thing to remember is that bosses *also* have the capacity to change. Just as we shouldn't label co-workers into permanently dysfunctional roles, we shouldn't accuse our bosses of such permanent failings either. Our daily interactions with them will likely make them either better or worse at managing others. The way we respond to leadership, discipline, and advice has the power to transform supervisors from so-so to superior.

Here's one example. Imagine you want to suggest an alternate way of doing something. You can either bring this up humbly and carefully or blurt it out in an accusatory manner. Allowing everyone, but particularly your boss, the room to maintain his or her dignity is important. Never be critical or correct a boss in front of others. Respect is the key. If you frame your ideas as helpful suggestions, you have a much better chance of seeing them enacted.

Even if bosses seem completely incompetent and not up for the challenges of their post, it is not your responsibility to expose them or bring them down. God put them in your life, so learn what you can from them and realize your relationship is only for a season. It won't last forever; either they will go, or you will. Nothing is permanent. Until then, help them the best you can to accomplish the overall mission. Make them look as good as possible. Remember that if the boss looks bad, the entire section or department may be viewed as bad also. It's just like out at sea: if the captain hits an iceberg, everyone on the ship sinks. Helping the boss navigate troubled waters may not only endear you to the captain but also others as well.

Although it is difficult for people to change at their core, you can bring out the best or worst in your supervisors. As another example, imagine you want to address your supervisor's tendencies to micro-manage you. If you calmly explain the problem to your supervisor, he or she might give you a chance to prove you don't need as much oversight. Or your supervisor might suggest you do *A*, *B*, and *C* to put his or her mind at ease, perhaps by copying them on actions at key points in the process. (Let the supervisor see your progress.) On the other hand, if you label the supervisor a micro-manager and don't talk to the person about it, you leave him or her with no room to change. This will put your supervisor in a box and will do nothing to help him or her learn healthier ways of managing.

A supervisor's tendency to helicopter around you may be in response to perceived shortcomings in your game, such as not closing the loop on significant tasks. Do you keep your boss informed (at the level he or she desires) when tasks are completed or delays interfere with deadlines? Some supervisors desire more feedback than others. Figure it out and manage your boss's expectations appropriately. Whether he or she wants constant updates or an occasional check-in, make sure you understand the expectations and adjust your feedback accordingly. This will save you considerable frustration.

Responding to Critical Leaders or Co-workers
Next, let's look at some of the ways to respond when our leaders and co-workers show just how human they can be toward us.

Responding With Kindness
While noticing the faults of others comes naturally, responding in a Christ-like fashion will take practice, patience, and discipline. Looking honestly at our own imperfections will infuse us with the grace we need to extend to others. We must seek to understand the motivations of our leaders, even when they aren't offering us the same courtesy. "Let your speech always be with grace, seasoned with salt, that you may know how you ought to answer each one" (Colossians 4:6). Grace means undeserved favor. We need it from God and we owe it to others.

Responding By Blessing, Not Cursing
Our words are powerful—probably more powerful than we realize—and Scripture warns us to stay positive when it comes to other people. "Bless those who persecute you; bless and do not curse" (Romans 12:14). Based on thirty-three years as a Christian in the workforce, believe me when I say there are all kinds of negative consequences that follow disrespecting your leaders. Just a few include morale plummeting, productivity tanking, and teamwork disappearing. Even if your boss isn't as gracious as the princess in a fairy tale, continue to bless him or her and let God handle the rest.

We shouldn't respond in kind when our boss or co-workers come at us with unfair criticism. "A soft answer turns away wrath, but a harsh word stirs up anger" (Proverbs 15:1). The more we maintain self-control, the more we will come out looking professional when others go low. Even if a boss is downright evil, remember Jesus stepped down from heaven into a world overwhelmed by evil. He fought back by modeling good in every aspect of His life. By responding in a peaceful way, our tone may be transformative for our boss. "Where there is no wood, the fire goes out; and where there is no talebearer, strife ceases" (Proverbs 26:20).

Responding With Humility

Humility is about understanding the depths of our own immaturity. (If we truly knew the limits of our understanding, it would be hard for us to have a prideful attitude.) If God chooses us to help our boss improve, we need to do it with meekness, knowing our wisdom is coming from God and not from within ourselves. No one responds well to anyone with a prideful attitude.

We must strive to keep our own behavior in line with Scripture and our faith. Paul suggested to the Christians in Rome, "Bless those who persecute you; bless and do not curse. Rejoice with those who rejoice, and weep with those who weep. Be of the same mind toward one another. Do not set your mind on high things, but associate with the humble. Do not be wise in your own opinion" (Romans 12:14–16). Generally, we can cover almost any topic with anyone if we state our opinion with meekness and exhibit genuine concern for the person's best interest. "Who is wise and understanding among you? Let him show by good conduct that his works are done in the meekness of wisdom" (James 3:13).

Responding With Forgiveness

The number one arrow in the quiver of the Christian is forgiveness. When we fire a flaming arrow of forgiveness at our enemies, they often melt. Whether it be a co-worker who did us wrong or a supervisor who overlooked us for a promotion, forgiveness defuses all the bad feelings and tension. "Bearing with one another, and forgiving one another, if anyone has a complaint against another; even as Christ forgave you, so you also must do" (Colossians 3:13). Notice Paul doesn't say that because Christ forgave us, we *might* choose to forgive others. We must forgive because hate and its lesser cousins are not acceptable in God's eyes and make for miserable roommates.

Acts Of Goodness

At each stage in our relationship with another person, we have the choice to forgive or not forgive. Whenever we choose unforgiveness, it sets the relationship down the path to deterioration:

1 *Remedy Stage:* "Let's fix the problem."
2 *Responsibility Stage:* "Who caused the problem?"
3 *Rights Stage:* "I'm right, so you must be wrong."
4 *Removal Stage:* "Get rid of those people."
5 *Revenge Stage:* "Make someone pay."

If we find ourselves in this cycle, it is time for prayer. "You shall not take vengeance, nor bear any grudge against the children of your people, but you shall love your neighbor as yourself: I am the LORD" (Leviticus 19:18). There are two ways we can avert this cycle.

First, *do not be overcome by evil.* Evil compounds evil. When we get defensive and try to fight back, our bosses or co-workers might just escalate the situation. Our fallen human nature whispers "retaliation" in the ear of the aggrieved, but love commands us to overlook the slight and trust God for the answer. As Christians, we don't believe in karma, but we do believe a just Father protects His children unless there is a larger point to be made through our suffering.

King David expressed natural contempt for his enemies, even as he turned his right to retaliate over to the LORD. "As for the head of those who surround me, let the evil of their lips cover them; let burning coals fall upon them; let them be cast into the fire, into deep pits, that they rise not up again" (Psalm 140:9–10).

Second, *overcome evil with good.* Many times, evil can only be overcome with good. Our acts of goodness toward those who mean to harm us will put them in a difficult situation. They must either change their attitude toward us or override their conscience to continue the fight. Our loving gestures toward them becomes a testimony before God. "If your enemy is hungry, give him bread to eat; and if he is thirsty, give him water to drink: for so you will heap coals of fire on his head, and the LORD will reward you" (Proverbs 25:21–22).

David again provides advice on how to do this:

> Fierce witnesses rise up; they ask me things that I do not know. They reward me evil for good, to the sorrow of my soul. But as for me, when they were sick, my clothing was sackcloth; I humbled myself with fasting; and my prayer would return to my own heart. I paced about as though he were my friend or brother; I bowed down heavily, as one who mourns for his mother (Psalm 35:11–14).

Angry Fix

There is one approach to definitely avoid when dealing with leaders: *getting angry*. Don't give in to angry fixes for problem behaviors. Losing your cool will seldom solve a situation, and there is great risk to your career and witness when you cede control to unbridled emotions. Instead, focus on the *remedy* to bad behavior and take responsibility for your own side of the street. If you did anything to trigger your co-worker's bad behavior, take note of your actions and pray you learn not to incite the perpetrator. Apologize if appropriate. Don't focus on your rights or the other person's wrongs but on promoting peace in the office. "For the wrath of man does not produce the righteousness of God" (James 1:20).

If you find that your emotions are getting away from you, you may need to remove yourself from the troubling situation and take a break. Give up any feelings of entitlement to revenge. "Repay no one evil for evil. Have regard for good things in the sight of all men. If it is possible, as much as depends on you, live peaceably with all men. Beloved, do not avenge yourselves, but rather give place to wrath; for it is written, 'Vengeance is Mine, I will repay,' says the LORD" (Romans 12:17–19). Trust God to make everything right in the end.

Instead of giving in to angry emotions, give them away. Of course, your best example in this will be Christ.

> For to this you were called, because Christ also suffered for us, leaving us an example, that you should follow His steps: 'Who committed no sin, nor was deceit found in His mouth'; who, when He was reviled, did not revile in return; when He suffered, He did not threaten, but committed Himself to Him who judges righteously (1 Peter 2:21–23).

Some claim that Christ, being part man and part God, had an advantage to us, but He is to be your example in all things. You may not live up to His example, but your charge is to try your best.

Maturing as a Christian means giving up fleshly defense mechanisms in favor of heavenly ones. Due to several unpleasant experiences from my youth, I determined the best defense included a nuclear response to any hurt. If someone said something that intentionally or even unintentionally hurt my feelings, I hit back harder—trying to cut my attacker to the quick. As I've grown in the Lord, this human frailty occasionally tries to slip back into my life. Prayer reminds me, "Bearing with one another, and forgiving one another, if anyone has a complaint against another; even as Christ forgave you, so you also must do" (Colossians 3:13).

Summary

Most work problems are people problems. Although it's important to be task-focused and accomplish our part of the company's mission, our future effectiveness will depend on the relationships we cultivate with co-workers, supervisors, and customers in the workplace. For this reason, we need to understand several problematic co-worker behaviors and the human frailties of our leaders so we can know how to use kindness, blessing, humility, and forgiveness to deal with these people in our work lives. If we have deteriorating relationships at work, acts of goodness may be able to save the day. We must always avoid the angry fix. While an angry response may feel good in the moment, we will pay a price later in addition to grieving God.

Spotlight Feature
Eric Walker

Eric Walker has climbed the ranks from novice to senior professional during the course of his twenty-plus year career in the complex world of information technology. His stops have included government, large government contractors, and smaller information technology firms. His experience with state-of-the-art equipment and knowledge of technology systems has made him a sought-after expert and has led to promotions, awards, and new opportunities.

A devout Christian and native Oklahoman, Eric takes his faith to work and tries to maintain a good witness with his co-workers. Although he is human, he practices his profession with high ethical standards and prides himself on helping his employers do things the right way.

More than once in his career, Eric has encountered serious ethical dilemmas when his supervisors asked him to misclassify equipment costs or mischarge labor to the wrong accounts. In one case, he had to hold the line against substantial pressure to misclassify a $1 million piece of Cisco equipment to replace a failed component, which could not be properly charged to a current contract. Eric's company also asked him to use alternative identification numbers so the part could be inappropriately charged to a government contract.

It didn't take a lot of prayer or Bible study for Eric to know the request was just plain wrong. The situation tested his faith and determination, but he held strong and refused to falsify the information. Eric's moral stand proved unpopular with management. Although he had previously been considered a top performer (receiving excellent performance ratings and awards), he was abruptly labeled "not a team player." Three years later, he became the first person laid off when the company downsized, though at the time he ranked as his team's top performer. Eric didn't argue what seemed like a reprisal for his unwillingness to go along with the improper charging, and God quickly provided another job for him.

One of Eric's major motivators for working is giving to his local church and various Christian causes. He is motivated by Hebrews 7:8, which states, "Here mortal men receive tithes, but there [Jesus] receives them, of whom it is witnessed that he lives." Eric knows that when he gives, he is storing up riches in heaven and helping real people here on earth.

When he gets discouraged after a particularly hard day at work, Eric reminds himself of Jesus' words from Matthew's Gospel:

> Do not lay up for yourselves treasures on earth, where moth and rust destroy and where thieves break in and steal; but lay up for yourselves treasures in heaven, where neither moth nor rust destroys and where thieves do not break in and steal. For where your treasure is, there your heart will be also (Matthew 6:19–21).

Spotlight Questions

What could you identify with in Eric's story?

What action steps occurred to you about taking God to work?

Study Questions

1   *Read Romans 12:18.* What are some bad behaviors you've seen in your workplace?

2   How is it possible to live at peace with your co-workers in
    spite of their behaviors you find annoying?

3   *Read Romans 12:14–16.* When was a time you had to bless
    those who cursed you or treated you badly at work?

4   How can kindness overcome evil or make a bad situation
    better?

5   What does it mean to be high-minded or wise in your
    own opinion?

6   *Read James 3:13–18.* How does good conduct show that your
    works are done in "the meekness of wisdom"?

7   In what way would bitter envy and self-seeking cause a
    person to boast against the truth?

8   How is pride at the root of many workplace disagreements?
    Give an example.

9   *Read Romans 12:17–19 and 1 Peter 2:21–23.* How can respond-
    ing in anger make things worse instead of better?

10 How can Jesus' example help you respond correctly to issues
    in the workplace?

11 What is involved in committing yourself to God during
    your trials?

12 *Read Psalm 140:9–10 and Proverbs 25:21–22.* How can you
    keep from being overcome by evil?

13 What are some concrete ways you've overcome evil with
    good in the workplace?

14 What is one step you can take this week to help a leader
    or co-worker who exhibits less-than-productive or even
    destructive behavior?

Prayer

*Heavenly Father, thank You for Your most amazing creation: people.
Teach me how to love all those You have placed in my life for this
season. Show me how to learn from even the most difficult co-workers
and bosses while trusting You to mediate our differences. Bring peace*

to every area of my life as I yield the control to You. Show me how to care for the most unlovable people in my workplace. Teach me to get along with everyone by maintaining a humble spirit, a helpful attitude, and appropriate boundaries when needed. Show me how to overcome evil with good. Mostly, just remind me to come to You when I have difficulties with people. Guide me back to Your loving counsel and wisdom. In the name of Jesus, amen.

What will you do to take God to work this week?

9

LIVING BEYOND
PAYCHECK TO PAYCHECK

But seek first the kingdom of God and His
righteousness, and all these things
shall be added to you.
Matthew 6:33

CHALMA DIDN'T CONSIDER HERSELF A MODEL EMPLOYEE at the Department of Energy, but she worked hard just the same. She stayed late several occasions each month, and her performance appraisals reflected an above-average aptitude for her position. Her career occupied an important place in her life. So, a call from Jeremy at the Security Office surprised her on what had been a glorious Tuesday morning.

"Is this Chalma Brown?" the gruff voice on the other end asked.

"Yes, it is. How may I help you?"

"We need you to come over to the Security Office today and discuss some issues with us. Are you available at 2:00 PM?"

Chalma looked at her schedule and indicated her availability to come for the meeting at two o'clock. Immediately her mind raced, wondering why security would want to talk to her.

The sun shone bright and the trees sported new light green leaves, apropos for late spring in the District of Columbia. The ride on the shuttle from her building over to the Security Office on the main campus gave her plenty of time to think. Although jittery inside, her outward demeanor stayed cool as a cucumber.

Chalma's mind raced as she sat in the Security Office waiting room. She kept trying to figure out why she had been summoned. Although single, she had not been dating anyone, so that wasn't the issue. She hadn't travelled out of the country since a mission trip with her church a few years earlier to Haiti. Then it dawned on her.

Her hopes sank. When she had been given a government security clearance, she had signed on to regular credit checks and committed to avoiding serious credit issues. Her personal finances had gone steadily downhill during the past two years. She had loaned some money to a family member and never received repayment, and as a result she had gotten seriously behind on her car loan. The car had almost been repossessed. She had since used the opiate of instant gratification to steady her nerves about her financial problems. Ultimately, she had lost track of how much she owed on her many credit cards.

Fortunately, the Security Office gave Chalma sixty days to get her credit scores up to the acceptable level. Although it took extreme measures, she found a way to keep her job through radical plasectomy (cutting up her credit cards), raiding her retirement account, and selling her Lexus automobile. Painful, these accommodations to her situation fixed the problem. As she realized how close she had come to the brink, Chalma turned her financial life around and now has a credit score well above the minimum her organization requires to avoid being a security risk.

Financial Shipwreck

Personal finances wreck many a career. Most places of employment now have standards for their employees about maintaining their financial affairs, even if it's as simple as a prohibition against getting collection calls at work. People make wrong choices. Sometimes these unproductive choices come from a lack of knowledge. Other times, disaster comes from rebelliousness or spiritual blindness or trying to keep up with peers.

There is little excuse today not to know how to conduct our financial affairs. Sound financial education is as close as a computer or public library. For Christians, Dave Ramsey remains the dean of financial education. Many churches across the country teach his courses, including Financial Peace University (see www.daveramsey.com/classes). Ramsey's mentor, the late Larry Burkett, also captured many timeless biblical principles in his writing. Burkett's organization, Crown Financial Ministries, continues this legacy of biblical teaching with many resources and programs (see www.crown.org).

Financial ignorance aside, most of our financial mistakes come within earshot of sound financial advice. We choose short-term wants over long-term security. A vacation sometimes takes a higher priority than aggressively paying down credit cards. Buying a new car takes precedence over making do with a used one. It doesn't have to be that way. We can choose to delay gratification and put financial security ahead of momentary pleasures.

The rise of modern financial management skewed the value proposition of work by separating our work from payment for our efforts. Direct deposit means most of us don't even see our paycheck. If we use automatic bill payment through our bank, we may have only a couple hundred dollars of discretionary spending power each month. The rest is spoken for before the deposit comes into our checking account. Is it any wonder that many young people today fail to embrace the value of working?

Over the years, the purposes behind working have expanded beyond just salary. Most of us expect full-time jobs to provide health insurance, life insurance, and retirement savings matching.

Beyond tangible benefits, people want fulfillment, and most need to understand their work is contributing to the greater good in some way. We all want significance—to make a difference in the world. This latter motivation can be stronger in some people than even the desire to meet their basic needs. How can an accountant derive meaning in keeping track of the construction costs associated with a new superstructure? The answer is only if the accountant can tie his or her actions to the eventual value added by the new high-rise. God intends for His people to grasp this concept. Our work contributes to His care for the world.

What God Values

As Christians, we want to understand how our jobs tie into God's greater mission for mankind. Whether we mow lawns, cut hair, or run a multi-billion-dollar company, our work helps to care for the people God created. This value proposition surpasses the idea of working to make a living or creating worthwhile services or products. To really embrace our calling to work in the secular world, we must understand this view.

We must grab hold of the understanding we are acting as the very hands and feet of God by caring for His world through our work. Our products and services manifest God's care for our fellow human beings. When we involve God in our work, He becomes part of our attempts to bless His world. "Now then, we are ambassadors for Christ, as though God were pleading through us: we implore you on Christ's behalf, be reconciled to God" (2 Corinthians 5:20). The way we do our job should shout, "Be reconciled to God!"

Internalizing our higher calling allows us to work each day as unto God. We see with the eyes of the Holy Spirit though the clutter of our natural existence to the spiritual essence of our eternal life in God's kingdom. Before we depart earth for heaven, our great calling, our eternal work has already begun. Each new day is a fresh opportunity to show God's love through working. Realizing the freedom of willingly participating in this great calling is vital to staying energized throughout a long career.

At an even higher level, something we say or do may cause an eternal effect on someone we meet. As we co-labor with God, we may influence where that person spends eternity and the quality of the rest of his or her life on earth. Our significance becomes mind-blowing as we understand our potential in the hands of God.

Work Ethic

As a pastor, I would be the first to tell you beliefs are both taught and caught. My parents played a critical role in teaching me and my brother about the importance of a strong work ethic. Their example made a deep impression on us. Neither of my parents graduated from high school or earned high salaries. Dad worked at a factory, and Mom worked for the city recreation department. They faithfully went to work day in and day out, year after year. They didn't complain about their bosses or imply their wages were unfair.

Mom and Dad often volunteered for overtime at their jobs. They took God to work, did their jobs to the best of their abilities, and managed their money well. God blessed their work ethic and respect for biblical principles. At home, my brother and I were assigned chores and were expected to perform them without pushing back. Somehow, the way my parents involved us in the work of keeping up our house made us eager to help. Both my brother and I sought part-time jobs in our teens, even though I also played football in high school.

Today, my parents enjoy a nice retirement. Because of their efforts and emphasis on education, my brother became the first one in our family tree (to our knowledge) who graduated from college. Fortunately, I earned a scholarship to play football in college, but my parents still helped with some of my expenses, like clothing and incidentals.

By watching how they conducted their lives, I caught their work ethic and made it my own. My commitment to giving my all at work and at home came from them. I've tried to teach my children the same values, and I'm often proud of their accomplishments as well.

If you are a parent, recognize the important role you play in the lives of your children and how they will or will not take God to work. Talk to them about the spiritual side of working for the glory of God. Show them how they can use work to take care of God's world. Your kids are watching how you work, and it will influence how they live their lives. Your contribution to your children's value system elevates your work life beyond living paycheck to paycheck.

Sound Financial Footing

The Bible talks about money as much as any other subject. Money has been a major source of interest for human beings since its inception. The following are just a few of the key biblical principles regarding money.

1 God owns it all, and we are managers of His resources.
2 Work is essential to supporting ourselves and our families.
3 A tenth of what we receive should be given back to God.
4 The only way to prosper is to spend less than we earn.
5 A borrower is servant to the lender.
6 God will provide for those who are following Him. This provision usually involves work—which He, in turn, will bless.
7 Being content with the earnings from our labor is a gift from God, which comes from experience.

8 Earthly riches don't last and should not be pursued to the detriment of our spiritual health, our families, or our physical health. "Will you set your eyes on that which is not? For riches certainly make themselves wings; they fly away like an eagle toward heaven" (Proverbs 23:5).

How to Escape Living Paycheck to Paycheck

Living paycheck to paycheck means being under constant financial stress and knowing we are only a paycheck away from financial disaster. A CareerBuilder research report released August 24, 2017, revealed that seventy-eight percent of U.S. workers live paycheck to paycheck to make ends meet.[3] As Christians, we need not fall into this trap. However, once we are ensnared, we need to be willing to take the following strong medicine to escape.

Ask For God's Help

If anything deserves prayer, our financial lives need this kind of help. Healthy finances form a foundational stone to almost every productive person's life. Money affects our ability to drive, eat right, live where we feel called, and give to spread the gospel. Sometimes, we hold back this part of our lives because we really don't want God's advice and wisdom. Many of us would rather shop and mindlessly run up our credit cards than stay home and eat beans and rice.

Remember to pray about your financial decisions and your daily ability to live within your means. Repent of past mistakes and seek God's help for the future. "But the end of all things is at hand; therefore be serious and watchful in your prayers" (1 Peter 4:7).

Keep Good Records

One of the tenets of good stewardship is the principle of diligent accounting. We want what we want when we want it. In my own life, many of my financial mistakes stemmed from purposeful ignorance. Stopping to consider the long-term effects can save us from these particularly boneheaded moves. "Be diligent to know the state of your flocks, and attend to your herds; for riches are not forever, nor does a crown endure to all generations" (Proverbs 27:23–24).

A proper accounting sounds complicated, but it isn't. There are four essentials we need to know about our finances: (1) what we owe, (2) what we own, (3) what we earn, and (4) where it goes.

Do Financial Check-ups

Most trips to the financial pit are long and gradual. We tell ourselves fiscal salvation will come down the road somewhere via a job promotion, salary increase, inheritance, selling our home, and the like. The truth is that it is always possible to outspend any salary, windfall, or inheritance, particularly if we start the spending before the increase is received.

The best way to avoid financial doom is to do regular check-ups and get in front of trends that point us in the wrong direction. The prophet Haggai's warning holds true as we consider finances:

> Thus says the LORD of hosts: 'Consider your ways! You have sown much, and bring in little; you eat, but do not have enough; you drink, but you are not filled with drink; you clothe yourselves, but no one is warm; and he who earns wages, earns wages to put into a bag with holes.' Thus says the LORD of hosts: 'Consider your ways!' (Haggai 1:5–7).

Plan Your Spending

The key to controlling spending is budgeting. God wants us to enjoy the fruit of our labors. He takes delight in seeing us earn money and spend it appropriately. He wants to bless us with an abundance and with contentment. "The plans of the diligent lead surely to plenty, but those of everyone who is hasty, surely to poverty" (Proverbs 21:5). If we run out and spend each dollar as we make it, trouble lies ahead. Ignorance plus easy credit are a recipe for disaster.

As a young person, I had the mistaken impression that those who control credit would proactively keep me out of trouble. I thought they consulted reliable tables and charts to understand how much credit I could handle. Whatever they predicted would come to pass in my life, regardless of my behavior. Little did I know that lenders are incentivized to provide credit, not necessarily use good judgment. Car dealers want to sell us a car. They will find clever ways to justify loaning us the required money, even if they know we will have difficulty paying back the loan. The same is true of mortgage lenders, credit card companies, and furniture stores.

For this reason, it is totally up to us to budget and figure out how much we can afford before we make any major purchases. Jesus taught us, "For which of you, intending to build a tower, does not sit down first and count the cost, whether he has enough to finish it—lest, after he has laid the foundation, and is not able to finish, all who see it begin to mock him, saying, 'This man began to build and was not able to finish'?" (Luke 14:28–30). We need both a short-term and long-term plan.

Every Christian should have a budget that includes line items for tithes and giving. A tenth of our earnings belong to God. Beyond that, we give offerings to help those in need, support mission work, and participate in other worthwhile charities. But even this spending needs to be done in a disciplined way.

It is possible to put ourselves in financial peril by giving more than God approves of or to the wrong cause. So we need to pray about it. "Do not withhold good from those to whom it is due, when it is in the power of your hand to do so. Do not say to your neighbor, 'Go, and come back, and tomorrow I will give it,' when you have it with you" (Proverbs 3:27–28).

Give Obediently Back to God

As mentioned elsewhere in this book, God provides everything we receive. Paying tithes shows we understand this and appreciate His provision. Like saving, tithing is a practice that becomes a habit. The first thing we should always do with our income is to give obediently back to God. It is a commandment with promise. "Honor the LORD with your possessions, and with the first-fruits of all your increase; so your barns will be filled with plenty, and your vats will overflow with new wine" (Proverbs 3:9–10).

Tithing produces blessing! By remembering to honor the LORD, we open up the channels of blessing to flow back in our direction. As the prophet Malachi wrote, "'Bring all the tithes into the storehouse, that there may be food in My house, and try Me now in this,' says the LORD of hosts, 'if I will not open for you the windows of heaven and pour out for you such blessing that there will not be room enough to receive it'" (Malachi 3:10).

Act Your Wage

Some people believe feelings and urges are uncontrollable. This is simply not true. All types of feelings knock on our mind's door, but Christians must practice the discipline of weighing the spirits and sending the negative thoughts packing. Contentment is a feeling we can nurture through thankfulness. Stopping to bless each meal and thanking God for our homes each day will help to build contentment within us. We need to take time to be thankful for all God provides in our lives. "Let your conduct be without covetousness; be content with such things as you have. For He Himself has said, 'I will never leave you nor forsake you'" (Hebrews 13:5).

Experiencing pleasure should never be our primary purpose or motivating factor for living. Animals wander the earth looking for their next meal and their next pleasurable experience. Men and women have a higher purpose: to worship God and to serve Him and each other. "He who loves pleasure will be a poor man; he who loves wine and oil will not be rich" (Proverbs 21:17).

Addictions can cost more than just money, but most of them cost plenty. Spending time and energy letting an addiction run us around our town or city, draining our bank account, is not God's best for us. Instead, we need to get help and commit to loving the precious life that God provides to us. "Why do you spend money for what is not bread, and your wages for what does not satisfy?" (Isaiah 55:2).

Getting into debt is the quickest way to bondage. We have to learn how to live within our means and develop a plan to escape the burdens of debt and live free. The short-term pleasure of charging a vacation on our credit card pales in comparison to the pain of not being able to pay for our basic needs or even losing our marriage over long-term debt. "The rich rules over the poor, and the borrower is servant to the lender" (Proverbs 22:7).

Save For the Future

Saving is a habit. If we get accustomed to always living on less than we earn, there will always be a surplus for the lean times. One thing in life is certain, and that's the unexpected. No matter how smoothly things have been going, there will come a day when something different will happen. A booming economy will end and leaner times will start. Declining interest rates will change to rising interest rates. We need to be ready for changing times. "There is desirable treasure, and oil in the dwelling of the wise, but a foolish man squanders it" (Proverbs 21:20).

In addition to saving for our own retirement (be sure to divide retirement savings among multiple investments in case one or two of them don't perform well), there will be times when we will want to help someone in need. This might be our children or other relatives, or it might be a total stranger. "There is one who scatters, yet increases more; and there is one who withholds more than is right, but it leads to poverty. The generous soul will be made rich, and he who waters will also be watered himself" (Proverbs 11:24–25).

Giving to others takes money. Leaving money for our children and loved ones takes discipline. "A good man leaves an inheritance to his children's children" (Proverbs 13:22).

More Than Money

A woman named Rebecca had anger issues at work. As a long-time cashier for a major grocery store chain, she lived in fear of customer complaints and failure to live up to her employer's demands. The pressure of her job was not in her interactions with customers—she actually liked many of them. Rather, her concern involved fear of being unfairly judged during those times when her line didn't move as fast as some of the other cashiers.

At her store, the customers were invited to help bag their groceries if they so desired. Sometimes, several customers in a row would decline or just couldn't physically help with the bagging. Rebecca stayed fastidious about carefully bagging like items together and avoiding combinations that could damage one product or another. Yet even with the care she took, one time a customer complained because she put two onions (surrounded by their own plastic bag) in the same outer bag as a bunch of bananas. This earned Rebecca a talking-to by her manager.

Over the years, the pressure and fear took a toll on Rebecca, and she became discouraged. She needed God to change her attitude and take away her fear and anger. After hearing one of the messages in the *Taking God to Work* series at Capital Baptist Church, she could feel a transformation begin inside her.

On a particularly busy day, her line started slowing down because several customers in a row didn't help with bagging. The person who came along next was an older lady with many items in her basket. She looked frail and obviously wasn't going to do her own bagging. As Rebecca turned to begin bagging the woman's groceries, she heard God speak to her within her spirit. He said, "Rebecca, will you bag these groceries for Me?"

When she happily replied that she would, the years of anger and fear lifted off her shoulders. God set Rebecca free from her fears and put her to work *for Him*, not just for an employer. More than a paycheck, Rebecca began taking care of God's world that day.

Later, she heard the song, "The King of Heaven Wants Me." It solidified her worth, knowing that no matter what others thought of her, God finds her beautiful. Since then, Rebecca has brought a new attitude to her work. Joy has replaced anger and meaning took the place of resentment. Now she does her cashier job with intention, as unto the LORD. She finds it an honor and a privilege to help people for the Master.

Financial Stability

Many people confuse being financially stable with being independently wealthy. Financial stability means bills are paid on time and money is available for a reasonable standard of living. It also usually implies the stable person has an emergency fund (bank account) with three to six months of living expenses safely tucked away. If someone is independently wealthy, it means they don't need to work in the future. Their fortune is sizable enough that their money and/or interest from safe investments will adequately pay their living expenses and reasonable desires for their expected lifespan.

It's easy for the average worker to get confused about these two concepts, throw up his or her hands, and say, "I will never be financially well!" This may be true if you mean financial independence from working. However, almost anyone can eventually become financially stable.

Getting Free From Debt

Many of us have found ourselves deeply in debt at one time or another. Sometimes, this is directly attributable to bad choices we have made (such as spending more than we've earned, burying ourselves in student loans, or risking large amounts of money in shaky investments.) At other times, we may end up in significant debt due to no fault of our own (such as through an illness that causes huge medical bills, a spouse acting deceptively about finances, or tough economic times shuttering our employer).

When the debt level is high, financial stability may seem a long way off. Our subconscious mind may play tricks on us to sabotage plans for getting out of debt and becoming financially stable. However, with God's help and our determination, most can find a way out of debt and into financial stability. The problem is we really don't *want* to feel the pain of financial discipline. By throwing up our hands and saying it's hopeless, we can go out and spend fifty dollars on dinner for two instead of cooking chicken and rice at home for less than ten dollars.

Financial stability is not only a worthy goal but also an amazing accomplishment. Once we feel the security and stability of sustainable financial practices, we won't know how we survived without them. God wants to show us that life is about more than constantly fighting with creditors or letting ourselves down because of broken finances. If we trust Him, He will teach us how to manage our money and find stability.

"The blessing of the LORD makes one rich, and He adds no sorrow with it" (Proverbs 10:22). With determination and God's blessing, we can find financial security.

Summary

Living paycheck to paycheck is all too common today, even though the way we handle our personal finances can greatly impact the trajectory of our careers. If our financial ship is in danger of running aground, it makes sense to revisit the value proposition of work. Are we spending too much or earning too little? It could be a combination of the two. By inviting God into our finances, keeping good records, doing check-ups of our financial condition, and planning our spending, it is possible to pay down debt and eventually increase savings. One of the key concepts is to "act our wage" and not overspend just because others seem to be getting away with it. Obediently giving back to God and saving are key practices that God often rewards with financial blessings.

Spotlight Feature
Ola Kabazzi

Ola Kabazzi, a contractor for a government agency, found herself battling the demands of the Washington, DC, metroplex for the future of her family. She started her day early in the morning and drove to a commuter lot near her home. There, she stood in line for a ride with a total stranger who coveted her personhood enough to drive her into the city. (By finding two extra people, drivers may use high occupancy vehicle lanes in the Virginia suburbs, which are reserved for vehicles with three or more persons. This cuts the driving time for the driver and the riders. The practice is affectionately known as "slugging.")

Once Ola was in downtown Washington, she found her way to the office and put in a full shift. The pressure to perform and keep her customers happy competed with her desire to be at home more for her three children. After retracing her steps in the evening, she arrived home tired but eager to serve her family. Ola felt she had to work. It seemed the only way for her to make ends meet for her family.

As Ola's children grew, she became increasingly concerned about their education and spiritual development. God led her to a passage of Scripture that convicted her heart: Acts 17:24–27. Based on these verses, Ola came to believe that God had called her to her specific town, block, and household. By running all over the city, she could not minister effectively where God had placed her for the present time.

Without telling her husband (at first), Ola enrolled the two of them in a homeschool convention. As the date of the conference drew near, she finally asked her husband if he would go along. He agreed to attend but told her up front that he didn't feel homeschooling fit their family. By the end of the conference, he had changed his mind. He agreed with Ola that they would make ends meet somehow based on his salary alone. His agreement had been one of the conditions Ola told God she needed to make homeschooling possible for their family.

Ola traded her corporate job for the full-time job of taking care of her family. The pressures of commuting and pleasing customers segued into hours with her children and helping them with their studies. Her primary focus became her family and her children's education and spiritual development. Since that time, God has met all of her and her family's financial needs and proven Himself faithful.

Like many homeschoolers, Ola's children attend labs and other technical classes once a week at a consortium. This gives them socialization with other students and a wider range of curriculum. Ola helped out at the consortium for a year, running several of the administrative functions like collecting fees, paying the teachers, buying supplies, and distributing them to the instructors.

Although Ola's new life is not devoid of pressures, the many external stressors have been replaced by internal questions about

how to serve God and her community better. The encouragement of Scripture and other homeschool mentors have been
essential to her success. She reminds herself that Ephesians
6:5–9 says she keeps working as unto God and not to please
men. Philippians 2:14 reminds her not to grumble or complain.
And 1 Thessalonians 5:18 teaches her to give thanks in all things.
These passages have elevated Ola and her family far beyond
living paycheck to paycheck.

Spotlight Questions

What could you identify with in Ola's story?

What action steps occurred to you about taking God to work?

Study Questions

1   *Read Matthew 6:6.* What does living paycheck to paycheck
    mean to you?

2   What does this verse recommend doing with financial
    issues?

3   *Read Proverbs 27:23–24 and Haggai 1:5–7.* Do you perform
    regular financial check-ups? Do you live by a budget?
    Explain.

4   Do you know what you owe? What you own? What you
    earn? Where it goes?

5   *Read Proverbs 3:27–28, 21:3, and Luke 14:28–30.* How can
    you be diligent about planning?

6   How is your Christian witness tied into your handling of
    financial affairs?

7   Without naming names, what example comes to mind
    about a person's financial situation that has impacted his
    or her work?

8   *Read Proverbs 21:17, 22:7, Isaiah 55:2, and Hebrews 13:5.* How
    does covetousness drive human behavior?

9   Why is addiction to pleasure a pathway to poverty?

10   In what way is a borrower the servant to the lender?

11   *Read Proverbs 11:24–25, 13:22, 21:20, and Malachi 3:10.* What practices help you save money?

12   What temptations strongly pull at you to squander money?

13   What is God's promise for the tither?

Prayer

Dear Father in heaven, thank You for the resources You provide. Thank You for my salary, my benefits, and the other financial blessings I've received. Thank You for Your guidance, as reflected in the Bible and taught by Christian men and women through books and other resources. Where education or training is needed, help me to learn how to effectively manage my financial affairs. When the issue is self-control, strengthen my resolve to live by a budget and avoid overspending. Teach me to be an effective steward of the resources You've provided by tithing, giving, paying my bills, and sharing resources with the less fortunate. Help me break my addictions to things that have previously inhibited me from living my financial life in a way pleasing to You. Show me how to be a good financial witness of the power of the gospel. Help me to avoid any appearance of financial impropriety, either in my work or in my personal affairs. I give You the glory for all of Your generous blessings. In the name of Jesus, amen.

What will you do to take God to work this week?

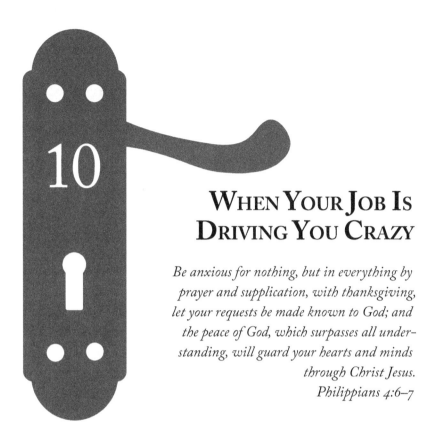

WHEN YOUR JOB IS DRIVING YOU CRAZY

Be anxious for nothing, but in everything by prayer and supplication, with thanksgiving, let your requests be made known to God; and the peace of God, which surpasses all understanding, will guard your hearts and minds through Christ Jesus.

Philippians 4:6–7

SARAH, A SUPERVISOR in a mid-size manufacturing company, strived for excellence each day. Her boss, Katie, was a strong leader with the company. She had mentored Sarah for many years, even before Sarah had joined the management team. Yet in spite of Katie's many positive attributes, she could come across as quite cutting and direct. She bullied some of the other managers, though Sarah did not usually draw her ire.

One day, Sarah sat in the conference room, waiting for the manager's weekly staff meeting to begin. Her colleagues filed in and found places around the crowded boardroom table. Gentle chitchat continued until Katie whirled into the room like a human tornado. Her dark brown hair coifed to perfection, Katie's expensive suit betrayed her love of life's finer things.

"Whoever is putting eggs in the microwave has got to stop," she said with disgust. "It stinks out there. If they don't stop it, I'm going to have all the microwaves ripped out of here. It's going to be too bad, so sad."

Sarah twisted her necklace chain and tried not to look nervous. It bothered her that the leader of this large organization raised her voice about something as mundane as microwave smells coming from the kitchenette.

"I want to hear about end-of-quarter numbers from each of you," Katie continued menacingly. "Sarah, we'll start with you."

Sarah nearly swallowed her tongue as she opened the manila folder sitting in front of her place at the table. Although she felt prepared, Katie's aggressive management style had set her on edge. "Boss, production rose six percent over the last quarter and four percent year over year."

"Tell me something I don't know," Katie fired back. "How many more orders do you expect from customers through year end? Come on, people, you need to be in touch with your customers. Don't just spew numbers at me. What do they mean?"

"No problem," Sarah replied. "I have the latest figures right here. New work should be five percent below last year. So, even though we lost one person, we should have plenty of capacity to meet our year-end production goals. The total number of orders is 190."

Although the answer placated her boss and she moved on to the next person, Sarah felt acid climbing into her esophagus. No breakfast and an extra cup of coffee conspired to bring on acid reflux. Sarah tried not to throw up in her mouth. The stress nearly overwhelmed her. Even when she had the right answers, it never seemed to be enough. She simply had to find a new job, and soon.

Processing Workplace Stress

Stress is a major problem for American workers today. According to the American Institute of Stress website:

- Forty-four percent of Americans feel more stress than they did five years ago
- Twenty percent report being under extreme stress
- Seventy-five percent of doctor visits are for stress-related ailments
- Stress increases the risk of heart disease by forty percent and stroke by fifty percent
- Forty-four percent of Americans report losing sleep every night over stress
- Stress costs American industry $300 billion each year[4]

Fear Increases Stress

One of the major roots of stress is fear. *What if we fail? What if the boss loses faith in us? What if we lose our job? What if the next guy gets the promotion instead of us?* Fear represents a lack of faith. If we believe God's Word about His plans for us, there is no rational reason for fear. We can take comfort that nothing can happen to us at work that Jesus can't eventually make right. If we are in God's will, we can survive almost anything. Trouble can and will come into any life, but as Christians we can depend on our LORD to sort it out with us.

It is impossible to escape from the love of God that has taken hold of our lives as believers. Not only is He the "hound of heaven," but He is also the lover of our souls. He always has another job, another way out, or another plan should things fall apart. What's more, He doesn't want us to live in fear and dread. "For God has not given us a spirit of fear, but of power and of love and of a sound mind" (2 Timothy 1:7).

The remedy to a job that is driving us crazy is to grasp onto God's love for us and those around us. Finding that place of comfort in God each day releases us from fear. Like the waiting arms of a loving parent, God's loving care guards our minds from excessive concern about temporal circumstances.

It is also important for us to gain perspective on our situation when our job is driving us crazy. Christians all over the world have found themselves in extremely difficult situations. Persecution, torture, and starvation represent just a few of the things suffered today by Christians somewhere in the world. If those folks can find solace in Scripture in the midst of such troubles, we ought to be able to find the same for our less odious problems.

If we never felt discomfort, we might never seek the Comforter. We can find hope even when we feel like Paul, who wrote, "We are hard-pressed on every side, yet not crushed; we are perplexed, but not in despair; persecuted, but not forsaken; struck down, but not destroyed" (2 Corinthians 4:8–9). God is there to comfort us.

Don't Worry

Parrots are worriers. If you've owned one of these furry friends, you know their small brains are endlessly curious and constantly concerned about potential threats. It is a dichotomy that keeps them fed and alive in their native jungle habitats. They like the familiarity of their cages and homes, but they become bored if left in a small environment for too long. On the other hand, too many new stimuli in their lives can make them agitated and scared.

My favorite pet parrot enjoyed riding around on my shoulder, pirate-style. Bruno could have spent hours just hanging out and doing whatever I did, *unless* I went to the basement. Although it was furnished, the lower level of my home held no comfort for Bruno. Being below ground did not sit well with her, and she froze in position if I started down the basement stairs. (Bruno got her name before she had a DNA test that revealed her sex.) She didn't do her familiar head bobs or looking around. I could feel the tension in her talons as she held onto my shirt tightly.

She felt petrified, no matte r how many times I tried to desensitize her from fear of the basement. At one point or another, she would release her bowels on my shoulder and send us both upstairs—me for a fresh shirt, and her for the safety of her cage.

I can relate to Bruno's fear. As a lifetime acrophobic (a person afraid of high places), merely looking at a skyscraper could cause my brain to go on tilt. I know, it is irrational to be standing safely on the sidewalk outside a tall building and be scared of a bunch of steel and concrete. Going up in a building beyond ten floors or so was not something I wanted to do.

God carefully planted me in Washington, DC, where the height of buildings is restricted to no taller than the Washington Monument (555 feet tall). This restriction kept my fear manageable and taught me to rely on God for those rare occasions when work or other situations (like jury duty) required me to go near the top of one of our city's mini-skyscrapers.

Like a parrot, I tended to hide my anxiety. In the jungle, prey animals do not want their predators to know of their fear when they draw near. So, parrots put on a strong demeanor and try to hide injuries and illnesses until they are near death. In Washington, DC, I thought the same defense mechanism might be in order for my government career. Little did I know that this coping skill would lead me farther from peace and the help I needed from God.

Finding New Life From a Sabbatical

In 2009, just six years short of retirement age (fifty-five), my anxiety grew to a barely manageable level. Panic attacks suddenly became frequent reminders that something felt dramatically wrong with my life. A trip to the emergency room for a faux heart attack and numerous bouts of dizziness made me realize I could no longer hide my condition. I began to wonder about my ability to continue functioning at a high-stress job. Something had to give.

Eventually, through many circumstances and confirmations, God led me to the decision that I needed substantial time away from work. Although it sounded strange to quit a well-paying and secure government job just six years before retirement, I cashed in my 401(k), took myself out of the game, and opted for a life-saving sabbatical. During the next five months, I renewed my close relationship with God, and He taught me many things about myself and life. The experience became so fulfilling that I wrote a book about it titled *Sabbatical of the Mind: The Journey from Anxiety to Peace*. In the book, I explain how God led me to analyze those parts of my life that caused fear, unhappiness, and disappointment.

God showed me how to find healing from anxiety and more meaning in everyday life. Frankly, I doubt I could have learned so much or changed in so many ways without taking extended time to be alone (mostly) with God. His Word, as revealed in the Bible, and His wisdom, as explained by other godly Christian writers, saved me from the mental turmoil that had robbed me of my peace. After the sabbatical, I returned to my role as a government manager and worked another five-and-a-half year stretch until retirement.

There are times in life when the cumulative burden of stress overcomes us. Work, family obligations, church duties, and other responsibilities have crowded out rest time for so long that taking just one day off fails to soothe us. Even a short vacation may not be enough to reset our mental clock. In such times, God may be calling us—like He did me—to come away with Him for a more extended season of rest and focusing on Him.

A sabbatical implies *active* resting. It isn't just laying around napping in the sunroom (though I did some of that). During my time off, I read dozens of books, improved my physical conditioning, looked up old friends to have lunch, prayed for long periods, and just basked in the presence of God. During this quiet season, God's Word, the Bible, gave me new insights into my phobia and other fears. I came to realize that at the heart of my anxiety lay a failure to apply faith to the immediate concerns around me. Truth be told, we all face fears of some sort. But if deep inside we know our next stop is heaven, there isn't much to fear—even in death.

Due to finances or other pressures, not everyone can take extended time off work. But that doesn't have to prevent you from reserving periods of time to focus on your relationship with God. Whether it be alone time or a Christian retreat or a conference, you can spend a few moments to take the focus off mundane daily tasks and put the focus on your heavenly Father. He wants to communicate with His people and show you just how much He loves you. It's a jungle out there!

Four Steps to Exchanging Stress For God's Peace

1. Trust God Completely

"Be anxious for nothing, but in everything by prayer and supplication, with thanksgiving, let your requests be made known to God" (Philippians 4:6). Stress is carrying a burden that God never intended for you to bear. As previously noted, the root cause of most stress is a lack of faith. If we completely trusted God, there would be nothing to fear or feel stressed out about! Jesus gave the following advice:

> And which of you by worrying can add one cubit to his stature? If you then are not able to do the least, why are you anxious for the rest? Consider the lilies, how they grow: they neither toil nor spin; and yet I say to you, even Solomon in all his glory was not arrayed like one of these. If then God so clothes the grass, which today is in the field and tomorrow is thrown into the oven, how much more will He clothe you, O you of little faith? (Luke 12:25–28).

The Giver of all wisdom is ready, willing, and able to provide you with the answers to your problems. When anxiety begins to creep into your daily life, the words of James 1:5 can help. My rough paraphrase: If you need answers, you can ask God, who is eager to tell you. Once you know the answer, you can ask for anything you need without doubting. Doubting won't get you anywhere with God or in life.

An endless fountain of peace is available to you as a believer. You just have to figure out how to tap into it. "You will keep him in perfect peace, whose mind is stayed on You, because he trusts in You. Trust in the Lord forever, for in YAH, the Lord, is everlasting strength" (Isaiah 26:3–4). The key to finding an overcoming faith is to keep your mind and heart on the Prince of Peace. Consciously find ways to keep God at the forefront of your day, whether that means reading bits of Scripture on cards placed strategically in your desk or listening to a Christian radio station playing in your ear.

There are many other tangible ways that you can practice the presence of God in your workday. Pulling the promises of God into your consciousness will bring transformational change to your mind. "For whatever is born of God overcomes the world. And this is the victory that has overcome the world—our faith" (1 John 5:4).

2. Pray Continually

"Pray without ceasing" (1 Thessalonians 5:17). Prayer is a mighty weapon in the fight against anxiety. But it needs to be a way of life—not just an emergency call for help once our panic is triggered. When stress pushes us to our knees, we are in the perfect position to pray.

The psalmist wrote, "Cast your burden on the Lord, and He shall sustain you" (Psalm 55:22). Take time before the day begins to talk things over with God. Commit your agenda, your meetings, your work products, and your communications to the Lord. Ask for His help to do everything with excellence and in peace.

Once you are in the middle of the fight of life, it's not too late to call on the Lord. He cares about you and wants to help. "Casting all your care upon Him, for He cares for you" (1 Peter 5:7). There is no problem too big for God's power or too small for His concern.

Pray specifically about everything with thanksgiving. You are loved children, and you don't need to slink around and be afraid of God. "Let us therefore come boldly to the throne of grace, that we may obtain mercy and find grace to help in time of need" (Hebrews 4:16)

Remember to be patient in prayer. Sometimes, the answer won't be immediate. Hang in there and keep praying and believing. At some point, change over from requesting answers to just thanking God for what He has already provided and the answers that are on the way. Even if you don't know it yet, God will send a fix to your problem. "Continue earnestly in prayer, being vigilant in it with thanksgiving" (Colossians 4:2).

3. Adjust Your Thinking

Stinking thinking leads to stressful living. Have you ever gotten into such a funk that you can almost smell the bad fragrance of your thoughts? The Christian life is not one mountaintop experience after another, but neither should it include prolonged periods of anger, crabbiness, and unforgiveness. Paul teaches that you can decide what thoughts you allow to hang around in your mind. "Finally, brethren, whatever things are true, whatever things are noble, whatever things are just, whatever things are pure, whatever things are lovely, whatever things are of good report, if there is any virtue and if there is anything praiseworthy—meditate on these things" (Philippians 4:8).

Your thought life matters to God, and it greatly affects changes to your mood. "For as he thinks in his heart, so is he" (Proverbs 23:7). Your daily life is governed by the thoughts you allow to dominate your mind. In just one day, thousands of thoughts may rumble through your brain, but the key is to ponder the good stuff and cast out the bad. You—the real you, the inner person of the heart to which Scripture refers—is different from your mind and should be the boss of your entire being. Your regenerated soul needs to be the gatekeeper over your thoughts and only allow things that are good to remain there. This is the key to letting the Holy Spirit control your life and bring you consistent peace of mind.

If specific thoughts are troubling you, bring them to the foot of the cross and leave them there. If the thoughts insist on coming back, cast them away using Scripture. "Casting down arguments and every high thing that exalts itself against the knowledge of God, bringing every thought into captivity to the obedience of Christ" (2 Corinthians 10:5). As a Christian, you do not have to live in a cesspool of unredeemed thoughts at work or anywhere else.

Let's go back to Philippians and look at the approved list again. These are tried-and-true standards to protect your thought life:

- Is it true?
- Is it honest?
- Is it just?
- Is it pure?
- Is it lovely?
- Is it of a good report (something positive and uplifting)?

Don't be just like everyone else at your office or workplace. Embrace a redeemed attitude about life and be a light to co-workers and managers alike. "And do not be conformed to this world, but be transformed by the renewing of your mind, that you may prove what is that good and acceptable and perfect will of God" (Romans 12:2).

4. Obey Constantly

At some point, your thoughts and prayers need to move you to physical action. Don't just *hear* but *do* the Word of God by putting into practice what you've read in the Bible, heard preached on Sundays, and believed during prayer times. "The things which you learned and received and heard and saw in me, these do, and the God of peace will be with you" (Philippians 4:9).

Do the right thing and you will feel the right way. Peace follows right actions. Disobedience produces stress. It will make you feel out of sorts and cause you to question yourself. If you have gotten into the habit of taking inappropriate or improper shortcuts at work, turn over a new leaf with the help of the Holy Spirit. Ask God to help you change and become a person you can respect again. "Good understanding gains favor, but the way of the unfaithful is hard" (Proverbs 13:15). Don't make your way difficult by doing sketchy things.

Obedience produces peace. Habitually doing what is right will eliminate the need for guilt and disappointment in yourself. Twelve step programs have a motto: "Do the Next Right Thing." When life feels too complicated, there is almost always a "next right thing" to do, even if it's just the laundry. By following God's Word and taking care of life's chores, things usually get better—though it may take time to work through the wreckage of your past.

This will be true of your work life *and* your home life. Trust Jesus and His process for getting you to heaven and help a bunch of people along the way. "Therefore, having been justified by faith, we have peace with God through our LORD Jesus Christ" (Romans 5:1).

Women and Stress

Men and women experience many of the same stressors in the workplace. A demanding boss, inadequate personnel resources, and market changes affect everyone. However, as women continue to expand their presence in the workforce, studies are being done about the ways in which the genders process stress and to what extent it matters.

According to a U.S. government website, "Women often cope with stress in different ways than men. Women 'tend and befriend,' taking care of those closest to them, but also drawing support from friends and family. Men are more likely to have the 'fight or flight' response. They cope by 'escaping' into a relaxing activity or other distraction."[5] The website suggests several tips that can help women (and men) reduce stress:

- *Develop a new attitude.* Become a problem solver, be flexible, get organized, and set limits.
- *Relax.* Take deep breaths, stretch, massage tense muscles, and take time to do something you want to do.
- *Take care of your body.* Get enough sleep, eat right, get moving, and don't deal with stress in unhealthy ways (such as drinking too much alcohol, using drugs, smoking, or overeating).
- *Connect with others.* Share your stress by talking with friends or family, get help from a professional, and help others.

The Cleveland Clinic urges women to slow down long enough to think about how the negative effects of stress might be affecting them.[6] According to the website, women either choose or are forced to take on multiple roles at home, caring for children and parents in addition to work. Stress can lead women to work harder and reach higher in their careers, but it can also cause health problems if not dealt with properly. The bottom line is that women need to focus on stress management activities such as exercise, expressing themselves, keeping a positive outlook, participating in loving relationships, and finding purpose in their lives.

God's Correction

Sometimes our craziness at work or in life is not everyone else's fault. There are times when our behavior contributes greatly to our rough circumstances. God may be allowing some of our chickens to come home to roost to teach us how to live better. God may allow challenges into our lives with the express purpose of helping us grow and change.

In my early twenties, I viewed myself as quite the comedian. Laughter is great, but my way of expressing humor sometimes wandered into disrespecting those I cared about the most. One time at the Christian fellowship I attended, a beautiful young German lady caught my eye. For some reason, she was willing to date me. Although she had my utmost respect, I found myself clowning around with her too often. Eventually, she pulled me aside and asked if I had lost respect for her.

The speech she gave cut me to the quick. When she first met me, I had invited her to my scruffy college house and made her a pretty good lasagna dinner. My manners and willingness to wait on her had won her heart. But in a matter of weeks, I had managed to undo all that work by poking fun at her rigid nature and several other things she held dear. Although our relationship ended with a whimper, I learned a couple of important lessons. People could love the real me without me putting on a comedy show to win them over.

Although it may sting for a moment, God's correction means we are His children. "My son, do not despise the chastening of the LORD, nor be discouraged when you are rebuked by Him; for whom the LORD loves He chastens, and scourges every son whom He receives" (Hebrews 12:5–6). When we find ourselves in a tough situation of our own making at work, we can call on the LORD. He will help us, even when we must suffer a rebuke.

Finding Peace In All Circumstances

At one time or another, your job will drive you at least a little bit crazy. Whether it's the people, the work, the working conditions, the deadlines, or other external factors, circumstances can threaten your inner tranquility. Learning to hold on to the Word of God during such moments will give you great peace.

When your job is driving you crazy, the LORD will provide just the right comfort through a Scripture, a prayer, or a spiritual song—if you give Him the time to do so. "Great peace have

those who love Your law, and nothing causes them to stumble"
(Psalm 119:165). Memorize this or another Scripture to help
you hold on to peace of mind when difficult moments pop up.

Crises will tend to draw you back into God's Word. So, if
your world is going a little crazy just now, make sure to spend
time in your Bible. The solid rock of Jesus is available to you
through God's Word. It gives you something strong to hold on
to when the wind seems to be blowing everything else around.

One of the biggest gifts Jesus left behind on earth is peace. It
became His parting gift as He ascended into heaven following
His resurrection. "Peace I leave with you, my peace I give to
you; not as the world gives do I give to you. Let not your heart
be troubled, neither let it be afraid" (John 14:27). Pursue it and
grab hold of it.

Maybe It's Your Industry

Sometimes, you may find yourself in an industry to which you
are ill suited. If you've held several jobs in your field and are
continually finding yourself miserable, it could be that you are
in the wrong field.

For example, if you are person who hates conflict, jobs that
require negotiation will not be your best fit. If you are person
who loves adventure, accounting won't be the right industry for
you. If you like constantly exploring and learning new things, a
highly routine job will not be one in which you will excel.

As stated elsewhere in this book, all discomfort in a job does
not mean it is time to jump ship. Realize that certain lines of
work invite unethical persons more than others. God may have
planted you in a difficult industry precisely because you live by
His principles. Just realize the baggage that may come with
your journey.

What Are You Thinking About?

The key to having peace in your mind is to guard your thought
life. If your job or any other part of your life is driving you crazy,

the problem usually rests not with other people, places, or things but in your own mind. If you find yourself with such a "thinking problem," the cure is quite simple. Think about something else.

Do you find yourself focusing on the co-worker who doesn't seem to be pulling his or her weight? Replace the negativity, fear, and bitterness with better thoughts, as defined in Philippians 4:8–9. The battle is in the mind. The secret is swapping out negative thoughts, talk, and actions with positive thoughts, talk, and actions.

So instead of going on and on with a lunch buddy about how horrible the other political party is acting, discuss what God is doing in your life. Instead of focusing on what you see as a bonehead move by management, think about how you can boost productivity in your business unit. Instead of complaining about how much work must get done by the end of the day, thank God for your job and praise Him for helping you complete the work by quitting time.

Summary

There are times in our lives when our job will drive us crazy. Stress plays a major part in our lives, which is a problem because it leads to all kinds of diseases that can diminish our effectiveness and shorten our life expectancy. Fear and worry are two of the big drivers behind stress. We need to follow Paul's advice and "be anxious for nothing, but in everything by prayer and supplication, with thanksgiving, let your requests be made known to God; and the peace of God, which surpasses all understanding, will guard your hearts and minds through Christ Jesus" (Philippians 4:6–7).

Depending on how stressed out we become, an extended break may be required. In my book *Sabbatical of the Mind: The Journey from Anxiety to Peace,* I recount my battles with stress and anxiety in the Washington rat race. My sabbatical journey, and the lessons I learned through it, provide a blueprint for coming back from stress. This includes four important steps to peace that could prove the antidote to our job insanity: (1) trust God completely, (2) pray continually, (3) adjust our thinking, and (4) obey to the best of our ability. Philippians 4:8–9 gives us things to think about instead of what is stressing us out.

Spotlight Feature
Pam Nicholson

"Lord, help me," Pam Nicholson lamented one day. "These millennials are driving me crazy." Sitting at her desk in the modern office building, she could hear another person down the hall calling her name. Instead of getting up and walking to her desk, several of her young co-workers preferred to holler down the hall and hope Pam would come to them. While Pam doesn't mind helping, the generation gap often has her at wits' end. Why would her co-workers expect someone three times their age to get up and walk to where they were sitting? "It's not only disrespectful, but lazy," Pam reminds God in an often-repeated prayer.

Although her official title is director of nursing, many in the office call on Pam as the voice of experience. Unfortunately, the demands of her own position keep her plenty busy training and supervising home health aides, who are then assigned to clients across northern Virginia. The company Pam works for was founded by immigrants from Ghana, and many of the employees either immigrated from there or are related to someone from that country. While she applauds the heart behind the company's mission, there is often a language barrier between not only her and the new recruits but also between her clients and some of the home health aides. This is just one of many problems Pam must sort out as she works to match the aides with clients.

Pam enjoys doing intake with new customers. She travels to their homes, often in a place like Warrenton, Virginia, a distant suburb of Washington, DC. Pam determines exactly what is needed for the patient's care. While her firm is not permitted under law to provide medical nursing services, she is a registered nurse and served for many years in emergency room care in Brooklyn, New York.

Pam believes her work is an extension of God's care for her clients. She decides which services the client will need and then assigns a home health aide who might help with bathing, feeding, or other essential needs of the homebound or differently abled. After placing one of her staff in the home, she keeps tabs on the service provided and intervenes if any issues develop. By working with the clients and her staff, she seeks to provide quality care within the parameters of the social or private insurance covering the clients.

Part of Pam's role is to mediate when things aren't going well between a home health aide and a client. "I tell the clients these relationships are like shoes," she says. "If they don't fit, I have more waiting. Matching the right clients and aides is important." Having been in and around nursing for forty-three years, she takes great pleasure in making sure everyone has a smile on their face. If clients are feeling bad, she prays for them and does her best to improve their situation. "If I can leave someone with a smile on their face," she says, "I've been successful."

Nursing of any kind is challenging—both physically, mentally, and spiritually. Although Pam is glad the twelve-hour shifts at the hospital are behind her, she uses her faith every day to deal with troublesome people and difficult circumstances. "Some of the clients we provide services for are very poor," she says. "They need everything. I often end up praying for God's wisdom in how to help." More than anything else, she wants to make sure everyone is satisfied with the services they are receiving. "It really is God's work."

Spotlight Questions

What could you identify with in Pam's story?

What action does Pam's story suggest for you?

Study Questions

1   *Read Philippians 4:6–9.* What makes you anxious in your job?

2   How can prayer help relieve the stress you are feeling?

3   What is the value of adding thanksgiving to prayer?

4   *Read Luke 12:25–28.* What does Jesus say about worrying?

5   What is the relationship between stress and faith?

6   *Read James 1:5.* How can God's willingness to give you wisdom bring comfort from anxiety?

7   *Read 1 Thessalonians 5:17.* How often should you pray?

8   *Read 1 Peter 5:7.* It is a fact that God loves you. How does this verse encourage you to activate His concern for others?

9   *Read Proverbs 23:7 and 2 Corinthians 10:5.* Why is it important to manage your self-talk?

10 What should you do if negative, unhelpful thoughts come to mind?

11 *Read Proverbs 13:15 and Romans 5:1.* If disobedience causes stress, how can you avoid stress?

12 Your justification is by faith. How can the works—which demonstrate your faith—bring peace into your situations at work?

Prayer

Dear Father, I sometimes find my job difficult. Whether it be the people, the tasks, or the situations, my employment wears me down on occasion. Honestly, it makes me feel like I can't endure it for much longer. But You, Lord, are like a fountain of refreshing water. Your Spirit cleanses and refreshes me. Restore to me the joy of my salvation. Help me to live out Your desire for me not to fear but to have power, strength, and a sound mind that I might serve You. Teach me to rest properly when I'm weary. Show me how to commit my days to You and to invite You into every workplace situation. And for all these things, I will thank You and praise You. You are my strength and my joy. In the name of Jesus, amen.

What will you do to take God to work this week?

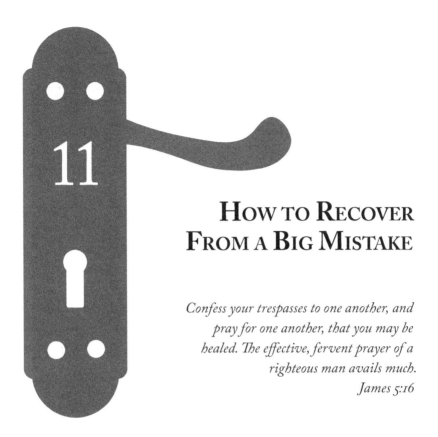

HOW TO RECOVER
FROM A BIG MISTAKE

*Confess your trespasses to one another, and
pray for one another, that you may be
healed. The effective, fervent prayer of a
righteous man avails much.*

James 5:16

ON A COOL NOVEMBER DAY IN 1984, I prepared for another day
at my desk job at Tinker Air Force Base, located near Oklahoma
City. Little did I know the pandemonium that lurked ahead.

Building 3001 on the base could only be described as behemoth. It served as a repair hangar for large, military jet aircraft
and as an office building for hundreds of civilian employees.[7]
Throughout the acres of shop area were different types of solvents
and other flammable compounds, used by workers to strip paint,
repair, and repaint aircraft.

On that day a small-business contractor, working to repair
a pipe on the roof, ignited the insulation around a pipe and

set fire to the tar-sealed roof. The welder went to get help, and the first firefighter arrived and began dousing the roof with an extinguisher. The blaze temporarily went out but reignited twice more.

Within minutes, it became clear the fire had penetrated the exterior roof and now grew inside a cavity separating the ceiling of the work areas and the roof itself. Soon the firefighters began roaring in, sirens screaming, from every nearby town and city. They headed into the building, and I and many others were evacuated.

It took forty-nine hours and fifteen million gallons of water to extinguish the fire completely. All told, the inferno damaged more than seventeen acres of roof. Area hospitals treated 115 firefighters for smoke-related illnesses during and after the fire. Regular business office employees like myself had several days off with pay as the firefighters worked to extinguish the fire and air out the noxious fumes.

The welder's mistake cost $154 million and took six months of work to repair. While contractors are required to be bonded for such work, the bond is usually no more than a couple of million dollars. In the end, the taxpayers paid for the error.

Fortunately, most of our mistakes are not as large or costly as the Tinker Air Force Base fire of 1984. But none of us are immune to miscues. In this chapter, we will look at errors.

Getting Personal About Mistakes

One of my first significant mistakes involved meeting my new co-workers in a small office on my first day of work at the Chicago Office of Naval Research. The administrative officer walked me around to make introductions. I proudly smiled and shook hands with each of the fifteen or so Navy employees. Most acted quite friendly, but others gave me the oddest stares and even seemed reluctant to shake my hand. I didn't expect an "ahoy there, matey," but the arms-length treatment made me wonder.

I tried to decipher the mixed signals as I returned to my desk. Moments later, I was horrified to find the zipper on my pants had been in the down position the whole time. Not a little bit down, but *all* the way down. Talk about making a first impression! Thankfully, I sported clean boxer shorts for the occasion. Later, one of my co-workers, once he knew me better, remarked that I had seemed "quite open and friendly" at that first meeting.

Historically Momentous Mistakes

Mistakes are a story as old as time. Adam and Eve certainly made a sizable blunder when they allowed sin into their lives and doomed the rest of humanity to living in a fallen world. (In their defense, any one of us would have likely made the same mistake.) And what about the crew of the Titanic not bringing enough lifeboats for all the passengers because builders deemed it unsinkable?

We all make mistakes, but some missteps are definitely bigger than others. The good news is that none of them are too big for God to forgive. The bad news is that sometimes our slip-ups harm others. Making amends might require more than simply expressing regret at the error. Here are a few more of history's greatest mistakes, where a simple "I'm sorry" would definitely not adequately fix the situation:

- Construction of the Tower of Pisa, which began to lean due to being built on an inadequate foundation.
- Decca Records Company turning down the Beatles, because they labeled the music "unsellable."
- Napoleon invading Russia during the winter.
- Russia selling Alaska to the United States for two cents an acre.
- Japan attacking Pearl Harbor with no U.S. aircraft carriers in port (the damage would have been much greater to the U.S. fleet had the Japanese eliminated even one aircraft carrier).

Next, we will look at how to recover from some more common errors.

Mistakes Affecting Only Our Own Work

Everyone makes mistakes in day-to-day tasks. We all forget to do small tasks or omit key data in reports from time to time. Many times, you will discover the snafu before it goes out and be able to fix it. No one finds out about the problem, and it doesn't affect anyone. In those cases, there is no harm done, and you need not bring it up to anyone else.

But what if the flub causes you to lose days or even weeks in accomplishing a project? At some point, this type of error grows beyond the category of affecting only your own work. The right move is to confess your mistake to those affected, offer to jump into fixing the problem, and pray for grace from your employer.

Mistakes Affecting Our Co-Workers

Some misadventures will affect your co-workers. If, after providing input to someone else, you find a submission contains an error, the right thing to do is notify those involved. Timing matters. If the mistake does not immediately affect a task the other co-workers are doing, it's best to get the correct information first and then tell them you need to provide an amended work product. If the project is urgent and there is the possibility they could pass the faulty information up the chain of command or use it to make an immediate decision, you probably should immediately notify all those affected.

Never is quality more important than when fixing an error. Making errors on top of errors will dramatically erode your credibility and be doubly damaging to your reputation. There is nothing funny about a comedy of errors. Before submitting a fix, make sure you have double-checked the correction, whether that means going back to source material, proofreading a revised document from the beginning, or getting a second set of eyes to help you ensure quality.

The hallmark of the Christian worker should be humility and a willingness to accept the consequences for his or her mistakes. Praying for God's help to eliminate mistakes and obtain mercy from our bosses and co-workers should be part of our recovery process.

Mistakes Significantly Affecting Our Employer

Sometimes, blunders significantly affect our bosses or the company as a whole. For example, let's say the information technology lead provides a set of metrics to the CEO of the company. Two weeks later, she discovers inaccurate data caused a key metric to be reported incorrectly. Her bogus data could lead to significant business decisions being made incorrectly—if she doesn't quickly fix the metric and report the mistake.

Although it may cost her job, she must discern how the mistake happened, correct the underlying data, put safeguards in place to prevent a recurrence, and report the revised data to the CEO. Most wise leaders want their employees to feel free to correct mistakes, particularly when the data is heavily relied upon for business planning. Even if this company's CEO didn't respond by giving her another chance, she would have done the right thing.

People-pleasers are those who would rather look good to others than do the right thing. Our purpose first and foremost should be to please God. In his letter to the Galatians, Paul asked, "For do I now persuade men, or God? Or do I seek to please men? For if I still pleased men, I would not be a bondservant of Christ" (Galatians 1:10). It's all about being self-centered or Christ-centered. The life of a Jesus-follower is one that puts others first—even ahead of his or her own reputation.

Mistakes That Cost Us Our Job

People lose their jobs for many reasons that have nothing to do with poor performance or inappropriate conduct. Companies go out of business all the time, and many people lose their jobs as a result. However, in this case, we are talking about blunders that lead to your own job loss. What should you do when your failure costs you your job?

- First, take the failure to God in prayer and ask Him what to do next. Remember He isn't surprised or taken aback. He will no doubt throw in a few lessons to be learned. Ask Him up front what you can learn from the whole situation.

- Understand why you failed. Go deeper than the official reason provided in your termination. Get to the bottom of what factors set you up to fail and figure out how to avoid making the same mistake in the future. If needed, get help from mature Christian friends or a counselor who can help you sort out what happened.

- Recover from the loss. Whether or not your mistake warranted the dismissal, it represents a loss in your life. Pause and regroup. Don't be too hard on yourself. Don't get stuck in hating the personalities and events of the past.

- Based on your understanding of why you failed and what you learned while recovering from the loss, apply for new work that meets your needs, offers you opportunities to serve others, and gets you back in the game of life.

There are situations where the punishment, including job loss, greatly exceeds the magnitude of the transgression. Put simply, you may have gotten fired for a minor offense. In such cases, the organization may have had a different reason for firing you, such as a desire to downsize higher-paid employees to cut costs or to reshape the skill set of their workforce. Whatever the reason, you are still out of the job and need to bounce back. All you can do is analyze what you might have done better. Learn from the situation and seek God for the next steps.

Mistake Versus Failure

If sin is willful wrongdoing, then what is the definition of mistake? I prefer to think of mistakes as either willfully or accidentally doing the wrong thing. Turning down the wrong road might be a driving mistake that costs us an extra fifteen minutes of travel time. We didn't intend to go the wrong way, but we did it without understanding the facts. A mistake becomes sin when we willfully do what we know to be wrong. For example, taking someone else's possessions without their consent is sin.

The primary aggrieved party for sin is always God. When we know our actions fall into the sin category, our first stop in fixing the mistake should be to repent before God. King David of the Old Testament provided a great model of this kind of repentance when he said:

> Have mercy upon me, O God, according to Your lovingkindness; according to the multitude of Your tender mercies, blot out my transgressions. Wash me thoroughly from my iniquity, and cleanse me from my sin. For I acknowledge my transgressions, and my sin is always before me. Against You, You only, have I sinned, and done this evil in Your sight (Psalm 51:1–4).

Obviously, some sins go beyond just offending God. Our willful wrongdoing can cause great harm to others that isn't easily undone. In those cases, we need to own our errors and try our best to make them right. We need to allow God to lead us to the correct actions to fix the problems. By committing ourselves to restitution, we will eliminate cheap grace and focus on undoing the wrong to the greatest extent possible.

How to Recover From Moral Failure

There are times when our mistakes are specific moral failures. We recognize our sin and realize the only path is repentance and cleansing from the LORD. The following is a roadmap for overcoming failure.

Keep Trusting God

The first step to maintaining our trust in God is to recognize His goodness. Although He doesn't condone or uphold us in our sin, He is merciful and loving. He provides for us, often in spite of our waywardness. The book of Isaiah put it this way: "I will mention the lovingkindnesses of the LORD and the praises of the LORD, according to all that the LORD has bestowed on us, and the great goodness toward the house of Israel, which He has bestowed on them according to His mercies, according to the multitude of His lovingkindnesses" (Isaiah 63:7). Remember the loving nature of God. It is the very essence of who He is— "for God is love" (1 John 4:8).

Keep Loving God

We demonstrate our love for God by keeping His commandments. Talking is one thing but doing is another thing entirely. The Gospels repeat this theme throughout. "Jesus said to him, 'You shall love the LORD your God with all your heart, with all your soul, and with all your mind.' This is the first and great commandment" (Matthew 22:37–38).

Our Great Teacher went on to explain how we prove our love. "If you love Me, keep My commandments" (John 14:15). Part of this love relationship includes God's willingness to use our failures to correct our sins. Like a good parent, God is more than the provider of treats whenever we want them. David wrote, "It is good for me that I have been afflicted, that I may learn your statutes" (Psalm 119:71).

Keep Imitating God

Following Jesus is not one long, futile attempt to abide by a list of rules and regulations. Our walk with the Master is about learning His ways and imitating Him. "As you therefore have received Christ Jesus the LORD, so walk in Him" (Colossians 2:6). A big part of avoiding moral failure is to learn how to appropriate God's power in our lives. We can overcome our lesser nature by yielding to God as He crucifies our fleshly appetites. In other words, we don't fight the good work He is doing in us.

As we imitate Christ by following Him, it will have a trans-forming effect on us. Paul writes about this in his second letter to the Corinthians: "But we all, with unveiled face, beholding as in a mirror the glory of the LORD, are being transformed into the same image from glory to glory, just as by the Spirit of the LORD" (2 Corinthians 3:18). While we don't see God's nature face to face in this life, the glimpses we receive from Scripture, through nature, and through the actions of fellow believers let us know that God is worthy to be followed.

Being transformed into "little Christs," or Christians, includes suffering through the crucifixion of our sinful nature. It can be painful to go through the cleansing of our moral failures, espe-cially as we realize the depth of our depravity and how we have fallen short of God's best for us. Looking to Christ and all He suffered for our sins can bring us into fellowship with Him as we are cleansed. Paul wrote, "I also count all things loss ... that I may know Him and the power of His resurrection, and the fellowship of His sufferings, being conformed to His death" (Philippians 3:8, 10).

Failures That Cost Us Our Witness

Sometimes our mistakes cost us not only our job but also our Christian reputation. One member of Capital Baptist Church told the following story in front of the whole congregation.

> I made a significant mistake at work. I became sexually involved with a female co-worker. I knew it wasn't right. While the tryst did not progress into a relationship, my co-worker became pregnant from our encounter. I had to figure out what I should do next. Everyone at work found out about it. Some kidded me about my faith. After witnessing to my co-workers about Jesus, I had fathered a child out of the bonds of marriage. Needless to say, I felt embarrassed about the circumstances and took some deserved grief from my co-workers.

Then I got back on the right track. I knew what I had to do. I took full responsibility and accepted my role as father to the child. My daughter (from this relationship) is one of the best gifts I have ever received. I treasure her and support her. Although the situation could not be described as God's best for me or for my Christian witness, I didn't compound the damage. I did everything possible to make the situation right and move on with my life. Eventually, I left that employer and found another job.

This member's story touched many in the congregation. Everyone has seen his love for his daughter as he brings her to Sunday School. His commitment to helping her grow up with a father in her life is truly a positive outcome. Although the circumstances temporarily blew up his witness at that company, over time he proved how he intends to live his life: as a follower of Jesus.

Helping Others Get Back On the Right Track

When someone is in the process of making a significant mistake, the Bible instructs us to attempt, with humility, to turn that person back to the right path. "Brethren, if anyone among you wanders from the truth, and someone turns him back, let him know that he who turns a sinner from the error of his way will save a soul from death and cover a multitude of sins" (James 5:19–20).

At work, this principle still applies. If we help a friend who is falling into a bad attitude, our support may be the thing that leads him or her back into many more years of successful service with the employer. Gently encouraging a team member who is feeling down after a major blunder could save that person a great deal of self-doubt. Many times, the consequences of our errors at work entirely rests with our supervisor. He or she can either overlook it, dole out severe penalties, or do something in between.

When we are the supervisor in charge, it's important (when possible) for us to pray through these situations before addressing them. Our leadership should always be redemptive but may require the person who messed up to face some consequences. There are times when the only way to get through to someone about the seriousness of the error is to require him or her to face disciplinary action. I used formal discipline only a couple of times during my twenty years in management. Both times, the employee and the organization sorely needed action to be taken to rectify the unproductive behavior. And both times, it significantly improved the employee's conduct and performance as well as the organization's ability to function effectively.

Forgiving Others

There are times when our mistake will not be handled well by our supervisor or colleagues. We may have done everything possible to be honest and up front about our mistake. We may have worked to fix the problem we caused. Yet others might still hold the episode against us. Rivals might put us down or continually tease us about the blunder. In these cases, our only response is forgiveness.

> Repay no one evil for evil. Have regard for good things in the sight of all men. If it is possible, as much as depends on you, live peaceably with all men. Beloved, do not avenge yourselves, but rather give place to wrath; for it is written, 'Vengeance is Mine, I will repay,' says the Lord. Therefore 'if your enemy is hungry, feed him; if he is thirsty, give him a drink; for in so doing you will heap coals of fire on his head (Romans 12:17–20).

Trusting the Lord to have our back, even when we err, is the sign of a mature relationship with God.

Coming Back From Failure

Life deals us many blows. Sometimes we feel like fighters who have been beaten, vanquished, and permanently injured. Our career may be in shambles. Perhaps mistakes have compounded failures, which have piled on personal pain. We may feel like we have nothing left to give.

As always, the best place to turn is to the Lord. No matter what we've done or how others have reacted, God still loves us and has a plan to restore us. God always has another strategy for redemption, even if we've messed up the last one. The Lord is knowledge incarnate. Even if our situation seems hopeless, Jesus knows the answer. His Father invented work and knows what we can still do to make the world a better place and get paid for our labor.

God Can Miraculously Provide

When Jesus and Peter came to the town of Capernaum during their travels, the local tax man approached Peter and asked if Jesus would pay his temple tax. This particular "tax" was actually a scheme the local religious leaders used to rip off strangers who visited their area. Peter knew the disciples had no money at that moment and brought the issue to Jesus.

The Savior's response proved He always has one more miracle up his sleeve. He said to Peter, "Go to the sea, cast in a hook, and take the fish that comes up first. And when you have opened its mouth, you will find a piece of money; take that and give it to them for Me and you" (Matthew 17:27). If Jesus can cause a coin-laden fish to swim up to Peter on cue, He can come up with a new job for us or temporary provision apart from a job—if that is the true need.

No matter how down we've been, God's plan is to bring us back up. God is a future maker. He has hope for us. When we call out to Him, we will be amazed at the results.

> When the LORD brought back the captivity of Zion, we were like those who dream. Then our mouth was filled with laughter, and our tongue with singing. Then they said among the nations, 'The LORD has done great things for them.' The LORD has done great things for us, and we are glad. Bring back our captivity, O LORD, as the streams in the South. Those who sow in tears shall reap in joy. He who continually goes forth weeping, bearing seed

for sowing, shall doubtless come again with rejoicing, bringing his sheaves with him (Psalm 126:1–6).

A Major Miscalculation About Time

Perhaps the biggest mistake we can ever make is to put off a decision to serve Christ. Eventually, all of us will run out of time. The tricky part is that actuarial tables aren't reliable down to the individual level. Few of us know if we have another year to live or thirty more years. It is never a good idea to put off living for Jesus. Now is the right time to use our talents and energy to take care of His world. David wrote, "So teach us to number our days, that we may gain a heart of wisdom" (Psalm 90:12).

Summary

There is a difference between mistakes and sin. Sin is a subset of mistakes that involve disobedience to God's law. Work mistakes are often not sin, but they may require us to own up to the miscues to avoid harming our co-workers, supervisors, or the company as a whole. We should be encouraged that recovery is possible, even from mistakes that cost us our jobs. Moral failure is more serious, but it can be overcome through repentance and cleansing from God. In these instances, we must keep trusting God, keep loving God, and keep imitating God. Repentance may include restitution if our actions have materially hurt others. Our hope is that any persons we've wronged will forgive us, and as Christians, we owe forgiveness to those who have sinned against us. The most serious error anyone can ever make is to put off knowing Christ. At some point, all of us will run out of time on earth. It is imperative that we accept Jesus before we miss our opportunity.

Spotlight Feature

Johnny Curtis

As co-owners of Freedom Tree Service, Johnny Curtis and his brother operate their company in the DC suburbs according to Christian principles. The name of the company took shape in part from John 8:36: "Therefore if the Son makes you free, you shall be free indeed." The name also stems from their mother's commitment to be a freedom fighter for God and country.

From its inception, Johnny has run the firm according to biblical principles. "It sets us apart from some of the competition," he says. Perhaps pun intended, he notes that "trees are a shady business," and it is easy to shine if you treat people right. Johnny's Christian values have proven effective in his twelve years in business. "If you don't overcharge and you clean up after yourselves, the word spreads," he says.

"We have very good reviews on Angie's List and Yelp! because we treat people right."

Johnny doesn't insist that new hires to the company be acknowledged Christians, but he does explain to them that the business will be run by biblical principles. "It's good for business," he states. "Employees also see that we pray at the beginning of each work day. We huddle up to pass out the various job assignments for the day. At the conclusion of that meeting, I always lead a prayer and ask the Lord's blessing on the day."

Johnny has every intention of doing things God's way, yet mistakes still happen in both Christian and secular business. Freedom Tree has fourteen employees during the busiest season of the year, and multiple crews are in several locations. In one memorable incident, Johnny's nephew and another man were running a stump grinder to eliminate the remnants of a fallen tree. Johnny got a call from his nephew that day. "I think we dented a car," he said. Although the facts seemed sketchy, his nephew felt confident the stump grinder threw out a rock or other debris, which then hit a neighbor's vehicle.

After inspecting the car, it became obvious it had incurred other bumps and bruises besides just what would have been caused by the impact of the rock from the grinder. At first, Johnny asked his nephew if he was certain they had been responsible for the dent. When his nephew confirmed he thought they had done it, Johnny felt he had no choice but to offer to pay for the damage.

"In those moments, your integrity is challenged," Johnny says. "Would it be easier to pretend it didn't happen? Did anyone else see the incident? But I realized it isn't just about me. How would my nephew feel if I didn't handle it ethically? My witness was on the line." The result of notifying the neighbor cost the business $700.

"Biblical principles are the way to long-term success," Johnny says. Momentary temptations to take shortcuts may seem right in the short run, but people will see through us. The Bible is the way to lasting success. Scripture is the best business guidebook.

Spotlight Questions

What could you identify with in Johnny's story?

What action steps occurred to you about taking God to work?

Study Questions

1   Read James 5:16. What is a mistake you've made at work?

2   How did you handle the mistake? Did you admit it? Did you find forgiveness?

3   Read Galatians 1:10. What does it mean to be a people pleaser?

4   Why is it important to care more about pleasing God than pleasing other people?

5   How do you try to avoid being a people pleaser?

6   Read Romans 12:17–20. What is an on-the-job incident where you thought about repaying evil for evil?

7   What part does forgiveness play in living peaceably with others?

8   How does this passage recommend you treat those who have sinned against you?

9   Read Psalm 90:12. What does it mean to "number our days?"

10 How does remembering the limited time everyone will live lead you to pray about seemingly insignificant things?

11 Read James 5:19–20. Why should you help co-workers who are falling into bad attitudes or bad behaviors at work?

12 When was a time you helped someone at work who later gave you credit for turning him or her around from the wrong path that person was on?

Prayer

Lord, You understand my frailty better than I do. Please forgive me for mistakes I've made as a result of my sinful nature, desires, or actions. Grant me complete repentance of heart and mind that I might serve You in holiness. Because of Your grace to me, I forgive those who have sinned against me, and I pray You would not hold them accountable for those mistakes that harmed me. Show me how to make amends for those wrongs that I have committed against others. Grant me the integrity not to hide my sin but to bring it to You and allow You to completely heal me. For all these things, I thank You and live in Your debt. In the name of Jesus, Amen.

What will you do to take God to work this week?

Winning the Spiritual Endgame

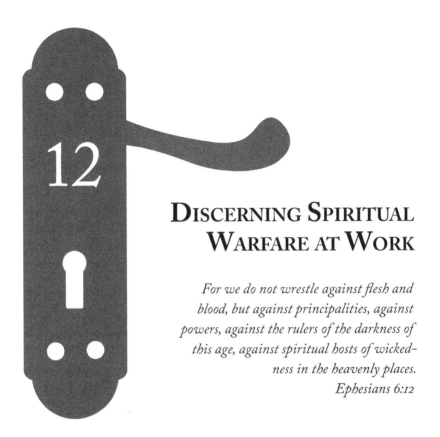

12

DISCERNING SPIRITUAL WARFARE AT WORK

For we do not wrestle against flesh and blood, but against principalities, against powers, against the rulers of the darkness of this age, against spiritual hosts of wickedness in the heavenly places.
Ephesians 6:12

QUIET FILLED THE OFFICE THAT DAY. After a morning chocked full of business calls, meetings, and paperwork, the files on my desk pointed to a long, boring afternoon of searching property records. While this task was not my favorite part of the contracting officer job, I knew it had to be done. Property management paperwork usually took a back seat to more time-sensitive matters, and on long-running contracts like the one before me, the property may have been transferred many times, creating a morass of intertwined claims and issues. Someone—me, in this case—eventually had to figure it all out so the contract file could be closed and the final payment made. While not complicated, the process proved tedious and time-consuming even with my trusty bottle of Diet Pepsi for company.

Several inches deep into the large brown file, eye-strain and tedium had induced an almost hypnotic state on my mind. Suddenly, I heard shouting coming from the nearby copier room. The male voice spoke in even tones, but the woman shrieked and screamed. Her voice became louder as she rebuked the devil and called out to God.

"Get behind me, Satan!" Brenda shouted. "You have no authority here. Take your evil host and get out of this office forever!"

"Yes, I'm the all-powerful one, your boss," Jason responded. "I'm ordering you to get back to your desk before I write you up for insubordination."

I peeked out of my office and saw Brenda running back to her desk along one wall of the large open area. She cried loudly, and tears ran down her face as she plopped dejectedly into her chair.

Jason stomped authoritatively across the large open area to his office. Once there, he slammed the metal and glass door, which echoed with a clunky reverberating sound. Although not usually in charge, he served as acting manager that afternoon while our mutual boss went across town for a meeting.

I returned to my desk and tried to get back into the large property file. A few minutes later, Janis, a co-worker, ducked into my office and closed the door behind her. In our small ten-person office, it took little effort to see who went where. I knew why Janis had come to see me and, most likely, so did everyone else on the staff.

Janis raised her eyebrows and gave me her best surprised look.

"What's going on out there?" I asked.

"Apparently, Brenda thinks Jason is the Antichrist of the Bible and is populating the office with his evil host of demons."

"That's interesting," I responded, not sure how to interpret any of this. Gossip wasn't my thing, and none of this sounded like something I wanted to jump into.

"Jason egged her on at first, because he found the whole thing ludicrous. He's not the most spiritual guy in the world, but I don't think he's in a position to become a world leader. So, I doubt he is the embodiment of Satan on earth. But I'm worried Brenda might get a gun and go postal."

My curiosity peaked at the idea that any of us might be in danger. "I hear you," I said. "I have my trusty government-issued tape dispenser if violence breaks out. My back-up security plan is to wail it at the shooter." My attempted humor did little to set Janis at ease. "Seriously though, the shouting is disruptive. Do you think Brenda will get into major trouble for the outburst? Jason *is* the manager in charge."

"Brenda claims she is going to file some kind of complaint because Jason harassed her. According to her, he comes into the copier room every time she goes in there to pray. That's how she discerned 'evil' was at work in the office. He claims he just needs to make copies and the timing has been a coincidence."

Our regular boss had left Jason in charge, but I wondered if he had the clout to actually take disciplinary action. Brenda's yelling at him certainly had to be considered inappropriate, if not insubordinate.

Later, I ended up in the copier room with Brenda. She brought up the situation to me and quickly became emotional. "You have to believe me," she said adamantly. "Jason and his evil host are at work in this office. He can't fool me. I know what's going on here. The devil is behind it."

I didn't know what to say. And I still don't.

The situation with Brenda and Jason may sound extreme, but it reflects actual events that happened during my career with the federal government. What began as an attempt at humor by Jason turned into a volatile situation with Brenda. She literally believed that Jason, a rather mild-mannered-looking engineer, represented a serious evil presence, if not the Antichrist described in the book of Revelation.

Although at the time I had been a Christian for fifteen years, I felt none of the evil my co-worker sensed. Jason seemed like a normal guy, though with a goofy sense of humor. He claimed to be a practicing Catholic. As I prayed about the situation, my gut told me personality conflict gone awry, more so than legitimate spiritual warfare.

Although neither employee suffered serious consequences for the outburst, Brenda soon accepted another job elsewhere, which included a pay bump. I lost touch with her when she transferred out. Only God knows for sure, but time has proven that Jason is not the Antichrist of the Bible. His career continued to flourish as he accepted a promotion in another city and faded into government oblivion.

Personality Conflict or Spiritual Warfare?

As followers of Christ, we are called to be aware of spiritual forces. As mentioned previously, Paul put it this way: "For we do not wrestle against flesh and blood, but against principalities, against powers, against the rulers of the darkness of this age, against spiritual hosts of wickedness in the heavenly places" (Ephesians 6:12). So, how do we tell the difference between a personality conflict, like the one described above, and real spiritual conflict?

We pray and ask God for discernment. He must grant us spiritual eyes to see beyond the personalities to understand if there is more at work in the spiritual realm. The Holy Spirit inside us has many purposes, and one of these may be to help us figure out what's going on spiritually and how we should pray. The name of Jesus is greater than any force in the universe. As believers, we have authority, granted by Jesus, to clear away any evil spiritual forces in our workplaces. Jesus said, "Behold, I give you the authority to trample on serpents and scorpions, and over all the power of the enemy, and nothing shall by any means hurt you" (Luke 10:19).

Think that over. God intended for us to bring the light of Jesus into our workplace, shine it all over, and cause dark forces to flee. Although this authority is significant, it barely registers in comparison to our eternal salvation. That is the most amazing gift. Jesus drove this point home when He said,

> I saw Satan fall like lightning from heaven. Behold, I give you the authority to trample on serpents and scorpions, and over all the power of the enemy, and nothing shall by any means hurt you. Nevertheless, do not rejoice in this, that the spirits are subject to you, but rather rejoice because your names are written in heaven (Luke 10:18–20).

If our motives are pure and we continually get resistance to the good things we are trying to accomplish, we need to bring the matter to the LORD. He will teach us to pray for peace, order, and success at our workplace. God knows everything that is going on. We don't know and probably *won't* know exactly how much of our conflict is rooted in spiritual opposition. But God may grant us a small part to play in bringing spiritual peace to our own corner of the company, government organization, or other place of employment.

We have to realize that not everyone who rubs us the wrong way is necessarily overcome with evil. It is a big, beautiful world with all kinds of personalities in it. People come to work from an infinite number of environmental factors that have shaped their personalities. An angry father, a distant mother, a mentally ill brother, or a drug-addicted aunt may have taught your co-worker coping mechanisms that are not helpful. This doesn't make them evil. But when their human frailty rubs up against our own immaturity, fireworks can ignite. The key is to bring these situations to God in prayer.

Pray For Spiritual Wisdom

God does not want His children to be ignorant of the spiritual forces in the world around us. He also doesn't want us to fear them. Jesus is LORD of all because He conquered death and the grave. There is no evil that can overcome Christ. The king of evil tried to subdue God's Son but failed. Our charge is to rest in the wisdom of Scripture and rely on the guidance of God's Spirit to discern what's going on around us. Paul prayed that "the God of our LORD Jesus Christ, the Father of glory, may give to you the spirit of wisdom and revelation in the knowledge of Him" (Ephesians 1:17).

Careful With Saying, "God Told Me"

When it comes to God and the world of work, Christians must be careful of two extremes. At the one extreme is a totally secular workplace where believers check their faith at the door, put their heads down, and work without thoughts of God until the closing bell rings. At the other extreme is an overly spiritualized view where believers perceive that every action is prompted by either God or the devil.

While God wants us to pray without ceasing, He doesn't expect us to find spiritual nuggets in every shovel of dirt we scoop. There lurks neither a demon behind every setback nor an angel guiding our every success. Applying God's principles to our work will likely lead us to many successes and help us overcome challenges as well. The LORD will use our difficulties to build our character and refine our personalities to be more like Jesus.

As we try to live being more aware of God at our workplaces, we may be tempted to believe that God is giving us all kinds of advice for other people. This can happen, but more often we just end up giving out our own advice to our co-workers and attribute it to God. The practice of saying, "God told me," can be spiritually hazardous for ourselves and for the recipient of the advice.

If God really did say something to us for the other person, that's fine. But if God's voice wasn't truly behind the word of advice, the recipient may become confused or even undertake some activity that is definitely not in God's plan for them. More often, God speaks individually and directly to His children through Scripture, sermons, or other teachings. He does use conversations with other believers, but usually this is to confirm the point His Holy Spirit has already shown to that person. For this reason, if we have an *opinion* we want to share with a friend, we need to do so without attributing it to God.

As brothers and sisters in the Lord, God may lead us to carefully give counsel with another believer, particularly in an area where we have experience. We need to do so humbly and without getting hung up about whether the advice is immediately well received. Sometimes, people need to think about a matter and mull it over in light of Scripture.

Obviously, the Bible is a sure foundation and authoritative voice—more so than what people say. But whatever the source, God will confirm His words to us in our hearts. "My sheep hear My voice, and I know them, and they follow Me" (John 10:27). God is good, and He wants us to clearly understand the right path He wants us to take.

Indicators Of Spiritual Warfare

Previously, we asserted that most work problems are people problems. This is certainly true on a human level. By working through our issues with other people, we grow, learn about ourselves, and come to understand more about God. But beyond the human world we see is a world of spiritual forces. The key verse for this chapter reminds us that our battle as Christians is really not against other people but against principalities, powers, rulers of the darkness of this age, and spiritual hosts of wickedness in the heavenly places.

This realization matters, because our tendency is to look at our roadblocks as only skin deep. Once we've embraced our God-given giftedness and begin taking care of His world, we

become partners with Him in all that is good and right. As we
serve other people in the name of Jesus, our witness cries out
"there is a God" and "He loves you."

Why on earth would anyone not support someone doing
good and bringing glory to God? The answer is simple: there are
enemies of God. Evil exists, and it wants to supplant and oppose
those who long for God's glory, His praise, and His power to be
released. Satan and his spirits work through people to discredit
God and His people. He does not want God's kingdom to pre-
vail in heaven or on earth. But how can we know whether our
opposition is truly supernatural? We can't know for sure, but
here are some warning signs:

- Our efforts meet constant resistance for no logical reason.
- Those who oppose us make it personal and attack us instead
  of the proposed solution or change.
- No matter how much we attempt to bring clarity, the project or service is repeatedly thrown into confusion.
- The opposition uses discouragement and often makes us
  want to quit.

At this point, you may be considering setting the book down
and going for a walk. Hang in there with us. This book about
taking God into the workplace would not be complete without
an understanding of those times when normal human measures
don't fix our problems. As the world continues to become more
corrupt and more decadent, Christians need to know, more than
ever, how to respond to assaults on their belief system.

Spiritual Battle

Before His death, Jesus prayed for those of us who would believe
on His name in the future. Just as Jesus did nothing without the
Father's approval, we will find power and beauty as we increase
our unity with God and with other believers.

In a poignant and beautiful prayer, Jesus showed His compassion for us as we shine His light into a dark and sometimes

cruel world. His compassion and understanding of us offers great encouragement. His prayer went like this:

> I do not pray for these alone, but also for those who will believe in Me through their word; that they all may be one, as You, Father, are in Me, and I in You; that they also may be one in Us, that the world may believe that You sent Me. And the glory which You gave Me, I have given them, that they may be one just as We are one: I in them, and You in Me; that they may be made perfect in one, and that the world may know that You have sent Me, and have loved them as You have loved Me (John 17:20–23).

God knew we would face spiritual battles, so He also offers us spiritual armor to help us at work and beyond. "Put on the whole armor of God, that you may be able to stand against the wiles of the devil... Therefore take up the whole armor of God, that you may be able to withstand in the evil day, and having done all, to stand" (Ephesians 6:11, 13).

Praying through our business situations will give God an opportunity to show us how to deal with the spiritual forces we encounter. Our unity with God and His purpose will overcome many obstacles. Again and again in my career with the government, I learned the importance of praying before meetings. When I remembered to do so, it often amazed me how much more God accomplished during the meeting.

If you are experiencing opposition and it appears to be spiritual, don't be afraid to take authority over any power or principality in the name of Jesus. Order it to go and never return by the power of Jesus.

Sometimes we know all the right things to do. We've prayed and trusted God for the result. We've taken authority over evil and exercised our faith. In these situations, the only thing left to do is stand and trust that God is working to fix our problem.

> Stand therefore, having girded your waist with truth, having put on the breastplate of righteousness, and having shod your feet with the preparation of the gospel of peace; above all, taking

the shield of faith with which you will be able to quench all
the fiery darts of the wicked one. And take the helmet of salvation, and the sword of the Spirit, which is the word of God
(Ephesians 6:14–17).

Like a sports team that slacked off on practice, sometimes it
takes losing to remind us of the power of prayer and Bible study.
When the fiery darts start flying at work, they often drive us
back to our knees to talk it over with the LORD.

Be careful about taking personal advice from unbelievers at
work. Those who don't share our worldview may suggest paths
that would lead us away from God. Many marriages have been
derailed when one partner or another listened to ungodly advice
at work.

Indicators and Remedies For Personality Conflicts

There are probably an infinite number of reasons why two
people might immediately like or dislike each other. Reasons
for disliking another person are infinite: looks like someone
who hurt us once, smells like our ex-boyfriend or uses sarcasm
inappropriately. Whatever the cause, as Christians we have a
calling to try to live peacefully with our colleagues and respect
the authority of our bosses.

In those situations where we find ourselves just wanting to get
away from another person, it is usually worth the time to figure
why we are reacting this way. God will help us figure it out if we
invite Him into the situation. He will even help us to love the
"unlovable" people if we garner the courage to ask for His help.

One practical remedy for resolving a personality conflict
includes developing empathy for the other person. Try to figure
out what might have bent that person in the direction that
annoys you, and then use that knowledge to give that person
grace should he or she trespass on one of your boundaries. If
you don't know the person well, take a few minutes to chat with
him or her. Sometimes a few minutes waiting for a meeting to

start can provide you with valuable insights. If you learn things about the person that are admirable, it may counteract some of your aversion to him or her. Finally, try to imagine what Jesus might see in the person. He tended to find the good or the potential in almost everyone.

Whether you are encountering legitimate spiritual warfare or just a personality conflict, use your spiritual armor and your relationship with God to find out the best way to handle it.

Have No Fellowship

To adopt the Christian walk is to cast off our sinful past. When we separate our Christian walk and our life at work, we run the risk of living out our work hours apart from the benefits and protection of our faith. Whether we like to admit it or not, we need our faith at work—maybe more so than when we are safely in our homes on the couch.

Work environments sometimes include pockets of spiritual wickedness. Those under the power of the evil one may try to draw us into conversations, thoughts, and actions that are anathema to our commitment to Christ. Living out the light that is within us has the potential to drive out the darkness, but it isn't automatic. Our charge is to recognize when we have stepped near the boundaries of darkness and refuse to proceed into fellowship with evil.

> For you were once darkness, but now you are light in the LORD. Walk as children of light (for the fruit of the Spirit is in all goodness, righteousness, and truth), finding out what is acceptable to the LORD. And have no fellowship with the unfruitful works of darkness, but rather expose them. For it is shameful even to speak of those things which are done by them in secret. But all things that are exposed are made manifest by the light, for whatever makes manifest is light (Ephesians 5:8–13).

This doesn't mean you can't speak to, or work with, non-Christian people. It just means that some situations, some conversations, and some joking around aren't right for you. Listen to the Holy Spirit within you to discern when it's time to withdraw your fellowship from people who are tearing you down or harming your faith. God will talk to you. Just yield to His quiet suggestions and head back to your desk or work area.

The same advice applies when dealing with Christians who have fallen for false teaching or false teachers. If you find yourself in serious disagreement with another professing Christian about a point of doctrine, there may be a time when you should agree to disagree and move on. Arguing seldom changes the mind of another person, unless God does the work.

Make sure you understand the difference between false teaching and different points of emphasis. Paul used the analogy of a body in 1 Corinthians 12:12–31 to describe the church, and it has many parts. He warns believers not to think that every person will have the same function in the body of Christ. Hands don't do what feet are supposed to do.

Every person in the body came from a spiritual background or heritage. If you view that heritage as particularly rich or safe, you may be quick to judge others who don't understand every doctrine the same way you see it. The Bible gives you a firm foundation for your beliefs. If you find allies in the Christian faith at work, don't waste the resource of their fellowship over one or two less important doctrines that may separate you.

Beating Discouragement With Joy

One of the enemy's most common weapons is discouragement. Every time you love someone in the name of the Father, you are bringing His kingdom to the earth. By witnessing to others with your love and care for them, you are acting as a mighty force for good. The secret of a successful Christian life is to keep going, keep doing good, keep loving, and keep showing people the Jesus inside of you. "But as for you, brethren, do not grow weary in doing good" (2 Thessalonians 3:13).

Work and Our Spiritual Life

God wants us to work, take care of His world, and enjoy the fruit of our labor. The Christian worker is intended to be a witness of God's love, grace, and provision. Don't underestimate the good you are doing by living an authentic Christian life at your job. Chances are you are doing a world of good in the physical and spiritual realms.

> But we urge you, brethren, that you increase more and more; that you also aspire to lead a quiet life, to mind your own business, and to work with your own hands, as we commanded you, that you may walk properly toward those who are outside, and that you may lack nothing (1 Thessalonians 4:10–12).

Restoring Order

Spiritual battles and personality conflicts strain relationships and upset the orderliness of our workplace. Words are said that can't be taken back, and relationships can be badly damaged. As salt and light, Christians should be willing to speak up when things aren't going well. At the Department of Homeland Security, I got a reputation as a turn-around specialist for our troubled business units. This began with reshaping a single underperforming division. Later, my bosses asked me to take over other struggling divisions and improve their performance and morale. With God's help, I used this six-part approach to achieve these goals.

1. Calm Everyone Down

First, I calmed everyone down and worked to promote an atmosphere of peace in the office. At that point I had more than ten years of management experience under my belt, and God used that preparation for the challenges I faced. In my first post as a manager at the Department of Homeland Security, I quickly detected a lot of tension and even yelling back and forth in the office. Employees gossiped about each other, the customers, and management. By refocusing everyone on the tasks at hand and shutting down the gossip, internal relations and relationships with our customers greatly improved. I reminded my folks that professional conduct must be demonstrated at all times. The new requirement to keep their voices at a normal volume eventually took hold. After a couple of months, the office atmosphere became noticeably more peaceful and quiet.

2. Emphasize the Importance Of the Mission and Customer Service

The Department of Homeland Security workforce was united by a common goal of protecting their families, friends, and fellow countrymen. The department was formed after the September 11, 2001 terrorist attacks. Its mission was to protect the United States homeland from natural and manmade threats. In the office, I asked the employees to work more closely with their customers to eliminate some of the "us versus them" mentalities. As the customers grew to understand our needs in trying to serve them, we all became better at producing the end product: quality contracts for goods and services. The mission gave everyone a vision of where the future might lead and took away some of the fear that our efforts would be ineffective.

3. Value Quality Work

When people feel appreciated, they go to great lengths to reward their managers and their organization with a great volume and quality of work. Admittedly, at one point I encouraged a couple of key trouble makers to job hunt. These individuals had become rigid in their opinions and were the first to gossip when things didn't go their way. Even worse, they encouraged others to take sides in a non-existent war of popularity. Fortunately, they found comparable employment where, hopefully, they were more content. Beyond these bad apples, I valued and rewarded the contributions of everyone else. Understaffing posed the biggest problem when I first took over as a division director, and several of the employees continued doing heroic things to keep up with the demands of our customers.

4. Stick Up For Important Principles

Employees want to follow leaders who stick to admirable principles. When a new president appointed new leadership at the Department of Homeland Security, political types at the top of the organization promulgated a controversial terror watch list. It included many conservative organizations, including my MBA alma mater, Regent University, founded by Pat Robertson. I suspected the school had made the list because of Robertson's conservative beliefs.

Any organization that embraced biblical standards was perceived as a threat by the new leadership. I and dozens of other workers at the Department of Homeland Security used our positions to push back on this outrageous persecution of Christian organizations. While not all of my employees agreed with my political bent, they understood the importance of leaving politics out of things like defining terrorist organizations.

5. Make It Clear That People Matter

Due to inadequate staffing at the Department of Homeland Security and the demands of our mission, some of the employees began breaking down physically and mentally. One of my first acts as the new boss involved supporting vacations and sick leave. Although we needed more hands and the vacation time seemed counterproductive, I knew that fresh employees would accomplish a lot more than worn-out troops. It was hard for the people to be at their best when they were exhausted and getting them out of the office for needed breaks changed a lot of attitudes.

6. Share Your Faith Judiciously

God led me to share my faith in specific ways with specific individuals, though only rarely and in key moments of their lives. Being the boss meant people told me things about their personal situations and problems. On occasion, this opened doors for me to offer hope, encouragement, or other guidance. If the employee or colleague came from a Christian background,

I would offer to pray for him or her. In all cases, I tried to point the person to the LORD.

Only a few times over the years did this end badly. One time, a gay employee facing a difficult personal situation took offense at the mention of God. He had been raised by a father who served as a pastor. My employee had grown up playing piano in church. When I tried to bring up God, he screamed and warned me to never to broach the subject again. I respected his request, but I still prayed for him often.

In my thirty-three-year career with the federal government, I experienced many ups and downs. During my twenty-plus years in management, I faced serious situations that caused great stress and even physical difficulty. However, the blessings far outweighed the problems. The friendly faces greatly outnumbered the angry ones, and the joy of the LORD lifted me up day by day. While some took my demeanor to mean that I never had a serious problem, the truth is that I knew the problem solver. God always made Himself available to help sort out any situation. Business meetings went much better when I prayed first. God became a partner in many business dealings and brought numerous promotions, awards, and adventures.

Summary

The Christian's fight is usually not against a flesh and blood enemy, so we must depend on God's help to fight our spiritual battles. Half the battle is simply being aware that spiritual forces may oppose us as we attempt to care for the world in Jesus' name. We may need to pray for discernment so we can tell the difference between a simple personality conflict and spiritual opposition. Some addictions, certain sins, and various agendas can't be overcome simply by using our human efforts. We must call on the LORD in prayer for spiritual wisdom.

Getting prepared means putting on the whole armor of God as described in Ephesians 6:10–20. The major offensive weapons are God's Word and the Holy Spirit. The good news is that Jesus already came and won the war. He conquered the grave, and when we are willing to submit our lives to Him, our enemies have little power except to temporarily disrupt God's plan as it unfolds through Christ's followers.

Spotlight Feature
Deby Allen

Deby Allen, the owner/operator of Special Effects Styling Salon in New Carlisle, Ohio, takes her faith to work each day. Although she has run the salon for twenty-seven years, her spiritual awakening came eighteen years ago. She credits one of her longtime employees for praying Christ into their workplace. "I'm sure she wore out the knees of her pants praying for me," Deby says. Since that time, she has tried to put God first in everything.

Deby grew tired of the negativity of the outside world and the gossip that dominated her profession. So, she decided to change the music to a Christian station, KLOVE radio. The positive Christian music and her own decision to put God in charge changed the atmosphere of her salon and led to big results. "I got so tired of all the negative stuff," Deby says. "God just changed everything. Switching to KLOVE, it got really peaceful in the shop. I don't have to worry about trashy commercials. People like the uplifting messages. It's like getting away from the outside world and all the bad things that are happening."

In addition to changing the radio station, Deby tries to make Special Effects a peaceful oasis. "We stopped nitpicking, gossiping, and using inappropriate language. Bringing God into the picture transformed Special Effects." Subscribing to fifteen magazine subscriptions, Deby throws out any with trashy covers.

God taught Deby to get her priorities in order. "He told me to put Him first," she says. "People second. I'm third. I pray for my clients and for my staff. The day goes much better when I do it that way. Everything flows better. I ask God to guard and guide my words, thoughts, and deeds."

When things go wrong for a client, Deby puts her faith in action by trying her best to fix any missteps. "With long-time clients, there aren't many problems," she says. "But occasionally, a newer client will not like something, and we find a way to fix it." This might mean not charging for a particular treatment or re-dying someone's hair a different color. The key is to treat others fairly, as we would want to be treated, she says.

Eighteen years ago, Deby learned that putting God first meant making major changes in the way she ran her business. "It changes how you deal with money," she says. "It keeps you honest. I don't want to cheat God. Nobody knows about the little things, but God does. Follow His Word in all your practices. I've learned from trusting Him that I don't need to comment when people bring up a gossipy subject. I don't need to share it or get into that conversation."

To Deby's surprise, over the years God has done amazing things in the lives of her staff and her clients. Working in a Christian environment even led one of her employees to faith in Jesus. The breakthrough came through a gradual process. "She started going to church," she says, "and made a profession of faith, eventually being baptized." Nothing beats the feeling of helping someone find the LORD through your business.

Spotlight Questions

What could you identify with in Deby's story?
What action steps occurred to you about taking God to work?

Study Questions

1   *Read Ephesians 6:12.* What comes to mind when you imagine a spiritual battle?

2   Why do you think the Bible states that you are not wrestling against flesh and blood but against principalities, powers, and rulers of the darkness of this age?

3   How can prayer help you battle against unseen powers?

4   *Read 2 Corinthians 10:4.* Why do you think Paul said the Christian's weapons are not carnal?

5   What spiritual weapons does the Christian possess that could help tear down strongholds?

6   What does it mean to bring thoughts into the captivity of Christ?

7   *Read 1 Timothy 1:18–19.* In what ways do Christians today wage warfare in the workplace?

8   Faith and a good conscience will help to wage warfare. How has this worked for you?

9   *Read 1 Thessalonians 4:10–12.* How does living peaceably with all men fit in with waging spiritual warfare?

10   How can waging spiritual warfare actually contribute to your reputation with those outside the Christian faith?

11   *Read 2 Timothy 2:4.* What worldly entanglements could prevent you from being a good soldier for Christ?

12   How can you be a good spiritual soldier in your workplace this week?

Prayer

Dear God, thank You for each of the co-workers, bosses, and employees that You have placed in my world. Thank You for those easy-to-get-along-with colleagues and also for those who rubbed me the wrong way. Thank You for the lessons I learned from the pleasant people I came to call friends and for the difficult individuals who may have tried purposefully to harm me. Your wisdom is higher than mine. My cognitive powers are tiny compared with the Creator of the Universe. Even so, I humbly ask that You grant me the discernment to know the root causes of any personality conflicts, disagreements, and spiritual battles that come my way. Remind me through Your Holy Spirit to bring each situation to You, listen at Your feet, and glean answers from Your Holy Scriptures. Allow me to live at peace with all men and women, as far as possible, while holding true to my Christian values. In the name of Jesus, amen.

What will you do to take God to work this week?

SHOULD CHRISTIANS RETIRE?

Surely there is a reward for the righteous;
surely He is God who judges in the earth.
Psalm 58:11

MILESTONES CAN BE BEAUTIFUL. When I look back over a thirty-three-year career, I can point to hundreds of times when I believe God blessed me because of my relationship with Him. From the time in my twenties when I yielded my work life to God, until my eventual retirement with Homeland Security at the end of 2015, I can see God's hand directing me at each twist and turn. Even when I made or contemplated huge mistakes, He spoke to me in one way or another and often redirected my path.

In my years with the government, I saw major reorganizations, received a wall full of awards, got promoted numerous times, traveled to nearly every major city in the continental

U.S., hugged employees with cancer, cried with co-workers at funerals, and experienced a lifetime of memories. All the laughter I experienced and generated through those thirty-three years could fill a laugh-track three days long.

Working for research and science organizations allowed me to preview amazing technological advances, work with very smart people, and understand the diversity of mankind a little better. (Did you know that most scientists don't like to chitchat on the elevator?) From a naval ship that could travel at sixty knots, to technology that could make planes invisible to radar, every day became a learning experience. One of my favorite projects involved merging two different types of body armor to improve protection of our warfighters.

But even with all these exciting programs, the best part remained the people. My ability as a manager to speak into the lives of employees and colleagues, using a biblical perspective, probably amounted to my most important contribution. Many of my Christian co-workers and employees did the same for me.

What Do You Hope to Accomplish With Your Life?

At the beginning of our careers, most of us merely want to earn a living. Perhaps we have no idea where we even want to live. Thirty or forty years sounds like an eternity to a twenty-year-old. We don't yet understand the value of work or why it's important, and we may look at the prospects of forty years behind a desk as depressing and even daunting.

However, over time and with maturity, we come to realize the beauty of God's plan regarding work. In addition to supporting ourselves and our families, we find our work to be an extension of God's care for people, places, and things. At some point, retirement will come into sight—maybe ten years or less into the future. It's time to think about our career end game.

When you reach the terminus of your career, what accomplishments will be significant to you? To God? To those you love?

What is the type of contribution that will make you feel you wisely spent your most important resource here on earth—*time?* Will you be proud of building a large company or founding a nonprofit organization? Will you feel good about policies you developed that made things better for the poor or elderly?

Perhaps you will be proud of a new scientific discovery that brought healing to millions of people or the fact you created new jobs for hundreds or thousands of people. You may even take satisfaction from helping an employer earn billions of dollars because of some innovation you developed. Regardless, we hope this book has helped you evaluate or re-evaluate how you would like to help care for God's world.

If you are still far from retirement, the good news is you can alter the trajectory of your career. Even though the first part may have been all about you, the rest of your career can be all about God and helping Him care for His Creation.

Perspective

When we are in the middle of the forest, it can be difficult to gain perspective about the expanse of our career. At work, our opinion may only matter because of our rank or position. Five minutes after we retire—sometimes sooner—loyal employees and even friends will likely turn their attention to our successors. Think about it. Do your current employees spend hours worrying about what previous bosses or departed co-workers think of changes to the organization? They obviously don't give it more than a passing thought. So, what is really important to you? Friendships? Character? Souls won to Christ? Employees mentored? Lives nurtured? The way you cared for God's world through your job?

Our partnership with the Almighty unlocks untold blessings on those we serve. In no way are we equal partners or even deserving of our supporting roles, but God chooses to give us a part to play. As we are filled with the love He birthed in us, it is our incredible opportunity to love the world through our work. When we say goodbye to our workplace or our career, perhaps the most important thing is to know we tried our best to please God each day. The everyday miracles created by a surrendered life reveal the best way to maximize our talents: one day at a time.

The Calling of Our Partnership

Our inadequacy to fulfill this calling on our own should drive us to our knees in prayer. "Therefore I exhort first of all that supplications, prayers, intercessions, and giving of thanks be made for all men" (1 Timothy 2:1). Not every day on earth will be an adventure in paradise. Our efforts will sometimes be misunderstood. Our concern will sometimes be mislabeled as micro-management. Our acts of love will sometimes be spurned. Still, we must carry on with our divine purpose of caring for others through our work. This calling transcends our thirty to forty years in a "job." It is a lifetime calling. In the process, we may need take up more than a cross or two along the way.

> And he who does not take his cross and follow after Me is not worthy of Me. He who finds his life will lose it, and he who loses his life for My sake will find it. He who receives you receives Me, and he who receives Me receives Him who sent Me. He who receives a prophet in the name of a prophet shall receive a prophet's reward. And he who receives a righteous man in the name of a righteous man shall receive a righteous man's reward. And whoever gives one of these little ones only a cup of cold water in the name of a disciple, assuredly, I say to you, he shall by no means lose his reward (Matthew 10:38–41).

This passage is meant to reassure us that when we feel deprived of some earthly reward, God will eventually make it worthwhile. There will be instances when our calling causes us to miss time with family, a personal convenience, or some leisure-time activity. No matter how balanced we try to live, serving others exacts a price. It is unrealistic to think fulfilling our calling will come without a cost, but God wants us to know that none of our efforts in His name will be wasted. We will reap a reward for the times we give our best to care for others. That's why it is essential to connect our earthly job to our heavenly calling of caring for creation.

Memories Make the Best Mementos

More than a few workers have been underwhelmed by the farewell presents given at their retirement. What gift could sum up a career full of experiences, memories, and toil? A gold watch used to be the typical retirement gift. But in truth, by the time we get to retirement, most tangible mementos hold little value. If anything, we are thinking of downsizing, not collecting a bunch of additional hardware to display or store.

The best remembrances of a career well spent are memories, triggered by photos. As you go along in your career, make sure to collect a few snapshots. Document the big occasions and the everyday fun. Some of my favorite work moments probably have been forgotten, but my most cherished possessions from work are almost always photos. A picture is just a quick moment of time, but takes me back to the people, places, and fun that punctuated the hard work and accomplishment. So, take note of milestones reached, projects successfully completed, and happy moments at the holiday party or company picnic. Later, you will be glad to have the reminders of precious people you've known and mountains you've climbed.

Transition Preparation

Many of us go through a great deal of preparation to begin our work life or progress to the journeyman level. For those in professional careers, this meant lots of education. After thirteen years of elementary and secondary school, we may have headed off to college for four or five more years. Then we might have chosen an internship to stick a toe in the water of our chosen career. Somewhere in our mid-career, we might have gone back to school for even more study in the form of a Master's Degree.

For those in the trades, our jobs might have required technical school training or on-the-job instruction. Perhaps we began in our field shortly after high school. Years of learning or apprenticeship may have led to us achieving great skill in our trade. By putting in long days and showing great hustle, we built a business either for ourselves or our employer.

Throughout our working years, we likely spent hours understanding the financial implications of retirement and investing for it. Now, we need to show that same kind of preparation and interest in the activities that will follow our eventual retirement. Just because our employer and society agree on an age range as to when we *may* retire, it doesn't mean we *should* retire from a particular job or field. Before selecting a date, we need to pray it out, leave the decision to God, and make sure we are ready for another adventure—another phase of life.

Leisure time can get old fast. Many retirees find that painting watercolors is not as fascinating as they hoped. Staying home and watching television will lose its allure quickly. Depending on the rigors of your job, you may well enjoy a few months at a slower pace before launching into your second act. The important thing is to explore and again find your place of ministry to God's world.

Retirement for the Christian should just be a transition to a different type of service. It may not involve the same rigid schedule or demands of a nine-to-five job, but God knows many ways you can useful. He wants to plug you into your next opportunity. If you follow Him, even in retirement, He just might make it the most eternally productive time of your life.

Concrete Steps to Finding Your New Passion

Check Out the United Way Website in Your Area

The United Way has an exhaustive list of volunteer activities.

I found my first volunteer organization, the Pediatric Aids Care Program (PACP), through the federal employee equivalent of United Way. I decided that if I gave my money to PACP, perhaps I could give my time there as well. If I hadn't looked at the federal website or checked out their booklet, I wouldn't have known PACP existed. Do some research and stick a toe in before jumping in with both feet.

Take a Class
Perhaps you will discover your true passion has nothing to do with your previous career. A painting class, writer's conference, or woodworking seminar may be just the thing to get you started.

Go Deeper With Your Church
If you are like most folks, work may have interfered with some of your desired church activities. For example, you may not have been able to serve in Vacation Bible School because you were too busy with your primary career. Rethink some of those "never" choices you made when you were working and decide what you can do with your additional availability.

Try a Short-term Missions Trip
Maybe God is leading you to help out a ministry in another part of the world. If so, consider a short-term missions trip where you could help build a structure, feed the hungry, or teach a course. You may not choose to dive into full-time missionary work, but perhaps you can become an advocate for the ministry in your hometown and beyond.

Take Care Of a Family Member
Perhaps one of your dreams for retirement is to be available to care for a family member. God's economy is not like our own, and not all service projects need to be national in scale. Perhaps watching your grandchildren after school is the best use of your time to help them get started well on life's journey.

Get a Part-time Job

Maybe you enjoyed your career and felt ready for retirement but not ready to stop working completely. After retirement, I drove for Uber and Lyft, though it paid much less than I received from my federal job. I used it for five months as research for my first novel—the riders and experiences provided much fodder for a mystery I wanted to write about a Christian Uber driver who wandered into a murder scene and got accused of the crime.

Try Out For a Play or a Movie

Have you always harbored secret desires to do something artistic? If so, use retirement to explore those passions. Perhaps you will find an aptitude that you didn't know existed in you.

Teach or Consult

You will have gained a wealth of experience after a career of working in a certain industry or trade. Put that experience to use by teaching at a community college or online. Or perhaps you could consult and earn extra money in retirement. Depending on your field, you may be paid handsomely to work on special projects for your old firm or another in the same industry.

Never Done Working

Until God calls you to your eternal home, you have not completed your earthly work. Retirement from a career is merely a gateway to your next assignment. As long as there are hurting people, churches with open doors, neighborhoods with untended public gardens, or town councils with vacancies, there will be plenty for you to do. As long as there are at-risk youth needing a tutor, books that need to be written, or disabled folks who need a meal and a smile, you need never want for work.

Finishing your life strong requires diligence. Retiring from a career should just be a transition to even more rewarding service. You are wiser now and know your gifts, talents, and abilities better than when you started. Many have started new ministries and nonprofit organizations in retirement. Others have launched new businesses with their first retirement checks. Whatever you do, pick something that will help you continue to take care of God's world. Jesus' cause is too important for you to rest on your laurels. "Look to yourselves, that we do not lose those things we worked for, but that we may receive a full reward" (2 John 1:8).

Perhaps you began this study feeling you are coasting on autopilot in your job. Your salary is a necessity, and you didn't see any reasonable alternatives to your chosen career. In this study, we have not suggested that anyone must or even should leave his or her current employment. The choice is between you, the Lord, and those who depend on you. But know that the Lord may have something better for you out there—and it is always okay to ask Him.

Throughout these chapters, our heart has been to help you see that by changing your perspective, your current workplace could become the ideal place for you and God to take care of people. If you are sure it's time to go, I hope you've gathered courage to look around, with God's help. Life is a vapor, so get on with whatever your divine purpose may require. As James wrote, "Whereas you do not know what will happen tomorrow. For what is your life? It is even a vapor that appears for a little time and then vanishes away" (James 4:14).

God knows everything you need, and He's even aware of the things you want. He won't keep any good thing from you, but He might recommend a different timetable than the one you have in mind. Trust me, His timing is a lot better than yours! There is no safer ride than a journey wrapped in the arms of the Father.

Heaven

The main feature in heaven is God's presence. "He will dwell with them, and they shall be His people, and God Himself will be with them and be their God. And God will wipe away every tear from their eyes; there shall be no more death, nor sorrow, nor crying; and there shall be no more pain, for the former things have passed away" (Revelation 21:3–4). Can you imagine a world without death or even sorrow?

Our sinful lives before we came to Christ led us nowhere, but the fruit of our resurrected life in Christ will lead us to holiness and eventually eternal life in heaven. Our work for the kingdom is an outgrowth of the eternal life that Jesus bought for us. The journey leads to heaven, with many interesting stops along the way. The Holy Spirit within us is a deposit, showing God's good faith to eventually bring us to Himself.

Our work lives become a symphony as we yield this important part of our existence to the Maestro of the Universe. "But now having been set free from sin, and having become slaves of God, you have your fruit to holiness, and the end, everlasting life. For the wages of sin is death, but the gift of God is eternal life in Christ Jesus our Lord" (Romans 6:21–23).

God's Approval

When it comes down to it, God's approval is the best recognition for our work. No person or group knows more about our accomplishments, our unrealized potential, or our motives than God. He sees the inside and the outside of us. He knows whether our accomplishments are made of eternal gold, silver, or something less valuable. Others may give us more credit than is due, or they might not recognize the importance of our intangible contributions. But when our work life comes before the ultimate Judge, He will know everything He needs to know. All we want to hear is, "Well done, good and faithful servant."

Summary

Before retirement sneaks up on us, it's important for us to review what we hope to accomplish during our work years. Perspective can help us realize what is really valuable and what is not. Our partnership with God, while an unequal one, gives us the possibility of adventure, joy, and fulfillment in our careers. Memories will be our best mementos, so we need to make sure to take snapshots so we can remember those with whom we worked through the years. We are making our own history. As our retirement nears, we need to take steps to make the transition to new service projects easier. Christians don't retire—they just get promoted to more service.

Spotlight Feature
Cheryl Rogers

In many ways, Cheryl Rogers's work life has gone exactly as planned. When her four children were young, she stayed home and poured herself into their lives. Eventually, they went off to school, and she began her first job outside the home. Although she enjoyed working in a busy procurement office, she found the mission of the large manufacturing company uncompelling. So, she accepted a job change to become territory manager for an in-home comfort care firm. Her duties included scheduling and managing non-medical aides who provided services for (mostly) elderly people in their homes.

Over time, Cheryl found the distance between herself and the services she provided left her wishing for a different kind of job. This evolution is typical of many Christians who continue to grow and learn about their giftings. Although effective at her job, she wanted to impact customers directly.

The next logical leap for Cheryl was to accept a position as an office manager in a doctor's office. Although motherhood remained her primary concern, the hours and demands of her position at the doctor's office fit well into her family's schedule. Almost immediately, she knew this job represented a sweet spot where she could serve Jesus and others effectively. For many years, she continued working in this field and felt fulfilled by the contributions she made.

Cheryl might have been content staying in that environment until retirement, but God had other plans. The office politics turned south, and Cheryl unexpectedly found herself job hunting again. It became a watershed moment in her work life.

Cheryl went through the rigors of job hunting and found a position with an addiction treatment facility near Cincinnati, Ohio. While her first job with the company included plenty of human contact with patients, their families, and other staff members, she soon received a promotion. The move into addiction treatment management was not Cheryl's first choice, but it became obvious the position fit her perfectly. "Part of the job is still to work with patients," she says. "It is so rewarding to hear them talk about getting clean and sober. Their lives totally change. Some weren't even able to be around their families due to their addictions. Now they can spend the holidays with relatives again. They are so grateful for life's blessings."

Cheryl works closely with her staff on human resources matters but still finds herself in close contact with patients and their families. God is welcome at this facility, and Cheryl finds enough room there to share her faith when appropriate. Over time, her ability to care for others has become an obvious part of her skillset. Although she is still ten years or so away from retirement age, she intends to continue serving others as long as she is able. "There are many opportunities at my church that I hope to have more time to participate in," Cheryl says. "My goal is to stay healthy and continue doing what I can until Jesus comes."

Spotlight Questions

What could you identify with in Cheryl's story?

What action steps occurred to you about taking God to work?

Study Questions

1   *Read Psalm 58:11.* What did you hope to get from this study?

2   What is the promise of this verse?

3   Think of a practical definition of righteousness. How can you obtain it? (Hint: the cross of Jesus is involved.)

4   *Read Matthew 6:6.* Why is personal prayer time important?

5   When do you pray?

6   What tools do you use to remember prayer concerns?

7   *Read Matthew 10:38–41.* In what ways are Christians asked to take up their cross?

8   Do you recognize situations where God has asked you to lay down your life for His purposes? Give an example or two.

9   What does it mean to receive a righteous man in the name of a righteous man (see verse 41)?

10 *Read 2 John 1:8.* What does it mean to "look to yourselves, that we don't lose those things we've worked for?"

11 What can you do to ensure you receive a full reward in heaven?

12 *Read Colossians 3:23.* What will you do heartily, as to the LORD and not to men?

Prayer

Thank You, gracious heavenly Father, for Your purpose and plan for my life. Thank You for the vocation to which You have called me and Your help in finding the right situation where I can use my gifts. Open my eyes to the ministry opportunities around me and to those lost and broken ones whom You place in my path. Equip me with Your love, Your wisdom, and Your freedom for the journey. Make me fruitful for Your kingdom and teach me to take care of Your world through my work. At the end of my earthly life, may I be worthy of Your praise for the stewardship of the gifts, talents, finances, and relationships that You have entrusted to me. In the name of Jesus, amen.

What will you do to take God to work this week?

Epilogue

On a clear day in Washington in September 2011, my office at the Department of Homeland Security Office of Procurement Operations buzzed along busily as usual. Employees popped in and out as I tried to prepare for a meeting later in the day. Then, in a moment, everything changed. The whole building began to shake. I got up from my chair and walked into the hallway. The employee in the next office, a diminutive lady, became quite animated.

"Dave," Misha asked, "what's happening?"

"It feels like it might be an earthquake," I said without much conviction. My mind went first to terrorist attack or perhaps a nuclear bomb aimed at the Capitol or White House, both just blocks away.

"I don't want to be alone," Misha said.

"Come in my office," I responded. "You can get under the credenza, and I will get under the desk in case something falls from the ceiling."

As we crawled into cubby holes in the office furniture, I spoke a simple prayer that God would protect us and help us find out what happened. A new set of shakes and rattles began. After a minute or so, the rumbling stopped. The electricity in our building went off, including all but the emergency lights. The windows produced enough light for us to see that we were unharmed and that the office remained intact.

After a minute or two, we emerged from our hiding places and checked on the other people in our group. I used the combination to the secure room and opened the door. With no windows, the employees there had been plunged into complete darkness. Soon, they all made their way into the hallway. Without any other ideas, we filed down the staircase. Some people remained scared and wanted to hurry down. Others encouraged everyone to remain calm.

On that day, I felt glad that I brought God to work. In times of uncertainty, those around us need our faith, and we must be prepared for anything. Beyond just living to be a witness for Christ, people need our help in difficult times. Although these contributions to our colleagues and customers may seem minor at times, our entire presence turns into a reflection of a much greater light: Jesus. Our work life, like the other parts of our lives, isn't really about us. It's all about God and our ability to illuminate a path to Him. "So then neither he who plants is anything, nor he who waters, but God who gives the increase" (1 Corinthians 3:7).

Prayer

Dear Father, only You know the full potential You placed into my life. Show me how to work as unto You. Teach me patience, selfless love for my co-workers, respect for my supervisors, and freedom from low expectations. Show me how to embody superior customer service, beginning with You and extending to all those who depend on the goods and services I provide. Grant me wisdom in every aspect of my job or profession. Let me become a witness that pleases You. In the name of Jesus, amen.

Notes

1. "Religious Discrimination," U.S. Equal Employment Opportunity Commission, https://www.eeoc.gov/laws/types/religion.cfm as noted on February 21, 2018.

2. "More Than Half of U.S. Workers Are Satisfied with Their Jobs," The Conference Board, September 1, 2017, https://www.conference-board.org/press/pressdetail.cfm?pressid=7184, as noted on February 21, 2018.

3. "Living Paycheck to Paycheck Is a Way of Life for Majority of U.S. Workers, According to New CareerBuilder Survey," *Career-Builder,* August 27, 2017, http://press.careerbuilder.com/2017-08-24-Living-Paycheck-to-Paycheck-is-a-Way-of-Life-for-Majority-of-U-S-Workers-According-to-New-CareerBuilder-Survey.

4. "Stress Is Killing You," The American Institute of Stress, www.stress.org/stress-is-killing-you/, as noted on January 18, 2018.

5. "Stress and Your Health," U.S. Department of Health and Human Services, www.womenshealth.gov/a-z-topics/stress-and-your-health, as noted January 18, 2018.

6. "Women: Work, Home, Multiple Roles, and Stress," Cleveland Clinic, https://my.clevelandclinic.org/health/articles/5545-women-work-home-multiple-roles-stress.

7. "'It's on Fire!' Tinker Remembers Bldg. 3001 Inferno of 1984," *Tinker Take Off,* November 12–18, 2004, vol. 62, issue. 45, http://journalrecord.com/tinkertakeoff/category/2004-nov-12-nov-18-vol-62-iss-45/.

Acknowledgements

Pastor Steve Reynolds and David L. Winters would like to acknowledge the substantial support, assistance and friendship provided by the following:

Debbie Reynolds

Susan Fouty

Elizabeth Brown

Gary Hall

Kyle Hansen

Norah Harmon

Nirvana Blatchford-Rodriguez

Andrew Margrave

Byron McKinnon

Mabinty Quarshie

James Raeford

Latonya Stewart

Ana Sufitchi

Danielle Brow

Both authors owe a debt of gratitude to their parents for leading by example in demonstrating a strong work ethic. Thank you Alfred and Betsy Reynolds and Estil and Fern Winters.

Other Titles by Steve Reynolds

Bod 4 God: Twelve Weeks to Lasting Weight Loss

Get Off the Couch: 6 Motivators to Help You Lose Weight and Start Living

The Healthy Renegade Pastor *

Wise Up! *

(* co-authored books)

Other Titles by David L. Winters

Sabbatical of the Mind: The Journey from Anxiety to Peace

Driver Confessional

CPSIA information can be obtained
at www.ICGtesting.com
Printed in the USA
BVHW04*1226010918
525409BV00002B/5/P